Tricolore

5ᵉ édition

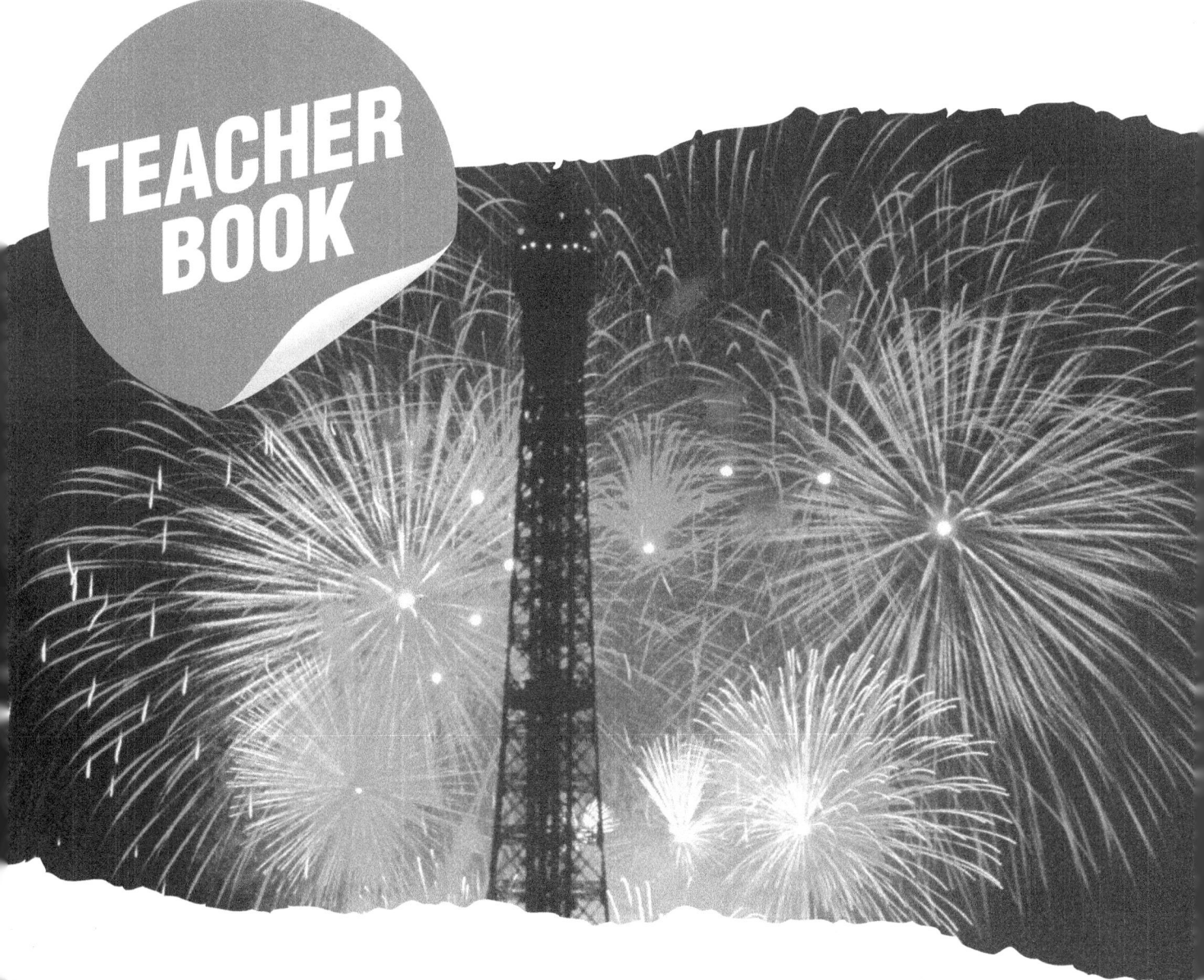

TEACHER BOOK

Sylvia Honnor
Heather Mascie-Taylor
Michael Spencer

OXFORD
UNIVERSITY PRESS

OXFORD
UNIVERSITY PRESS

Great Clarendon Street, Oxford, OX2 6DP, United Kingdom

Oxford University Press is a department of the University of Oxford.
It furthers the University's objective of excellence in research, scholarship,
and education by publishing worldwide. Oxford is a registered trade mark of
Oxford University Press in the UK and in certain other countries

Text © Sylvia Honnor, Heather Mascie-Taylor and Michael Spencer 2014

The moral rights of the authors have been asserted
Tricolore first published in 1980 by E. J. Arnold and Sons Limited
Encore Tricolore first published in 1992 by Thomas Nelson and Sons Limited
Encore Tricolore nouvelle edition first published in 2000 by Thomas Nelson
and Sons Limited
Tricolore Total first published in 2008 by Nelson Thornes Limited
Tricolore 5e édition first published in 2014 by Oxford University Press

All rights reserved. No part of this publication may be reproduced,
stored in a retrieval system, or transmitted, in any form or by any
means, without the prior permission in writing of Oxford University
Press, or as expressly permitted by law, by licence or under terms
agreed with the appropriate reprographics rights organization.
Enquiries concerning reproduction outside the scope of the above
should be sent to the Rights Department, Oxford University Press,
at the address above.

You must not circulate this work in any other form and you must
impose this same condition on any acquirer

British Library Cataloguing in Publication Data
Data available

978-0-19-839506-5

1 3 5 7 9 10 8 6 4 2

Printed in the United Kingdom

Acknowledgements

Cover: Photolibrary

The author and publisher would like to thank the following people for their
help and advice: Hilary Bates and Christine Dalton for editing the materials;
Hilary Attlee, Elizabeth King, Jackie Coe, Ruth Smith, Sue Hotham and
Bethany Honnor for their feedback during the writing of the course.

Cover photograph: Carol Havens/Getty Images

Although we have made every effort to trace and contact all
copyright holders before publication this has not been possible in all
cases. If notified, the publisher will rectify any errors or omissions at
the earliest opportunity.

Links to third party websites are provided by Oxford in good faith
and for information only. Oxford disclaims any responsibility for
the materials contained in any third party website referenced in
this work.

Contents

Section 1
General information

Introduction	iv
Components	iv
Student's Book	iv
Teacher's Book	iv
Tricolore 5ᵉ édition Kerboodle components	v
Grammar in Action	viii
Planning the course	ix
Tricolore 5ᵉ édition and the National Curriculum from 2014	xi
Tricolore 5ᵉ édition and the Scottish Curriculum for Excellence	xii
Tricolore 5ᵉ édition and the Curriculum in Northern Ireland	xii
Teaching approach	xiii
Developing listening skills	xiii
Developing speaking skills	xiii
Developing reading skills	xiii
Developing writing skills	xiv
Developing independence in learning and using the target language	xiv
Developing understanding and application of grammar	xiv
Developing translation skills	xiv
Developing cultural awareness	xiv
Cross-curricular links	xiv
Differentiation and building on earlier language learning	xv
Assessment	xv

Section 2
Games and songs

Games for language learning	xvii
1 Number games	xvii
2 General vocabulary games	xviii
3 Flashcard games	xix
4 Mini-flashcard games	xx
5 Games for practising verbs	xx
6 Spelling games	xxi
Songs	xxii

Section 3
Teacher's notes

Unité 1 Bonjour!	1
Unité 2 J'habite ici	14
Unité 3 Chez moi	26
1–3 Consolidation and assessment	41
Unité 4 Les animaux	45
4 Consolidation and assessment	60
Unité 5 Des fêtes et des festivals	64
5 Consolidation and assessment	85
Unité 6 Qu'est-ce que tu fais?	90
6 Consolidation and assessment	109
Unité 7 En ville	114
7 Consolidation and assessment	134
Unité 8 Une journée scolaire	140
8 Consolidation and assessment	161
Unité 9 C'est bon, ça!	166
9 Consolidation and assessment	183
Unité 10 Amuse-toi bien!	189
10 Consolidation and assessment	206
Contrôles	213

Section 1 General information

Introduction

Tricolore 5ᵉ édition builds on the proven strengths and approach of *Tricolore*, *Encore Tricolore* and *Tricolore Total*, incorporating new features to bring it into line with current teaching requirements.

The course features:

- lively, interesting and motivating materials for learning the French language
- a systematic and comprehensive approach to grammar progression, with clear explanations and extensive practice
- material to develop cultural awareness through authentic contexts and activities from France and other French-speaking countries
- systematic training in language learning, study and thinking skills
- user-friendly reference sections to encourage independent learning
- opportunities for differentiation through flexible use of activities, but a common core of material for all students.

Key features of the new edition are:

- on-the-page extension activities for students to stretch those with prior knowledge of French, or those in need of a challenge
- new focus on sound-spelling links to support pronunciation, spelling and transcription
- fully integrated next generation Kerboodle, containing an extensive bank of teaching materials and classroom resources, such as videos, interactive tasks, assessment materials, presentations, visuals and worksheets.
- up-to-date design and themes to support the tried and trusted Tricolore method
- amendments to incorporate the new official French spelling reforms, approved by the *Académie française*. These include the use of hyphens in compound numbers, removal of hyphens in some words, removal of circumflex accent with i and u, standardisation of some anomalies etc. For further details, see http://www.orthographe-recommandee.info/index.htm

Components

Tricolore 5ᵉ édition 1 covers one complete year's work.

The components are:

- Student's Book
- Teacher's Book
- Kerboodle resource, including: Resources, Audio, Copymasters, Assessment, Flashcards (see page v for more information)
- Audio CD pack (material is also available online as part of the Kerboodle subscription)
- Kerboodle Book
- Grammar in Action 1

Student's Book

The Student's Book is the main teaching tool of the course and contains the essential core material and reference sections. It comprises:

- **10 units**

  Each unit is organised in spreads and each spread is a self-contained entity with explicit learning objectives and a full range of activities to practise language and thinking skills. Every unit finishes with a unit summary (*Sommaire*). (The *Sommaires* are also provided on copymasters, available online as part of your Kerboodle subscription.) In *Tricolore 5ᵉ édition*, grammar explanations are given in *Dossier-langue* boxes and skills are covered in *Stratégies* boxes. Activities suitable for students with prior knowledge of French are indicated by a plus sign, while *Phonétique* boxes help students learn French sounds and recognise how these sounds are written.

- **Au choix**

  This section contains further practice and extension tasks for each unit. Most of these require reading and writing skills only, but a few involve listening.

- **Presse-Jeunesse**

  Starting after *Unité* 4 and at regular intervals throughout the book, these four magazine-style sections provide material for reading for pleasure and to enhance cultural awareness. They can be used flexibly and are intended for students to work on alone. Although they use mainly the vocabulary and structures previously taught, they also contain a small amount of additional language.

- **Rappel**

  These double-page, revision sections are placed after *Unités* 3, 5, 7 and 9, alternating with the *Presse-Jeunesse* sections. Each *Rappel* section provides reading and writing activities, suitable for students working independently, for homework or during cover lessons. They contain a variety of tasks including practice of vocabulary, grammar and topic revision.

- **Grammaire**

  The reference section covers the main grammar points and irregular verbs taught in *Tricolore 5ᵉ édition* 1.

- **Glossaires**

  French–English and English–French glossaries at the end of the Student's Book encourage students to use reference sources.

Teacher's Book

The Teacher's Book has three sections:

Section 1:

This provides general information, such as details of components, reference and planning documents, etc.

Tricolore 1 Teacher's Notes

Section 2:

This includes details of games and songs which can be used at various points in the course.

Section 3:

This provides detailed teaching notes and solutions for all items in the Student's Book and in the online Copymasters. It also includes a full transcript of all recorded items, ideas for starters and plenaries and notes on formative assessment (*Épreuves*) and summative assessment (*Contrôles*).

Each unit begins with an overview grid to help with planning. This summarises the objectives, key language, grammar, skills and sound–spelling coverage. The teaching suggestions follow the sequence of spreads in the Student's Book and include ideas for starters, plenaries, Assessment for Learning and differentiation. The Section 3 notes indicate linked online activities (available in the *Tricolore 5ᵉ édition* Kerboodle resource) in their suggested teaching sequence. Notes for the online copymasters are also included in this section.

The following symbols are used in the Teacher's Book:

66

Student's Book page number

3 Task number

Kerboodle

Online material (audio, interactive, worksheet, copymaster, video) available on Kerboodle

gia 1 p12

Grammar in Action 1 page number

🔊 Recorded item

Tricolore 5ᵉ édition Kerboodle components

Audio Tracks and Transcripts

Tricolore 5ᵉ édition offers a wide variety of lively listening material, recorded by French native speakers and at a speed and level which the students can understand. The audio tracks, together with editable transcripts of each recording, can be accessed online as part of your Kerboodle subscription. The recordings can also be purchased separately as an Audio CD pack.

List of CDs	Student CD (CD 6)
CD 1: Unités 1–3	Tu comprends? Unités 4–10
CD 2: Unités 4–5	Chantez! Unités 2, 3, 6, 8, 9, 10
CD 3: Unités 6–7	
CD 4: Unités 8–9	
CD 5: Unité 10 and Contrôles	

Interactive activities and online worksheets

Interactive activities

These self-marking activities link to the Student's Book to consolidate and extend content:

Phonétique, Stratégies and Grammar interactives are linked with appropriate items in the Student's Book

Listening and reading interactives offer additional stimulus material, usually in the form of audio recordings and text, but sometimes using videos and animations

Online worksheets

There is a wide variety of online worksheets, focussing on grammar, speaking, reading, writing and language-learning strategies, which can be customised and edited before they are assigned to students.

Presentations, e-books and songs

Presentations

These include:
- Editable grammar and vocabulary PowerPoints for front-of class use
- Kim's Game presentations for practising new vocabulary – students compete to remember which items have gone missing

e-books

The e-books help students to read longer stories, poems and informative texts right at the start of their language learning. This is in line with the new KS3 Programme of Study requirement that students read literary texts in the language and expand understanding of the language and culture. Audio versions of the stories are also included.

Songs

The songs that are featured on the Audio CD also appear as presentations, enabling the lyrics to be displayed centrally to encourage students to sing along, if wished.

Kerboodle Book

The **Tricolore** Kerboodle Book provides a digital version of the Student's Book for use with students at the front of the classroom.

Teacher access to the Kerboodle Book is automatically available as part of the Resources and Assessment package. A set of tools is available with the Kerboodle book, which include the following:

- Every teacher and student has their own digital notebook for use within their Kerboodle Book. The teacher can choose to share some of their notes with students, or hide them from view; all student notes are accessible only to the student making the notes.
- Sticky notes, bookmarks, and pen features enable users to personalise each page.

The facility to zoom in and spotlight any part of the text.

Like all other resources offered on Kerboodle, the Kerboodle book can be accessed using a range of devices.

Copymasters

The copymasters provide a wide variety of material for practice in all four skills.

Some worksheets are intended to be expendable, e.g. those containing crosswords, word searches or listening grids. Others can be cut up and used for pair or group activities. The *Sommaire* and grammar practice sheets can be stuck into the student's exercise book or file for future reference.

Mini-flashcards

These worksheets are initially used for a writing activity, but can then be cut up and used for group or pairwork activities and games.

Tu comprends?

These self-instructional listening tasks are used with the accompanying recordings for homework or for independent work in class.

Assessment

All assessment items can be accessed via the Assessment tab in Kerboodle. Correct answers are provided in one document in the Solutions folder.

Épreuves

These are informal assessments in listening, reading, writing and grammar, supplied as worksheets and audio files. The first set of *Épreuves* appears after *Unité* 3 (covering all of the first three units), after which there are a set of *Épreuves* at the end of each unit. Transcripts are also provided for the listening.

Contrôles

Three formal assessments in listening, reading, writing and speaking are included. These are grouped as follows:

- Unités 1–4
- Unités 5–7
- Unités 8–10

Record Sheets are provided to help you keep track of student progress.

Quizzes

Four self-marking interactive quizzes are included. These can be assigned to individual students, with scores automatically recorded in the Kerboodle Markbook.

List of Copymasters and Assessment worksheets

Below is a list of the Copymasters and Assessment worksheets that appear on Kerboodle, with information on where to find each item.

Resource	Location
1/1 La France	Resources > Introduction
1/2 Écoutez bien!	Resources > Unité 1 > Copymasters
1/3 Sommaire	Resources > Unité 1 > Sommaire
2/1 J'habite en France	Resources > Unité 2 > Copymasters
2/2 Trois conversations	
2/3 Les jours de la semaine	
2/4 Sommaire	Resources > Unité 2 > Sommaire
3/1 La famille Techno	Resources > Unité 3 > Copymasters
3/2 Masculin, féminin	
3/3 À la maison	
3/4 C'est où?	
3/5 Sommaire	Resources > Unité 3 > Sommaire
3/6 Épreuve: Écouter	Assessment > Épreuve: Unités 1–3
3/7 Épreuve: Lire	
3/8 Épreuve: Écrire et grammaire	

Resource	Location
4/1 Les animaux [mini-flashcards]	Resources > Unité 4 > Copymasters
4/2 Les animaux de mes amis	
4/3 C'est moi!	
4/4 Questions et réponses	
4/5 Des conversations au choix	
4/6 Tu comprends?	
4/7 Sommaire	Resources > Unité 4 > Sommaire
4/8 Épreuve: Écouter	Assessment > Épreuve: Unité 4
4/9 Épreuve: Lire	
4/10 Épreuve: Écrire et grammaire	
5/1 Des dates	Resources > Unité 5 > Copymasters
5/2 Être	
5/3 Les numéros	
5/4 Des vêtements [mini-flashcards]	
5/5 Jeux de vocabulaire	
5/6 Des cadeaux et des vêtements	
5/7 avoir	
5/8 Des descriptions	
5/9 Tu comprends?	

Tricolore 1 Teacher's Notes

Resource	Location
5/10 Sommaire	Resources > Unité 5 > Sommaire
5/11 Épreuve: Écouter	Assessment > Épreuve: Unité 5
5/12 Épreuve: Lire	
5/13 Épreuve: Écrire et grammaire	
6/1 Le temps [mini-flashcards]	Resources > Unité 6 > Copymasters
6/2 Vocabulaire: la météo et les saisons	
6/3 La météo A, B	
6/4 Tom et Jojo	
6/5 Les verbes	
6/6 Des activités	
6/7 Des cartes postales	
6/8 Tu comprends?	
6/9 Sommaire	Resources > Unité 6 > Sommaire
6/10 Épreuve: Écouter	Assessment > Épreuve: Unité 6
6/11 Épreuve: Lire	
6/12 Épreuve: Écrire et grammaire	
7/1 En ville (1) [mini-flashcards]	Resources > Unité 7 > Copymasters
7/2 Vocabulaire – les endroits	
7/3 C'est quelle direction?	
7/4 Où va-t-on?	
7/5 C'est où?	
7/6 En ville (2) [mini-flashcards]	
7/7 Ma ville/mon village	
7/8 Un plan à compléter A, B	
7/9 aller	
7/10 Tu comprends?	
7/11 Sommaire	Resources > Unité 7 > Sommaire
7/12 Épreuve: Écouter	Assessment > Épreuve: Unité 7
7/13 Épreuve: Lire	
7/14 Épreuve: Écrire et grammaire	
8/1 Quelle heure est-il? [mini-flashcards]	Resources > Unité 8 > Copymasters
8/2 Qui est-ce? A, B	
8/3 Jeux de vocabulaire: les matières	
8/4 La vie scolaire	
8/5 On fait beaucoup de choses	
8/6 Mon, ton, son	
8/7 Des questions et des réponses (notre/nos, votre/vos)	
8/8 Tu comprends?	

Resource	Location
8/9 Sommaire	Resources > Unité 8 > Sommaire
8/10 Épreuve: Écouter	Assessment > Épreuve: Unité 8
8/11 Épreuve: Lire	
8/12 Épreuve: Écrire et grammaire	
9/1 On mange et on boit [mini-flashcards]	Resources > Unité 9 > Copymasters
9/2 C'est quel mot?	
9/3 Des jeux de vocabulaire	
9/4 La forme négative	
9/5 À table	
9/6 Qu'est-ce qu'on va faire?	
9/7 Tu comprends?	
9/8 Sommaire	Resources > Unité 9 > Sommaire
9/9 Épreuve: Écouter	Assessment > Épreuve: Unité 9
9/10 Épreuve: Lire	
9/11 Épreuve: Écrire et grammaire	
10/1 Faire	Resources > Unité 10 > Copymasters
10/2 Grands mots croisés: la musique	
10/3 Les loisirs	
10/4 Manon et Clément A, B	
10/5 La semaine dernière	
10/6 24 heures	
10/7 Qu'est-ce que tu as fait?	
10/8 Tu comprends?	
10/9 Sommaire	Resources > Unité 10 > Sommaire
10/10 Épreuve: Écouter	Assessment > Épreuve: Unité 10
10/11 Épreuve: Lire	
10/12 Épreuve: Écrire et grammaire	
Premier contrôle: Écouter	Assessment > Premier contrôle: Unités 1-4
Premier contrôle: Parler	
Premier contrôle: Lire	
Premier contrôle: Écrire	
Deuxième contrôle: Écouter	Assessment > Deuxième contrôle: Unités 5-7
Deuxième contrôle: Parler	
Deuxième contrôle: Lire	
Deuxième contrôle: Écrire	
Troisième contrôle: Écouter	Assessment > Troisième contrôle: Unités 8-10
Troisième contrôle: Parler	
Troisième contrôle: Lire	
Troisième contrôle: Écrire	
Contrôles: record sheets	Assessment > Premier contrôle: Unités 1-4

Flashcards

There are 100 visuals for colour flashcards available on the *Tricolore 5e édition* Kerboodle resource. This allows the teacher to view and print images individually and in groups, as needed. They are used to present vocabulary and for oral work and games. (See TB page xix).

List of flashcards

1 happy face
2 sad face

Places
3 town
4 village
5 house and garden
6 flat
7 farm
8 street
9 grocer's shop
10 supermarket
11 café
12 cinema

Rooms
13 bedroom
14 kitchen
15 bathroom
16 lounge
17 dining room

Animals
18 hamster
19 dog
20 cat
21 rabbit
22 fish
23 horse
24 mouse
25 budgerigar
26 guinea pig

Weather
27 hot weather
28 cold weather
29 raining
30 fine sunny weather
31 windy weather
32 snow
33 fog

Activities
34 watching TV
35 listening to radio/CDs/iPod
36 doing homework
37 using computer
38 playing table tennis
39 playing basketball
40 playing volleyball
41 playing with games console
42 playing cards

Places in town
43 market
44 restaurant
45 swimming pool
46 campsite
47 museum
48 town hall
49 school
50 tourist office
51 youth hostel
52 hospital
53 post office
54 station
55 church
56 castle
57 mosque
58 ice rink
59 library
60 football pitch

Food and drink
61 ham
62 roast chicken
63 roast red meat
64 fish
65 omelette
66 potatoes
67 chips
68 carrots
69 peas
70 cauliflower
71 cabbage
72 French/green beans
73 lettuce
74 apple
75 orange
76 pear
77 peach
78 banana
79 grapes
80 strawberries
81 baguette
82 croissants
83 cheese
84 yoghurts
85 cake
86 wine
87 mineral water
88 lemonade
89 coke
90 fruit juice
91 coffee
92 tea
93 hot chocolate
94 milk

Leisure activities
95 playing chess
96 skate-boarding
97 roller skates/blades
98 mountain bike
99 drumkit
100 drawing

Grammar in Action 1

This expendable workbook provides additional practice of the grammar introduced in Stage 1. The workbook is designed for independent use by students and includes clear explanations, exercises at a range of levels and reference material. It provides a useful reference and revision resource for students to retain for personal use. The teaching notes for each spread indicate useful Grammar in Action activities for reinforcement. A solutions card is provided with each pack of eight books.

Planning the course
Stage 1 Overview

Unité 1 Bonjour! SB Page 8		
greet and say goodbye to a French-speaking person tell someone your name and age and ask their name and age ask someone how they are and tell them how you are talk about school items and things in the classroom understand simple classroom instructions	numbers up to 20 the gender of nouns (masculine and feminine) make nouns plural	using prior knowledge working out new meanings (cognates) comparing French and English pronunciation *phonétique* – the letters 'c', 'i', 'y'
Unité 2 J'habite ici! SB Page 14		
understand people saying where they live say where you live and ask someone where they live days of the week use the French alphabet	numbers up to 30 use *dans*, *à*, *en* to say 'in' for homes, towns or countries ask how to say things in French	using clues to work out meaning (1) memorising numbers getting help with words *phonétique* – the letters 'ch', 'j', 'ge', 'gi', 'é'
Unité 3 Chez moi SB Page 20		
talk about your family and your home talk about other people's homes and families say who things belong to describe where things are in a room read a poem in French	the definite article, *le* and *la* (the) the indefinite article, *un* and *une* (a/an) possessive adjectives, *mon*, *ma*, *mes* (my) and *ton*, *ta*, *tes* (your with *tu*) using *de* + name to show possession the singular of the verb *être* (to be) and *avoir* (to have) numbers up to 70 use prepositions *sous* (under) and *sur* (on) more about masculine and feminine words	using clues to work out meaning (2) remembering the gender of nouns remembering vocabulary *phonétique* – the letters 'è', 'a', 'à', '-as','-at' 'u', 's' (between vowels), 'z'
Rappel 1 – revision activities SB Page 30		
Unité 4 Les animaux SB Page 32		
talk about animals, especially pets describe animals and other things ask questions talk about your preferences and give opinions and descriptions	make adjectives agree understand the negative, *ne … pas* (not) use *Est-ce que*, intonation and question words the singular of the verb *avoir* (to have) more about plurals using *tu* and *vous*	using qualifiers expressing opinions memorising vocabulary *phonétique* – the letters 'ou', 'oi', 'qu'
Presse-Jeunesse 1 – magazine section SB Page 42		
Unité 5 Des fêtes et des festivals SB page 44		
ask for and give the date learn about saints' days and other festivals use correct greetings for special days talk about birthdays and presents discuss prices talk about clothes describe yourself and other people	the pronoun *on* the full present tense of the verb *être* (to be) the plural form of nouns and adjectives the full present tense of the verb *avoir* (to have) numbers 0–100	spelling and pronouncing the months using clues to work out meaning learning irregular adjectives with a noun 3 kinds of words – nouns, verbs and adjectives developing and practising your listening skills *phonétique* – the letters 'ui', 'ille'

Tricolore 1 Teacher's Notes

Rappel 2 – revision activities + tips for learning vocabulary SB Page 60		
Unité 6 Qu'est-ce que tu fais? SB Page 62		
talk about the weather say what the temperature is talk about months and seasons talk about sport find out about *les bandes dessinées* talk about family activities say what you do at weekends talk about different activities according to the weather	some regular *–er* verbs more practice of the pronoun *on* use *quand* + a phrase in a sentence	using some 'high frequency' words (*souvent, quelquefois, normalement*) translating from French to English practising and improving speaking skills *phonétique* – the letters 'au', 'aux', 'eau', 'eaux', 'am', 'an', 'em', 'en', '-er', '-et', '-ey', '-ez'
Presse-Jeunesse 2 – magazine section SB Page 76		
Unité 7 En ville SB Page 78		
learn about the French town, La Rochelle talk about places in a town say what happens regularly on a particular day ask for and understand directions and information understand and say how far away places are talk about your own town and area understand tourist information	use *le* + day of the week/time of day more about adjectives (irregular forms, position) the preposition *à, au, à la, à l', aux* (to, at) other prepositions *devant* (in front of), *derrière* (behind), *entre* (between), etc. use *il y a …* and *il n'y a pas de …* use the verb *aller*	remembering the gender of nouns using connectives, *et, mais, aussi, parce que, au contraire* reading and listening to longer texts *phonétique* – the letter 'h' at the beginning of a word, the letters 'th', the letters '–t' or '-te' at the end of a word
Rappel 3 – revision activities SB Page 92		
Unité 8 Une journée scolaire SB Page 94		
ask about and tell the time arrange a time to meet talk about daily routine and a typical day talk about school subjects say what you think of school subjects find out about Senegal, a French-speaking country in Africa talk about your school and prepare a presentation	the verb *faire* (to do, make) possessive adjectives *son, sa, ses* (his, her, its); *notre, nos* (our); *votre, vos* (your, plural or formal); *leur, leurs* (their) some examples of reflexive verbs (*je* form only) ask questions using *quel* use of the definite article	English and French spelling patterns: *–y* and *–ie* using qualifiers translating phrases (*le prof d'histoire*) working out the meanings of new words improving writing and speaking skills preparing a presentation *phonétique* – the letters 'im', 'in', 'r'
Presse-Jeunesse 3 – magazine section SB Page 110		
Unité 9 C'est bon, ça! SB Page 112		
meals in France talk about food and drink fruit and vegetables healthy eating discuss what you like to eat and drink having a meal with a French family plan some meals and picnics festival foods in other countries	the partitive article *du, de la, de l', des* (some) the verb *prendre* (to take) the verb *manger* (to eat) the negative *ne … pas* (not) *pas de* – (not any) use *aller* + infinitive to talk about the future	saying 'please' and 'thank you' improving your reading tackling gap-fill activities recognising false friends developing your written work reading for gist and detail *phonétique* – the circumflex accent, the letters 'gn', 'c', 'k', 'qu'

Rappel 4 – revision activities SB Page 124		
Unité 10 Amuse-toi bien! SB Page 126		
talk about sport talk about music and the *Fête de la Musique* discuss other leisure activities give opinions describe a special day understand and talk about what you did last weekend/last week find out about *Astérix* and the *Parc Astérix* use the 24-hour clock	*faire* + *de* + activity *jouer à* + sport *jouer de* + instrument recognise and use some phrases in the perfect tense (*je* and *tu* forms only)	read and write messages about leisure translating from French to English planning your writing learning and revising vocabulary *phonétique* – the letters 'un', 'um', 'x', '-sion', '-tion'
Presse-Jeunesse 4 – magazine section SB Page 140		
Au choix SB Page 142		
Extra activities to practise and extend the language learnt in *Unités* 1–10.		
Grammaire SB Page 160		
Glossaire Français–anglais SB Page 167		
Glossaire Anglais–français SB Page 173		

Tricolore 5ᵉ édition and the National Curriculum from 2014

The new National Curriculum for England and Wales can be accessed from the website of the Department for Education:

https://www.gov.uk/government/publications/national-curriculum-in-england-languages-progammes-of-study

Key differences from the previous curriculum include:

Compulsory MFL at Primary level

From September 2014, MFL will be compulsory at Key Stage 2. The teaching can be of any language (ancient or modern) with an aim to "enable pupils to understand and communicate ideas, facts and feelings in speech and writing, focused on familiar and routine matters, using their knowledge of phonology, grammatical structures and vocabulary".

Tricolore 5ᵉ édition has been planned and written with an understanding that a Year 7 class may well include pupils who have had different lengths of exposure to different languages. The course aims to help those with prior knowledge of French to capitalise on their head start, while tapping into the language awareness of students who have not yet learned French in a formal setting. On-the-page extension activities (indicated by a plus symbol) allow students with a background in French to tackle something more challenging, while the *Stratégies* features encourage all students to draw links with languages they have encountered previously. See also the section on differentiation in Teaching Approach (page xiii).

Removal of Attainment Targets

The former National Curriculum Attainment Target level descriptors no longer apply but it is understood that some teachers may still wish to use them for reference. *Tricolore 5ᵉ édition* Stage 1 covers attainment levels 1–4 (and some aspects of levels 5 and 6). A mark scheme showing how assessment tallies to levels is provided with the *Contrôles* in Kerboodle.

Initiating and developing of conversations

The new Key Stage 3 Curriculum asks that students "initiate and develop conversations, coping with unfamiliar language and unexpected responses, [and] making use of important social conventions such as formal modes of address". Many activities practise this throughout the course e.g. *Inventez des conversations* and numerous pairwork activities. Questions using *Est-ce que* are introduced in *Unité* 4, with other question words and forms used throughout. There are also *Stratégies* support features on keeping conversations going and speaking more confidently.

Emphasis on grammatical understanding and accuracy

A rigorous approach to grammar has always been a key strength of *Tricolore*. Grammar is explained in the *Dossier-langue* sections of the Student's Book and presented and practised extensively in print and online.

Translation and transcribing

The new Curriculum asks students to "transcribe words and short sentences that they hear with increasing accuracy". The *Phonétique* boxes that feature throughout the Student's Book, supported by practice activities online and in the Audio CD pack, enable students to develop a strong awareness of sound-spelling links to help with this. Translation skills are developed through the *Stratégies* boxes and online worksheets.

Reading from a range of different sources, including literary texts

Tricolore students are encouraged to read for personal interest and enjoyment, and to develop their own cultural awareness, through the e-books, songs, poems and Presse-Jeunesse magazine-style section. Authentic printed materials are used in the Student's Book where appropriate.

Becoming independent learners

In *Tricolore 5ᵉ édition*, students are encouraged to apply a deductive approach to understanding grammar, to use former knowledge to work out meanings, and to consider how new language can be used in different contexts. The *Dossier-langue* and *Stratégies* sections in particular focus on the development of these independent learning skills. The Student's Book contains clear reference sections, *Grammaire*, *Glossaire* (*Français–Anglais* and *Anglais–Français*) so students can look up information and meanings independently. Together with the *Dossier-langue* and *Stratégies* sections, these help to encourage the development of independent learning skills.

Tricolore 5ᵉ édition and the Scottish Curriculum for Excellence

The structure, content and teaching approach of *Tricolore 5ᵉ édition* is closely aligned to the principles of the Scottish Modern Languages Experiences and Outcomes.

Listening and talking

Strategies for listening are developed throughout the course, allowing students to gain confidence in understanding language from a variety of sources, including unfamiliar speakers. Speaking skills are practiced throughout the Student's Book in pairwork activities and online in the Record and Playback interactives. Creativity and fluency are encouraged in *Inventez des conversations* activities. Talking with others and expressing opinions are a focus of *Stratégie* features, covering topics such as speaking more confidently, listening with focus and keeping your conversation going.

Skills in planning and organising information are covered in *Unité* 8, while knowledge about language is developed through the *Stratégies*, *Phonétique* and *Infos* features.

Reading

Students are encouraged to read independently from a variety of sources (Presse-Jeunesse, e-books, songs, poems, websites). Appreciating other cultures – from la Rochelle to Senegal – is a key feature of the *Tricolore* course, with stimulus materials on festivals, traditions and everyday customs. The *Stratégies* features provide support in working out meanings, identifying patterns, tackling new language and analysing different texts.

Writing

Writing frames and worksheets help students to plan their writing effectively, while the focus on grammar and vocabulary gives students the tools they need to experiment with words and phrases, including expressing opinions. Knowledge about language is developed through the *Phonétique*, *Dossier-langue* and *Infos* features.

Tricolore 5ᵉ édition and the Curriculum in Northern Ireland

Tricolore 5ᵉ édition is fully in line with the learning outcomes and objectives of the MFL curriculum in Northern Ireland. Students are encouraged to become effective and creative communicators, with opportunities to develop awareness of language, to make inter-cultural comparisons, to use previously learnt language in new contexts, etc. The varied activities enable students to research and manage information, think critically, develop creativity and work effectively with others, etc.

1 Developing pupils as Individuals

There are many opportunities for students to communicate an understanding of self and others (personal conversation in several units); to explore issues relating to lifestyle and choice (hobbies *Unités* 6, 10, healthy eating *Unité* 9); to contribute actively to a positive learning environment (class interaction, *vocabulaire de classe*); to develop an awareness of cultural similarities and differences (*Unités* 5, 8, etc.).

2 Developing pupils as Contributors to Society

Students have opportunities to explore social issues which relate to everyday lives (giving opinions *Unités* 4, 8, expressing future plans *Unité* 9, reporting recent events *Unité* 10); to make inter-cultural comparisons (festivals *Unité* 5, food *Unité* 9); to develop an awareness of media and media resources (use of websites and authentic resources throughout the course); to discuss ethical issues (environment *Unité* 7).

3 Developing pupils as Contributors to the Economy and Environment

This objective is developed more fully in Stages 2 and 3.

Teaching Approach

Developing listening skills

Training in careful listening for detail and for gist is a key feature of the course and should be developed from the outset. Two key strategies are:

- Building confidence by introducing language gradually with clues for what is to be listened for. This will help convince students that they can understand spoken French.
- Encouraging guesswork, especially of cognates, and emphasising that you don't need to understand every word.

There are no 'paused' recordings so the teacher can judge when there should be pauses, and the speed of building up from simple to more demanding tasks. The only exception to this is in the *Contrôles*, which simulate examination-type conditions.

Recorded listening material can be broadly grouped as follows:

- **Intensive listening**

  Students know what to listen for and have to select specific information from the recorded text and listen in sufficient detail to respond, e.g. by matching a description to a picture or answering simple *Vrai ou faux?* questions. In many cases, students are also encouraged to listen for an opinion or for additional details.

  Most of the listening practice in *Tricolore 5e édition* 1 is intensive.

- **Listening for gist**

  Students listen to find out what happened at the end of a story or to discover the type of information. Students should not worry if they can't understand every word but should just listen for the main points, as they probably will do when they hear real French people talking.

- **Interrelationship between sounds and writing**

  This is reinforced by the *Phonétique* activities on Kerboodle. The *Phonétique* feature boxes are also supported by recorded material on the Audio CDs, so students can listen and repeat.

- **Independent listening**

  From *Unité* 4 onwards, there are recorded listening items, with linked tasks on the online copymasters. These *Tu comprends?* sections are based on the language content of the unit and are graded in difficulty.

- **Listening strategies**

  Students are encouraged to use their knowledge of French pronunciation to help them make sense of spoken French and to develop techniques for improved listening comprehension, such as anticipating language which might be used, using the context and other clues to infer meaning.

Developing speaking skills

The 2014 National Curriculum states that students should

- speak coherently and confidently, with increasingly accurate pronunciation and intonation
- express and develop ideas clearly and with increasing accuracy
- initiate and develop conversations

Tricolore 5e édition supports this with, for example:

- individual pronunciation practice. The *Phonétique* sections provide a structured approach to understanding and practising French sounds to improve pronunciation and listening comprehension skills.
- using the target language for class activities and in rubrics. Students are expected to use French for class activities, and to use English only when necessary (for example, when discussing a grammar point or when comparing English and the target language).
- questions – using *Est-ce que* (*Unité* 4), asking for personal details (*Unités* 1–4), more general questions (*Unités* 5–10).
- pairwork and role-play practice and 'information gap' activities, using the online copymasters.
- 'colour-coded conversations', called *Inventez des conversations*. Students practise a basic conversation, then vary and adapt it by substituting other words and expressions from the colour-coded sections.

Speaking strategies

These sections help students to develop techniques for speaking with more confidence and to keep a conversation going.

The *Tricolore 5e édition* online resource provides a record and playback facility, particularly useful for practice in pronunciation and speaking.

Developing reading skills

There is a wide range of reading material, including practice in intensive reading and reading for gist.

Reading strategies

These sections encourage students to work out meaning through finding cognates, looking for patterns, recognising types of words, using existing knowledge, linking pictures and titles to a text, etc. Students are encouraged to use techniques for skimming and for scanning written texts in order to find information and for gist comprehension.

Presse-Jeunesse

These magazine-style sections provide additional reading material which is both informative and entertaining. Each section includes comprehension activities for students to work on independently.

Reading skills

The *Tricolore* online resource includes e-books for class or individual use and several interactive reading tasks allowing students to work on reading texts at their own pace.

Using dictionaries and other reference material

There is regular practice in using dictionaries and the French–English and English–French glossaries.

Developing writing skills

There is systematic training in writing through a range of activities.

Copywriting

In the early units, the main emphasis is on copywriting of words and phrases to help familiarise students with spelling patterns. Some simple creative work can be introduced quite quickly, through word games, sorting words and making labels or posters for the classroom.

Learning new words

The *Sommaire* sections, at the end of each unit and on copymasters, encourage students to learn and practise lists of vocabulary on a regular basis.

Adapting a model by substituting text/ adapting known language to new contexts

These begin with simple sentence work, using substitution tables. More creative and open-ended writing is gradually introduced, especially through the *Dossier personnel* items in which students adapt the language they have learnt to their personal situation, state likes and dislikes and express opinions.

Writing strategies

These sections encourage students to develop and improve their writing skills by adding detail and opinions, by using connectives, by learning spelling patterns and by checking their work to improve interest and accuracy.

Re-drafting writing to improve its accuracy

Although this is quite advanced work for students using *Tricolore 5e édition* 1, early training is given by the following types of task:

- *Vrai ou faux?* tasks, followed by correcting false statements
- *Chasse à l'intrus* activities in which students add explanations for their answers
- sentence completion tasks, based on information from short articles or letters
- working on the computer with text re-sequencing activities
- unjumbling and completing sentences
- using substitution tables.

Developing independence in learning and using the target language

Students are encouraged to use dictionaries and other reference materials appropriately.

Students are given suggestions for memorisation and grammar strategies, e.g. learning nouns with their gender, using spider diagrams, using visual imagery, making associations, looking for grammatical patterns, etc.

Grammar is explained in English in the *Dossier-langue* and *Grammaire* sections.

The *Sommaire* sections at the end of each unit bring vocabulary and grammar points together for easy reference. This gives a sense of progress and emphasises the importance of regular learning as an essential language-learning skill.

To assist with independent work in the *Au choix* and *Rappel* sections, rubrics are given in English and French.

Developing understanding and application of grammar

Grammar is a central feature of *Tricolore 5e édition*. New grammatical structures are introduced in context and students are encouraged to work out rules for themselves. Key points are explained in the *Dossier-langue* sections, which is immediately followed by practice activities so students absorb the grammatical patterns and use them. There is a grammar reference section, including verb tables, and students are encouraged to make up their own electronic verb tables.

Grammar in Action

Grammar in Action is a series of self-instructional workbooks to accompany each stage of *Tricolore 5e édition*. The books provide extensive practice in French grammar to reinforce and extend the correct use of grammar.

Developing translation skills

Translation is given greater coverage in later stages of *Tricolore*, but Stage 1 includes some material to develop skills in translating from French to English, and to explain how certain phrases are expressed in French, through activities such as *Comment ça se dit en français/anglais?*

The *Dossier Langue*, *Stratégies* and *Infos* sections also draw out comparisons between French and English.

Developing cultural awareness

Tricolore 5e édition features many aspects of everyday life in France (meals, daily routine, school life, leisure) and also other French-speaking countries, such as *Sénégal* (*Unité* 8). The French town of La Rochelle provides the background for *Unité* 7. There is coverage of popular festivals in France (*Unité* 5) and around the world (*Unité* 9), the *Fête de la science* (*Unité* 6) and the *Fête de la musique* (*Unité* 10). Authentic materials and websites are used to extend knowledge about the French-speaking world.

Cross-curricular links

Tricolore 5e édition provides cross-curricular links with other subjects such as English (comparisons between grammar and vocabulary); technology (standard terminology, use of internet sites, software applications, the *Tricolore* online resource, etc);

Tricolore 1 Teacher's Notes

maths (using numbers, simple statistics, prices); PHSE (healthy eating); citizenship (politics, history and culture of other countries) and geography (towns, areas and climate of France, French-speaking countries in Africa, etc.).

Differentiation and building on earlier language learning

It is understood that some students may have had sustained exposure to French at Key Stage 2 while others may be encountering the language for the first time. The Student's Book extension activities (indicated by a plus sign) show which activities would be most suitable for those with prior knowledge during lessons or as homework.

The *Au choix* section of the Student's Book provides material for extension (harder items) and consolidation (more practice at the same level). Rubrics are given in English as well as French in this section, and in most cases, students can work on these tasks independently.

The online copymasters provide flexibility and include some support and some extension work. Many have an incline of difficulty, to allow even the less experienced students to try harder items if they wish.

The range of learning resources will enable teachers to tailor their teaching to different learning needs.

Pairwork can play a useful part in integration and continuity, maybe pairing a more experienced language learner to help a newer learner. 'Carousel' sessions can also be organised with some groups of students working on harder items than others, but all linked with a common theme.

Another way to build on diversity is for groups of students with prior knowledge to prepare presentations to help other groups. Some of these could involve internet research using websites about e.g. La Rochelle, schools in France, the French-speaking world, food and shopping.

Some more able students might also communicate directly with a linked French school or town, writing simple e-mails and reporting back to the class on their findings.

Differentiation by outcome

Some tasks, especially the open-ended ones such as the *Dossier personnel*, can be used at various levels according to ability and prior learning. For example, to offer more support for the less able, the task could be treated as a class activity and a description built up on the board to be copied down. In other cases, gap-filling tasks can be made easier by giving students options to choose from, which can be written on the board and copied.

Selective use of items

The teaching of each new area of language follows a sequence of steps: presentation, discovery and explanation of new language, practice of new vocabulary and structures, leading to full communicative use.

The initial presentation, through oral/aural work, the explanation of new structures and some practice is appropriate for all.

After this, there is room for selection, for example, by choosing appropriate tasks, games and Kerboodle activities.

Assessment

There are two types of assessment test:
- *Épreuves* (formative assessment)

  These appear after *Unité* 3 and all subsequent units. Full details (solutions, mark allocations) are given with the relevant unit notes. The skills tested are listening, reading and writing combined with grammar.

  The *Épreuves* relate specifically to the unit just completed and could be used during two lessons: one for listening and another for reading and writing.

  There is an incline of difficulty, starting with easy tasks at Level 1. Students will find the *Épreuves* useful to check their own progress and pinpoint areas for further revision. They can be used for continuous assessment or more informally in class, for homework or as extra practice and consolidation.

- *Contrôles* (summative assessment)

Tricolore 5e édition 1 includes three blocks of formal assessment in all four skills. The student's sheets are included in the Assessment tab in Kerboodle and the teaching notes are given at the end of Section 2. These should be used as follows:

- *Premier contrôle* – after *Unité* 4
- *Deuxième contrôle* – after *Unité* 7
- *Troisième contrôle* – after *Unité* 10

The *Contrôles* have been designed to provide:

- a means of checking how much of the language and structures in preceding units has been assimilated
- evidence to help determine the levels, based on previous National Curriculum targets, attained by students in each of the four language skills
- a way of recording progress made by students – a Record sheet for students is provided for this purpose
- a pointer towards lack of progress (enabling the teacher to take the necessary steps for support)
- an introduction, at a basic level, to the type of target language testing used in formal examinations, giving students a head start in developing the examination techniques they are going to need at a later date.

The three *Contrôles* each provide a series of tasks at various levels, with an incline of difficulty within each paper, so that all students can start together at the beginning and work through the tasks as far as they are able.

- *Premier contrôle*: Levels 1–2
- *Deuxième contrôle*: Levels 1–3
- *Troisième contrôle*: Levels 2–4 (+ some elements of Levels 5 and 6)

Full details are given on pp xxviii–xxxiv.

The following points should be borne in mind in relation to the various sets of papers:

Listening

These papers are designed to be expendable.

Each item is recorded twice, without any sound effects or interruptions and is clearly spoken by a native French speaker. It must be remembered that playing the material a third time, except where specified, could affect a student's performance and cause an artificially high score to be obtained.

Speaking

These sheets are designed to be re-used and there is no need for students to write on them.

The teacher is best placed to decide when to give out the tasks prior to the assessment and whether to allow students to record their own work.

Reading

These papers are designed to be expendable.

The use of dictionaries should not be permitted.

Writing

These sheets are designed to be re-used.

The use of dictionaries should not be permitted.

Because these tasks are open-ended, the marking is quite complicated, but full details are provided in the individual mark schemes.

Finally, it is important to remember that the assessment tasks of the three *Contrôles* are designed to supplement rather than replace knowledge accumulated by the teacher from everyday assessment of student performance as they work through the various activities.

Section 2 Games, songs and contrôles

Games for language learning

Many of the games described here can be used for a wide range of language practice. A game which is particularly appropriate for a specific area is mentioned in the relevant unit notes.

In many games the teacher is the caller at the beginning, but students can soon be encouraged to take over this role.

1 Number games

Continue!

The caller counts aloud, stopping at intervals and pointing at someone, who must say the next number or s/he is out.

Chef d'orchestre

This is a more complicated version of *Continue!* The class is divided into two teams (*en avant* and *en arrière*). The 'conductor' says any number and points to one of the teams who must call out the next or the previous number depending on which team is indicated.

Dice games

Ordinary dice can be used for number games or special ones made using higher numbers or with words on, such as the six persons of the verb paradigm, etc. The simplest form of dice games is for a player to throw the dice and say aloud the number or word that they throw. One group can throw for another and students unable to say the right words are out.

Loto! (Bingo)

Students can make a class set of Bingo cards, and play with buttons as counters. Similarly, they can play a simpler version by just writing any four numbers on a scrap of paper and crossing them off as they are said by the caller. This game is useful when the numbers are learnt as words, as the winner must show her/his paper to the teacher and will be eliminated if the words are incorrectly spelt.

This type of Bingo is also an excellent standby for practice of almost any set of vocabulary, days of the week, colours, etc. For example, when learning the date, students write four days in words on a piece of paper and cross them off as the caller says them, saying *Loto!* when all four have been said. (For a sample set of cards, see TB page xix.)

Le dix magique

This is a pontoon-type game. The French for pontoon is *vingt et un*, but this version uses a total of ten so is called *Le dix magique*. Students make a simple set of cards with numbers 1–10. They place the cards upside down and turn them over one at a time, saying the number, until they get exactly 10. If they get 11 or more they are 'bust' (*fichu!*) and they must start again. The best of five turns is the winner.

Onze!

Students stand up and take turns to call out numbers in sequence i.e. *un, deux, trois, quatre, cinq, six, sept, huit, neuf, dix, onze*. Students may choose to call out one number, two numbers or three numbers. Whoever calls out *Onze* has to sit down. It can get very tactical with the boys trying to get rid of all the girls and vice versa. When it gets down to the last two then the one going first should win if they think carefully. Whoever says *sept* will lose.

Countdown

This is a familiar game show format based on the long-running French show called *Le jeu des Chiffres et des Lettres*. It is played as a whole class activity and practises numbers as well as simple arithmetical operations such as *plus, moins, multiplié par, divisé par* and *égale*. Someone nominates and gives six numbers – four single-figure digits and two numbers which must be 25, 50, 75 or 100. Write them on the board. (Alternatively you can download a Countdown random number generator if you look around on the web.) You then 'randomly' put a three figure number on the board and the class have two minutes to arrive at that figure using some or all of their chosen numbers. They must not use a number more than once. When a student thinks they have solved the calculation you get them to explain it whilst you write it up on the board. To help them write up the terms they will need to explain the calculation.

This game works well with near beginners up to intermediate. Classes could use calculators, but it is probably better for them to use pencil and paper solutions.

Zut-alors (Fizz-buzz)

Another mental arithmetic game for the whole class. Explain that you are going to count up to 100, but whenever you get to a number with a 5 in, or a multiple of 5, they must say ZUT. When they arrive at a number with 7 in, or a multiple thereof, they must say ALORS. When 5 and 7 are involved they must say ZUT-ALORS. It takes about 15 minutes to get to 100.

Quelle heure est-il?

This is a 'signalling' game in which the caller holds her/his arms upright to symbolise the hour, to the right to symbolise quarter past, to the left to symbolise quarter to and downwards to symbolise half past and the class or individuals say the time.

The game could be played in the manner of *Jacques a dit* (see TB page xx), with the teacher saying the time and the students doing the hand signals. Alternatively, students could write down a sequence of times signalled and check them back orally.

2 General vocabulary games

These can be used for practising numbers and areas of vocabulary, e.g. food, pets, etc.

Attention!

Everyone in the class is given a word or number at the beginning of a week and a list of these is written on a notice or at the side of the board. At any odd time during the French lessons for that week, the teacher will call out one of the words or numbers listed and the correct student should stand up. If not, s/he is out and crossed off the list. The winners are those still in at the end of the week.

Tricolore 1 Teacher's Notes xvii

This game can be used to practise any vocabulary, each member of the class being allocated a colour, fruit, part of a verb, etc.

Effacez!

Numbers, pictures or words are displayed in random order. When the caller names an item on the board, a student must rush out and delete the item.

This can be played by the teacher just pointing at the next student, who has five seconds only to locate and delete the right item. It can also be played in groups or in teams. In the latter case it is advisable to write two sets of items, each in a different colour. If the teacher wants the items left on for further practice they could be highlighted instead of being deleted. This is an excellent game for matching the written word to vocabulary previously met only aurally.

Les deux échelles (a dice game)

Two or more six-rung ladders can be drawn on the board with a number (or word, part of verb, etc.) on each rung. Each team or group throws the dice and reads out the number or word and, if it is the next on the ladder, it is crossed off and the team moves up to the next rung. No number or word must be crossed off until that rung is reached and the first team to reach the top of the ladder wins.

See also Dice games and *Loto!* (TB page xvi).

Qu'est-ce qu'il y a dans la boîte?

This game can be played with any selection of objects linked with a recent vocabulary topic, e.g. classroom objects, pictures of animals, clothes, etc.

First show the class the things to be used and practise the vocabulary. The objects are then taken out of sight and placed one at a time in a box for the class to guess which one is there each time.

Vrai ou faux? (True and false chairs)

This is a useful game for mixed or lower ability classes as it does not involve all the class in speaking or writing. Each team has two chairs labelled *vrai* and *faux*. The teacher (or a student) makes any statement and a member of each team comes out and sits on the true chair if s/he thinks the statement is true and on the false one if not. Sitting on the right chair wins a point for that team. (If the teams are too level, points can be given for the first child to sit on the right chair each time.)

Je touche

This is a cumulative game (chain game), in which the first person gets up and touches something, saying what he/she is doing, e.g. *Je touche le livre de Jean*, and then chooses someone to continue. The next person repeats what has been said and adds on something else, and so on.

For writing practice the class could try to write the whole list down from memory at the end.

Another alternative is to make, from memory, a numbered list of drawings. This list can be used again for pairwork, e.g. *Numéro 4, qu'est-ce que c'est?*

Touché-coulé (Battleships)

This well-known game (best played in pairs) can be adapted to practise various bits of language. In its simplest form students are given the area of vocabulary to be practised, e.g. a verb paradigm, numbers, days of the week, etc. or a set of flashcards is put up as a reminder. Each person writes down on paper any three of the alternatives. Each player in turn guesses one item that the other person has written and if guessed correctly, the player must cross it out. The first one to eliminate their partner's items has won.

More complicated versions, nearer to the original, involve writing the items in a particular place on squared paper or a plan so that one player says to their opponent, e.g. A3, *tu as …*!

Using Battleships to practise the verb 'être'

(as for *Unités* 3 or 5)

Each partner marks where s/he is on a simple plan of a house or flat. Then each asks the other, in turn, e.g. *Es-tu dans la cuisine?* answering, e.g. *Oui, je suis dans la cuisine* or *Non* if incorrect. The first one to discover where the other is has won.

When the whole paradigm has been learnt, the game can be extended to include the third person and the plural persons of the verb, e.g. *Les enfants sont dans le salon*, etc.

Je pense à quelque chose

The basic guessing game, in which someone thinks of a word (within a given range) and the others have to guess it by asking *C'est un/une …?* (See *Unité* 1 – SB p9.)

Le jeu des Scarabées (Beetle)

Again, various areas of vocabulary which can have visual interpretation can be adapted to this, e.g. Beetle house. Students draw a square divided into six for a house. They throw the dice and fill in the correct parts as follows:

1 la cuisine
2 la salle à manger
3 la salle de bains
4 la chambre
5 la porte
6 le jardin

The first to complete her/his house has won. Other possible subjects are pets (*Unité* 4), clothes (*Unité* 5), lessons on a timetable (*Unité* 8) and courses of a meal (*Unité* 9).

Jeu de mémoire (Kim's game)

Everyone looks at a set of objects, words or information for a set time (say, two minutes). Then one or more of these is removed or the whole lot are covered up, and the class has to remember as many objects, facts or words as possible.

3 Flashcard games

For guessing games involving flashcards the class should always be shown all the cards to be used first and the French for these should be practised or checked before the game begins.

Qu'est-ce que c'est? (Guess the back of the flashcard)

It is better to limit the cards to a single topic, so that there are not too many to choose from.

The pile of flashcards is shuffled and the caller holds up a card with the picture facing her/him and says *Qu'est-ce que c'est?* Other students ask *C'est un/une* (+ noun)? and the person who guesses correctly comes out and acts as caller.

Qu'est-ce qu'il/elle fait?

This game is similar to the one above but is played with flashcards depicting actions (e.g. flashcards 34–42 and 95–100).

Quel temps fait-il?

This is played in the same way as above, but with cards 27–33.

Ce n'est pas … (Guess what the card isn't)

This is played with the whole class, as a group game or in pairs. One player holds up a card, face away, and the other person(s) guess what it is not, e.g.

– *Ce n'est pas un chien.*
– *Vrai.*
– *Ce n'est pas une souris.*
– *Vrai.*
– *Ce n'est pas un lapin.*
– *Faux – c'est un lapin.*

This is a good morale booster as the answer is more often right than wrong!

Des questions

The teacher picks up one of a group of flashcards and asks a question about it. S/he gives the card to the student who answers correctly. When all the cards are given out, the students with them come to the front and ask a question about their card to someone else in the class who then receives the card if s/he answers correctly. This goes on until all the class have had a turn.

Où vas-tu?

To practise the verb *aller*, all the flashcards referring to places should be put up around the room. The teacher or a student tells someone, e.g. *Va à la gare!* The student gets up and goes to the relevant place and on the way is asked *Où vas-tu?* If s/he answers correctly s/he continues and the teacher asks someone else *Où va-t-il/elle?* If s/he replies incorrectly s/he sits down and someone else is told to go somewhere. If s/he replies correctly and arrives at the destination s/he has a point.

Trois questions (Mind reading)

This is good for practising verbs + nouns. Tell students that you are going to read their minds. Put up a number of flashcards and tell a student to think hard about one of them (get the thinker to tell her/his neighbour or write down which s/he has chosen, as a safeguard). Then ask three questions and if you have read her/his mind by then you get a point, if not the class gets a point.

Examples:
1. *être* (+ room)
   Teacher: *Tu es dans la salle à manger?*
   Student: *Non, je ne suis pas dans la salle à manger.*
   Teacher: *Tu es dans le salon?*
   Student: *Non, je ne suis pas dans le salon.*
   Teacher: *Tu es dans la cuisine?*
   Student: *Oui, je suis dans la cuisine.*
   or *Non, je ne suis pas dans la cuisine.*
   or *Non, je suis* (+ correct place)
2. *avoir* (+ pets)
   Teacher: *Tu as un lapin.*
   Student: *Oui, j'ai un lapin.*
   or *Non, je n'ai pas de lapin*, etc.
3. *aller* (+ place)
   Teacher: *Tu vas à l'église.*
   Student: *Oui, je vais à l'église.*
   or *Non, je ne vais pas à l'église*, etc.

This game can be adapted for use with a wide range of structures and can be played teacher v class, group v group, team v team, girls v boys, etc.

4 Mini-flashcard games

The flashcard games which follow can be played in pairs or small groups, with the sets of mini-flashcards made from the worksheets.

Pelmanism (group or pair game)

Use double sets of word cards, mini-flashcards or picture cards + matching word cards. In turn, students turn over a pair of cards to see if they match. They say the word on or represented by the cards, then turn them face downwards again in the same place – unless they form a pair, in which case they pick them up and keep them.

Le jeu des sept familles (Happy Families or Fish!)

Using four sets of mini flashcards for each group, or a set of home-made cards, this game can be played as normal, using *As-tu …?/Oui, j'ai/Non, je n'ai pas …*

Loto de vocabulaire (Flashcard Bingo)

Students could make their own sets of *Loto* cards with pictures of four items. Each group of students could make sets of cards dealing with a different vocabulary area. The example below uses vegetables and fruit.

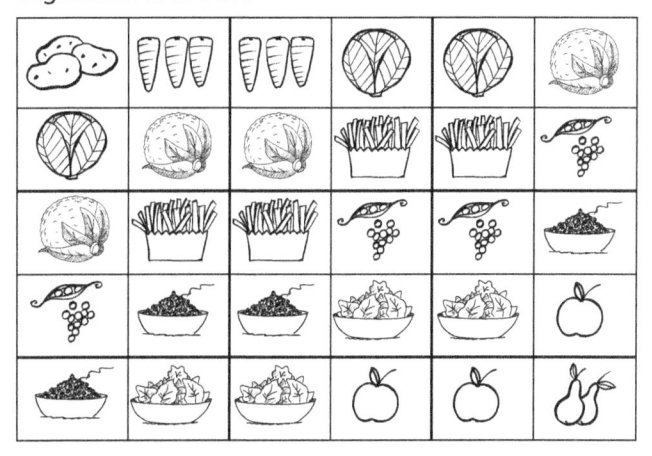

Tricolore 1 Teacher's Notes xix

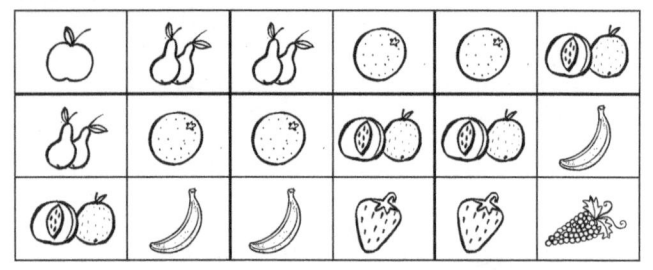

Players need four counters or buttons each.

The caller should shuffle the relevant flashcards and turn them up one at a time saying *Voilà des pommes de terre*, etc.

The winner (who must shout *Loto!*) is the player whose card is first full and who can also say the four things shown on it in French. If the first to finish cannot say the words in French s/he is out and the caller continues until the next card is full.

Suitable vocabulary areas for this are *En ville, À la maison, Les animaux* and weather.

The statements to be made by the caller can be extended to practise relevant structures, e.g. *J'aime les pommes de terre. Il y a des carottes.*

For a text-based item, teachers could use the grid in the *Tricolore 5ᵉ édition Kerboodle* resource, Starters and Plenaries section. This is a grid for 34 different cards (enough for one each in a fairly large class) using text for various items (e.g. *Unité* 3 covers 15 items of vocabulary on rooms and contents). Teachers could adapt the grid for other vocabulary topics and just replace a word or a picture.

'Carousel' version

Each group could have sets of flashcards, each on a different subject. The groups could rotate after five minutes or so to practise different sets of vocabulary.

Games with 2 sets of cards

Bataille! (Snap)

Flashcard snap in which they say the name of each card as they put it down. The first player to call *Bataille* wins the pile of cards.

Contre la montre

This is a race against time in which each student sorts their cards into fruit and vegetables, masculine and feminine, good and bad weather, inside or outside, as appropriate.

Mots et images

One player says the name of an object from their hand. The other player selects the appropriate card from their own hand and puts it on the table. Then this player says a name and the first player puts the appropriate card on the table, and so on.

5 Games for practising verbs

These are in addition to those already mentioned.

Verb dice

Make a big cardboard dice, but instead of numbers write on it *je, tu, il/elle/on, nous, vous, ils/elles*. Students throw the dice in turn and must say or write the correct part of the verb. The verbs could also be used in sentences, e.g. *Je suis à l'épicerie*.

Loto des verbes

Students write down three or four persons of a verb on their paper and play as before. Alternatively, about ten infinitives (of regular verbs) should be put on the board and everyone writes down the same person of four of them (this enables one person + relevant ending to be practised at a time).

Le jeu des mimes (Miming)

Students take turns to mime an action. The teacher or group leader says *Qu'est-ce qu'il/elle fait?* Students guess the action by asking *Tu regardes la télévision? Tu écoutes la radio?* etc. The actor answers *Oui, je regarde la télévision* or *Non, je ne regarde pas la télévision*, as appropriate.

Le jeu des mimes (Group version)

Students could work in groups of four or five, a representative of each group doing a mime in turn, and the members of the other groups writing down a guess for each mime. When enough mimes have been done (say, two or three per group), the groups can then be asked to guess in turn and to score a point for each correct guess. The points are totalled to find the winning group.

Chef d'orchestre

(See Number games, TB page xvi.) The teams must give the next person before or after the one quoted, in the standard paradigm or any agreed order. (Some classes will need the pronouns in order on the board as a visible prompt.)

Les verbes en cercle (Circle paradigm practice)

A number of subjects (nouns and pronouns) are written on the board, in random order, in the form of a circle, e.g.

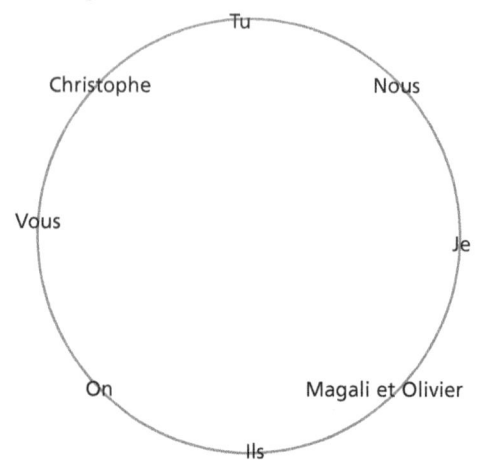

The teacher calls out a sentence, e.g. *Je joue au tennis*, and then points to any of the subjects in the circle and asks someone to modify the sentence accordingly. The person chosen then continues clockwise round the circle until stopped by the teacher. This practice drill should move quickly, with frequent changes of speaker, sentence and points on the circle. Different nouns and pronouns should be used whenever this is played.

Tricolore 1 Teacher's Notes

Jacques a dit (or Simon dit)

An old favourite in which students carry out actions preceded by *Jacques a dit (or Simon dit)* but not otherwise, e.g. *Jacques a dit (Simon dit): jouez au football! Asseyez-vous!* etc.

Les verbes en désordre (Scrambled verbs)

Write the pronouns and the six (or nine) parts of the verb in random order on each side of the board. One from each team comes out and rings *je* and the part which goes with it. Then, when this is done correctly, the next marker comes out and rings *tu* and the verb in a different colour, and so on until one team has correctly unscrambled the verb.

6 Spelling games

Dix secondes

Words linked with a particular topic are written on the board. A member of each team in turn has to see how many of the words s/he can spell correctly in, say, ten seconds. (The speller stands facing away from the board.) The words are crossed out or ticked when spelt so the choice gets smaller.

Je vois (I spy)

Play as in English: *Je vois quelque chose qui commence par …*

This game is particularly useful from *Unité* 2 onwards, when the French alphabet has been introduced.

Spelling consequences

Students in groups spell words one letter at a time, in turn. Each group has to say a new letter and must be 'on the way' to making a French word that makes sense, preferably from a given vocabulary area, e.g. *En ville* or *Les fruits et les légumes*.

If anyone thinks they know the word, they put their hand up, the spelling stops and they guess. If correct, their group gets a point and takes over, starting a new word. If wrong, the speller says which word they were spelling and the speller's group starts a new word, gaining one point. If anyone suspects that a group has added a letter when they had not got a word in mind, they can challenge. If they were right, they gain a point and take over with a new word. If wrong, the speller's group gets a point and starts a new word.

Songs

There are six songs on CD and Kerboodle, especially written and performed for *Tricolore*. The words of the songs and musical scores, comprising melodies, guitar chords and words, are on photocopiable pages of this Teacher's Book, TB pages xxii–xxvii. There is no music for *Attention, c'est l'heure!* which is a rap.

Un, deux, trois (Unité 2)

L'alphabet (Unité 4)

Le premier mois (Unité 6)

Attention, c'est l'heure! (Unité 8)

Pique-nique à la plage (Unité 9)

Samedi, on part en vacances (Unité 10)

There are two recorded versions of each song, one version including the words and the other an instrument only version.

The version of each song which includes the words can be:
- listened to by the students simply for enjoyment
- used as the stimulus material for various types of listening comprehension tasks or games
- used as a device to teach the song to students – they may be able to sing along with this version, or sing along with the teacher (who may choose to play the accompaniment or not) independently of the recording.

The instrument-only version of each song may be used in class as a means of encouraging students to perform the song without vocal support from the recording, and thus this version lends itself to independent preparation and performance by small groups. (The publishers recommend that students preparing the song independently of the teacher use a security copy in order to prevent the risk of damage to the master CD; OUP copyright conditions allow one such security copy to be made per purchasing establishment.)

Students preparing the songs in this way may be encouraged to perform them in extra- or cross-curricular contexts, for example departmental parents' evenings, school assemblies or as projects in conjunction with performing arts departments within the school.

The instrumental backing of the songs has been designed to be accessible and relatively simple in terms of musical structure and progression; thus, students with some musical training (in conjunction with music teachers or musically-able language teachers) might be expected to be able to produce full instrumental and vocal interpretations of these songs, by studying the recording and melody/guitar chords score.

Attention, c'est l'heure!

This rap 'song' practising times can be used at any appropriate point in *Unité* 8 or later.

Déjà sept heures moins dix, dix, dix,
Vite, vite, je vais être en retard.
Sept heures et quart je me prépare,
Je quitte la maison, enfin je pars.
Attention, c'est l'heure!
Ça y est, huit heures du mat, matin,
On entre en gare, j'arrive en train.
La cloche sonne à huit heures vingt,
Je suis au collège, tout va bien.
Attention, c'est l'heure!
Enfin midi, j'ai faim, faim, faim,
On va manger à la cantine.
Il est cinq heures, viens Géraldine,
La fin des cours, vive les copines.
Attention, c'est l'heure!
Il est six heures du soir, soir, soir,
Je fais mes devoirs, ouf, ça y est!
Huit heures, on prend tous le dîner,
Et puis, on regarde la télé.
Attention, c'est l'heure!
Besoin d'un bon dodo, dodo,
Très fatigué, je vais au lit.
Eh oui, il est dix heures et demie,
Alors à bientôt, bonne nuit.
Attention, c'est l'heure!

2 Words and music for the songs

L'alphabet

Moi, je sais l'al - pha - bet. E - coute, est-ce que c'est bon? A B C D E F G

1st time H... Ça con - tin - ue com - ment?

2nd time H I J K L M N O P... Ça con - tin - ue com - ment?

3rd time H I J K L M N O P Q R S

Tricolore 5ᵉ édition © Oxford University Press 2014

Un, deux, trois

- 1, 2, 3,
  Salut! C'est moi!
  4, 5, 6,
  J'habite à Nice.
  7, 8, 9,
  Dans la rue Elbeuf.
  10, 11, 12,
  Et toi?
- Toulouse.
  13, 14, 15,
  Dans l'avenue de Reims.
  16, 17,
  Je m'appelle Colette.
  18, 19, 20,
  C'est la fin!
  Recommence au numéro un …

Tricolore 5e édition © Oxford University Press 2014

Le premier mois

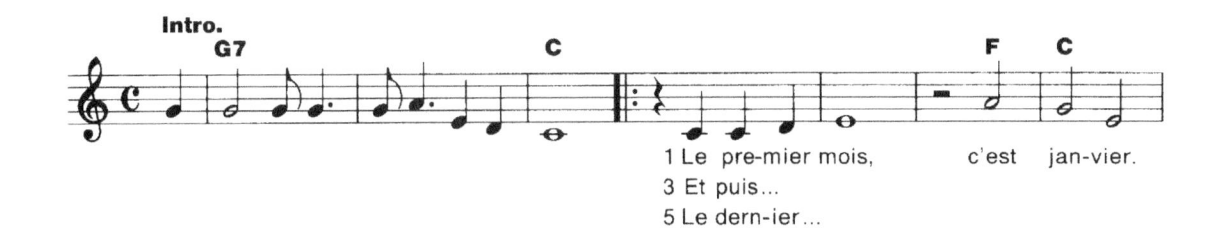

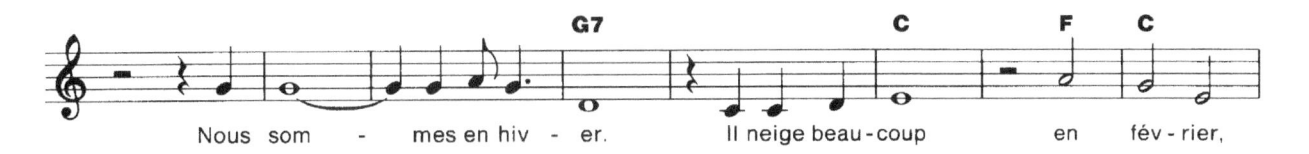

1. Le premier mois, c'est janvier.
   Nous sommes en hiver.
   Il neige beaucoup en février,
   En mars, il fait mauvais.

2. Au mois d'avril, il pleut, il pleut.
   Nous sommes au printemps.
   Il fait très beau au mois de mai,
   La météo dit: beau temps!

3. Et puis c'est juin, et juillet, août.
   Nous sommes en été.
   Il fait très chaud pour les vacances,
   Ma saison préférée.

4. Au mois de septembre la rentrée.
   Octobre, c'est l'automne.
   Du brouillard pendant novembre.
   Oh! qu'est-ce qu'il fait du vent!

5. Le dernier mois, on fête Noël.
   Nous sommes en décembre.
   Il fait très froid, mais moi, j'ai chaud –
   Je reste dans ma chambre!

Tricolore 5ᵉ édition © Oxford University Press 2014

Pique-nique à la plage

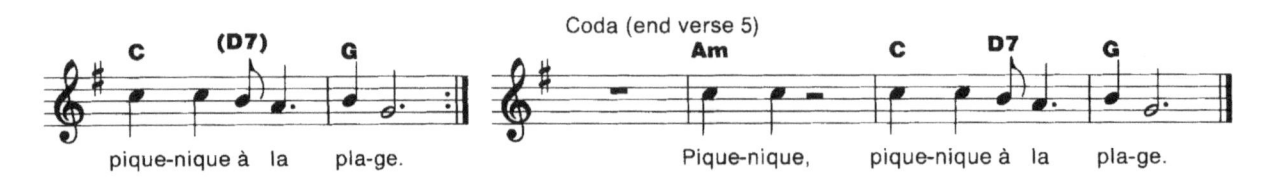

1. Bonne journée! Bonne journée!
   Tout le monde va pique-niquer.
   Va chercher le panier!
   Pique-nique, pique-nique à la plage.

2. Bonne journée! Bonne journée!
   Qu'est-ce que nous allons manger?
   Des sandwichs, une grande quiche.
   Pique-nique, pique-nique à la plage.

3. Bonne journée! Bonne journée!
   Regarde dans le panier.
   Oh, chouette, une galette!
   Pique-nique, pique-nique à la plage.

4. Bonne journée! Bonne journée!
   Il ne faut pas oublier
   Les chips, le vin, les petits pains.
   Pique-nique, pique-nique à la plage.

5. Quelle journée! Quelle journée!
   Tout le monde va pique-niquer.
   Allons trouver le soleil!
   Pique-nique, pique-nique à la plage.

Tricolore 5ᵉ édition © Oxford University Press 2014

Samedi, on part en vacances

Samedi, on part en vacances.
Samedi, on part en vacances.

1. Nice et Cannes, Toulouse et Sète,
   Ma valise est presque faite.
   Samedi, on part en vacances.
   Samedi, on part en vacances.

2. Oui, c'est vrai, on part demain.
   Où est mon maillot de bain?
   Nice et Cannes, Toulouse et Sète,
   Ma valise est presque faite.
   Samedi, on part en vacances.
   Samedi, on part en vacances.

3. Pour le soleil, mes lunettes,
   Pour le volley, mes baskets.
   Oui, c'est vrai, on part demain.
   Où est mon maillot de bain?
   Nice et Cannes, Toulouse et Sète,
   Ma valise est presque faite.
   Samedi, on part en vacances.
   Samedi, on part en vacances.

4. Faire du vélo, faire du ski,
   Faire du camping, allons-y!
   Pour le soleil, mes lunettes,
   Pour le volley, mes baskets.
   Oui, c'est vrai, on part demain.
   Où est mon maillot de bain?
   Nice et Cannes, Toulouse et Sète,
   Ma valise est presque faite.
   Samedi, on part en vacances.
   Samedi, on part en vacances.

5. Sète, Toulouse et Nice et Cannes,
   Nous allons en caravane.
   Faire du vélo, faire du ski,
   Faire du camping, allons-y!
   Pour le soleil, mes lunettes,
   Pour le volley, mes baskets.
   Oui, c'est vrai, on part demain.
   Où est mon maillot de bain?
   Nice et Cannes, Toulouse et Sète,
   Ma valise est presque faite.
   Samedi, on part en vacances.
   Samedi, on part en vacances.

6. Que nous avons de la chance,
   C'est bientôt les vacances!
   Sète, Toulouse et Nice et Cannes,
   Nous allons en caravane.
   Faire du vélo, faire du ski,
   Faire du camping, allons-y!
   Pour le soleil, mes lunettes,
   Pour le volley, mes baskets.
   Oui, c'est vrai, on part demain.
   Où est mon maillot de bain?
   Nice et Cannes, Toulouse et Sète,
   Ma valise est presque faite.
   Samedi, on part en vacances.
   Samedi, on part en vacances.

Tricolore 5e édition © Oxford University Press 2014

# Unit 1

Tricolore 1 Unité 1 Bonjour! Pages 8–13

Introduction page 3		
• Introduce France • Learn where some places are in France		
Grammaire	**Stratégies**	**Phonétique**
• None	• None	• None
Resources		
Key language: see page 2 Audio: None Copymasters: 1/1 *La France* Worksheets: None	Interactive activity: None PowerPoint: None Grammar in Action: None	

1A Toi et moi pages 8–9		
• Greet someone, ask their name and age and tell them yours • Ask someone how they are and tell them how you are		
Grammaire	**Stratégies**	**Phonétique**
• Use numbers 1–20	• Using what you know	• The letter 'c'
Resources		
Key language: see page 2 Audio files: **1** *Bonjour*; **2** *Ça va?* or CD 1, tracks 2 and 3 Flashcards: 1, 2 Copymasters: None Worksheets: Starters and plenaries	Interactive activity: *Bonjour! Ça va?* (L) Phonétique: The letter 'c'; *Qui parle?*, or CD 1, track 4 Grammar in Action: None	

1B Qu'est-ce que c'est? pages 10–11		
• Use numbers 1–20 with things in the classroom		
Grammaire	**Stratégies**	**Phonétique**
• Learn about gender (masculine and feminine) • Learn how to make singular nouns plural	• Working out meaning	• None
Resources		
Audio files: **1** *Des affaires scolaires*; **2** *Qu'est-ce que c'est?*; **4** *Qu'est-ce qui manque?*; *Dossier-langue*; *Stratégies* or CD 1, tracks 5, 6, 7, 8, 9 Copymasters: 1/2 *Écoutez bien* Worksheets: Starters and plenaries; *Une ou un?* (G); *Singulier ou pluriel?* (G)	Interactive activity: *Les affaires scolaires* (V) PowerPoint: Kim's game: *Les affaires scolaires* Grammar in Action: None	

1C En classe pages 12–13		
• Understand classroom commands and vocabulary • Practise some questions and answers		
Grammaire	**Stratégies**	**Phonétique**
• Giving instructions	• Remembering the gender of nouns (1)	• The letters 'i', 'y'
Resources		
Audio: **1b** *Donner un ordre*; **2** *Des instructions*; **3** *Un, deux, trois*, or CD 1, tracks 10, 12, 13 Copymasters: 1/3 *Sommaire* Worksheets: Starters and plenaries; *Dans la salle de classe* (R)	Interactive activity: *Vocabulaire de classe* (V) Ph The letters 'i', 'y', or CD 1, track 11 PowerPoint: *Un, deux, trois* (song) Grammar in Action: None	

Tricolore 1 Teacher's Notes   1

Introduction

Key language

Greetings, names and ages (1A)
Bonjour!
Salut!
Comment t'appelles-tu?
Je m'appelle …
Au revoir!!
Quel âge as-tu?
J'ai … ans.

Numbers 1–20 (1A)

Asking people how they are (1A)
Ça va?
Ça va bien, merci.
Comme ci comme ça.
Non, pas très bien.

Classroom items (1B)
Qu'est-ce que c'est?
C'est …
un bic
un cahier
un cartable
un carnet
un classeur
un crayon
un feutre
un lecteur MP3
un livre
un ordinateur (portable)
un portable
un sac (à dos)
un smartphone
un stylo
un surligneur
un tableau interactif
un taille-crayon
un trombone
une boîte
une calculatrice
une chaise
une clé USB
une fenêtre
une feuille de papier
une gomme
une porte
une poubelle
une règle
une table
une trousse

Classroom commands (1C)
Asseyez-vous.
Complète … /Complétez …
Compte … /Comptez …
Copie … /Copiez …
Écoute … /Écoutez …
Écris … /Écrivez …
Ferme … /Fermez …
Jouez à deux.
Levez-vous.
Ouvre … /Ouvrez …
Prends … /Prenez …
Range … /Rangez …
Regarde … /Regardez …
Répétez.
Réponds …
Travaillez à deux.
Trouve …

Introduction   page 3

- Introduce France
- Learn where some places are in France

Grammaire	Stratégies	Phonétique
• None	• None	• None
Resources		

Key language: see page 2
Audio: None
Copymasters: 1/1 *La France*
Worksheets: None

Interactive activity: None
PowerPoint: None
Grammar in Action: None

Tricolore 1 Teacher's Notes

1A Toi et moi   pages 8–9

- Greet someone, ask their name and age and tell them yours
- Ask someone how they are and tell them how you are

Grammaire	Stratégies	Phonétique
• Use numbers 1–20	• Using what you know	• The letter 'c'

Resources

Key language: see page 2
Audio files: 1 *Bonjour*; **2** *Ça va?* or CD 1, tracks 2 and 3
Flashcards: 1, 2
Copymasters: None
Worksheets: Starters and plenaries

Interactive activity: *Bonjour! Ça va?* (L)
Phonétique: The letter 'c'; *Qui parle?*, or CD 1, track 4
Grammar in Action: None

Worksheet

Starters (pages 8–9)

The material required for starters and plenaries can be found on online worksheets for each unit. They can be used to display on the interactive whiteboard or to print out.

1 **5-4-3-2-1** This is the first of a regular type of starter. Display the words in random order and ask students to find 5 towns/cities, 4 rivers, 3 mountains, 2 seas and 1 country.

Solution:

des villes	des rivières	des montagnes	des mers	un pays
La Rochelle	Garonne	Alpes	Atlantique	France
Lyon	Loire	Pyrénées	Méditerranée	
Marseille	Rhône	Vosges		
Paris	Seine			
Strasbourg				

If the online map activity has not yet been used, students could use that and talk briefly about France, before beginning to learn greetings, etc.

2 (Use after task 2 and the follow-up activities.) For a quick revision of introducing people, walk around the class, suddenly pointing to someone and asking the class *Qui est-ce?* When they reply, ask the person concerned *Comment t'appelles-tu?*

As this is simple revision, it needs to be done quickly, pointing to students behind you, on the other side of the class, etc. After a short while, able students could have a turn at this random pointing and questioning.

Introduction

Greetings

Introduce the class to French greetings and appropriate replies, both when addressed as a class and when addressed individually, e.g.

1 – *Bonjour, les enfants/les élèves/la classe!*
   – *Bonjour, Monsieur/Madame/Mademoiselle.*
2 – *Bonjour, Ellie/Olivia/Jack/Noah,* etc.
   – *Bonjour, M./Mme/Mlle.*

Greet individuals by name, perhaps shaking hands with them.

Explain the use of *Salut* as a more informal greeting (Hi!) and bring this into the conversation as well: *Salut, Lauren. Salut, Harry,* etc.

Introduce the other titles one at a time by using cards with names on, e.g. *M. Duval, Mme Cresson, Mlle Leclerc*.

Give out one or two cards and introduce those holding them to the class.

– *Voici Monsieur Duval. Répétez.*

– *Bonjour, Monsieur,* etc.

To make things more amusing, you could attach the name labels to hats which can then be put on a variety of children, who, in turn, exchange greetings with the class or individuals. When the class is confident with this, introduce *Au revoir* and practise in a similar way.

🔊 8

1 Bonjour!

The class listens to the greetings while looking at the photos.

Ask pupils what they think they'll be learning, before eliciting the lesson objective, e.g. by the end of the lesson you will be able to meet and greet someone in well pronounced French.

Then play the recordings again, this time with the students repeating after the speakers and then try out the conversations without the support of the recording. As you do this, begin to introduce some classroom commands, e.g.

Écoute! Écoutez! Ouvrez le livre à la page …

Regardez le livre.

Comment, if you wish, on the fact that shaking hands and sometimes kissing each other on the cheek, as shown in the photos, is quite usual in France for boys, girls and adults.

Tricolore 1 Teacher's Notes   **3**

1A Toi et moi

> 🖱 🔊 CD 1 Track 2
>
> ### Bonjour!
> 1 – Bonjour, Cécile.
>   – Bonjour, Sébastien.
> 2 – Salut, Olivier!
>   – Salut, Camille!
> 3 – Au revoir, Isabelle.
>   – Au revoir, Loïc.
> 4 – Bonjour, Monsieur Marcuse.
>   – Bonjour, Madame Lucas.
> 5 – Comment t'appelles-tu?
>   – Je m'appelle Océane. Et toi, comment t'appelles-tu?
>   – Je m'appelle Clément.

Use a selection of follow-up activities to consolidate the phrases learnt in task 1:
- after a short demonstration, ask students to get up and each say hello, then goodbye to four other people in French.
- integrate with greetings the teaching and practice of the commands: *Lève-toi/Levez-vous, Assieds-toi/Asseyez-vous, Viens/Venez ici* and *Retourne à ta place*. The game *Jacques a dit* (TB page xx) could be used here as a class activity to consolidate understanding of the new classroom commands.
- after playing the recording, introduce yourself: *Je m'appelle* (+ name) and then point to several students and get them to say *Je m'appelle* (+ name).
- gradually start to ask the question *Comment t'appelles-tu?* and practise this question and answer work until most students can answer correctly. The illustrated dialogue shows the printed form and should prove a useful prompt for practice in pairs. Make sure that everyone understands the rubric *Travaillez à deux*. As a follow-up, get students to go round the class asking four different people their names before they sit down.

Introduction

C'est ...?

The aim of the next activities is to be able to introduce people. Point to a student and ask *Comment t'appelles-tu?* The student replies. Then point to the student and say to the class. *C'est ...*

Gradually expand this as follows:
1 Teacher: *C'est ...? Oui/Oui, c'est ...*
2 Teacher: *Qui est-ce? C'est ...? Oui? Oui, c'est ...*
3 Teacher: *Qui est-ce?*
   Student: *C'est ...*
   Teacher: *Oui, c'est ...*
4 Teacher: *Qui est-ce? C'est* (+ wrong name)? *Non, c'est* (+ correct name).
5 Teacher: *Qui est-ce? C'est* (+ wrong name)?
   Student: *Non, c'est* (+ correct name).

> **Jeu**
>
> ### Devinez le prénom
> (Use at any point after task 1)
>
> Write a selection of about ten common French *prénoms* on cards and spread them out, face down. Students take turns to pick up and look at one of the cards, which then becomes his/her name. Other students are asked to guess the card-holder's name (*Qui est-ce?*) finally asking *Comment t'appelles-tu?* The student who guessed correctly picks a card next. Continue until all the names have been used.
>
> Several students could pick up cards and ask each other's names as a chain game. As an alternative version, one student picks up a card and the others have three chances to guess her/his correct name.
>
> Each pupil could keep a card and it could become his/her 'French name'.

> 📖 🔊 8 FC1–2   AfL
>
> ### 2 Ça va?

Tell the class they are going to learn how to ask people how they are or if they're OK. The class repeat *Ça va?* several times. Then get some students to ask you the question and, showing flashcard 1 (happy face), say *Oui, ça va bien, merci*. After a while, add to this *Et toi?* Hand the card to the questioner and get her/him to reply.

When everyone has practised this, introduce the possibility of not feeling too good, miming pain or sadness and using flashcard 2 (sad face) to teach *Non, pas très bien*.

Students copy down the names of the six people illustrated in silhouette or just write the numbers, then listen to the conversations between Julie and her friends and put a tick or a cross to show if each person is OK or not.

Pause the recording after the first conversation, referring to the example to make sure everyone knows what to do before playing the rest of the recording. Eventually correct the item orally with the class, perhaps playing the recording again and stopping after each conversation to say *Ça va? Oui ou non?*

> **Solution:**
> 1 *Lauryne* ✓, 2 *Julien* ✓, 3 *Sanjay* , 4 *Chloé* ✗,
> 5 *Léa* ✓, 6 *Alexandre*

1A Toi et moi

CD 1 Track 3

Ça va?

1. – Bonjour, Lauryne.
   – Ah, bonjour, Julie. Ça va?
   – Oui, ça va bien, merci, et toi?
   – Oui, oui. Ça va très bien.
2. – Bonjour, Julien, c'est Julie.
   – Ah, bonjour, Julie. Ça va?
   – Oui, ça va bien, merci, et toi?
   – Oui. Ça va très bien, merci.
3. – Bonjour, Sanjay.
   – Ah, salut Julie.
   – Ça va, Sanjay?
   – Oh, comme ci, comme ça.
4. – Bonjour, Chloé.
   – Qui est-ce?
   – C'est Julie. Ça va, Chloé?
   – Non, Julie. Ça ne va pas très bien.
5. – Bonjour, Léa.
   – Qui est-ce? C'est Julie?
   – Oui, oui, c'est moi. Ça va, Léa?
   – Ah, salut, Julie! Oui, oui, ça va bien, merci.
6. – Bonjour, Alexandre, c'est Julie.
   – Ah, bonjour, Julie. Ça va?
   – Oui, ça va bien, merci, et toi?
   – Bof, comme ci, comme ça.

For further practice, choose pairs of students to come out and ask each other *Ça va?* and cue their replies with the flashcards. This practice could continue as pair or group work and is an opportunity for peer assessment, with mini-flashcards made quickly by the students.

Interactive activity

Bonjour! Ça va?

Numbers 1–20

Many students will have at least some idea of the French numbers, but it is important to get pronunciation right at this point. It is a good idea to teach the numbers three at a time with students repeating them after you, and only move on to the next three when the previous group is properly learnt. Tell pupils that our brains recall information best when it's remembered in chunks.

Number games

There is a wide selection of these (see TB page xvi) e.g. *Loto!*, *Continue!*, *Onze* and *Le dix magique*. For games which have a winner, teach *J'ai gagné* and *(Name) a gagné*. The numbers need plenty of practice, so one or two number games could be played in each lesson during the first few weeks of French, with higher numbers being added unit by unit as they are introduced. *Zéro* could also be taught, perhaps as part of a 'countdown'.

If further practice of numbers 1–20 is required at this point, refer to 1C (page 10) where the numbers song can be used.

142 Au choix

1 C'est quel nombre?

9

3 Quel âge as-tu?

Students look at the question and answer printed at the top of the task and can be helped to work out how to slot different ages into the same answer structure. They can then go on to practise this with the puzzle.

1. Students follow the lines and work out each person's age, perhaps noting them down, e.g. Célia 11.
2. They work in pairs, in turns asking the age of their partner who replies for the person named, as in the example.

> **Solution:**
> Théo 5, Claude 10, Célia 11, Manon 7, Noah 3, Camille 18, Julien 8, Marine 17

Interactive activity

Qui parle?

Dialogue

Students could now add age to the dialogue previously used to ask each other's name (see SB page 8, task 2).

First revise greetings and asking names, demonstrating with a student.

Teacher: (shaking hands) *Bonjour.*
Student: *Bonjour, M./Mme/Mlle.*
Teacher: *Comment t'appelles-tu?*
Student: *Je m'appelle …*
Teacher: (shaking hands) *Au revoir, (name).*
Student: *Au revoir, M./Mme/Mlle.*

Get students to practise this in pairs, choosing a few to demonstrate this to the class. Then add in the new question and answer and get pairs of students to practise the complete dialogue, perhaps recording some of them.

9 Stratégies — AfL

Using what you know

This item provides consolidation of the questions and answers learnt so far, and is a good opportunity for peer assessment. Remind students of the spread objectives and agree the criteria for success. Students work in pairs to see how long a conversation they can make up. This could then be developed into a class competition to see which pair's conversation is the longest (as well as being correct).

Presentation

Quel âge?

Tricolore 1 Teacher's Notes

1B Qu'est-ce que c'est?

4 Salut!

a This is a follow-up to the *Stratégies*. Students complete the conversation with their own or made up details.

b The extension activity gives previous learners something to work at and could also be attempted by the more able linguists, even at this early stage. Encourage students with previous knowledge of French to use other relevant questions and expressions if they can. This will, of course, depend on other students understanding any language introduced. Strategies for dealing with unfamiliar language could be presented, e.g.:

Je ne comprends pas.

Comment ça se dit en anglais?

'[word]', c'est quoi en anglais?

See Unité 2C, (SB p19) for more practice.

Interactive activity

The letter 'c'

9 Phonétique

The letter 'c'

A full explanation of the sound of the letter 'c' is given on *kerboodle!*, together with interactive practice which includes differentiating between hard and soft 'c' sounds.

a Say the word *cinq* with the appropriate gesture (e.g. holding up five fingers). Students repeat the word with the same gesture. Then read out the other soft 'c' words with students repeating each one. The words are also included on the recording for optional use (part a).

Then say the word *cartable* with the appropriate gesture (e.g. carrying a schoolbag). Students repeat the word with the same gesture. Then read out the other hard 'c' words with students repeating each one.

Parts **b**, **c** and **d** can be used to practise pronunciation of the hard and soft 'c' sounds:

b Display the soft 'c' words (**a** *cinq*, **b** *Cécile*, **c** *un garçon*, **d** *ça*, **e** *c'est*) and ask students to match the words they hear to the written form (**e, d, b, a, c**);

c Display the hard 'c' words (**a** *comme*, **b** *M. Marcuse*, **c** *écoute*, **d** *Camille*, **e** *cartable*) and ask students to match the words they hear to the written form (**d, b, a, e, c**);

d Students listen to the silly sentences and note down the number of hard 'c' sounds (4) and soft 'c' sounds (3) they hear. They can then repeat the sentences to help them remember these sounds.

CD 1 Track 4

The letter 'c'

a cinq, c'est, Cécile, un garçon, ça
   cartable, Camille, comme, M. Marcuse
b c'est, ça, Cécile, cinq, un garçon
c Camille, M. Marcuse, comme, cartable, écoute
d Écoute, c'est Lucas au collège. Il dit: Comment ça va, Célia?

Worksheet

Plenaries (pages 8–9)

1 Students write down two sentences summarising the lesson, then share these with the class. Discuss the key points to remember and what aspects might cause difficulties.

2 Discuss strategies for remembering words and phrases and urge students to practise at home – maybe with brothers and sisters.

1B Qu'est-ce que c'est?   pages 10–11

- Use numbers 1–20 with things in the classroom

Grammaire	Stratégies	Phonétique
• Learn about gender (masculine and feminine) • Learn how to make singular nouns plural	• Working out meaning	• None

Resources
Audio files: 1 *Des affaires scolaires*; 2 *Qu'est-ce que c'est?*; 4 *Qu'est-ce qui manque?*; *Dossier-langue*; *Stratégies* or CD 1, tracks 5, 6, 7, 8, 9 **Copymasters:** 1/2 *Écoutez bien* **Worksheets:** Starters and plenaries; *Une ou un?* (G); *Singulier ou pluriel?* (G)	**Interactive activity:** *Les affaires scolaires* (V) **PowerPoint:** Kim's game: *Les affaires scolaires* **Grammar in Action:** None

Tricolore 1 Teacher's Notes

1B Qu'est-ce que c'est?

> Worksheet

Starters (pages 10–11)

1. Everyone stands up. Go quickly round the class asking people questions, alternating between their name, age and if they are well. If they answer correctly they sit down, until all are seated.

2. (Use before task 2) The lesson could start with a game to see if students remember the classroom vocabulary, e.g. *Jeu de mémoire* (Kim's game – see TB page xviii) or *Je touche* (TB page xvii). Use actual objects in the classroom, or the PowerPoint game below (Jeu de mémoire: Mes affaires d'école).

> Introduction

Gender

Grammatical gender is still a difficult concept, to be introduced gradually, stressing its importance but not making it sound too difficult.

The words *garçon* and *fille* have occurred in the number games, but in any case they are good ones to start with.

Revise the questions and answers learnt already and move on from *Qui est-ce? C'est Jean.* to *Qui est-ce? C'est un garçon. C'est un garçon? Oui, c'est un garçon.*

The best way to teach classroom objects, initially, is to handle them, introducing the words orally. A good standard teaching sequence is as follows:

Écoutez!/Répétez! C'est un(e) …

Oui ou non?/Choix – c'est un stylo ou un crayon?

Corrigez-moi. C'est un crayon.

Non, c'est un stylo.

Qu'est-ce que c'est? etc.

Introduce the French for five masculine classroom objects (*un livre, un stylo, un cahier, un crayon, un cartable*) and practise them with the question *Qu'est-ce que c'est?*

Then help students to deduce that the word for 'a' used with the other words is *un* (like *un* before *garçon*).

Next point to a girl and say *C'est un garçon?* (In single sex classes, use alternatives such as flashcards or a PowerPoint presentation.) When you get the answer *Non*, say *Non, c'est une fille. Répétez. C'est une fille*. Elicit the difference in sound from pupils.

Now teach five feminine objects (*une chaise, une règle, une table, une gomme, une boîte*) with *Qu'est-ce que c'est?*

Draw attention to the word *une* and link it with *une fille*.

Explain briefly that, in French, all objects are either *un* or *une* words, and mention the terms masculine and feminine. Tell the students to make sure that they always learn whether a word is masculine or feminine. You could introduce an ongoing presentation technique with PowerPoint: use one colour background for masculine words, one for feminine and one for plurals and get pupils to always do the same. Tell the students this is helpful as we learn in three ways – through seeing, hearing and doing, and this particular technique helps visual memory.

Or give each student two pieces of card, one in blue for masculine nouns, one in red for feminine nouns. When practising new vocabulary, students hold up the blue or red card as appropriate. This makes them think about the gender, and the colour helps cement the gender for some students. (See the Unité 1 Starters & Plenaries file in the online resource for a printable version of these cards.)

Next, teach a few more classroom objects (*un ordinateur, un classeur, un sac à dos, un trombone, un taille-crayon, une calculatrice, une trousse*) and practise these as before.

As further practice, play some fast-paced vocabulary games at the end.

Stress that masculine/feminine is not to do with the essence of the thing – stereotypically manly things are not necessarily masculine or girly things feminine.

> Interactive activity

Les affaires d'école

> Presentation

Jeu de mémoire: Mes affaires d'école

🔊 10

1 Des affaires d'école

Ask the class to look at the pictures of classroom objects, noticing that they are divided into masculine (*un*) and feminine (*une*) words (surrounded with red or blue frames as an added reminder).

Explain *affaires* if they have not already met the phrase *Rangez vos affaires!*

Students write down the numbers from 1–15, listen to the recording and write down the letter for each object as it is mentioned in the recording.

This task could be corrected by playing the recording again and stopping to check each answer in turn.

Reinforce gender here by asking students, as they listen, to say whether they heard *un* or *une* and what that, therefore, tells them about the noun, i.e. that it is masculine or feminine (*c'est masculin/féminin*).

The written form of the names for classroom objects can be introduced as soon as students are confident enough in their pronunciation. They should refer to the list in the *Sommaire* on page 13.

This is a suitable time for students to start their own vocabulary books, perhaps adopting the idea of writing or underlining masculine words in blue and feminine ones in red.

> **Solution:**
> **1** C, **2** I, **3** J, **4** A, **5** E, **6** N, **7** B, **8** D, **9** F, **10** H, **11** M, **12** L, **13** K, **14** O, **15** G

1B Qu'est-ce que c'est?

🔊 CD 1 Track 5

Des affaires d'école

1 – Qu'est-ce que c'est?
– C'est un cahier.
2 – Et ça? C'est une règle?
– Ah oui, c'est une règle.
3 – Qu'est-ce que c'est?
– C'est une gomme.
4 – C'est un livre?
– Oui, c'est un livre.
5 – Qu'est-ce que c'est?
– C'est un cartable.
6 – Et voici une chaise.
– Oui, oui, c'est une chaise.
7 – Et ça, qu'est-ce que c'est?
– C'est un stylo.
8 – Voici un crayon.
– C'est vrai. C'est un crayon.
9 – Et ça, qu'est-ce que c'est?
– C'est un taille-crayon, c'est mon taille-crayon.
10 – Et voici un bic.
– Oui, un bic. C'est important, ça!
11 – Et une calculatrice, regarde!
– Ah bon, c'est ma calculatrice, ça!
12 – Oui? Dans la trousse? C'est ça?
– Oui, oui. Dans la trousse.
13 – Et ça, c'est une boîte?
– Oui, c'est une boîte.
14 – Et ça, c'est une table.
– Oui, c'est vrai, c'est une table.
15 – Et voici un ordinateur.
– Oui, un ordinateur. Ça, c'est très important!

10 Dossier-langue

Masculine and feminine (gender)

Draw students' attention to this brief *Dossier-langue*, which sums up the gender of nouns.

If students already have the necessary dictionary skills, point out that the gender of a noun is listed after all nouns in a dictionary. They could try looking up some nouns and check if they are followed by m or f. Similarly, the *Glossaire* shows the gender of all nouns by including an article and using m/f where necessary.

140 Au choix

2 Télé-jeu: 30 secondes

Worksheet

Un ou une?

🔊 10   AfL

2 Qu'est-ce que c'est?

a Revise the classroom objects already taught using the structure *Qu'est-ce que c'est?*

– C'est un [bic/cahier/cartable/crayon/livre/ordinateur/stylo/taille-crayon.]

– C'est une [boîte/calculatrice/chaise/gomme/règle/table/trousse.]
– Voici/Voilà un/une …
– Oui/Non.

Then teach **un** tableau interactif, **un** portable, **un** carnet, **un** lecteur MP3, **un** classeur, **un** sac à dos, **un** trombone, **un** feutre, **un** surligneur, **une** clé USB, **une** feuille de papier, **une** poubelle, **une** fenêtre, **une** porte. Use flashcards, objects or the online presentation (Les affaires d'école).

When students are familiar with the new vocabulary, they can do the listening activity. For this they listen to French children playing the game *Je pense à quelque chose*, using a mixture of masculine and feminine nouns. Before they do this, explain simply how the game works, e.g.

– *Je pense à quelque chose. Qu'est-ce que c'est?*
– *C'est un livre?*
– *Non, ce n'est pas ça.*
– *C'est un feutre?*
– *Oui, c'est ça. Très bien!*

Play the game with them a few times, using first the objects in the masculine box (*un*), then in the feminine box (*une*). Play a few more rounds with students taking the teacher's role. Students can then listen to the recording and write down the numbers of any objects mentioned.

Solution:
4, 8, 10, 1, 7, 5, 3

🔊 CD 1 Track 6

Qu'est-ce que c'est?

– Je pense à quelque chose. Qu'est-ce que c'est?
– C'est un classeur.
– Non, ce n'est pas ça.
– C'est un feutre?
– Non, ce n'est pas ça.
– C'est une fenêtre?
– Non, ce n'est pas ça.
– C'est un tableau interactif?
– Oui, c'est un tableau interactif. Très bien!
– Je pense à quelque chose. Qu'est-ce que c'est?
– C'est un trombone?
– Non, ce n'est pas ça.
– C'est un sac à dos?
– Non, ce n'est pas ça.
– C'est un portable?
– Oui, c'est ça. C'est un portable.

b Students can now play the game in pairs or groups, using both masculine and feminine singular nouns. This is an opportunity for peer assessment. Remind students of the spread objectives and agree the criteria for success. Show how their work can be improved by praising good examples and letting them demonstrate to other groups or the whole class.

For further practice, students could play a version of *Je pense à quelque chose* using mini whiteboards. Working in pairs, they each draw (in secret) three items they might find in a pencil case/classroom. They have to guess their partner's items by asking,

Tricolore 1 Teacher's Notes

1B Qu'est-ce que c'est?

e.g. *Un stylo, s'il te plaît*. If their partner has drawn this item, they get another go; if not, they swap over. The winner is the person who identifies all three with the fewest guesses.

11 Dossier-langue

Plural nouns

This explains plurals. The listening activity focuses on the sound of singular and plural forms. Students should then look at the difference between French and English plurals. Elicit from them that the final *s* in French is silent and practise other words in the singular and plural.

CD 1 Track 7

Plural nouns

1	un crayon neuf crayons	4	une solution trois solutions
2	une table cinq tables	5	un parent deux parents
3	un article sept articles	6	un sport quatre sports

11

3 Au collège

a Students read through the statements about Mathilde's possessions, and copy down only those which match the picture.

Solution:

1 Il y a quatre crayons, 3 Il y a une trousse, 4 Il y a trois livres, 5 Il y a un portable

b This time, students refer to the picture and write complete sentences to describe it.

Solution:

*Dans le sac de Thomas, il y a **un** taille-crayon. Il y a **deux** classeurs. Il y a cinq **règles**, une **calculatrice**, quatre crayons et **un** carnet.*

c An extension activity where students have the opportunity to write phrases independently.

Interactive activity

Combien?

Worksheet

Singulier ou pluriel?

142 Au choix

3 C'est quelle image?

cm 1/2

Écoutez bien!

11 Stratégies

Working out meaning

This short item focuses on the French pronunciation of cognates that are easy to recognise when read. Play the recording and get students to repeat the French.

CD 1 Track 8

Working out meaning

1 *France*, 2 *Paris*, 3 *table*, 4 *sport*, 5 *animal*, 6 *action*, 7 *télévision*, 8 *orange*, 9 *violet*, 10 *intelligent*

11

4 Qu'est-ce qui manque?

Students listen to the conversation and look at Carine's birthday presents to work out which ones are missing. First get students to read the introductory text and work out or look up the meaning of *anniversaire, cadeaux* and *Qu'est-ce qui manque?* Then ask them to name the presents shown (*un portable, deux livres, un tee-shirt*) – the last one could be presented as a cognate to reinforce earlier *Stratégies*.

They then listen to the conversation of the girl speaking on the phone and see if they can spot and write down the three presents that are not shown in the picture.

Solution:

un sac à dos; deux bics; un ordinateur

CD 1 Track 9

Qu'est-ce qui manque?

– Comme cadeaux d'anniversaire, j'ai reçu un portable et deux livres et un sac à dos.
– C'est super bien.
– Et aussi, il y a un tee-shirt et deux bics et un ordinateur.
– Un ordinateur?! C'est fantastique!

Possible group or class follow-up activities include:

1 Students could choose three or four of the objects learnt on the spread and say that they received them for birthday gifts. The other students note down their 'gifts'.

2 They could use actual classroom objects and work in a group naming all the objects. One of the objects is then taken away and the other students answer the question *Qu'est-ce qui manque?*

3 They could play a cumulative game. Student 1 starts with one object, e.g. *Comme cadeau d'anniversaire, j'ai reçu un ordinateur*. The next student repeats this and adds on a second object, e.g. *… et un stylo*. Students continue to add on objects until the list is exhausted. This is a good activity for those who have done French before as they could use previously learnt vocabulary.

Tricolore 1 Teacher's Notes

1C En classe

> **Worksheet**

Plenaries (pages 10–11)

1 Use the game *Qu'est-ce qu'il y a dans la boîte?* (see TB page xvii). Make sure that there are sometimes several of the same object in the box. When students have identified an object, encourage them to think about whether they should use *un/une* or a number and how they remembered which to use. If there is only one object, ask how to make this plural. Similarly, for plural objects, elicit whether one of them would be *un* or *une*. A number of images are provided on the online worksheet for a version of this activity if required.

2 Follow up the *Stratégies* item on this spread by leading a discussion of the correlation between sound and spelling, based on place names on the map (SB page 3), e.g.

France – looks like English: sounds totally different

Paris, Calais – final consonant not sounded

Lyon/Lyons – languages often spell towns differently

Honfleur – silent 'h'

This could lead into a further discussion about learning strategies and identifying patterns in language (including comparisons with patterns in English). Some words are provided on the online worksheet for a version of this activity if required.

1C En classe   pages 12–13

- Understand classroom commands and vocabulary
- Practise some questions and answers

Grammaire	Stratégies	Phonétique
• Giving instructions	• Remembering the gender of nouns (1)	• The letters 'i', 'y'

Resources

Audio: 1b *Donner un ordre*; 2 *Des instructions*; 3 *Un, deux, trois*, or CD 1, tracks 10, 12, 13
Copymasters: 1/3 Sommaire
Worksheets: Starters and plenaries; *Dans la salle de classe* (R)

Interactive activity: *Vocabulaire de classe* (V)
Ph The letters 'i', 'y', or CD 1, track 11
PowerPoint: *Un, deux, trois* (song)
Grammar in Action: None

> **Worksheet**

Starters (pages 12–13)

1 As all the items on this double page spread are intended to consolidate the language covered in the first weeks of learning French, another look at the online map of France would be appropriate.

Students could see how quickly they can identify the places on the map and then work in groups to see how many of the words on the map and how many snippets of information about France they can remember.

2 5-4-3-2-1 game. Display the list of words in random order, then ask students to name 5 electrical/electronic items, 4 things to write with, 3 containers, 2 pieces of furniture, 1 book.

> **Solution:**
>
> *un lecteur MP3, un ordinateur, un portable, un tableau interactif, un smartphone; un bic, un crayon, un feutre/un surligneur, un stylo; une boîte, un sac (à dos)/un cartable, une trousse; une chaise, une table; un cahier/un livre/un carnet*

Introduction

Classroom instructions

Gradually introduce *s'il te plaît* and *merci bien* and, if wished, *Je ne sais pas/Je voudrais un …*

Begin to use as often as possible such commands as *regardez, ouvrez, fermez, écrivez*, so that the class gets used to the lesson being conducted in French.

🔊 12

1 Donner un ordre

a Students read the classroom commands and match them to the illustrated activities.

> **Solution:**
>
> **1** C, **2** A, **3** H, **4** B, **5** G, **6** J, **7** D, **8** I, **9** E, **10** F

b Students listen to the recording and write down the letter for the correct picture.

> **Solution:**
>
> **1** E, **2** C, **3** G, **4** F, **5** B, **6** I, **7** H, **8** J, **9** A, **10** D

10 Tricolore 1 Teacher's Notes

1C En classe

CD1 Track 10

Donner un ordre
1. Asseyez-vous.
2. Écoutez.
3. Écrivez.
4. Fermez le cahier.
5. Levez-vous.
6. Ouvrez le livre à la page 10.
7. Prenez un stylo.
8. Rangez vos affaires.
9. Regardez.
10. Répétez.

c This activity provides written practice of the classroom commands in context. Students could read out their answers and direct other students or the teacher to follow the appropriate instruction.

Solution:
1. *Écoutez la chanson.*
2. *Comptez les crayons.*
3. *Ouvrez le carnet.*
4. *Fermez la fenêtre.*
5. *Regardez le tableau interactif.*
6. *Trouvez un bic.*
7. *Regardez le livre.*
8. *Fermez le cahier.*

Interactive activity

Vocabulaire de classe (1)

12

2 Des instructions
a This activity provides written practice of the classroom commands in context. Students could read out their answers and direct other students or the teacher to follow the appropriate instruction.

Solution:
1 c, 2 d, 3 a, 4 e, 5 b

b For this extension activity, students design posters illustrating the key commands to display around the classroom.

Worksheet

Dans la salle de classe

12 Dossier-langue

Giving instructions

Some students might like to look up the imperative in the grammar section. It is formally introduced and practised in *Unité* 7, but imperatives form an essential part of rubrics on every page, so they are important to recognise and can be fun to use creatively (e.g. by students bossing each other around, creating silly commands or instructions, etc.).

Follow-up suggestion: students role play in groups of 3–4 – the one being the teacher gives the commands and the rest act them out. Students who have prior knowledge of the imperative could act as the teacher.

The game *Jacques a dit* is also a useful one to play at this point.

Interactive activity

The letters 'i', 'y'

12 Phonétique

The letters 'i', 'y'

A full explanation of the sound of the letters 'i' and 'y' is given on *kerboodle!*, together with interactive practice.

a Say the word *livre* with the gesture for book (turning palms up as if opening a book). Students repeat the word with the same gesture. Do the same for *stylo* (with a writing action). Then read out the other words with students repeating each one. The words are also included on the recording for optional use (part **a**).

Parts **b**, **c** and **d** can be used to practise pronunciation of the 'i' and 'y' sound.

b Display these words: a *dix*, b *unité*, c *merci*, d *un bic*, e *il y a*, f *un stylo*. Students listen to the recording and write the letter of the word they hear (a, e, c, d, f, b).

c Display these words: *six, écris, livre, dis, oui, fille*. Students should say them, then listen to the recording to check their pronunciation. Play the recording again, pausing for students to repeat each word.

d Students listen to the silly sentence and note down how many times they hear the sound (7). They can then repeat the sentence to help them remember this sound.

CD 1 Track 11

The letters 'i', 'y'

Écoutez et répétez:
a stylo, livre, souris, Paris, merci
b dix, il y a, merci, un bic, un stylo, unité
c six, écris, livre, dis, oui, fille
d Sylvie la souris lit dix livres à Paris.

Tricolore 1 Teacher's Notes

1C En classe

12 Stratégies

Remembering the gender of nouns (1)

A memorisation strategy to help reinforce the gender of nouns. Students should be encouraged to use colour coding in their personal vocabulary books.

142 Au choix

4 Trouve la question

13

3 Un, deux, trois

Students read the song as they listen to it, then listen again and join in. There is also an instrumental-only version of the song for students to sing along without the words as support.

See TB page xxi for notes on using the songs.

For reference, the numbers 1–30 are listed in the *Sommaire* for *Unité* 2 (SB page 19).

CD 1 Tracks 12–13

Un, deux, trois

- 1, 2, 3,
  Salut! C'est moi!
  4, 5, 6,
  J'habite à Nice.
  7, 8, 9,
  Dans la rue Elbeuf.
  10, 11, 12,
  Et toi?
- Toulouse.
  13, 14, 15,
  Dans l'avenue de Reims.
  16, 17,
  Je m'appelle Colette.
  18, 19, 20,
  C'est la fin!
  Recommence au numéro un …

13 cm 1/3

Sommaire

This is a summary of the main language and structures taught in this unit. It is also on copymaster for ease of reference.

Interactive activity

Vocabulaire (1)

Worksheet

Plenaries (pages 12–13)

1 Get students to construct a mind map. Provide a blank sheet with headings for the topics covered (greetings, name and age, health, numbers, classroom objects, classroom commands). Students write notes or vocabulary for each of the headings, based on their learning so far, then discuss these with the teacher.

2 Referring to the *Sommaire* for help, students work in pairs to see how long a conversation they can make up, using greetings, questions and answers about name, age and health and also about what things are and how many of them there are. Encourage discussion about what students have learnt, what parts are easier and what proved more difficult.

Au choix

142 Au choix

1 C'est quel nombre?

This provides practice in understanding numbers, used alone and with nouns.

Solution:
1 F, **2** C, **3** A, **4** H, **5** J, **6** G, **7** B, **8** D, **9** E, **10** I

CD 1 Track 14

C'est quel nombre?

1 six
2 dix-huit
3 deux
4 douze
5 dix
6 trois livres
7 trois cahiers
8 sept crayons
9 deux gommes
10 quatre stylos

142 Au choix

2 Télé-jeu: 30 secondes

This is a fun listening item for practice of classroom vocabulary. Ask students to look at the picture, then explain it briefly:

Voilà, c'est un jeu à la télé. Regardez les prix. Chloé gagne quatre choses et Max gagne six choses.

Explain *gagne*, if not guessed. Some teachers may wish to give their class the written words (on the board in random order). As follow-up, students can play the game themselves. One student sees how many prizes s/he can win in thirty seconds, without looking at the book and with suitable applause from the class. Soon, a student can play the quizmaster, or the game can be played in groups. More prizes could be added.

Solution:
Chloé 1, 2, 4, 6 **Max** 1, 3, 5, 7, 8, 9

12 Tricolore 1 Teacher's Notes

1C En classe

▶ 🔊 CD 1 Track 15

Télé-jeu: 30 secondes
- Voilà, Chloé et Max, regardez les prix – ce sont des prix fantastiques, non?
- Oui, oui, fantastiques!
- Bon, tu as trente secondes: 3 … 2 … 1 … zéro!
- Eh bien, numéro un, c'est un ordinateur portable et deux, euh, c'est un smartphone.
- Très bien, super! Continue!
- Alors trois, numéro trois, c'est … c'est une télé?
- Ah, non. Mais …
- Ah non, euh, la télé, c'est numéro quatre. Et numéro six, euh, c'est un lecteur MP3 …
- Trente secondes! Très bien, Chloé. Tu as gagné un ordinateur portable, un smartphone, une télé et un lecteur MP3.
- Oh, merci, merci, monsieur.
- Et maintenant, Max. Ça va?
- Euh … oui, oui, ça va.
- Tu as trente secondes: 3 … 2 … 1 … zéro! Commence!
- Numéro un est un ordinateur portable, euh … oui, numéro trois, c'est une calculatrice; numéro cinq, des crayons; numéro sept, un classeur; numéro huit, une poubelle, numéro neuf, un cartable et …
- Trente secondes! Fantastique, Max! Tu as gagné six prix, six! Voilà: un ordinateur portable, une calculatrice, des crayons, un classeur, une poubelle et un cartable. Félicitations et au revoir!

📖 142 Au choix

3 C'est quelle image?
Students match the conversations to the pictures.

Solution:
1 B, **2** A, **3** G, **4** C, **5** D, **6** E, **7** F, **8** H

📖 142 Au choix

4 Trouve la question
Students find the appropriate question to match the answers supplied.

Solution:
1 c, **2** e, **3** f, **4** a, **5** d, **6** b

Copymasters

🔊 cm 1/2

Écoutez bien!
A listening quiz on language taught in this unit. Students write down 'Section 1' and numbers from 1–5. They look at the pictures and write the letter of the correct one as they hear it.

Solution:
1 d, **2** b, **3** e, **4** a, **5** c

In Section 2, the class number again from 1–5, then listen for the age of each speaker.

Solution:
1 e, **2** a, **3** b, **4** d, **5** c

In Section 3, students number from 1–10, then listen for classroom objects.

Solution:
1 j, **2** c, **3** b, **4** d, **5** g, **6** a, **7** i, **8** f, **9** h, **10** e

▶ 🔊 CD 1 Tracks 16–18

Écoutez bien!
Section 1
1 Bonjour! Je m'appelle Pierre.
2 Bonjour! Je m'appelle Françoise.
3 Bonjour! Je m'appelle Catherine.
4 Bonjour! Je m'appelle Jean-Pierre.
5 Bonjour! Je m'appelle Michèle.

Écoutez bien!
Section 2
1 – Quel âge as-tu?
– J'ai six ans.
2 – Quel âge as-tu?
– J'ai quatre ans.
3 – Quel âge as-tu?
– J'ai douze ans.
4 – Quel âge as-tu?
– J'ai cinq ans.
5 – Quel âge as-tu?
– J'ai dix ans.

Écoutez bien!
Section 3
1 C'est une gomme.
2 C'est un livre.
3 C'est un cartable.
4 C'est une règle.
5 C'est une boîte.
6 – Qu'est-ce que c'est?
– C'est un crayon.
7 – Qu'est-ce que c'est?
– C'est un cahier.
8 – Qu'est-ce que c'est?
– C'est une table.
9 – Qu'est-ce que c'est?
– C'est un stylo.
10 – Qu'est-ce que c'est?
– C'est une chaise.

cm 1/3

Sommaire
A summary of the main vocabulary and structures in the unit. This copymaster provides a reference for students to file or annotate as they wish. They could apply colour coding to the nouns to help them memorise the genders.

Tricolore 1 Teacher's Notes

Unité 2

Tricolore 1 Unité 2 J'habite ici   Pages 14–19

2A Venez en France pages 14–15		
• Understand people saying where they live		
Grammaire	Stratégies	Phonétique
• Learn how to say 'in' a place	• Using clues to work out meaning (1)	• The letters 'ch'
Resources		
Audio: 1 *J'habite en France*; or CD 1, track 19 Copymasters: 2/1 *J'habite en France* Worksheets: Starters and plenaries	Interactive activity: *J'habite en France* (L, R) Ph The letters 'ch', or CD 1, track 20 PowerPoint: Kim's game : *Où habites-tu?* Grammar in Action: None	
2B Où habites-tu? pages 16–17		
• Say where you live • Ask someone where they live		
Grammaire	Stratégies	Phonétique
• Use numbers up to 30 • Asking a question	• Memorising numbers	• The letters 'j', 'ge', 'gi'
Resources		
Audio: 2 *Et toi? Où habites-tu?*; 3 *Qui habite où?*; 5a *Inventez des conversations* or CD 1, tracks 21, 22 and 24 Copymasters: 2/2 *Trois conversations* Worksheets: Starters and plenaries; Prepositions used for locations (G); Numbers 1–30 (V), *Carte d'identité* (W); *J'habite à …* (W)	Interactive activity: Numbers 1–30 (V) ; Memorising numbers (Strat) Ph The letters 'j', 'ge', 'gi' , or CD 1, track 23 Video: *Une nouvelle famille dans la rue* Grammar in Action: None	
2C Comment ça s'écrit? pages 18–19		
• Say what day of the week it is • Spell words using the French alphabet		
Grammaire	Stratégies	Phonétique
• None	• Getting help with words	• The letter 'é' with acute accent
Resources		
Audio: 1 *La semaine de Lou*; 5 *Tu habites où?* Copymasters: 2/3 *Les jours de la semaine*, 2/4 *Sommaire* Worksheets: Starters and plenaries e-book: *Le lecteur MP3 d'Anne-Sophie*	Interactive activity: Days of the week (V); Identifying days of the week (L); Classroom commands (2) Ph The letter 'é' with acute accent, or CD 1, track 29 PowerPoint: *L'alphabet* (song) Grammar in Action: None	

Key language

Where people live (2A and 2B)

Où habites-tu? (Tu habites où?)
J'habite …
dans une maison
dans un appartement
dans une ferme
dans un port
dans une ville
dans un village
à la maison
à la montagne
au bord de la mer
à Londres
près de Paris
en France
en Angleterre
en Écosse
en Irlande (du Nord)
au pays de Galles

Numbers 1–30 (2B)

Days of the week (2C)

Quel jour sommes-nous?
lundi
mardi
mercredi
jeudi
vendredi
samedi
dimanche

The French alphabet (2C)

Asking for help (2C)

Comment ça s'écrit?
Comment dit-on […] en français?
Comment dit-on […] en anglais?

2A Venez en France   pages 14–15

- Understand people saying where they live

Grammaire	Stratégies	Phonétique
• Learn how to say 'in' a place	• Using clues to work out meaning (1)	• The letters 'ch'

Resources

Audio: 1 *J'habite en France*; or CD 1, track 19
Copymasters: 2/1 *J'habite en France*
Worksheets: Starters and plenaries

Interactive activity: *J'habite en France* (L, R)
Ph The letters 'ch', or CD 1, track 20
PowerPoint: Kim's game : *Où habites-tu?*
Grammar in Action: None

Worksheet

Starters (pages 14–15)

1 Display words and phrases from the previous unit randomly on the screen (see below or the online worksheet for a suggested list). In pairs, students create as many different phrases as they can.

11 ans	as-tu	Au revoir	Bonjour
calculatrice	Ça va	Comment	elle
il	j'ai	je	m'appelle
Non	ordinateur	Oui	pas très bien
portable	Quel âge	sac	s'appelle
Salut	t'appelles	très bien	tu
un	une		

2 (For use after *habite à* is taught.) Make up a *Vrai ou faux?* item about where famous people live. Start them off, then students make up their own statements, e.g.

David Beckham habite à Londres.
Le Prince Harry habite en Angleterre.
Homer Simpson habite à Springfield.
Nessie habite en Écosse.
Sherlock Holmes habite à Londres en Angleterre.

Introduction

Share the spread objectives with students at the start of each lesson. Give them every opportunity to demonstrate their knowledge and skills and to evaluate their progress.

Draw attention to these basic phrases.

Qui est-ce?	Il y a …
Qu'est-ce que c'est?	Oui, c'est ça.
C'est …	Non, ce n'est pas ça.
Ce n'est pas …	Voici …

Interactive activity

Introduction S

J'habite …

Teach how to say where you live using the online presentation (see above) and repetition of *J'habite à* (+ place). Then students say the phrase in answer to the question *Où habites-tu?* Finally, students could question others.

Using the presentation, gradually teach *C'est une ville/un village/un port* and ask: (Name of place), *c'est une ville? C'est un village?* Write the names of some well-known towns or villages in Britain and France on the board and use them for oral practice, e.g.

Teacher: (Student A), *Paris, c'est une ville?*
Student A: *Oui, c'est une ville.*

Alternatively, students could work on this in pairs, e.g.

Student A: *Paris.*
Student B: *C'est une ville.*

This provides an opportunity for the teacher to monitor who is able to say the words and who understands the work.

In a similar way, teach *une maison* and *un appartement*. Then ask *Tu habites dans une maison ou dans un appartement?* Teach *une ferme* and practise these nouns using a flashcard game (FC 3–7, see TB page xviii).

🔊 14

1 J'habite en France

Use the photos to teach or revise *garçon, fille, homme, femme*, e.g.

Voici une femme.
Elle s'appelle Mme Dumas. Elle habite ici.
Et voici une fille. Elle habite dans une maison.

Next look at all the pictures in turn, speaking briefly about them, e.g.

Voici Paris. C'est une ville? Oui, c'est une ville.
Et voici Strasbourg. C'est une ville aussi.
Répétez – Strasbourg.
Mme Dumas habite à Strasbourg.
Et voici une ferme. C'est un appartement? Non, c'est une ferme, près de Trouville.
Et voici un homme. Répétez. Il s'appelle M. Lebrun, etc.
Et voici une fille. La fille habite ici, dans la maison.

Now play the whole recording once while students follow in their books. Play it a second time, using the pause button to give them time to identify each speaker.

Tricolore 1 Teacher's Notes **15**

2A Venez en France

> **CD 1 Track 19**
>
> **J'habite en France**
> 1 J'habite à Paris. C'est fantastique!
> 2 Moi, j'habite ici, en Normandie. J'habite dans une ferme, près de Trouville.
> 3 Moi, j'habite à La Rochelle. C'est un port en France.
> 4 Moi, j'habite ici, à l'Île de Ré. C'est une île près de La Rochelle.
> 5 Moi, j'habite à Nice. C'est super.
> 6 Moi, j'habite dans un village, à la montagne. C'est dans les Alpes, près de Grenoble.
> 7 J'habite ici, à Strasbourg, avec ma famille. J'habite dans une maison en ville.
> 8 Moi, j'habite à Lille. J'habite dans un appartement en ville.

Presentation

Jeu de mémoire: Où habites-tu?

cm 2/1

J'habite en France

Interactive activity

The letters 'ch'

> **15 Phonétique**
>
> ### The letters 'ch'

A full explanation of the 'ch' sound is given on *kerboodle!*, together with interactive practice which includes recognising words which contain the sound.

a Say the word *chat* with the appropriate gesture (clawing motion like a cat's paws). Students repeat the word with the same gesture. Then read out the other words with students repeating each one. The words are also included on the recording for optional use (part **a**).

Parts **b** and **c** can be used to practise pronunciation and recognition of the 'ch' sound.

b Display the following words: **a** *chien*, **b** *chanson*, **c** *quelque chose*, **d** *chaise*, **e** *touche*, **f** *chocolat*. Students listen and repeat the words they hear, then note down the order in which they are said (**c, a, f, b, e, d**).

c Students listen to the silly sentence and note down how many times they hear the sound (4). They can then repeat the sentence to help them remember this sound.

> **CD 1 Track 20**
>
> ### The letters 'ch'
> Ecoutez et repetez:
> a chat, La Rochelle, la Manche, chose, chaise
> b quelque chose, chien, chocolat, chanson, touche, chaise
> c Choco le chat chante dans la douche.

> **15 Dossier-langue**
>
> ### Saying 'in' a place

Work briefly through the explanation and ask students to complete rules 1, 2 and 3. Encourage them to refer back to them as they do the next few tasks.

> **Solution:**
>
> **1** à, **2** en, **3** dans

Students could build up their own list of strategies for learning and remembering new language, e.g. in a personal file/exercise book. These rules could be added to their list.

> **15**

2 C'est où?

Students read the texts on SB page 14 and find the French for the phrases.

> **Solution:**
>
> 1 à Paris
> 2 dans un appartement
> 3 en ville
> 4 dans une ferme
> 5 dans une maison
> 6 un port en France
> 7 à la montagne
> 8 dans les Alpes
> 9 près de La Rochelle

> **15 Stratégies**

Using clues to work out meaning (1)

Some simple training in strategies for listening can be built into the materials from the outset (see also TB page xiii, Developing listening skills).

1 Build up confidence by introducing language gradually with clues for what is to be listened for. This will help convince students that they can understand spoken French.

2 Encourage guesswork and emphasise that you don't need to understand every word. For example, this item includes some new, but easily guessable, words: *super*, *moderne*, *important(e)*.

> **15**   AfL

3 Vrai ou faux?

a Teach *Vrai ou faux?* by making statements about members of the class or classroom objects, e.g. (holding up a book)

Voici une règle – c'est vrai ou faux? – C'est faux!

Use the example to check that everyone knows how to do the task.

2B Où habites-tu?

The task could be done as a class activity or individually with the answers checked orally. Some students might be ready to read out some of the statements being checked or they could just be repeated by the class. Students could then to try to make up further *vrai ou faux* statements about the photos.

> **Solution:**
>
> 1 *vrai*, 2 *vrai*, 3 *faux*, 4 *faux*, 5 *faux*, 6 *vrai*, 7 *faux*, 8 *vrai*, 9 *faux*, 10 *vrai*

b As an extension activity, students correct the false sentences. Several different answers are possible.

> **Solution (possible):**
>
> 3 *Camille habite dans un appartement (à Lille) en France.*
> 4 *M. Lebrun habite dans une ferme.*
> 5 *Mme Dumas habite dans une maison à Strasbourg.*
> 7 *Nicolas habite dans un port. / Lucas habite à Paris.*
> 9 *Julie habite près de La Rochelle (à l'Île de Ré).*

As follow-up, students could make up similar statements about their own town and set them as a class activity, e.g. *St Albans est en France. Huddersfield est en Angleterre. Liverpool est près de Paris*, etc.

As further follow-up and a simple but effective opportunity for AfL, ask students: How do you say (for example) 'in a house'? Students tell their partner, who checks and corrects if necessary. Take feedback from the class. This links to both objectives for this spread and allows students to demonstrate their ability to recall and generate the language they have learnt.

Worksheet

Plenaries (pages 14–15)

1 In pairs, students tell their partner three things about where they live. They then pair up with another two students – how many different phrases can they say? Take feedback from the class.

2 Sticky notes: students write one phrase (or more, depending on the class) about where they live (*j'habite à …, j'habite dans …, j'habite en …, c'est une ville …, c'est super/fantastique*, etc.). They stick the notes on an agreed place in the classroom (e.g. a display board headed *J'habite ici*). Teacher monitors the sticky notes for accuracy and uses this as an AfL opportunity, asking students to give feedback and suggestions for improvement. These can also be used to start the next lesson.

2B Où habites-tu?   pages 16–17

- Say where you live
- Ask someone where they live

Grammaire	Stratégies	Phonétique
• Use numbers up to 30 • Ask a question	• Memorising numbers	• The letters 'j', 'ge', 'gi'

Resources

Audio: 2 *Et toi? Où habites-tu?*; 3 *Qui habite où?*; 5a *Inventez des conversations* or CD 1, tracks 21, 22 and 24
Copymasters: 2/2 *Trois conversations*
Worksheets: Starters and plenaries; Prepositions used for locations (G); Numbers 1–30 (V), *Carte d'identité* (W); *J'habite à …* (W)

Interactive activity: Numbers 1–30 (V) ; Memorising numbers (Strat)
Ph The letters 'j', 'ge', 'gi', or CD 1, track 23
Video: *Une nouvelle famille dans la rue*
Grammar in Action: None

Worksheet

Starters (pages 16–17)

1 **Chain questioning** (Use this to revise personal information before SB page 17, task 4)

Display the questions *Comment t'appelles-tu? Quel âge as-tu?* and *Ça va?* and choose a student to ask someone one of the questions. If they answer correctly, that student asks another person one of the other two questions, and so on. This could be done as a competition in rows or groups,

2 Use a number game (see TB page xvi) to revise the numbers taught so far.

1 J'habite ici

Students find the correct words from the box to complete these core sentences.

They could just note down the numbers and matching letters and the answers could be checked orally, with students supplying the full sentence. Any students ready to start writing could copy down the complete sentences. This could be used as a homework task.

2B Où habites-tu?

Solution:
1 *b*, 2 *f*, 3 *c*, 4 *a*, 5 *e*, 6 *d*, 7 *h*, 8 *g*

16 Dossier-langue

Asking a question

This short item introduces the concept of inversion to form questions. Go over the example to ensure students recognise the change of word order. Some students may be able to make up other questions such as *Habites-tu en France/dans une maison/à Londres?* Avoid other parts of the verb at this stage.

16 — AfL

2 Et toi? Où habites-tu?

Students listen to the model dialogue, then make up their own answers and use them in conversation, based on the illustrated examples and the table. Students could learn the conversations for homework. This can be the basis of an early speaking assessment. It is also an ideal opportunity for peer assessment, allowing students to demonstrate their skills and to give or receive feedback.

CD 1 Track 21

Et toi? Où habites-tu?
– Où habites-tu?
– J'habite à Wakefield. Et toi, où habites-tu?
– Moi, j'habite dans un village, près de Leeds.

Worksheet

Où?

cm 2/2

Trois conversations

143 Au choix

1 C'est où?

143 Au choix

2 J'habite …

Worksheet

Écris des phrases

Teaching numbers up to 30

Revise numbers 1–20 and teach numbers up to 30 orally, using the *kerboodle!* activities (below), repetition and number games (see TB page xvi).

The song *Un, deux, trois* could be used to revise numbers 1–20 as preparation for the next group of numbers.

Presentation

Chantez! Un, deux, trois
See SB p13 for lyrics.

Interactive activity

Les nombres 1–30

Worksheet

Comptez

17

3 Qui habite où?

Revise the pronunciation of the names and ask the class to read aloud the numbers of the houses. Then play the recording, pausing after each speaker to look at the example, and for students to write down the correct answers.

Check the results orally, perhaps with further questions, e.g. *Qui habite au numéro sept? Où habite Magali?* etc.

Solution:
1 *Olivier 7*, 2 *Coralie 21*, 3 *Magali 25*, 4 *Loïc 30*, 5 *Sébastien 14*, 6 *M. Garnier 28*, 7 *Jean-Marc 5*, 8 *Isabelle 15*

This activity could also be used more competitively: say one of the people's names and students race to say the correct number. If considered appropriate, the 3rd person could also be introduce, e.g.

Teacher: *Magali.*

Student: *Élle habite au numéro 25.*

CD 1 Track 22

Qui habite où?

1 – Où habites-tu, Olivier?
 – J'habite à Paris, dans la Villa Violette.
 – C'est quel numéro?
 – Numéro sept.
2 – Et toi, Coralie? Où habites-tu?
 – J'habite à La Rochelle, dans la rue Gambetta.
 – Quel numéro?
 – Vingt et un.
3 – Salut, Magali. Est-ce que tu habites au numéro vingt-cinq?
 – Oui, c'est ça. Au vingt-cinq.
4 – Et toi, Loïc, tu habites dans cette rue, non?
 – Oui, j'habite au numéro trente.
5 – Salut, Sébastien.
 – Salut!
 – Où habites-tu, Sébastien?
 – À La Rochelle, au numéro quatorze, rue du Pont.
6 – Et vous habitez aussi dans la rue du Pont, M. Garnier. C'est vrai?
 – Oui, mais moi, j'habite au numéro vingt-huit.
7 – Et Jean-Marc, aussi. Il habite au numéro cinq.
 – Oui, c'est ça. Moi, j'habite au cinq.
8 – Et toi, Isabelle, où habites-tu?
 – Moi, j'habite à Rennes, dans la rue de Paris.
 – Quel numéro?
 – Quinze, j'habite au numéro quinze.

Tricolore 1 Teacher's Notes

2B Où habites-tu?

17

4 C'est moi!

This task is suitable for students ready for independent reading.

In part **a**, students match up the two halves of sentences. In part **b**, they write out the sentences in full.

> **Solution:**
> **a** 1 b, 2 a, 3 e, 4 f, 5 d, 6 c
> **b** 1 *Je m'appelle Sonia Charbonnier.*
> 2 *J'ai douze ans.*
> 3 *J'habite dans une maison.*
> 4 *Ma maison est dans un petit village.*
> 5 *Le village est près de La Rochelle.*
> 6 *La Rochelle est une ville en France.*

Interactive activity

Où habites-tu?

17 Stratégies

Memorising numbers

This memorisation strategy gives tips for helping students remember the numbers. Short term memory can generally deal with five items of vocabulary comfortably, so learning in groups of five is helpful for many students.

A number of online flashcard makers are available for students to use then play the associated games.

An oral game (like "Buzz") is useful for larger numbers, e.g. counting aloud and pointing to the next person to continue after two or three numbers.

Interactive activity

The letters 'j', 'ge', 'gi'

17 Phonétique

The letters 'j', 'ge', 'gi'

A full explanation of the soft 'j' sound is given on *kerboodle!*, together with interactive practice which includes differentiating between the soft and hard 'g' sounds.

a Say the word *bonjour* with the appropriate gesture (waving hello). Students repeat the word with the same gesture. Then read out the other words with students repeating each one. The words are also included on the recording for optional use (part **a**).

Parts **b** and **c** can be used to practise pronunciation and recognition of the soft 'j' sound.

b Students listen and repeat the words they hear. They then note down how many soft 'j' sounds they hear (7). One word (*Georges*) has the sound twice and they should listen very carefully for the difference between 'j' and 'ch' (from the previous *Phonétique*).

c Students listen to the silly sentence and note down how many times they hear the sound (7). They can then repeat the sentence to help them remember this sound.

CD 1 Track 23

The letters 'j', 'ge', 'gi'

Écoutez et répétez:
a bonjour, Julien, Georges, village, girafe
b bonjour, Georges, garage, jouez, Grenoble, je, gomme, âge, chaise
c Georgette la girafe joue dans le jardin avec Joël le gymnaste.

17 AfL

5 Inventez des conversations

a Students read and listen to the model conversation.

b In pairs, they then make up their own conversations based on the model.

c As an extension activity, students use previous knowledge to add extra details to the conversation. They could be encouraged to prepare and perform presentations of themselves (or a famous person or friend, in the first person), saying name, age, where they live and anything else they have learnt. They could do this in pairs, asking and answering as many questions as possible, using props and role play. The activity is fun and gives them a real sense of how much they have already learnt.

The pairwork activities offer a good AfL opportunity. First agree the criteria for success with students; they can then check their conversation with partners and know exactly what they must do to be successful.

CD 1 Track 24

Inventez des conversations

– Comment t'appelles-tu?
– Je m'appelle Roman. Et toi, comment t'appelles-tu?
– Moi, je m'appelle Jules. Quel âge as-tu?
– J'ai douze ans. Et toi? Quel âge as-tu?
– Moi, j'ai onze ans. Où habites-tu?
– J'habite près de Tours. Et toi? Où habites-tu?
– J'habite à Orléans. Au revoir, Roman.
– Au revoir, Jules.

Worksheet

Carte d'identité

Tricolore 1 Teacher's Notes   **19**

2C Comment ça s'écrit?

Interactive activity

Rue Danton: Une nouvelle famille dans la rue

This is a suitable point at which to use the first episode (covering *Unités* 1 and 2) of the video soap opera. The language is closely linked to the unit, but the video also provides some extension and valuable cultural background. The online activities help focus students on the key language.

Worksheet

Plenaries (pages 16–17)

1 Brainstorming session in which students work out how much they could now tell a French person about themselves, e.g. name, age, state of health, where they live, how many MP3 players etc. they have. This also could take the form of a mind map if preferred.

2 Students reflect on the objectives of the unit and how much they have achieved. They could find two things they've found easy, one thing they've found hard; say what is the most important fact they have learnt this unit and what is the oddest fact. They should comment on any aspects of French culture they have been exposed to (especially if they have watched the *Rue Danton* video) and compare these with their own.

2C Comment ça s'écrit? pages 18–19

- Say what day of the week it is
- Spell words using the French alphabet

Grammaire	Stratégies	Phonétique
• None	• Getting help with words	• The letter 'é' with acute accent

Resources

Audio: 1 *La semaine de Lou*; **5** *Tu habites où?*
Copymasters: 2/3 *Les jours de la semaine*, 2/4 *Sommaire*
Worksheets: Starters and plenaries
e-book: *Le lecteur MP3 d'Anne-Sophie*

Interactive activity: Days of the week (V); Identifying days of the week (L); Classroom commands (2)
Ph The letter 'é' with acute accent, or CD 1, track 29
PowerPoint: *L'alphabet* (song)
Grammar in Action: None

Worksheet

Starters (pages 18–19)

1 *Trouve les paires* Display a selection of sentences and phrases in French. Students match them to the English translations. (See online worksheet.)

1 *Ça va?* a In a flat.
2 *Il habite à la montagne.* b Not very well.
3 *Asseyez-vous.* c She's called Françoise.
4 *Dans un appartement.* d How are you?
5 *Pas très bien.* e Sit down.
6 *Où habites-tu?* f It's a town in France.
7 *C'est une ville en France.* g Where do you live?
8 *Elle s'appelle Françoise.* h He lives in the mountains.

Solution:
1 d, **2** h, **3** e, **4** a, **5** b, **6** g, **7** f, **8** c

2 *Chasse à l'intrus* Display groups of words from *Unités* 1 and 2. Students identify the odd word out of each group and justify their choice. (See online worksheet.)

A	B	C	D	E	F
crayon	Ça va.	une boîte	seize	je	maison
stylo	Copie	**un cartable**	sept	**jeudi**	ferme
classeur	Écoute.	une poubelle	six	il	**montagne**
feutre	Écris.	une trousse	**samedi**	elle	appartement

Days of the week

Present or revise the days of the week, perhaps using the *kerboodle* activity below, a weekly planner or a French calendar.

Interactive activity

Un calendrier

20 Tricolore 1 Teacher's Notes

2C Comment ça s'écrit?

1 La semaine de Lou

a Make sure students know the days of the week before presenting this item. See if they have spotted the link between *di* and day.

CD 1 Track 25

La semaine de Lou

Voici Lou Leroux. Il est reporter à Télé-France.
Il voyage beaucoup.
Lundi, il est dans un village en Écosse.
Mardi, il est à Londres, en Angleterre.
Mercredi, il est au pays de Galles.
Jeudi, Lou est à Belfast, en Irlande du Nord.
Vendredi, il est dans une ferme à la montagne, en France.
Samedi, Lou est à Paris.
Lou est à la maison. Ouf!! Lou adore le dimanche!

b Once students have heard, read and understood the text, they find the five true sentences. Follow this up with some oral work – teacher-led at first, then handed over to students, e.g.

C'est lundi. Où est Lou?

Il est en Angleterre – c'est quel jour?

Solution:

Sentences 1, 3, 5, 6 and 8 are true.

c As an extension activity, students write about the travels of a cyclist, Clara, in France. Discuss places Clara might visit and refer them to the map on SB page 3 or to a more detailed map of the country for ideas.

Students could be encouraged to do their own cartoon strip of the journey. Suggest sources for illustrating their work (presentation pictures or clip art of town, village, house, flat, farm, etc.). These could provide an interesting wall display and be a stimulus for further oral work.

2 Quel jour sommes-nous?

Students look at the abbreviations of the days of the week and work out which day is represented.

As follow-up, students could practise in pairs. Give the instruction: *À deux. A indique une abréviation, B dit le jour.*

Student A: [points to *ma*, for example]

Student B: *Mardi*.

Student A: *Oui, c'est ça!*

You could have the days displayed in the classroom to remind you, with the title *Quel jour sommes-nous?* Go over the question and the answer (*Nous sommes*) *lundi*, etc.

As a memorisation strategy, students could practise saying the day in French every day (including the weekend).

Interactive activity

L'alphabet

Introduction

L'alphabet

Before doing the remaining SB activities, the French alphabet should be taught. Use the online presentation (above) or the song (below) or follow this suggested sequence:

- The class repeats a few letters at a time – ask them to spot the 'catches' as they arise (*e/i*, *g/j*, etc.).
- Gradually work up to the whole alphabet using such strategies as stopping and seeing if the class or one group can go on alone, dividing the class into two or more groups and 'conducting' them, moving swiftly from one group to another, one group carrying on as the other leaves off.
- Teach students to spell their names and introduce *Comment ça s'écrit?*
- Help the class to get used to asking the teacher to spell any word they are not sure of.
- Practise spelling a few words regularly and perhaps play a spelling game, e.g. *Ton nom s'écrit comme ça?*
- The teacher, and later one of the class, spells out someone's name in French. Anyone who thinks their name is being spelt should stand up. If the wrong person stands up or the person named fails to stand up, they lose a point. If the person named stands up, they have the next turn at spelling a name.

When students have learnt the alphabet, suggest that every time they learn a new French word, they should try to spell it in French. The introduction of the French alphabet could be linked with ICT, providing a good opportunity to explore the keyboard, which would be useful for those students with poor keyboard skills.

The most basic activity is *Trouve la touche*. Dictate spellings or phrases by saying, for example, *Tapez 'd', tapez 'e', tapez 'u', tapez 'x' – C'est quel mot?*

Presentation

Chantez! L'alphabet

3 L'alphabet

Students listen to the song and could follow it using the online presentation (above). They then listen again and join in. The 'karaoke' version can also be used once students are familiar with the song.

Tricolore 1 Teacher's Notes

2C Comment ça s'écrit?

L'alphabet
CD 1 Tracks 26–27

– Moi, je sais l'alphabet,
  Écoute est-ce que c'est bon?
  A, B, C, D, E, F, G, H …
– Ça continue comment?
– A, B, C, D, E, F, G, H,
  I, J, K, L, M, N, O, P …
– Ça continue comment?
– A, B, C, D, E, F, G, H,
  I, J, K, L, M, N, O, P,
  Q, R, S, T, U, V, W …
– Ça continue comment?
  A, B, C, D, E, F, G, H,
  I, J, K, L, M, N, O, P,
  Q, R, S, T, U, V, W,
  X, Y, Z.
– Ça continue comment?
– Idiote, c'est tout, c'est bon!
  A, B, C, […] X, Y, Z.

Tu habites où?
CD 1 Track 28

1 – Tu habites où?
  – J'habite à Lyon.
  – Comment ça s'écrit?
  – L-Y-O-N.
2 – Moi, j'habite à Dijon.
  – Comment ça s'écrit?
  – D-I-J-O-N.
3 – Tu habites à Bordeaux. Comment ça s'écrit?
  – B-O-R-D-E-A-U-X.
4 – Moi, j'habite à Limoges.
  – Comment ça s'écrit?
  – L-I-M-O-G-E-S.
5 – Tu habites où?
  – J'habite à Villefranche.
  – Villefranche. Comment ça s'écrit?
  – V-I-L-L-E-F-R-A-N-C-H-E.
6 – Et moi, j'habite à Quimper.
  – Comment ça s'écrit?
  – Q-U-I-M-P-E-R.

C'est quel jour?
Now students are familiar with the alphabet, provide further practice of days of the week with a simple listening task. Spell out days of the week (in random order) and students either spot which one is being spelt from a calendar-type list or write it down.

cm 2/3

Les jours de la semaine

19 *AfL*

4 Comment ça s'écrit?
This pairwork activity consolidates the work on spelling. Students should act out the conversation in pairs then adapt it by changing the names to whatever they want. This activity provides another opportunity for peer assessment. Remind them of the objectives of the spread and agree the criteria for success before they proceed to demonstrate their skill.

19

5 Tu habites où?
Students write down the names of French towns as they are spelt out.

As follow-up, they could find the places on a map of France. This could link in with the cycling activity (**1c** above).

To link in with the phonics item (below), spell out some extra French towns with an é (*e accent aigu*), e.g. *Épernay, Chambéry, Béthune, Montélimar.*

19 Stratégies

Getting help with words
This provides some useful phrases for finding out new words, helping students to respond to face-to-face instructions, questions and explanations. Practise the questions and some answers with a quick quiz round the class.

Student A: *Comment dit-on 'jeudi' en anglais?*
Student B: *Comment dit-on 'book' en français?*
Student C: *Comment ça s'écrit?*

Interactive activity

The letter 'é' with acute accent

19 *Phonétique*

The letter 'é' with acute accent
A full explanation of the sound of the letter 'é' (*e accent aigu*) is given on *kerboodle!*, together with interactive practice which includes recognition of the sound.

a Say the word *éléphant* with the appropriate gesture (arm swaying and pointing up like a trunk). Students repeat the word with the same gesture. Then read out the other words with students repeating each one. The words are also included on the recording for optional use (part **a**).

Parts **b** and **c** can be used to practise pronunciation and recognition of the 'é' sound.

b Students listen and repeat the words they hear, all of which contain the letter e. They then note down which ones contain the 'é' sound (1, 2, 5, 8).

2C Comment ça s'écrit?

c Students listen to the silly sentence and note down how many times they hear the sound (6). They can then repeat the sentence to help them remember this sound.

The *Phonétique* in *Unité* 3 (SB page 21) contains practice of the 'è' sound and includes differentiation between 'é' and 'è' sounds.

> 🔊 CD 1 Track 29
>
> ### The letter 'é' with acute accent
> Écoutez et répétez:
> a éléphant, écoute, télé, détail
> b 1 école
>   2 télé
>   3 appartement
>   4 moderne
>   5 zéro
>   6 Grenoble
>   7 règle
>   8 écoute
> c Un éléphant en Écosse téléphone à l'école.

📖 19

L'alphabet

Some useful tips to help students remember the more difficult letters of the French alphabet. Encourage students to think up their own ideas as this helps cement the pronunciation in their minds. The key letters and words are recorded as a model for students, with sound effects which can reinforce the learning for some students.

> 🔊 CD 1 Track 30
>
> ### L'alphabet
> i – j … comme l'île de Fiji.
> g comme génie
> h comme hache
> C'est un VW, comme Volkswagen.

📖 143 Au choix

3 Qu'est-ce que c'est?

📖 143 Au choix

4 Jean-Pierre a des problèmes

Interactive activity

Vocabulaire de classe (2)

Worksheet

Presentation

Le lecteur MP3 d'Anne-Sophie

📖 19 cm 2/4

Sommaire

A summary of the main language and structures of the unit, also on copymaster for ease of reference.

Interactive activity

Vocabulaire (2)

Worksheet

Plenaries (pages 18–19)

1 Students agree on (for instance) 10 words that they are going to find more difficult to remember from this unit. They then suggest and discuss things they are going to do to remember them.

2 Students produce a spider diagram of everything learnt in the unit. This could be in groups or as a whole-class activity with students contributing to the mind map on the board.

Au choix

📖 143 Au choix

1 C'est où?

Students make up sentences, using the appropriate prepositions with the names of towns or countries. This could be an oral or written activity.

> Solution:
> 1 *Glasgow, c'est une ville en Écosse.*
> 2 *Manchester, c'est une ville en Angleterre.*
> 3 *Paris, c'est une ville en France.*
> 4 *La Rochelle, c'est une ville en France.*
> 5 *Bordeaux, c'est une ville en France.*
> 6 *Dublin, c'est une ville en Irlande.*
> 7 *Leeds, c'est une ville en Angleterre.*
> 8 *Belfast, c'est une ville en Irlande du Nord.*
> 9 *Swansea, c'est une ville au pays de Galles.*
> 10 *Aberdeen, c'est une ville en Écosse.*

📖 143 Au choix

2 J'habite …

This gap-fill activity practises the prepositions with places, towns and countries. Students could write out the full sentences or do the activity orally.

> Solution:
> **1** *dans, à,* **2** *dans, dans,* **3** *en, dans,* **4** *à, près, au,*
> **5** *en, dans, près*

Tricolore 1 Teacher's Notes

2C Comment ça s'écrit?

📖 🔊 143 Au choix

3 Qu'est-ce que c'est?

This activity gives further practice of singular and plural nouns with *c'est* and *voici*. (*Voici* has been used at this stage as *ce sont* is not explicitly taught in this unit.)

a Students listen and match the captions with the pictures.

Solution:
1 C, 2 A, 3 D, 4 E, 5 B, 6 G, 7 F, 8 H

🔊 CD 1 Track 31

Qu'est-ce que c'est?

1 C'est une boîte.
2 Voici des portables.
3 Voici des boîtes.
4 Voici des enfants.
5 C'est un portable.
6 C'est un surligneur.
7 C'est un enfant.
8 Voici des surligneurs.

b Students write sentences about the eight pictures, using the substitution table to help them.

📖 🔊 143 Au choix

4 Jean-Pierre a des problèmes

Students first listen straight through to get the gist of the story. They then look at the things the teacher asks for and listen to the recording, writing down the order in which the objects are asked for.

Finally see if the class can explain why Jean-Pierre has apparently come without a lot of his equipment.

Solution:
C, D, F, E, A, B

🔊 CD 1 Track 32

Jean-Pierre a des problèmes

- Jean-Pierre, donne-moi ton cahier, s'il te plaît.
- Oui, monsieur … euh … mon cahier … mais monsieur, mon cahier est dans mon cartable.
- Bien. Voici ton cartable. Donne-moi ton cahier de mathématiques.
- Mais monsieur, mon cahier n'est pas ici.
- Ah … ton cahier n'est pas là. Montre-moi ta calculatrice alors.
- Ma calculatrice … mais monsieur, ma calculatrice n'est pas dans le cartable.
- Jean-Pierre, c'est la leçon de mathématiques et ton cahier n'est pas dans ton cartable, et ta calculatrice n'est pas dans ton cartable! Alors, regarde bien dans le cartable. Il y a des crayons?
- Oui, monsieur, il y en a deux. Mais monsieur …
- Et il y a une gomme?
- Oui, monsieur, il y a une gomme, mais monsieur …
- Tais-toi, Jean-Pierre! Il y a une règle?
- Oui, monsieur, il y en a une, mais monsieur …
- Et un livre? Il y a un livre de mathématiques?
- Oui, monsieur …
- Bon, c'est bien, alors!
- Mais non, monsieur, ce n'est pas bien!
- Jean-Pierre, qu'est-ce qu'il y a, alors?
- Ça, c'est le cartable de Sébastien. Voilà mon cartable et voici mon cahier et ma calculatrice!

Copymasters

cm 2/1

J'habite en France

As a support activity to task 1 on page 14, students listen again to the recording, first identifying the speakers and noting down the names, then filling in the grid on the sheet. This activity is ideal for use with individual listening facilities.

Solution:

	Ville / port	village	île	maison	appt.	ferme
Lucas	✓					
Camille	✓				✓	
M. Lebrun						✓
Mme Dumas	✓			✓		
Nicolas	✓					
Maxime		✓				
Julie			✓			
Jean-Pierre	✓					

🔊 cm 2/2

Trois conversations

Students should first look through the illustrations for the conversations and the multiple choice items, before working on the recorded version and ticking the correct options. This item would be useful with individual listening equipment or in a multi-media facility.

Solution:
1 Ab, Bc, Cb, Dc
2 Aa, Bc, Ca, Da
3 Aa, Bb, Ca, Db

🔊 CD 1 Track 34

Trois conversations

1 **Première Conversation**
- Bonjour. Je m'appelle Monique. Comment t'appelles-tu?
- Je m'appelle Marcel.
  Quel âge as-tu, Monique?
- J'ai quatorze ans. Et toi?
- J'ai dix ans.

2 **Deuxième Conversation**
- Bonjour. Je m'appelle Marc. Comment t'appelles-tu?
- Je m'appelle Françoise. Tu habites où?
- J'habite dans un village, près de La Rochelle. Et toi?
- J'habite dans un village, près de Marseille.

3 **Troisième Conversation**
- Bonjour. Je m'appelle Philippe. Et toi? Tu t'appelles comment?
- Je m'appelle Martine. Tu habites où?
- J'habite à Sainte-Marie. C'est un village. Et toi?
- J'habite à Bordeaux. C'est une ville en France.

Tricolore 1 Teacher's Notes

2C Comment ça s'écrit?

Les jours de la semaine

This provides extra practice of the days of the week, numbers and spelling.

Solution:

1 *Mots mêlés*

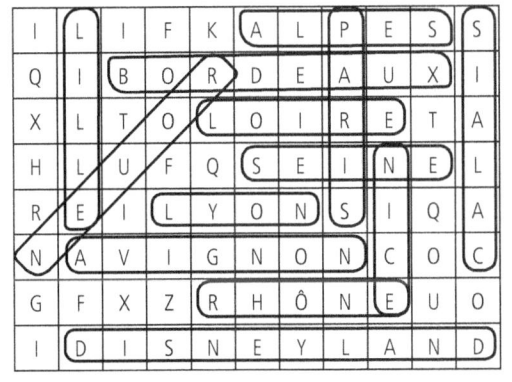

I	L	I	F	K	A	L	P	E	S	S
Q	I	B	O	R	D	E	A	U	X	I
X	L	T	O	L	O	I	R	E	T	A
H	L	U	F	Q	S	E	I	N	E	L
R	E	I	L	Y	O	N	S	I	Q	A
N	A	V	I	G	N	O	N	C	O	C
G	F	X	Z	R	H	Ô	N	E	U	O
I	D	I	S	N	E	Y	L	A	N	D

(The missing day is *mercredi*.)

2 *La semaine de Camille*

1 *Lundi, elle est à la ferme.*
2 *Vendredi, elle est à la plage (or Nice).*
3 *Samedi, elle est au match de foot.*
4 *Mardi, elle est à La Rochelle.*
5 *Mercredi, elle est à Paris.*
6 *Jeudi, elle est à la montagne.*
7 *Dimanche, elle est à la maison.*

Sommaire

A summary of the main language and structures of the unit on copymaster for ease of reference.

Unité 3

Tricolore 1 Unité 3 Chez moi   Pages 20–29

3A Ma famille pages 20–21		
• Talk about your family		
Grammaire	Stratégies	Phonétique
• Learn how to say 'the' and 'a' • Use the singular of *avoir* (to have)	• Using clues to work out meaning (2)	• The letter 'è' with grave accent
Resources		
Audio: 1 *Ma famille*; **4** *Trois familles*, or CD 1, tracks 35 and 37 **Copymasters:** 3/1 *La famille Techno* **Worksheets:** Starters and plenaries; *Des cartes d'identité* (W); *La famille Roland* (W)		**Interactive activity:** *La famille de Kévin* (L); *Des frères et des sœurs* (L) **Ph** The letter 'è' with grave accent, or CD 1, track 36 **PowerPoint:** *La famille* (V) **Grammar in** Action: None

3B C'est à qui? pages 22–23		
• Say which things belong to you		
Grammaire	Stratégies	Phonétique
• Use the words for 'my' and 'your' • Use *de* to show possession	• Remembering the gender of nouns	• The letters 'a', 'à' with grave accent, 'as', 'at'
Resources		
Audio: 3 *Mon numéro un*; **4** *Dani et Théo* or CD 1, tracks 38, 39 and 41 **Copymasters:** None **Worksheets:** Starters and plenaries; *Interview d'une vampire* (R,W); *C'est le crayon de …?* (W)		**Interactive activity:** *À moi, à toi* (G) **Ph** The letters 'a', 'à' with grave accent, '-as', '-at', or CD 1, track 40 **PowerPoint:** *Les articles* (G) **Grammar in Action:** pp6–7

3C Ma maison pages 24–25		
• Discuss your family and friends • Talk about your home		• Talk about your home
Grammaire	Stratégies	Phonétique
• Use the singular of *être* (to be)	• None	• The letter 'u'
Resources		
Audio: 4 *La maison de la famille Laurent*, or CD 1, track 42 **Copymasters:** None **Worksheets:** Starters and plenaries; *Le verbe être* (G)		**Interactive activity:** *Les pièces* (V) **Ph** The letter 'u', or CD 1, track 43 **PowerPoint:** *Des maisons françaises* (V) **Grammar in Action:** None

3D C'est où? pages 26–27		
• Describe where things are in a room		
Grammaire	Stratégies	Phonétique
• Use some prepositions • Learn more about masculine and feminine	• Remembering vocabulary	• None
Resources		
Audio: 1 *Notre chambre*; *Suzanne et Suzette Souris*, or CD 1, tracks 44 and 45 **Copymasters:** 3/2 *Masculin, féminin* **Worksheets:** Starters and plenaries; *Invente des phrases* (W): Remembering vocabulary (Strat)		**PowerPoint:** *C'est où?* (G) **Video:** *L'appartement de Manon et Hugo* **Grammar in Action:** p5

3E Une famille fantastique page 28		
• Read a poem in French		
Grammaire	Stratégies	Phonétique
• None	• None	• The letters 's' (between vowels), 'z'
Resources		
Audio: 1 *Alban et sa famille extraordinaire*, or CD 1, track 46 **Copymasters:** None **Worksheets:** Starters and plenaries **e-book:** *La famille Souris*		**Interactive activity:** Classroom commands (V) **Ph** The letters 's' (between vowels), 'z', or CD 1, track 47 **PowerPoint:** None **Grammar in Action:** None

Key language

Family members (3A)
Tu as des frères et sœurs?
Tu as des grands-parents?
J'ai …
un père
une mère
un beau-père
une belle-mère
une sœur
deux sœurs
un frère
trois frères
un demi-frère
une demi-sœur
un(e) cousin(e)
un grand-père
une grand-mère
des parents
des grands-parents
un oncle
une tante
Je suis fils unique / fille unique / enfant unique

Possessions (3B)
mon, ma, mes
ton, ta, tes
C'est le/la/l' … de …
une console
un jeu vidéo
un portable
une radio
un smartphone
une station d'accueil MP3
une télé
un vélo

Around the home (3C)
Dans ma maison, il y a …
la salle à manger
le salon
la cuisine
la salle de bains
la chambre
les toilettes
le garage
le jardin
un lit

Giving information about others (3C)
Il/Elle s'appelle comment?
Il/Elle s'appelle …
Il/Elle a quel âge?
Il/Elle a … ans.
Il/Elle habite où?
Il/Elle habite à …
Qui est-ce?
C'est …
Il/Elle est …
amusant(e).
sportif (sportive).

Prepositions (3D)
dans
sur
sous

Numbers 0–70 (3E)

3A Ma famille

3A Ma famille pages 20–21

- Talk about your family

Grammaire	Stratégies	Phonétique
• Learn how to say 'the' and 'a' • Use the singular of *avoir* (to have)	• Using clues to work out meaning (2)	• The letter 'è' with grave accent'

Resources

Audio: 1 *Ma famille*; **4** *Trois familles*, or CD 1, tracks 35 and 37
Copymasters: 3/1 *La famille Techno*
Worksheets: Starters and plenaries; *Des cartes d'identité* (W); *La famille Roland* (W)

Interactive activity: *La famille de Kévin* (L); *Des frères et des sœurs* (L)
Ph The letter 'è' with grave accent, or CD 1, track 36
PowerPoint: *La famille* (V)
Grammar in Action: None

Worksheet

Starters (pages 20–21)

1 Revise and practise days of the week and numbers up to 30. Each lesson, ask which day it is (*Quel jour sommes-nous? Aujourd'hui, c'est …*) and what the date is. Show a month page from a calendar (see online worksheet) and point to a date, asking, for example, *Le 15, c'est quel jour?* Follow this with questions such as *Deux jours après/avant le 15, c'est quel jour?*, reinforcing the use of *avant* and *après* by pointing at the appropriate date.

2 (use after task 3) Display a family tree on the board (see online worksheet) – two grandparents, two parents, three children. Use stick figure symbols to represent males and females and label the middle child *moi*. Write these family nouns on the board in random order: *le père, la mère, la sœur, le frère, le grand-père, la grand-mère*. Ask students to match them to the different members of the tree in relation to *moi*.

A number of activities and ideas are suggested for the introduction of reading in the course of the book (see TB xiii) and some of these could be used with this unit.

Presentation

La famille

📖 🔊 20

1 Ma famille

Speak about the Laurent family using the photos to introduce the recording. Students can go on to listen to the recorded text several times, with or without the printed version. For extra practice, the teacher could say a number from 1 to 5 and the name of a student who could then say the corresponding sentence aloud.

CD 1 Track 35

Ma famille

1 – Je m'appelle Thomas Laurent et j'ai douze ans. Dans ma famille, il y a cinq personnes: mes parents et trois enfants.
2 – Voici mon frère. Il s'appelle Daniel et il a dix ans.
3 – Voici ma sœur. Elle a quatorze ans.
 – Je m'appelle Louise et je suis la sœur de Thomas et Daniel.
4 – Voici ma mère, Madame Claire Laurent.
5 – Voici mon père, Monsieur Jean-Pierre Laurent.

📖 20 AfL

Students read through the statements and, referring back to the text if necessary, decide who is speaking or described each time. The activity could be corrected orally. This provides an opportunity for peer assessment if students read out the answers. They should review the objectives and agree the criteria first.

Solution:

1 *C'est Thomas,* **2** *C'est Louise,* **3** *C'est Daniel,* **4** *C'est M. Laurent,* **5** *C'est Louise,* **6** *C'est Mme Laurent,* **7** *C'est M. Laurent,* **8** *C'est Louise*

📖 20 AfL

2 La famille Laurent

a Students complete the description, orally or in writing, using the words in the box. They should read out the full sentence when correcting this task, which provides another opportunity for peer assessment. Review objectives and agree criteria first.

Solution:

1 *père,* **2** *mère,* **3** *famille,* **4** *fille,* **5** *fils,* **6** *frères,* **7** *sœur*

b As an extension activity, students describe an imaginary family using the previous sentences as a model and the picture as inspiration.

As follow-up, students could introduce their invented family to a partner. The partner could ask questions to elicit the information.

Tricolore 1 Teacher's Notes

3A Ma famille

20 Dossier-langue

Masculine and feminine

This short explanation should help to familiarise students with *le* and *la*. It is covered again later in the fuller item on gender (SB 27).

Interactive activity

La famille de Kévin

Worksheet

La famille Roland

21

3 Une grande famille

As preparation, tell the class you are going to ask them whether they have any brothers and sisters and ask *Tu as (As-tu) des frères et sœurs?* with just *Oui* or *Non* for the answers to begin with.

The short cartoon then introduces the printed version of the question *Tu as des frères et sœurs?* and supplies examples of how to answer it. Talk the class through the cartoon to check it has been understood, e.g.

Voici une fille. Elle dit, 'Tu as des frères et sœurs?'
Et voici un garçon. Il répond …
Regardez les photos. Le garçon dit, 'J'ai quatre sœurs' etc.

Write on the board:
Oui, j'ai … sœur(s).
Oui, j'ai … frère(s).

Then ask some students to answer more fully the question *Tu as des frères et sœurs?*, choosing first those you know to have siblings. Eventually teach orally *Non, je suis fille/fils/enfant unique*. Add this to the list on the board, and go on to the next item.

Interactive activity

21 Phonétique

The letter 'è' with grave accent

A full explanation of the sound of the letter 'è' is given on *kerboodle*, together with interactive practice which includes differentiating between è and é.

a Say the word *règle* with the gesture for ruling a line (running a pen along a ruler). Students repeat the word with the same gesture. Then read out the other words with students repeating each one. The words are also include in the recording for optional use (part **a**).

Parts **b** and **c** can be used to practise pronunciation of the *a/à/as/at* sound.

b Ask students to listen and repeat the words they hear. Then display the words **a** *très*, **b** *chère*, **c** *Val d'Isère*, **d** *père*, **e** *complète*, **f** *après* for students to match (**d, a, f, b, e, c**).

c Students listen to the 'silly sentence' and note how many times they hear the sound (4). They can repeat the sentence to remember this sound.

For further practice, write some additional words on the board to check that students can recognise the link between spelling and related pronunciation, e.g. *frère, mère, collège*.

CD 1 Track 36

The letter 'è' with grave accent

Écoutez et répétez:
a règle, frère, mère, père
b père, très, après, chère, complète, Val d'Isère
c Mon père est près de Genève cet après-midi.

Stratégies

Using clues to work out meaning (2)

This reading strategy focuses on using context, cognates and near-cognates to help work out meaning.

21 AfL

4 Trois familles

a First give the class a few minutes to look at the photos and text.

Add to the list on the board *demi-frère, demi-sœur, grand-père, grand-mère, grands-parents, cousin(e)*. Ask the class to repeat these words and work out the meaning.

Go through each of the statements with the class, pointing at the relevant words on the board as you say them, e.g.

Voici Talia. Elle est fille unique. Voici Simon. Il est fils unique.

Il habite avec sa grand-mère et son grand-père/avec ses grands-parents.

Voici Alice. Elle a un demi-frère et une demi-sœur.

Some students may want to know more about stepparents and siblings. They may be able to spot that *demi* is invariable whereas *beau* and *belle* agree. They could even look up the plurals in the glossary and find the 'mother/father-in-law' meaning, too.

Now use the recording, and incorporate a range of listening and reading strategies with varying amounts of support.

CD 1 Track 37

Trois familles

1 – Talia, tu as des frères et sœurs?
   – Non, je suis fille unique.
   – Tu as des cousins?
   – Oui, j'ai une cousine, Delphine et un cousin, Nicolas.
2 – Et toi, Simon, as-tu des frères et sœurs?
   – Non, je suis fils unique.
   – Et tu habites avec ta grand-mère et ton grand-père, c'est ça?
   – Oui, j'habite avec mon père et mes grands-parents.
3 – Et toi, Alice. Tu es fille unique aussi?
   – Non, non. Dans ma famille, il y a ma mère, mon beau-père et aussi mon demi-frère, David, et ma demi-sœur, Érika. Ils sont fantastiques!

29

3B C'est à qui?

b The reading task in part **b** is based on the photos and text above, but with the verbs in the third person. It could be done orally as a class activity or by students working in pairs, providing an opportunity for peer assessment. More able students, working alone, could write corrected versions of the false sentences.

> **Solution:**
> (suggested corrections): **1** faux (Talia est fille unique./Talia a deux cousins.), **2** faux (Simon a un père et des grands-parents/un grand-père et une grand-mère.), **3** vrai, **4** vrai, **5** faux (Simon est fils/enfant unique.), **6** faux (Alice a un demi-frère et une demi-sœur.), **7** vrai, **8** vrai, **9** vrai, **10** vrai

Interactive activity
Des frères et sœurs

Worksheet

Des cartes d'identité

143 Au choix — AfL

6 Ma famille

21 Dossier-langue

The singular of *avoir* (to have)

Students are reminded that they have now met all the singular parts of *avoir*, and about the use of *avoir* when talking about age.

21

5 Avoir

a This short task practises the singular paradigm of *avoir*.

> **Solution:**
> **1** j'ai, **2** tu as, **3** il a, **4** elle a, **5** ai, **6** as, **7** a, **8** a

b As an extension activity, students write a description of their imaginary family, using parts of *avoir*. Encourage them to use as much of their knowledge as possible.

As a follow-up speaking activity, students each invent a family for themselves and note down the details. They then work in pairs or small groups, finding out about these 'new families', by using the questions and answers learnt on this spread.

142 Au choix

1 Combien?

cm 3/1

La famille Techno

Worksheet

Plenaries (pages 20–21)

1 In pairs, students tell their partner three things about their family. They then pair up with another two students – how many different phrases can they say? Take feedback from the class.

2 In pairs or groups, students discuss strategies for remembering family vocabulary – *frère*, *mère*, *père* all rhyme; how to remember *sœur*? *enfant* is like which English word? (infant) **or** How many cognates or near cognates can students remember? (e.g. *unique*)

3B C'est à qui? pages 22–23

- Say which things belong to you

Grammaire	Stratégies	Phonétique
• Use the words for 'my' and 'your' • Use *de* to show possession	• Remembering the gender of nouns	• The letters 'a', 'à' with grave accent, 'as', 'at'

Resources
Audio: 3 *Mon numéro un*; 4 *Dani et Théo* or CD 1, tracks 38, 39 and 41 **Copymasters:** None **Worksheets:** Starters and plenaries; *Interview d'une vampire* (R,W); *C'est le crayon de …?* (W)	**Interactive activity:** *À moi, à toi* (G) **Ph** The letters 'a', 'à' with grave accent, '-as', '-at', or CD 1, track 40 **PowerPoint:** *Les articles* (G) **Grammar in Action:** pp6–7

3B C'est à qui?

> **Worksheet**

Starters (pages 22–23)

1 Display a number of words randomly on the board/screen (see below and online worksheet for suggestions). Students try pronouncing them silently to themselves putting the correct word for 'the' in front of each. After one minute, point to a word and then point to or name a student; the student says the word with *le/la/l'* in front.

appartement, lecteur MP3, boîte, chaise, crayon, fenêtre, gomme, livre, maison, ordinateur, taille-crayon, porte, poubelle, règle, stylo, trousse, village, ville

The rest of the class agree (*Oui, c'est ça/correct*) by calling out the correct article.

In this activity, students …
- are building up internal sound checking skills
- are encouraged always to sound out silently before trying words out loud
- are reminded that there is more than one form of the definite article.

2 (use before task 3) Revise days of the week and classroom objects, using one of the following:
- Give the days of the week with missing letters and ask students to fill in the gaps.
- Display jumbled spellings of the days of the week and ask students to write them correctly.
- Write the days of the week on the board in one location and a list of classroom items in another, then play a chain game in groups or as a class,

  e.g. *Lundi, j'ai un cartable. Mardi, j'ai un cartable et un lecteur MP3. Mercredi, j'ai un cartable, un lecteur MP3 et …*

  lecteur MP3, boîte, crayon, cahier, calculatrice, cartable, classeur, feutre, gomme, livre, portable, règle, stylo, taille-crayon, trousse

> **Introduction**

My and your

Teach *mon* and *ma*, *ton* and *ta* orally, by picking up classroom objects and saying *Voici mon crayon, Où est ton crayon?/C'est ta gomme, ça? Oui, c'est ma gomme*, etc. Go round the class 'stealing' possessions from students. When you have assembled a pile of these, ask students *C'est ton crayon/ta gomme?* etc. They can only claim their possessions back by correctly saying *C'est mon crayon* etc. Gradually extend this type of activity to include some plurals, *tes cahiers, mes livres*, etc. When most students are getting the idea, move on to the explanation on SB 22.

> **22 Dossier-langue**

The words for 'my' and 'your'

Ask the class to read through the explanation and see if they have worked out the rule and understood it, first by getting one or two of them to explain it to the class, then asking the whole class to work in pairs and explain the rule to each other.

For practice, divide the class in half, one team being 'my' and one 'your'. When you say a French word, perhaps also holding up an object, the members of each team take it in turns to say, e.g. *mon stylo/ta règle/mes affaires*, etc. The teams take it in turns to answer first and the winner is the first to get, say, 20 points for correct answers.

If students produced posters for SB 143 *Au choix* task 6 (see TB page 30), these could be used for pairwork, e.g. *C'est ta soeur? Non, c'est ma mère*, etc.

> **gia 1 pp6–7**

Further practice of the possessive adjectives *mon, ma, mes* and *ton, ta, tes*.

> **Interactive activity**

> **22**

1 La famille Corpuscule

Talk about this unusual family, using the illustrations and getting students to repeat the names of the family, preferably in short sentences, e.g. *Voici la famille Corpuscule. C'est une famille de Vampires. Voici le père. Il s'appelle Tombô. Voici la mère. Elle s'appelle Draculine*, etc.

Then move on to the task which involves supplying the correct possessive adjective either orally or in writing.

Voici Désastre. Il présente sa famille. Complète la description pour Désastre.

> **Solution:**
> **1** *Ma, mon,* **2** *mes,* **3** *Mon, mon,* **4** *Ma, ma,*
> **5** *mes, ma*

Les Corpuscule

As a follow-up speaking activity, put the names of the *Corpuscule* family on pieces of paper. Students pick one and have to say two things (or as much as they can) as if they are that person, e.g. *Je m'appelle Draculine. Mon fils s'appelle Désastre et ma fille s'appelle Enferina.*

Alternatively, students sit in the Hot seat and others ask them questions, e.g. *Ton fils, comment s'appelle-t-il?*

> **144 Au choix**

2 Des questions utiles

> **Worksheet**

Interview d'un vampire

Tricolore 1 Teacher's Notes **31**

3B C'est à qui?

22 AfL

2 Tu as tes affaires?

Further practice of the two possessive adjectives. Draw students' attention to the colour-coding suggested in the *Stratégies* box (masculine nouns in blue and feminine ones in red), indicating the thought process necessary to carry out the task. Remind students of the learning objectives and how this task will allow them to demonstrate their skills. Students could do this task orally in pairs, changing over roles half way through. More able students could then write the answers as consolidation (just possessives + noun).

Encourage students to check and correct each other's work, displaying correct answers as appropriate.

> **Solution:**
> **1** *ta; ma*, **2** *ta; ma*, **3** *tes; mes*, **4** *ton; mon*, **5** *ton; mon*

Dans mon cartable …

Working in pairs or small groups, each student puts two or three of their possessions in their school bag and they each have to ask questions in turn to find out what they are, e.g. *Tu as ton livre? Oui, voici mon livre* (puts it on the table) (or *Non!*). The first one to guess the possessions of all the others has won.

Introduction

C'est le/la … de …

Introduce this structure by going round the classroom and picking up objects, saying, e.g.

Voici la règle de Martin, et ça, qu'est-ce que c'est?

C'est le stylo de Linda.

C'est le crayon de David. Vrai ou faux?

Use some games for practice, e.g.

1. Put a few objects in a box. Take one out and hold it behind your back. Students guess what it is and who it belongs to, e.g. *C'est la règle de Chantal?*
2. *Je touche …* (See Games TB page xvi.)
3. *Je pense à quelque chose*, played as usual, but with each person guessing using the construction *C'est le livre de Caroline* etc. (See Games TB page xvi.)

The choice of objects could be limited in order to stop one person's turn from going on interminably.

22

3 Mon numéro un

a Students listen once for the actual objects and again to check whether it is *mon* or *ma*.

> **Solution:**
> **1** *ma guitare*, **2** *ma peluche*, **3** *mon smartphone*
> **2** **1** *mon portable*, **2** *ma liseuse*, **3** *mon chat*
> **3** **1** *mon chien*, **2** *mon smartphone*, **3** *ma tablette*
> **4** **1** *mon vélo*, **2** *ma tablette*, **3** *ma raquette de tennis*

CD 1 Track 38

1. – Mon numéro un est ma guitare – j'adore la musique. Mon numéro deux, c'est ma peluche. C'est un petit chien qui s'appelle Milou. Et mon numéro trois … mmm … ah oui, c'est mon smartphone.
2. – Tu as beaucoup d'affaires. Quel est ton numéro un?
   – Alors, mon numéro un, c'est mon portable – j'aime les ordinateurs. Et mon numéro deux, c'est … euh … c'est ma liseuse – j'ai beaucoup de livres électroniques.
   – Tu as un numéro trois?
   – Oui, mon numéro trois, c'est mon chat. Il s'appelle Gaston.
3. – Et toi, quel est ton numéro un?
   – Mon numéro un, c'est mon chien, oui, mon chien. Il est adorable! Et mon numéro deux … c'est mon smartphone. Mon numéro trois … quel est mon numéro trois? Hmm … c'est ma tablette … oui, c'est ça, ma tablette.
4. – Moi, j'adore le cyclisme, et mon numéro un, c'est mon vélo.
   – Et quel est ton numéro deux?
   – Mon numéro deux, c'est ma tablette … et puis mon numéro trois, c'est ma raquette de tennis. C'est super.

b If students need to look up words for their list or conversation (part **c**), go over basic dictionary skills if students are not already familiar with these.

c Students adapt the conversation, using as much previous knowledge as possible.

Présentation

Les articles

23

4 Dani et Théo

a Play the recording as students follow the cartoon strip. Then ask them some questions, on similar lines to those in the exercise which follows, e.g. *Regardez le lecteur MP3. C'est le lecteur MP3 de Dani? Non? C'est le lecteur MP3 de son frère? Oui, c'est ça.*

CD 1 Track 39

Dani et Théo

– Lundi, Dani est à la maison.
– Voici un SMS de mon frère, Théo. Il est à Nice.
– Aujourd'hui, c'est mardi. Dani est content.
– Voici le lecteur MP3 de mon frère. C'est cool!
– Mercredi, il est à la campagne.
– C'est le vélo de mon frère. J'aime le vélo!
– Jeudi, Dani a une liseuse.
– Il y a 45 livres électronique sur la liseuse de mon frère. Je lis le numéro 13.
– Vendredi, il cherche son cartable.
– Où est mon cartable? Ah, je prends le sac à dos de mon frère.
– Samedi, il est avec une amie.
– Je vais au cinéma. Voici la copine de mon frère.
– Mais dimanche … qui est-ce?!
– Aïe! Voici mon frère!

b Students write down the true statement in each pair. This can be corrected orally, with students reading out the full sentence each time, e.g.

32 Tricolore 1 Teacher's Notes

Regardez 'a'. C'est le lecteur MP3 de Dani? Oui? Non?

Et regardez 'b'. C'est le lecteur MP3 de son frère. C'est vrai?

Oui, c'est vrai.

Solution:
1 *b*, **2** *b*, **3** *b*, **4** *a*, **5** *a*, **6** *b*

Qu'est-ce qui manque?

As follow-up. this group speaking task provides practice of classroom objects + *de* + name. Everyone in the group puts something in the middle, e.g. pencil, ruler, rubber. They shut their eyes while the teacher mixes the objects up and removes one thing. Then in turn students pick up something and identify it saying, *C'est le crayon de Paul,* etc. At the end they are asked *Qu'est-ce qui manque?* and have to say what is missing.

> Worksheet

C'est le crayon de …?

> 23 Stratégies

Remembering the gender of nouns

This grammar memorisation strategy suggests ways of remembering the gender of nouns.

> 23 Dossier-langue

Explaining belonging

Go through the presentation of *de* + noun and ask students to give further examples to reinforce the new structure.

> Interactive activity

> 23 Phonétique

The letters 'a', 'à' with grave accent, 'as', 'at'

A full explanation of the sound of the letters 'a', 'à', 'as' is given on *kerboodle!*, together with interactive practice which includes differentiating between words that do and do not contain the 'a' sound.

a Say the word *sac* with the appropriate gesture (shouldering a bag). Students repeat the word with the same gesture. Then read out the other words with students repeating each one. The words are also include in the recording for optional use (part a).

Parts **b** and **c** can be used to practise pronunciation of the *a/à/as/at* sound.

b Ask students to listen and repeat the words they hear. Then display the words **a** *Lucas*, **b** *ami*, **c** *oh là là!*, **d** *pas*, **e** *famille*, **f** *rat* for students to match (b, e, d, a, f, c).

c Students listen to the 'silly sentence' and note how many times they hear the sound (5). They can repeat the sentence to remember this sound.

For further practice, write some additional words on the board to check that students can recognise the link between spelling and related pronunciation, e.g. *achat, madame, résultat, vas*.

> CD 1 Track 40

The letters 'a', 'à' with grave accent, '-as', '-at'

Écoutez et répétéz:
a sac, voilà, Thomas, chat
b ami, famille, pas, Lucas, rat, oh là là!
c Camille le chat aime le sac de mon ami Lucas.

> Worksheet

Plenaries (pages 22–23)

1 Students write down two sentences summarising the lesson, then share these with the class. Discuss the key points to remember and what aspects might cause difficulties.

2 Students shut their books and take stock of what they have learnt so far in this unit: vocabulary for members of the family, differences between masculine and feminine, using possessive adjectives, using the different word order of *le/la* (+ noun) *de* (+ name).

3C Ma maison   pages 24–25

- Discuss your family and friends
- Talk about your home

Grammaire	Stratégies	Phonétique
• Use the singular of *être* (to be)	• None	• The letter 'u'

Resources

Audio: 4 *La maison de la famille Laurent*, or CD 1, track 42
Copymasters: None
Worksheets: Starters and plenaries; *Le verbe être* (G)

Interactive activity: *Les pièces* (V)
Ph *The letter 'u'*, or CD 1, track 43
PowerPoint: *Des maisons françaises* (V)
Grammar in Action: None

3C Ma maison

Worksheet

Starters (pages 24–25)

1 Reinforce the focus on masculine and feminine. Present an assortment of 12–15 nouns learnt so far, without the articles (see below and online worksheet). Give each student two pieces of card, one in blue for masculine nouns, one in red for feminine nouns. Now read out the list of words. Students hold up the blue card if the word is masculine, red for feminine.

cahier, calculatrice, cartable, chaise, classeur, fenêtre, lecteur MP3, maison, porte, poubelle, sac, stylo, table, tableau interactif, village

2 (use after task 3) Play *Loto!* using visuals or text. Prepare a card for each student with any four rooms or items in the Laurent family's house in French (see online worksheet). Students pick them up as they enter the classroom. The first student to get all four places calls *Loto!* and has to say the four places in French. An alternative version of this is 'strip bingo' – items are listed vertically on a strip of paper and students can only tear items from the top or the bottom when they are called out.

24 Dossier-langue

The singular of *être* (to be)

As the singular parts of *être* have occurred in context, this is now explained and practised. The full paradigm is covered in *Unité 5*. If teachers wish to cover the full paradigm in this unit, an online task is provided below. For oral practice, use flashcards (13–17) for the rooms, giving them to students and asking questions, e.g.

- *Où es-tu?*
- *Je suis dans la chambre.*
- *Où est Richard? Il est dans la cuisine?*
- *Non, il est dans la salle à manger,* etc.

Worksheet

Le verbe être

24

The next three items are a set of e-mails to practise the singular of *être* and other vocabulary.

1 Un message d'Yvan

a Students read the e-mail from Yvan which could be followed by a brief discussion about the verbs used.

b Point out the word *sportif* in preparation for the feminine form which appears in the next e-mail.

> **Solution:**
> 1 *faux*, 2 *vrai*, 3 *vrai*, 4 *faux*, 5 *faux*, 6 *vrai*, 7 *vrai*, 8 *faux*

24

moi and *toi*

This item focuses on the use of emphatic pronouns *moi* and *toi*.

24

2 Un message de Karine

As the e-mail is sent by a girl, comment on the use of *sportive*.

> **Solution:**
> *Je suis ta correspondante; Il est amusant; Elle est fantastique!; Es-tu sportive comme moi?*

24

3 Salut!

a Students now write their own e-mail, filling in the gaps. More able students could add a few more sentences here.

b Encourage students to use all their knowledge and add as much detail as possible.

24

est (is), *et* (and)

This item focuses on the sound of *est* (is) and *et* (and). It is accompanied by a short listening differentiation task.

Both these words are often used. How different do they sound? Is each word always pronounced the same way?

Emphasise to students that understanding the context helps them work out which word is being used. Also mention that the final *t* of *est* is sounded before a vowel or silent *h*, but the *t* on *et* is never sounded.

> **Solution:**
> 1 *et*, 2 *est*, 3 *et*, 4 *est*, 5 *est*, 6 *est*, 7 *et*, 8 *est*

> **CD 1 Track 41**
> 1 J'ai une sœur et un frère.
> 2 Mon frère est très amusant.
> 3 Il a une souris et un rat.
> 4 La souris est amusante.
> 5 Mais le rat est horrible.
> 6 Ma sœur est très petite.
> 7 Elle déteste le rat et la souris.
> 8 Mais elle adore son petit chat. Il est fantastique!

Presentation

Des maisons françaises

Tricolore 1 Teacher's Notes

3C Ma maison

🔊 25   AfL

4 La maison de la famille Laurent

a First get the class to look at the plan of the house and familiarise themselves with the rooms. Play the recording while students follow the text. Use a range of reading strategies with varying amounts of support.

Look again at the plan and talk briefly about the rooms, e.g.

La salle à manger, c'est la lettre …?
La lettre A, c'est quelle pièce? C'est la chambre.
Et voici la cuisine. Regardez. Dans la cuisine il y a une radio, etc.

Once the students are familiar with the plan and have understood the text, ask questions about the plan, introducing *Qu'est-ce qu'il y a?* and *Il y a …* and gradually train the class to answer and then ask each other these, e.g.

- a – *C'est le salon?*
  – *Oui, c'est le salon./Non, c'est la salle à manger.*
- b – *Il y a une table/une radio/un lit dans la salle à manger/la cuisine/la chambre de Louise? Oui ou non?*
- c – *Où est le lecteur CD/l'ordinateur?*
  – *Dans la chambre de Louise/de Thomas et Daniel,* etc.
- d – *Qu'est-ce qu'il y a dans la chambre de Louise?*
  – *Dans la chambre de Louise, il y a un lit, un chat et une station d'accueil MP3.*

Finally play the recording again, this time with students not following the printed text.

🔊 **CD 1 Track 42**

La maison de la famille Laurent
Je suis Louise Laurent.
Voici notre maison et notre jardin.
Et voici le garage.
Dans la maison, il y a huit pièces: le salon, la salle à manger, la cuisine, les toilettes, la salle de bains et trois chambres.
Dans la chambre de mes parents, il y a un lit et un lecteur CD. Oui, il y a toujours un lecteur CD – ce n'est pas très moderne, quoi?!
Dans la chambre de Thomas et Daniel, il y a deux lits, une console de jeux et toutes les affaires de mes frères.
Il y a une télé dans le salon et un ordinateur dans la chambre de mes frères.
Il y a aussi un téléphone dans la chambre de Maman et Papa.
Dans la salle à manger, il y a une table et cinq chaises.
Dans la cuisine, il y a une radio et un téléphone.
Dans ma chambre, il y a ma station d'accueil MP3, mon portable et, regardez, sur mon lit, il y a mon chat Mimi!

b This matching task consolidates the vocabulary for rooms. Ask questions such as *Le salon, c'est où? La cuisine, c'est la lettre 'B', oui ou non?* Answers can be checked orally. Students could check each other's work in pairs as an opportunity for peer assessment. Refer to the spread objectives and agree criteria for success before assessing their work.

Point out the pronunciation and spelling of *accueil*, both of which can cause problems. Other uses of *accueil* can be mentioned, e.g. *page d'accueil* (= home page), *accueil (d'un hôtel)* (= reception).

Once all the areas of the house have been identified, do further oral practice of the new vocabulary, e.g. *La lettre 'D', c'est quelle pièce?*

For further practice, print the pictures from the PowerPoint presentation (above) as flashcards and play any of the flashcard games (see TB 24) or adapt the games for the whiteboard. A useful one here is 'Guess which room it is' or 'Guess which room it isn't'. Hold a flashcard face down, or hide the whiteboard picture, and ask, for example,

– *Ce n'est pas la cuisine?*
– *Vrai.*
– *Ce n'est pas la salle à manger?*
– *Faux, c'est la salle à manger. Regardez!*

If more oral work is required, give flashcards of rooms to a row of students, asking them questions, e.g.

Tu es dans le salon? Es-tu dans la cuisine? etc.

Then get students to make up *vrai ou faux* statements to ask others, e.g.

Corrie est dans la salle à manger. Tyler est dans la salle de bains, etc.

Solution:
1 J, **2** G, **3** H, **4** I, **5** A, **6** C, **7** B, **8** D, **9** E, **10** F

↖ Interactive activity

Les pièces

↖ Interactive activity

🔊 **25 Phonétique**

The letter 'u'

A full explanation of the sound of the letter 'u' is given on *kerboodle!*, together with interactive practice which includes differentiating between words that do and do not contain the u sound.

a Say the word *lune* with the gesture for moon (form a circle with thumb and forefinger and hold your hand up as if in the sky – the circle shape helps remind students of the shape their mouth should be in). Students repeat the word with the same gesture. Then read out the other words with students repeating each one. The words are also include in the recording for optional use (part **a**).

Parts **b** and **c** can be used to practise pronunciation of the u sound.

b Ask students to listen and repeat the words they hear. Then display the words **a** *sur*, **b** *une*, **c** *Luc*, **d** *musique*, **e** *tu*, **f** *salut* for students to match (**e**, **b**, **f**, **d**, **a**, **c**).

Tricolore 1 Teacher's Notes   **35**

3D C'est où?

c Students listen to the 'silly sentence' and note how many times they hear the sound (5). They can repeat the sentence to remember this sound.

For further practice, write some additional words on the board to check that students can recognise the link between spelling and related pronunciation, e.g. *Lucie, plume, rue, surligneur*.

CD 1 Track 43

The letter 'u'

Écoutez et répétez:
a lune, utile, rue, unique, amusant, une
b tu, une, salut, musique, sur, Luc
c Dans la rue des Dunes il y a une grande statue amusante.

---

25   **AfL**

5 Les pièces

This entails matching two halves of a sentence. Answers could be checked through in pairs first as an opportunity for peer assessment, then corrected orally to give practice in reading out the complete sentences.

Solution:
1 *b*, 2 *j*, 3 *g*, 4 *h*, 5 *e*, 6 *a*, 7 *d*, 8 *c*, 9 *f*, 10 *i*

---

145 Au choix

5 Samedi

CD 1 Track 49

Samedi

– C'est samedi chez la famille Laurent. Où sont les enfants?
– Où est Louise? Je pense qu'elle est dans sa chambre … Louise, tu es dans ta chambre?
– Oui, Maman. Je suis ici. J'écoute des CD.
– Et Thomas? Il est dans sa chambre aussi? Thomas, tu es dans ta chambre?
– Non, Maman. Je suis dans le salon. Je regarde la télé.
– Très bien. Mais où est Daniel? Daniel, tu es dans ta chambre?
– Oui, Maman, je suis dans ma chambre. Je range mes affaires.
– Tu ranges tes affaires?!
– Mais oui, Maman! Dimanche, c'est le concert rock en ville, non? Et moi, j'adore la musique!

---

25 Interactive activity

Ma famille et ma maison

Worksheet

Plenaries (pages 24–25)

1 Find out from students how they remember the spelling and pronunciation of the rooms and the objects in them. They work in pairs, then report back to the whole class. If necessary, provide some ideas to start them off, e.g. *salon* – like 'saloon'; *cuisine* – spell it rhythmically C-U … I-S … I-N-E.

2 Ask students to look at the objectives for SB pages 24–25: how well do they think they have done? Can they explain the main points to a partner? What did they find easy or difficult?

3D C'est où? pages 26–27

- Describe where things are in a room

Grammaire	Stratégies	Phonétique
• Use some prepositions • Learn more about masculin and feminine	• Remembering vocabulary	• None

Resources
Audio: 1 *Notre chambre*; *Suzanne et Suzette Souris*, or CD 1, tracks 44 and 45 **Copymasters:** 3/2 *Masculin, féminin* **Worksheets:** Starters and plenaries; *Invente des phrases* (W); Remembering vocabulary (Strat)   **PowerPoint:** *C'est où?* (G) **Video:** *L'appartement de Manon et Hugo* **Grammar in Action:** p5

Tricolore 1 Teacher's Notes

3D C'est où?

Worksheet

Starters (pages 26–27)

1 Write a random list of vocabulary items on one area of the board (see online worksheet – rooms, furniture, objects). Begin to draw any one of the items. Students tell you as soon as they know what it is. Bad drawing 'adds to the interest'. Students then continue in pairs. (This provides good preparation for the vocabulary used in work on prepositions.)

2 Show the picture of Thomas and Daniel's room (SB page 26 and Unité 3 Starters and Plenaries worksheet) and play *Sur ou sous?* Explain that holding your arms up means that an object is *sur*; holding them down means it is *sous*. Say sentences containing *sur* or *sous* (e.g. *la trousse de Thomas est sur la chaise*). Students listen and when they hear *sur* their arms go up, when they hear *sous* their arms go down under the desks. Alternatively, they could only do the action if the information is correct (as a version of *Jacques a dit …*).

Introduction

Où est …?

There are a variety of ways to teach and practise *sur*, *sous* and *dans*, e.g. with classroom objects, piling them up, putting them in, on or under things and asking questions beginning with *Où est …?* At first supply the answers too, then get the class to answer. Eventually students can ask and answer similar questions. The small diagram on SB page 26 gives the meaning of the three words. Several oral games provide useful practice, e.g. *Qu'est-ce qu'il y a dans la boîte?* (see TB page xvii).

Presentation

C'est où?

📖 🔊 26

1 Notre chambre

Use the picture for oral discussion. Students then listen to Thomas describing the room and guess which is his side.

After this first hearing, go through the whole item more thoroughly using the printed text. Use listening and reading strategies as appropriate.

Ask questions about the picture, e.g. *Où sont les livres de Thomas?/Où est le lit de Daniel? – Voici/Voilà …*

Où est le cartable?/Qu'est-ce qu'il y a dans la trousse? etc.

🔊 CD 1 Track 44

Notre chambre

Je suis Thomas Laurent, et Daniel est mon petit frère.
Voici notre chambre et voici notre console avec les jeux vidéo.
Voici mes affaires. Mes livres sont sur la table et mes crayons sont dans la boîte.
Mon stylo est sur le cahier et mes classeurs sont sous la table.
Et voilà mon lecteur MP3.
Et voici les affaires de mon frère Daniel.
Où est le sac? Ah oui, il est sur le lit!
Dans le sac, il y a une règle et des livres.
Et qu'est-ce qu'il y a sous le lit? Voilà!
Le smartphone de Daniel est sous le lit.
Et voici la trousse de Daniel: elle est sur la chaise.
Et qu'est-ce qu'il y a dans la trousse? Regardez!
Il y a une gomme dans la trousse, mais les crayons et le stylo sont sous la chaise!

📖 26

2 Dans la chambre

Students supply the word *sur*, *sous* or *dans* to complete these sentences. Most are given in the text, but one or two have to be discovered through the picture of the bedroom. The answers should be checked orally afterwards, with students reading aloud each completed sentence.

> **Solution:**
> 1 *dans*, 2 *sur*, 3 *dans*, 4 *sur*, 5 *dans*, *sur*, 6 *dans*, 7 *sous*, 8 *sur*

Use similar questions and answers to consolidate the new vocabulary and to introduce the pronouns *il* and *elle*.

Consolidation

The following worksheet and *Au choix* activities present a selection of differentiated activities which could be used here to consolidate work on rooms in the house, prepositions and expressing possession.

Worksheet

Invente des phrases

📖 144 Au choix

3 La maison de la famille Lambert

📖 144 Au choix

4 Jeu de mémoire

📖 26 Stratégies

Remembering vocabulary

Tricolore 1 Teacher's Notes 37

3D C'est où?

📢 26
Suzanne et Suzette Souris

This item focuses on the pronunciation of the sounds *ou* and *u*, already met in the words *sur* and *sous*. Students could try saying the sentences as a tongue twister.

> 📢 CD 1 Track 45
>
> **Suzanne et Suzette Souris**
>
> Suzanne Souris est sur la boîte.
> Voici sa sœur, Suzette Souris.
> La boîte est sous la table. Suzanne et Suzette Souris sont aussi sous la table.

📖 27 Dossier-langue
Masculine and feminine

By now students have met all the articles and several possessive adjectives and pronouns, so this item really serves as a reference table for revision, bringing the main examples together. Go through the table with students and check that they can complete it accurately. The completed table …

- sets out more fully the link between *un* and *le/une* and *la* (already mentioned on SB page 20)
- includes *l'* + vowel
- mentions the use of the pronouns *il* and *elle* to mean 'it'
- explains that gender applies to things as well as people in French.

If some students are not too clear about any of these points, give them more examples, e.g.

Voici un stylo. (Write *un stylo* on the board.)

C'est le stylo de Vivienne, oui? (Write *le stylo* under *un stylo*.)

Put the pen in a box, or any other suitable place.

Bon, le stylo de Vivienne est dans la boîte. Il est dans la boîte. (Write *il* under *le*.)

Coloured pens could be used to highlight masculine and feminine words.

Continue in the same way using feminine objects and with words beginning with a vowel, so that students can see the pattern.

📖 27
3 Où est …?

This task practises the prepositions *sur*, *sous* and *dans* and also involves matching the correct pronoun (*il* or *elle*) with a masculine or feminine noun.

Mention two things to look for when doing the task:
1 get the right preposition
2 match the genders (*il* for masculine noun, *elle* for feminine noun).

> **Solution:**
> 1 c, 2 a, 3 d, 4 b, 5 g, 6 e, 7 h, 8 f

C'est où?

For further practice of prepositions and pronouns, play a game. Someone places/hides objects around the classroom and asks where they are. Others reply using pronouns. This could be a team game – one mark for the correct place, one for the correct preposition, one for using the correct pronoun.

📖 27
4 Ma chambre

a Students could discuss this activity in pairs first, noting the phrases and vocabulary they will need. The task could then be done orally as a class activity, asking students questions such as: *Qu'est-ce qu'il y a dans ta chambre? Où est ton ordinateur? Tu as une télévision dans ta chambre?*

Students can then write out a short description of their room (or their ideal room, if they prefer). The final version of this can form part of students' *Dossier personnel*.

b Students could prepare a presentation using a variety of media, e.g. whiteboard, PowerPoint, video. Encourage them to include text that shows the amount of language they have learnt so far and to make the presentation as interesting as possible with visuals where possible.

As an alternative, students could write an extended text about their home, for example in the form of a blog:

Écris un paragraphe sur ta maison ou ton appartement (avec des photos ou des dessins, si possible).

cm 3/2

Masculin, féminin

gia 1 p5

Masculine and feminine

This grammar explanation and practice covers material in *Unités* 1–3 and can be used here for consolidation.

> 📌 Interactive activity

Rue Danton: L'appartement de Manon et Hugo

> 📌 Worksheet

Plenaries (pages 26–27)

1 In pairs, students tell their partner three things about where things are in their house or room. They then pair up with another two students – how many different phrases can they say? Take feedback from the class.

2 Show visuals of some of the items of vocabulary that students have met in this unit (and also from the first two units). Which, if any, do students find hard to remember? Is it easy to remember the gender? Discuss, as a class, ways of memorising the more difficult words.

3E Une famille fantastique   page 28

- Read a poem in French

Grammaire	Stratégies	Phonétique
• None	• None	• The letters 's' (between vowels), 'z'

Resources

Audio: 1 *Alban et sa famille extraordinaire*, or CD 1, track 46
Copymasters: None
Worksheets: Starters and plenaries
e-book: *La famille Souris*

Interactive activity: Classroom commands (V)
Ph The letters 's' (between vowels), 'z', or CD 1, track 47
PowerPoint: None
Grammar in Action: None

Worksheet

Starters

1 Display the numbers up to 30 in words in French on the board, out of sequence. Invite students to work out the right order silently to themselves and then to call them out in sequence. Point to the first student who starts – *un, deux*. Then point to another student (not the next one) who continues – *trois, quatre, cinq*. Point to a third student – *six* –, etc.

2 Display words with the vowels é and è missing. Students hold up a piece of paper with é or è on it. It is helpful if these are on different coloured paper, perhaps orange for é and green for è.

   Suggestions:

   écoute, réponse, numéro, stratégie, zéro, idée, vérifie, télé, téléphone, intéressant, vidéo, différent, vélo, père, mère, frère, pièce, complète, règle and one to really test them: *répète*.

1 Alban et sa famille extraordinaire

Students should listen for the rhythm, the rhymes and the intonation of the poem. Once they are familiar with it, they could read the poem aloud themselves. This could be done a line or a verse at a time around the class and it could be recorded or filmed.

CD 1 Track 46

Bonjour! Je m'appelle Alban.
J'ai quel âge? J'ai un an.
Et qui a cinq ans? Mon grand-père.
C'est bientôt son anniversaire.

J'ai trente frères et vingt-huit sœurs,
et j'ai aussi dix demi-sœurs.
Mes vingt-huit sœurs, elles habitent
dans la chambre de Marguerite.

C'est nul, chez elle: il y a des classeurs
et des livres, mais pas de lecteur!
Et où est le lit de mes sœurs?
Voilà! Il est sous l'ordinateur.

Pour moi, Alban, et mes frères,
c'est différent et c'est super:
on habite dans la chambre de Mathieu.
Il y a de la place pour trente-deux.

Chez Mathieu, pas de cahiers,
mais il y a une grande télé,
un portable et des jeux vidéo
et de la musique pop à la radio.

J'ai aussi plusieurs cousines;
elles habitent dans la cuisine.
Et où sont donc mes cousins?
Eh bien, dans la salle de bains.

Et toi, tu as des frères et sœurs?
Ou peut-être des demi-sœurs?
J'espère que tu n'es pas enfant unique;
une grande famille, c'est fantastique!

2 Alban et sa famille

a This task tests comprehension of the poem.

   Solution:
   1 *faux,* **2** *vrai,* **3** *vrai,* **4** *vrai,* **5** *faux,* **6** *vrai*

3E Une famille fantastique

b Students correct the false sentences.

> **Solution:**
> (Suggested): **1** *Alban a des frères et sœurs,* **5** *Son grand-père a cinq ans.*

c Students should write out full sentences so they use the words in context.

> **Solution:**
> **1** *an, (grand-père),* **2** *jeux vidéo,* **3** *trente, sœurs,* **4** *télé,* **5** *sous*

| Interactive activity |

| 28 Phonétique |

The letters 's' (between vowels), 'z'

A full explanation of the sound of the letters *s* and *z* is given on *kerboodle!*, together with interactive practice which includes differentiating between words that do and do not contain the 'z' sound.

a Say the word *zéro* with the gesture for for 'zero' (drawing a zero in the air). Students repeat the word with the same gesture. Then read out the other words with students repeating each one. The words are also include in the recording for optional use (part **a**).

Parts **b** and **c** can be used to practise pronunciation of the *z* sound.

b Ask students to listen and repeat the words they hear. Then display the words **a** *Louise,* **b** *les élèves,* **c** *amusant,* **d** *treize,* **e** *française,* **f** *cuisine* for students to match (**d, a, e, f, c, b**).

c Students listen to the 'silly sentence' and note how many times they hear the sound (5). They can repeat the sentence to remember this sound.

For further practice, write some additional words on the board to check that students can recognise the link between spelling and related pronunciation, e.g. *musée, résumé, besoin, allez-y!*.

| CD 1 Track 47 |

The letters 's' (between vowels), 'z'

Écoutez et répétez:
a zéro, chaise, maison, musique
b treize, Louise, française, cuisine, amusant, les élèves
c Isabelle parle avec sa cousine Louise à la maison à Toulouse.

| Worksheet |

Plenaries (page 28)

1. With their books closed, students reconstruct the different language they have learnt in this unit. Write up the information as a mind-map with *Chez moi* at the centre (see online worksheet).

   Surround *Chez moi* with some sentences/sentence starters, e.g.

   Dans ma famille, j'ai un frère, …

   Dans mon appartement, il y a …

   Dans ma chambre, j'ai …

   Mon ordinateur est sur la table, …

2. Discuss what students have been able to include in their *Dossier personnel* at the end of this unit. Students could assess how far they have come in the first three units (before moving on to the first *Rappel* section) and summarise what they now know.

| 29 Sommaire |

A summary of the main language and structures of the unit, also on copymaster for ease of reference.

Unité 3 Consolidation and assessment

Épreuves Unités 1–3

These worksheets can be used for an informal test of listening, reading and writing or for extra practice, as required. For general notes on the Épreuves, see TB page xv.

3/6 Écouter 1 tr 44–47

As the first item of each task is given as an example, each task is effectively out of 5, giving a total of 20 marks for the listening test.

A Des affaires scolaires

Solution:
1 b, 2 f, 3 e, 4 d, 5 a, 6 c
(mark /5)

CD 1 Track 50

Des affaires scolaires

Voici des affaires scolaires:
1 Regarde la trousse, c'est ma trousse.
2 Et voici un cartable. C'est le cartable de Suzanne.
3 Et où sont les cahiers? Ah oui, voici les cahiers.
4 Voici une console. C'est ma console.
5 Et voilà mes crayons. Il y a douze crayons.
6 Et où est ma règle? Ah oui, voici ma règle!

B C'est moi!

Solution:
1 a, 2 a, 3 a, 4 a, 5 b, 6 a
(mark /5)

CD 1 Track 51

C'est moi!

1 Salut! Je m'appelle Sophie.
2 J'ai douze ans.
3 Je suis fille unique.
4 J'habite dans une maison.
5 Voici ma chambre et voici mon baladeur.
6 Et voici ma mère dans la salle à manger.

C C'est quelle phrase?

Solution:
1 a, 2 a, 3 b, 4 b, 5 b, 6 b
(mark /5)

CD 1 Track 52

C'est quelle phrase?

Exemple: 1a
1 a Voici Michel avec ses deux soeurs.
  b Voici Michel avec ses deux frères.
2 a Voici Marie avec son demi-frère.
  b Voici Marie avec sa demi-soeur.
3 a Il y a un cahier sur la table.
  b Il y a un cahier sous la table.
4 a Voici une photo de mes grands-parents avec ma soeur et moi.
  b Voici une photo de mon grand-père avec ma soeur et moi.
5 a Voici une ville. Elle est près de Paris.
  b Voici un village. Il est près de Calais.
6 a Dans la cuisine, il y a une table et trois chaises. Il y a aussi une radio.
  b Dans la cuisine, il y a une petite table et deux chaises. Il y a aussi un téléphone.

D Je pense à quelque chose

Solution:
1 b, 2 e, 3 a, 4 c, 5 f, 6 d
(mark /5)

CD 1 Track 53

Je pense à quelque chose

– Je pense à quelque chose. Qu'est-ce que c'est?
– C'est un crayon?
– Non, ce n'est pas ça.
– Ce sont des gommes?
– Non, non. Ce n'est pas ça.
– Je sais, je sais, c'est une calculatrice.
– Non, ce n'est pas une calculatrice.
– Ce sont des livres?
– Des livres? Non, ce n'est pas ça.
– Zut … qu'est-ce que c'est, alors? C'est une règle, c'est juste?
– Non, non. Ce n'est pas juste.
– Alors, c'est un baladeur?
– Oui, fantastique! C'est un baladeur.

3/7 Lire

There are three reading tests, effectively out of 6, 7 and 7, giving a total of 20 marks.

A Notre maison

Solution:
1 g, 2 e, 3 d, 4 f, 5 b, 6 a, 7 c
(mark /6)

B C'est quelle image?

Solution:
1 f, 2 d, 3 a, 4 g, 5 e, 6 c, 7 b, 8 h
(mark /7)

Tricolore 1 Teacher's Notes   41

Unité 3 Consolidation and assessment

C Le télé-quiz

Solution:
1 vrai, **2** vrai, **3** faux, **4** vrai, **5** faux, **6** vrai, **7** vrai, **8** vrai
(mark /7)

3/8 Écrire et grammaire

There are three writing and grammar tests, effectively out of 6, 6 and 8, giving a total of 20 marks.

A Les mots corrects

Solution:
1 une maison, **2** une ville, **3** un village, **4** la France, **5** une porte, **6** des cahiers, **7** des livres
(mark /6)

B Les images et les descriptions

Solution:
1e Voici une fille.
2b Voici un garçon.
3f Les crayons sont dans la trousse.
4g Le livre est sur la table.
5a Voici un ordinateur.
6c La famille Lebrun.
7d La calculatrice est sous la boîte.
(mark /6)

C Un e-mail de Martin

Solution:
1 suis, **2** j'ai, **3** J'ai, **4** Mon, **5**

Rappel 1

30–31

This section can be used at any point after *Unité* 3 for revision and consolidation. It provides reading and writing activities which are self-instructional and can be used by students working individually for homework or during cover lessons.

1 Les nombres

a

Solution:
1 vingt-huit, **2** soixante-deux, **3** quarante-quatre, **4** quatorze, **5** cinquante, **6** trente-cinq

b

Solution:
1 five (10, 17, 18, 19, 70), **2** six (1, 21, 31, 41, 51, 61), **3** five (21, 31, 41, 51, 61)

2 Masculin, féminin

Solution:

masculin		féminin	
frère	mon	elle	mère
garçon	père	fille	sœur
il	ton	la	ta
le	un	ma	une

3 Un multi-quiz

Solution:
En France: **1** c, **2** b, **3** a
Au collège: **4** a, **5** b, **6** c
En famille: **7** c, **8** c

4 Le jeu des images

Solution:
1 B, **2** A, **3** D, **4** I, **5** E, **6** C, **7** F, **8** G, **9** H, **10** J

5 Des descriptions

This task requires production of vocabulary involving some knowledge of gender and number.

Solution:
1 une table, une chaise et un livre
2 des maisons et un cinéma
3 famille, fille, garçons, parents. La, ans

6 Les petits mots

This task requires production of articles and possessive adjectives.

Solution:
a **1** une, **2** une, **3** ton, **4** ta, **5** le, **6** ton
b **7** ma, **8** mon, **9** ma, **10** mon, **11** le

7 Questions et réponses

This is a predominantly open-ended task testing key language from *Unités* 1–3.

Solution:
1–5 open-ended, **6** sur la table, **7** sous la table, **8** Il est sur le livre, **9** une maison, **10** Non, c'est le chat de Louise.

Copymasters

CM 3/1

La famille Techno

This is an information-gap activity, based on a family tree. Students work in pairs, asking questions in turn to complete the ages of the people on their allocated family tree.

Hot seat

For further speaking practice, use the subject of one's family as a 'Hot seat' topic – one student answers questions asked by various members of the class for about a minute, e.g. *Ton frère/Ta sœur,*

Unité 3 Consolidation and assessment

comment s'appelle-t-il/elle?/Quel âge a-t-il/elle? etc.

cm 3/2

Masculin, féminin

This gives practice of gender. There is a built-in incline of difficulty, so less able students may need help with tasks 3 and 4.

> **Solution:**
>
> **1** *Les mots féminins*
>
> The following should be underlined: *la famille, la maison, une demi-sœur, la trousse, la mère, la télé, une carte postale, la radio, une calculatrice, la grand-mère*
>
> **2** 5-4-3-2-1
>
> 5 *un frère, une demi-sœur, le père, la mère, la grand-mère*
>
> 4 (any 4) *la télé, un ordinateur, un lecteur MP3, la radio, une calculatrice*
>
> 3 *samedi, vendredi, dimanche*
>
> 2 *un stylo, un crayon*
>
> 1 (any one) *une maison, un cinéma*
>
> **3** *Fais deux listes*
>
> | | |
> |---|---|
> | l'animal | la ferme |
> | le lecteur MP3 | la maison |
> | le grand-père | la rue |
> | le jardin | la sœur |
> | l'ordinateur | |
> | le sac | |
>
> **4** *Les blancs*
>
> This is an open-ended task.

Au choix

144 Au choix

1 Combien?

This activity gives further practice of question and answer work about families and could be done orally in class or used as a written extension activity. This is suitable as a written homework activity.

Students could go on to design various different families for each other, using pencil and paper and stick men (or on the computer or whiteboard). They then change over, answering questions about each other's families.

> **Solution:**
>
> **1** *J'ai deux frères et une sœur.*
>
> **2** *J'ai une sœur.*
>
> **3** *Je suis enfant unique.*
>
> **4** *J'ai quatre frères.*
>
> **5** *J'ai un frère et une sœur.*
>
> **6** *J'ai trois sœurs.*

> **7** *J'ai un frère.*
>
> **8** *J'ai un frère et deux sœurs.*

144 Au choix

2 Des questions utiles

Students supply the correct adjective: *ton, ta* or *tes*. This could be an oral exercise or the answers could be written and checked orally.

> **Solution:**
>
> **1** *Ton,* **2** *Ta,* **3** *Tes,* **4** *Ton,* **5** *ton,* **6** *Ton,* **7** *ta,* **8** *tes*

144 Au choix

3 La maison de la famille Lambert

This task is suitable for most students. Students listen to the recording and complete the text. This could be done as an oral exercise with students requiring extra support.

> **Solution:**
>
> **1** *maison,* **2** *chaises,* **3** *table,* **4** *salle à manger,* **5** *salon,* **6** *la télé,* **7** *un,* **8** *affaires,* **9** *la,* **10** *de*

> **CD 1 Track 48**
>
> ### La maison de la famille Lambert
>
> Voici la maison et le jardin de la famille Lambert.
> Dans la cuisine, il y a trois chaises et une table.
> Mme Lambert est dans la salle à manger.
> Anne-Marie Lambert est dans le salon. Elle regarde la télé.
> Voici la chambre de Christophe Lambert. Dans sa chambre, il y a un lit et aussi ses affaires.
> Voici la salle de bains.

144 Au choix

4 Jeu de mémoire

This brings together work on the rooms of the house and also revises possession. Students study the pictures on SB pages 25–26 before trying to identify the objects, using the substitution table to help them. The task could be done in writing and checked orally.

> **Solution:**
>
> **1** *C'est la radio de la famille Laurent.*
>
> **2** *C'est le lit de Thomas.*
>
> **3** *C'est le stylo de Daniel.*
>
> **4** *C'est le lecteur MP3 de Thomas.*
>
> **5** *C'est la télé de la famille Laurent.*
>
> **6** *C'est le chat de Louise.*
>
> **7** *C'est le sac de Daniel.*
>
> **8** *C'est le portable de Louise.*

Tricolore 1 Teacher's Notes

Unité 3 Consolidation and assessment

Optionally, this task could be followed by more oral questions about the objects shown, practising *C'est le* (+ noun) *de* (+ name).

Some students may be able to cope with the alternative structure *C'est à qui? C'est à* (+ name) – see *Grammaire 4.3* (SB page 160). This could be done first with the teacher asking questions, then with some students making up similar questions about the objects shown or about things in the classroom, e.g.

– *Le lecteur MP3, c'est à Louise? – Non.*

– *C'est à qui? – C'est à Simon.*

– *Et ce cahier, c'est à James? – Oui.*

– *Ah oui, c'est le cahier de James*, etc.

144 Au choix

5 Samedi

This item practises the verb *être* and also includes some possessive adjectives and rooms of the house. Go through the text and pictures with the class, commenting on where everyone is and asking questions such as *Où est Louise? Ah, voilà, elle est dans sa chambre*, etc. Students could then do part **b** in which they complete the sentences. They should then listen to the recording and follow the text, checking their answers as they go.

Solution:
1 *est*, **2** *est*, **3** *es*, **4** *suis*, **5** *es*, **6** *suis*, **7** *est*, **8** *es*, **9** *suis*, **10** *est*

CD 1 Track 49

Samedi

– C'est samedi chez la famille Laurent. Où sont les enfants?
– Où est Louise? Je pense qu'elle est dans sa chambre … Louise, tu es dans ta chambre?
– Oui, Maman. Je suis ici. J'écoute de la musique.
– Et Thomas? Il est dans sa chambre aussi? Thomas, tu es dans ta chambre?
– Non, Maman. Je suis dans le salon. Je regarde la télé.
– Très bien. Mais où est Daniel? Daniel, tu es dans ta chambre?
– Oui, Maman, je suis dans ma chambre. Je range mes affaires.
– Tu ranges tes affaires?!
– Mais oui, Maman! Dimanche, c'est le concert rock en ville, non? Et moi, j'adore la musique!

145 Au choix AfL

6 Ma famille

This brief item can be exploited with varying degrees of support, depending on ability, as an AfL task. Use the spread objectives as a focus for discussion and remember that it is important to model how to do tasks of this kind.

At the simplest level, students could design a poster for classroom display, including sketches or photos with labels. However, some students will be able to write a fuller description of their family, and this can form part of their *Dossier personnel*. This text could then be used as a basis for pair work.

As a variation, students could swap over and pretend to be someone else answering questions for them. Discuss how students' work has met the assessment criteria, and provide encouragement for improving skills where necessary.

Some posters could be put up in the classroom and used later for oral practice of *son/sa/ses*, e.g. *Son frère, comment s'appelle-t-il? Quel âge a-t-il?* etc.

The posters are also good for a guessing game. Cover the name at the top of the poster and say, for example: *Son frère s'appelle Thomas, sa sœur a 6 ans. Qui est-ce?*

Unité 4

Tricolore 1 Unité 4 Les animaux Pages 32–43

4A Tu as un animal? pages 32–33		
• Talk about pets		
Grammaire	Stratégies	Phonétique
• Use adjectives to describe colour and size	• None	• The letters 'ou'
Resources		
Audio: 2b *Vote, vote, vote!*; 4a *Tu as un animal?*, or CD 2, tracks 2 and 3 **Copymasters:** 4/1 *Les animaux* **Flashcards:** 18–26 **Worksheets:** Starters and plenaries; *Une souris, un chat …* (V)		**Interactive activity:** *Sondage sur les animaux* (L); *Les couleurs* (V) **Ph** The letters 'ou', or CD 2, track 4 **PowerPoint:** *Les couleurs* (V); *Les animaux* (V) **Grammar in Action:** None

4B Les adjectifs pages 34–35		
• Use adjectives to describe things		
Grammaire	Stratégies	Phonétique
• Make verbs negative	• Adding interest to your writing (1)	• The letters 'oi'
Resources		
Audio: 3 *C'est quel mot?*; 4a-b *Des animaux*, or CD 2 tracks 6 and 7 **Copymasters:** 4/2 *Les animaux de mes amis* **Worksheets:** Starters and plenaries; *Les adjectifs d'Albert* (G)		**Interactive activity:** *Masculin ou féminin?* (G) **Ph** The letters 'oi', or CD 2, track 5 **PowerPoint:** 1 S *Les animaux* **Grammar in Action:** p8

4C Tu as des questions? pages 36–37		
• Ask questions	• Talk about your home	
Grammaire	Stratégies	Phonétique
• Practise the singular of the verb avoir (to have)	• None	• The letters 'qu'
Resources		
Audio: 1 *Deux interviews*, or CD 2, track 8 **Copymasters:** None **Worksheets:** Starters and plenaries; *Mon animal* (W); The present tense of *avoir* (G)		**Ph** The letters 'qu', or CD 2, track 9 **PowerPoint:** None **Grammar in Action:** pp10–11, 12

4D Tu aimes ça? Et vous aussi? pages 38–39		
• Express opinions		
Grammaire	Stratégies	Phonétique
• Use some plural nouns • Understand two ways of saying 'you'	• Adding interest to your writing (2)	• None
Resources		
Audio: 1 *Des animaux extraordinaires*; 2a *Tu aimes ça?*, or CD 2, tracks 10 and 11 **Copymasters:** 4/3 *C'est moi!*, 4/4 *Questions et réponses*, 4/5 *Des conversations au choix* **Worksheets:** Starters and plenaries		**Interactive activity:** *Extraordinaire!*; Adding interest to your writing (Strat) **Video:** *Rue Danton: Alpha adore le foot* **PowerPoint:** *Tu ou vous?* (G); Kim's game: *Les animaux* **Grammar in Action:** p9

4E Le zoo extraordinaire pages 40–41		
• Understand and practise descriptions • Use some everyday phrases		
Grammaire	Stratégies	Phonétique
• None	• Remembering vocabulary (2)	• None
Resources		
Audio: 1 *Le zoo extraordinaire*, or CD 2, track 12 **Copymasters:** 4/6 *Tu comprends?*, 4/7 *Sommaire* **Worksheets:** Starters and plenaries; Remembering vocabulary (Strat) **e-book:** *Le-sais tu? Les animaux*		**Interactive activity:** Classroom commands (V) **Grammar in Action:** None

4A Tu as un animal?

Key language

Animals and pets (4A)

Est-ce que tu as un animal à la maison?
Oui, j'ai …
un chat/chien
les animaux
un chat
une chatte
un cheval / des chevaux
un chien
un cochon d'Inde
un hamster
un lapin
un oiseau / des oiseaux
un perroquet
une perruche
un poisson (rouge)
une souris
une tarentule

Adjectives and descriptions (4B to 4E)

De quelle couleur est-il/elle?
Est-ce qu'il/elle est gros(se)?
Il/Elle est comment?
Il/Elle est (assez/très) …
blanc/blanche
bleu/bleue
brun/brune
gris/grise
jaune/jaune
marron
noir/noire
orange
rouge
vert/verte
grand/grande
petit/petite
gros/grosse
énorme
méchant/méchante
mignon/mignonne
aimable

Asking questions (4C)

Est-ce que …?
Comment …?
Où est …?
Quel jour/âge …?

Preferences (4D)

Est-ce que tu aimes …?
J'adore …
(Oui), j'aime (beaucoup) …
Je préfère …
(Non), je n'aime pas (beaucoup) …
Je déteste …

Connectives (4D)

et
mais
aussi
parce que/qu'

4A Tu as un animal? pages 32–33

- Talk about pets

Grammaire	Stratégies	Phonétique
• Use adjectives to describe colour and size	• None	• The letters 'ou'

Resources

Audio: 2b *Vote, vote, vote!*; 4a *Tu as un animal?*, or CD 2, tracks 2 and 3
Copymasters: 4/1 *Les animaux*
Flashcards: 18–26
Worksheets: Starters and plenaries; *Une souris, un chat …* (V)

Interactive activity: *Sondage sur les animaux* (L); *Les couleurs* (V)
Ph The letters 'ou', or CD 2, track 4
PowerPoint: *Les couleurs* (V); *Les animaux* (V)
Grammar in Action: None

4A Tu as un animal?

> Worksheet

Starters (pages 32–33)

1 *Chasse à l'intrus* Play an odd-one-out game, based on language encountered in *Unités* 1–3. Display sets of words, e.g.

   seize, trois, quinze, crayon, vingt

   chambre, télé, cuisine, toilettes, salon

   mère, cousine, frère, grand-mère, demi-sœur

   habite, ai, est, suis, sur

   une chaise, un cahier, un crayon, un ordinateur, un livre

   une ferme, un village, un appartement, une maison, une famille

   Students write down the odd one out. Collate answers as a whole-class activity with students giving a reason for their choice (some of the above groupings are deliberately ambiguous).

2 **5-4-3-2-1** Play in small groups or as a class. Display the words below (or others) in random order.

   Suggestion: 5 rooms, (*chambre, cuisine, salle à manger, salle de bains, salon*), 4 classroom objects (*cahier, gomme, stylo, règle*), 3 words for 'in' (*à, dans, en*), 2 names of animals (*chat, souris*), 1 verb (*habite*).

   To revise the alphabet as well, this could be played as a team game, one team giving the word, the other spelling it out correctly.

> Presentation

Les animaux

> Introduction FC 18–26

Est-ce que tu as un animal à la maison?

Using the PowerPoint presentation (above) or flashcards 18–26, teach the names of the pets. Introduce them a few at a time, use repetition and ask: *Qu'est-ce que c'est?*

Eventually write the words on the board for a game of *Effacez!* or *Je pense à un animal*.

Start some simple copy-writing with a game of *Loto!*, in which students write down the names of four animals and the teacher or another pupil acts as caller.

When introducing the animals, use the vocabulary reinforcement techniques (see TB page xviii).

> Interactive activity

Sondage

> 32

Les couleurs

Introduce the colours using the presentation and the online activity below. When introducing the colours, use the vocabulary reinforcement techniques (see TB page xviii).

Teach colours with known vocabulary, e.g. *Voilà un stylo: il est bleu*, and with the animal pictures, e.g. *Voilà un lapin: il est blanc et noir*. Introduce *De quelle couleur est-il/elle?* and appropriate answers. Gradually encourage students to ask each other about colours, masculine nouns only.

Point out the broad difference between the use of *brun* for hair and *marron* for eyes.

Note that the end of the presentation covers masculine and feminine endings and can be used once these have been taught (SB page 35).

> Presentation

> Interactive activity

Les couleurs

> 32

1 Grand Concours National

Ask students if they can guess the meaning of the words *concours national* and *finalistes*.

Talk about the animals in the photos: *La photo A, c'est quel animal? Le chien, c'est quelle photo?*

Introduce the words *grand/gros* and *petit* and refer to classroom objects, etc. to emphasise the meaning.

Refer to the note on SB page 33 (*Dossier-langue*) about the use of *grand* and *gros*.

The feminine version of *chat* has been introduced as this is commonly used when referring to pets. It avoids students making sentences like *J'ai un chat. Elle s'appelle Mimi*. If appropriate for your students, you could also teach *une chienne*. Tell the class to read through the eight descriptions of the animals and do the simple task, matching the descriptions with the photos.

> Solution:
> 1 C, 2 A, 3 E, 4 F, 5 B, 6 D, 7 H, 8 G

This could be checked orally, e.g. *Numéro 2, c'est Minnie. C'est quelle photo?*

Further oral work could be based on the photos and descriptions, e.g.

Est-ce que Minnie est blanche/grise/noire?

Le hamster, comment s'appelle-t-il?

Est-ce que Samba est gros ou petit?

Est-ce que le lapin s'appelle Minou?

Il est noir et blanc. C'est Samba?

> cm 4/1

Les animaux

> Worksheet

Trouve les animaux

Tricolore 1 Teacher's Notes 47

4A Tu as un animal?

🔊 32

2 Vote, vote, vote!

a Draw students' attention to the *Pour t'aider* box which suggests different ways of answering. Ask students, *Tu préfères quel animal?* After a few oral answers, ask everyone to write their vote on a slip of paper as indicated. Add up the votes to find the class results – extra number practice can be given by getting the class to count out each animal's score aloud. Sort the votes into separate piles for each animal and give out the piles to individual students.

Alors qui a les votes pour Minou? Ellie? Bon, comptez les votes avec Ellie! ... Très bien – sept votes pour Minou, etc.

b A recording of the results is provided. The class can listen to the first part of the recording (up to *Et finalement, voici les résultats.*) jotting down the correct letters or the names in the order in which the nine finalists are mentioned.

Then play the rest of the recording so that the class can compare their results with those of the national competition.

Solution:

Order mentioned: 1C *(Samba)*, 2A *(Minnie)*, 3D *(Tally et Lily)*, 4E *(Flic)*, 5F *(Carotte)*, 6B *(Dodu)*, 7G *(Tricolore)*, 8H *(Fifi)*

Result: 1 *Dodu, le cochon d'Inde,* **2** *Samba, le chien,* **3** *Flic, le petit hamster*

🔊 CD 2 Track 2

Vote, vote, vote!

Bonsoir, bonsoir! Voici des résultats importants, les résultats du Grand Concours National. Il y a huit finalistes: Samba, un gros chien adorable; Minnie, la petite souris blanche; les deux chats, Tally et Lily; puis un petit hamster qui s'appelle Flic; Carotte, un lapin noir et blanc; un cochon d'Inde qui s'appelle Dodu; Tricolore, le petit poisson; et Fifi, la petite perruche bleue, verte et jaune.
Et finalement, voici les résultats.
En troisième place – le numéro trois ... c'est Flic.
Oui, Flic, le petit hamster, a gagné le troisième prix.
Le deuxième prix ... c'est pour Samba, le chien.
Alors, Samba est numéro deux.
Et finalement, le premier prix, le numéro un ... c'est pour Dodu, le cochon d'Inde. Alors, Dodu a gagné le concours, le grand concours national!
Félicitations à tous les animaux et bonsoir!

🔊 32

3 Mes préférences

a In pairs, students discuss which animals they like or do not like.

b As extension, students talk about other preferences using the same structures but including previous knowledge. Students could be referred back to 3B *Mon numéro un ...* (SB page 22) to revise other ways of expressing preferences.

As an alternative extension activity, students could write about their favourite animal, e.g.

Mon animal préféré est ... C'est un(e) ...
Il/Elle est ... (adjective).

🔊 33   AfL

4 Tu as un animal?

Students should first listen and follow the conversation, then listen again without looking at the text. Play the recording again, but pause at key places, asking students to supply the next word from memory, e.g.

C'est une ... Elle s'appelle ...
Oui, j'ai un ... Il s'appelle ...
C'est un ...

a Students write out the gapped text as completed sentences.

b They then make up three similar sentences about Noah and his pet.

c Students make up conversations in pairs, using the dialogue as a model. Suggest that if they do not have their own pet they can talk about a pet belonging to a friend or relation. Check that they understand the phrase *je n'ai pas d'animal*.

This conversation is for basic pair practice at this stage but will be expanded as the unit progresses, since agreement and position of adjectives are taught on the next spread. Teachers who wish to explain this straight away, can refer to task 5 and get pupils to deduce rules from this.

Some of the dialogues could be recorded or presented to the class.

Note: if students want to use the plural of *animal*, *cheval* or *oiseau*, direct them to the note on SB page 38 (*Dossier-langue*).

This activity offers an excellent opportunity for AfL. Agree the criteria for success with students. They prepare their work, check it against the agreed criteria, check with a partner, and then they could even record their dialogue. It can be a classic WALT and WILF exercise: We Are Learning Today ... and What I'm Looking For ...

As extension to part **c**, students could mention the size of their pet, or say that they have two pets. They can also put the conversation into the third person and talk about their partner's pet using *le/la ... de X* (as they have not yet learnt *son/sa/ses*).

Tricolore 1 Teacher's Notes

4A Tu as un animal?

Solution:

a **1** *une perruche,* **2** *Coco,* **3** *jaune*

b *Noah a un rat. Le rat s'appelle Roland. Roland est (gros et) noir.*

CD 2 Track 3
Tu as un animal?

J'ai un oiseau. C'est une perruche jaune. Elle s'appelle Coco. Et toi, Noah? As-tu un animal?
Oui, Sophie, j'ai un animal. Il s'appelle Roland.
Qu'est-ce que c'est?
C'est un rat, un gros rat noir!
Aïe!

33

5 C'est à qui?

This task practises recognition of colours. The maze puzzle is not quite as straightforward as might at first appear. Although students should have no trouble in tracing the owners of each animal by using the lines, they will have to look carefully to distinguish between the actual pets, since the puzzle includes three birds, two fish and two horses, all of different colours.

Note that both *brun* and *marron* are used in the colours as they are both in common usage for describing animals. Point out, when appropriate, that *marron* is invariable (see *Dossier-langue* SB page 35). Make sure everyone is clear what has to be done, e.g.

Regardez l'oiseau bleu et vert – il est mignon, non? Mais il est à qui? Suivez la ligne ... voilà – il est à Hugo.

Maintenant, regardez les descriptions des animaux ... Numéro 1, l'oiseau bleu et vert ... c'est ça.

Students can just write the number and the name (or initial) of the owner or they can write out the whole sentence for practice. When checking answers, ask for the full sentence. See TB page 64 for explaining the construction *c'est à* (+ name) if this has not already been done. Adjectival agreement is covered in the next spread, but can be briefly explained if students enquire about it.

Solution:

1 *Thomas,* **2** *Magali,* **3** *Coraline,* **4** *Eléna,*
5 *M. Lebrun,* **6** *Coraline,* **7** *Thomas,* **8** *Hugo*

For further practice, make up some true or false statements or questions, *Est-ce que M. Lebrun a un poisson? Thomas a un poisson rouge, orange et vert. C'est vrai?*

33 Dossier-langue

Adjectives (1)

Make sure students understand the difference between *gros, grand* and *petit*. Students could find examples of *gros* on these pages (e.g. *Le gros chien s'appelle Samba./C'est un rat, un gros rat noir.*)

Interactive activity
The letters 'ou'

33 Phonétique
The letters 'ou'

A full explanation of the *'ou'* sound is given on *kerboodle!*, together with interactive practice which includes differentiating between *'u'* and *'ou'*.

a Say the word *souris* with the appropriate gesture (hands below chin, twitching). Students repeat the word with the same gesture. Then read out the other words with students repeating each one. The words are also included on the recording for optional use (part **a**).

Parts **b** and **c** can be used for further practice.

b Say and display the words: **a** *trousse,* **b** *bonjour,* **c** *vous,* **d** *trouve,* **e** *douze,* **f** *Strasbourg.* Students listen to the recording, repeat the words and note down the corresponding letter (**c, e, a, f, d, b**).

c Students listen to the silly sentence and note down how many times they hear the sound (5). They can then repeat the sentence to help them remember this sound.

For further practice, write some additional words on the board to check that students recognise the link between spelling and pronunciation, e.g *où, Louis, cousine, tour.*

CD 2 Track 4
The letters 'ou'

Écoutez et répétez:
a souris, rouge, sous, écoute
b vous, douze, trousse, Strasbourg, trouve, bonjour
c Ils trouvent une souris sous le coussin rouge.

146 Au choix

1 Combien d'animaux?

Worksheet

Plenaries (pages 32–33)

1 Ask how many students can name at least one animal in French. All hands should go up. Two? Three? Keep going until only a few hands are left up, then challenge these students to name them. Follow this with a discussion on which animals students are most likely to remember. Why? Which memorisation techniques did they use?

2 Students find something in the classroom for each colour they have learnt. They touch it and say *C'est jaune,* etc. They then discuss different techniques they can use to help remember the colours and how to spell them, e.g. visualising the words spelt out in coloured letters, identifying a colour with a particular coloured item, etc.

Tricolore 1 Teacher's Notes   49

4B Les adjectifs

4B Les adjectifs pages 34–35

- Use adjectives to describe things

Grammaire	Stratégies	Phonétique
• Make verbs negative	• Adding interest to your writing (1)	• The letters 'oi'

Resources

Audio: 3 *C'est quel mot?*; **4a-b** *Des animaux*, or CD 2 tracks 6 and 7
Copymasters: 4/2 *Les animaux de mes amis*
Worksheets: Starters and plenaries; *Les adjectifs d'Albert* (G)

Interactive activity: *Masculin ou féminin?* (G)
Ph The letters 'oi', or CD 2, track 5
PowerPoint: 1 S *Les animaux*
Grammar in Action: p8

Worksheet

Starters (pages 34–35)

1 Display the first part of the transcript of *Vote, vote, vote!* with key words blanked out. Display the missing words in a random list (see online worksheet). Students work in pairs to decide which words go where. Finally, students try to read the gapped text, supplying the missing words from memory, but prompted by the list.

Solution:

(inserted words underlined)

Bonsoir, bonsoir! Voici des résultats importants – les résultats du Grand Concours National. Il y a huit finalistes: Samba, un gros chien adorable; Minnie, la petite souris blanche; les deux chats, Tally et Lily; puis un petit hamster qui s'appelle Flic; Carotte, un lapin noir et blanc; un cochon d'Inde qui s'appelle Dodu; Tricolore, le petit poisson; et Fifi, la petite perruche bleue, verte et jaune.

2 *En groupes* (use at some point after task 2)

Display a mixture of masculine and feminine adjectives in random order (see online worksheet and Solution below). Display a 3-column grid with the first word in each column already filled in. Students have to place the words in the correct box. As an extension they could give an example (*blanc – masculin – mon chat est blanc*).

Solution:

masc	fém	masc et fém
blanc	bleue	moderne
gros	brune	rouge
méchant	grise	énorme
noir	petite	jaune
petit	blanche	orange
vert	mignonne	fantastique

Alternatively, students could hold up cards for *masculin*, *féminin* or *masculin et féminin*.

Presentation

Les animaux

34

1 Une histoire de chats

This task gives practice with adjectives and feminine agreements. First introduce the words *mignon/mignonne* and *méchant/méchante*, e.g. using some of the animals from page 32 or using the PowerPoint images above: *Regardez Minnie/la souris. Elle est mignonne, non? Et voilà Lily/une chatte. Elle est mignonne aussi, elle n'est pas méchante.*

Write the words on the board. Refer to the *Dossier-langue* section (below) which gives a brief introduction to the negative. The class then reads through the story, first silently, then aloud. Ask them some questions, e.g.

Est-ce que César est jaune?

Est-ce que Mimi est grosse?

Est-ce que Minette est mignonne?

Est-ce que César est le chat de Monsieur Lenoir?

Est-ce que tu préfères Mimi ou César?

Eventually students can complete the sentences. More able students could act the story or make up a similar sketch.

Solution:

1 César, **2** Mimi, **3** Géant, **4** Minette, **5** César/Géant, **6** Mimi

34 Dossier-langue

The negative

A brief introduction to the negative.

Interactive activity

The letters 'oi'

Tricolore 1 Teacher's Notes

4B Les adjectifs

34 Phonétique

The letters 'oi'

A full explanation of the *'oi'* sound is given on *kerboodle!*, together with interactive practice which includes recognition of words which contain the sound.

a Say the word *oiseau* with the appropriate gesture (hand tweeting like a bird's beak). Students repeat the word with the same gesture. Then read out the other words with students repeating each one. The words are also included on the recording for optional use (part **a**).

Parts **b** and **c** can be used for further practice.

b Ask students to listen and repeat the words they hear. Then display the words **a** *moi*, **b** *toi*, **c** *soixante*, **d** *au revoir*, **e** *Poitiers*, **f** *boîte*. Students listen again and note the corresponding letter (**d**, **f**, **a**, **e**, **c**, **b**). Point out that the circumflex accent on *boîte* makes no difference to the sound.

c Students listen to the silly sentence and note down how many times they hear the sound (6). They can then repeat the sentence to help them remember this sound.

For further practice, write some additional words on the board to check that students recognise the link between spelling and pronunciation e.g. *trois*, *fois*, *bois*, *Blois*.

With some groups, the following rhyme could be used at this point (similar to 'one potato, two potato, …' for choosing turns): *Dans la cour de chez Dubois, il y a sept oies: une oie, deux oies, trois oies, quatre oies, cinq oies, six oies, c'est toi!*

Students would need the pun explaining as they haven't met *c'est toi / c'est à toi* etc.

CD 2 Track 5

The letters 'oi'

Écoutez et répétez:
a oiseau, poisson
b au revoir, boîte, moi, Poitiers, soixante, toi
c Moi, je vois un poisson noir dans une boîte de petits pois.

35 Dossier-langue   AfL

Adjectives (2)

This covers adjectival agreement (singular only) and the difference in position of some adjectives. Plurals are introduced receptively in *Unités* 1–5, but not fully explained until *Unité* 5.

Tell the class to spot the differences in the spelling of *blanc*, *petit* and *mignon* (in the description of the dog and the mouse) and work out and explain the reason for these.

Students could read aloud the masculine and feminine forms of the adjectives, perhaps with half the class saying the feminine form and the other the masculine, changing over from time to time.

Explain the two words for 'brown': *marron* is invariable, i.e. does not change for feminine or plural; *brun* is a regular adjective. The two words are largely interchangeable, but *brun* is normally used for hair and *marron* for eyes.

Working in pairs or groups, students spot as many adjectives as they can. Students read their list aloud in turns. Everyone with the same adjective gains 1 point. Any that no-one else has is worth 5 points. This activity is suitable for peer assessment, after reminding students of the spread objectives and agreeing the criteria for success.

35

2 Des adjectifs

This task gives routine practice of masculine and feminine forms of common adjectives and produces a useful reference table.

Solution:

masculin	féminin	anglais
brun	1 brune	brown
noir	2 noire	6 black
gris	3 grise	grey
blanc	4 blanche	7 white
jaune	jaune	8 yellow
rouge	5 rouge	9 red
gros	10 grosse	big/fat
grand	grande	15 large
petit	11 petite	16 small
énorme	12 énorme	17 enormous
méchant	13 méchante	nasty
mignon	14 mignonne	cute

Interactive activity

Masculin ou féminin?

Worksheet

Albert

35

3 C'est quel mot?

In this listening discrimination task, students have to choose the correct form of the adjective they hear repeated.

Solution:
1 *a*, 2 *b*, 3 *b*, 4 *a*, 5 *a*, 6 *b*

CD 2 Track 6

C'est quel mot?

1 blancs, blanches – blancs
2 vert, verte – verte
3 petit, petite – petite
4 grands, grandes – grands
5 gris, grise – gris
6 gros, grosse – grosse

Tricolore 1 Teacher's Notes   51

4B Les adjectifs

🔊 35

4 Des animaux

a Before listening to the recording, students could try to predict what is going to be said from looking at the pictures. They then listen and note which animal is mentioned.

b They listen again and focus on the adjectives in this true/false activity.

c As extension, students write their own description of two of the animals, then they draw another animal of their choosing and describe it. This could be their own pet, an animal belonging to a friend or an imaginary pet. Encourage students to use as much language as they can from previous language-learning experience. They should be encouraged to use qualifiers in their descriptions (see *Stratégies* below). Students could work in pairs, each checking the other's descriptions to see if adjectives agree and seeing how many qualifiers and different adjectives are used.

Solution:
a **1** C, **2** E, **3** A, **4** F, **5** D, **6** B
b **1** faux, **2** vrai, **3** faux, **4** vrai, **5** vrai, **6** faux

🔊 CD 2 Track 7

Des animaux

1 Voici mon chat. Il s'appelle Frodo et il est super mignon. Il est assez petit et il est gris.
2 C'est mon chien, Noiraud. Il est noir et très aimable.
3 Voici ma souris blanche. Elle s'appelle Chine, elle n'est pas très grosse, mais elle est assez méchante.
4 Tu n'aimes pas les tarentules? Moi, j'adore Arabelle, ma tarentule noire. Elle est énorme et elle est super mignonne!
5 Voici mon chien. Il est gros, il est noir et brun. Il est assez méchant, mais j'aime beaucoup Roger.
6 J'adore les poissons. Voici Georges – il est mignon, n'est-ce pas? Il est orange, blanc et noir.

35 Stratégies

Adding interest to your writing (1)

This grammar strategy covers qualifiers and their use in improving descriptions.

As follow-up, play a growing-sentences chain game. Remind students to use *et* and *mais* to lengthen sentences. Start them off with a sentence such as *J'ai un chat*. This could eventually grow into something like *J'ai un très petit chat noir et blanc et assez mignon mais pas très méchant et il s'appelle Frodo, mais ...* This could be played as a team game to see which team can build the longest sentence.

Jeu

Le message secret

This is an optional follow-up activity on adjectives and animals. Each student writes a 'secret message' on a piece of paper and signs it. The message is an instruction to draw and colour an animal (the message can be sensible or 'silly'), e.g. *Dessine un gros chien blanc et noir./ Dessine trois chats, un bleu, un vert et un orange.*

Some messages might contain more detail, e.g.

Dessine Georges. C'est un cochon d'Inde. Il est noir.
Dessine Lulu. C'est une souris. Elle est blanche et très mignonne.
Dessine Noiraud. C'est un chien. Il est gros – et il est très méchant.

The messages are folded, pooled and given out at random.

The person receiving each message must carry out the instruction correctly and show it to the teacher (or group leader) to prove that it has been understood.

To make further use of these drawings and descriptions, after students have written their names on the back, the papers could be pinned up or laid on tables around and numbered. They could then be used as a matching game in which students have to match up the descriptions with the resulting picture.

cm 4/2

Les animaux de mes amis

146 Au choix

2 Chat perdu

146 Au choix   AfL

3 Des animaux

gia 1 p8

Using adjectives – singular

These self-explanatory tasks give further practice in describing animals, etc. and would be useful for homework, or later for consolidation.

Worksheet

Plenaries (pages 34–35)

1 Students summarise in pairs the rules for making adjectives agree. They then make up an exercise to test other students' understanding of the rules. Discuss what sort of exercise they might make up, e.g. match question and answer, gap-fill (with missing words in a box), translation.

2 Ask students to look at the objectives for SB pages 34–35: How well do they think they have done? Can they explain the main points to a partner? What did they find easy or difficult?

4C Tu as des questions? pages 36–37

- Ask questions

Grammaire	Stratégies	Phonétique
• Practise the singular of the verb *avoir* (to have)	• None	• The letters 'qu'

Resources

Audio: 1 *Deux interviews*, or CD 2, track 8
Copymasters: None
Worksheets: Starters and plenaries; *Mon animal* (W); The present tense of *avoir* (G)

Ph The letters 'qu', or CD 2, track 9
PowerPoint: None
Grammar in Action: pp10–11, 12

Worksheet

Starters (pages 36–37)

1 *Loto!* Have cards with names of animals ready to hand out to students as they come into the classroom (see online worksheet). Vocabulary used: *un animal, un chat, une chatte, un cheval, un chien, un cochon d'Inde, un hamster, un lapin, un oiseau, un perroquet, une perruche, un poisson, un rat, une souris, une tarentule.* Hold up flashcards, saying the word for what is portrayed on each. When checking back, students must say the words correctly. Students need to listen carefully because you can say *un animal, un oiseau,* and *une chatte.*

2 *Chaque mot à sa place* Display the grid and the words below at random (see online worksheet). Give students a few minutes to read and work out the answers, then ask *Quelle est la bonne case pour chaque mot?* Students should give the number of the box before confirming the correct answer. The first row is done as an example. Some students might be able to explain what each category is.

words: *petite, une sœur, jaune, un livre, un chat, un cahier, un cheval, un chien, une cousine, un dictionnaire, grosse, marron, une mère, mignonne, rouge*

Solution:

1	2	3	4	5
un chat	jaune	petite	un livre	une sœur
un chien	rouge	grosse	un cahier	une mère
un cheval	marron	mignonne	un dictionnaire	une cousine

36

1 Deux interviews

Students look at the questions about the two interviews and listen to the recording. Pause the recording so that students can write *Oui* or *Non* after each question.

Solution:
1 Jean-Paul a *Oui* b *Oui* c *Non*
2 Charlotte a *Non* b *Oui* c *Non*

CD 2 Track 8

Deux interviews

Conversation 1
– Salut, Jean-Paul! Est-ce que tu as un animal à la maison?
– Oui, j'ai un chien. Il s'appelle Pirate.
– Est-ce qu'il est gros ou petit?
– Il est très gros et tout noir – très, très noir.

Conversation 2
– Bonjour, Charlotte.
– Bonjour.
– Est-ce que tu as un animal à la maison, Charlotte?
– Non, monsieur, mais mon frère a un animal. C'est un hamster.
– Tu n'aimes pas les animaux, toi?
– Ce n'est pas ça, monsieur. J'aime les animaux, mais notre famille habite dans un appartement à Paris.
– Ah bon, je comprends.

As a follow-up to these interviews, students could be asked to make up two more similar questions, using *Est-ce que …*, and put them to other students.

e.g. **1** *Est-ce que tu as un animal …?*
2 *Est-ce qu'il (elle) est …?*

36 Dossier-langue

Asking questions

Ask students to look at all the questions in *Deux interviews* (above) to see how they all begin with *Est-ce que …* Make sure that they fully understand that a sentence can be turned into a question just by putting *Est-ce que …* at the beginning. They could then practise turning more sentences into questions, e.g.

Charlotte habite en France.

Maman est dans la maison.

La radio est dans la cuisine.

Martin/Sandra est le frère/la sœur de Nicole.

This can be developed into a pair or team activity with one person making a statement and another turning it into a question. Students should be told to confine their statements to information about other people and things so they avoid such nonsensical questions as *Est-ce que je suis un garçon?* etc.

4C Tu as des questions?

Some of the questions could be written down on slips of paper and then re-used, one student picking out a question at random and another answering it.

Asking questions

First, revise the questions already learnt by playing a chain question game. One student asks someone a question and if it is answered correctly, the second student asks a question of a third person, etc. Students could refer back to *Unité* 3 for ideas.

📖 36

2 Des interviews

This brings together the work on questions and answers about animals and should be practised orally in pairs. The *Dossier-langue* reminds students of other question forms and question words that have been covered.

The feminine versions of cat and dog have been included as students often want to refer to their pet by its correct gender. If necessary, provide other feminine forms such as *une jument* (mare).

In part **c**, students with prior learning should be encouraged to record substantial interviews for an imaginary radio station, *Radio Tricolore*. They should include as much information as possible and use adjectives, qualifiers and negatives where possible.

Interactive activity

Interview

146 Au choix

4 Des questions

gia 1 pp10–11

Asking questions (1) and (2)

This full-page practice on the use of *Est-ce que …* (p10) and on asking questions with question words (p11) would be useful here for homework or for revision.

📖 37

3 Une description

Students should now be able to write (and perhaps record) a short description of one of their own or a friend's pets, using the models supplied here or the writing frame.

Worksheet

Tu as un animal?

📖 37 Dossier-langue

The verb *avoir* (to have)

Students find the parts of the singular paradigm of *avoir* in the conversations in *Des interviews* (above). They can also discuss the points made about shortening *je*. Ask students if they can think of any other examples of this. If you wish, tell them this is called elision.

Worksheet

Avoir

Interactive activity

The letters 'qu'

📖 37 Phonétique

The letters 'qu'

A full explanation of the 'qu' sound is given on *kerboodle!*, together with interactive practice which includes recognising the sound in context.

a Say the word *question* with the appropriate gesture (drawing a question mark in the air). Students repeat the word with the same gesture. Then read out the other words with students repeating each one. The words are also included on the recording for optional use (part **a**). Point out that 'qu', 'k' (not very common) and hard 'c' ('ca', 'co', 'cu') all produce the same sound.

Parts **b** and **c** can be used for further practice.

b Ask students to listen and repeat the words they hear. Then display the words **a** *curieux*, **b** *quel*, **c** *kilo*, **d** *quatre*, **e** *cartable*, **f** *copine* for students to match (**b**, **d**, **f**, **e**, **a**, **c**).

c Students listen to the silly sentence and note down how many times they hear the sound (5). They can then repeat the sentence to help them remember this sound.

For further practice, write some additional words on the board to check that students recognise the link between spelling and pronunciation e.g. *quarante*, *quatorze*, *quinze*, *quartier*, *quoi*.

CD 2 Track 9

The letters 'qu'

Écoutez et répétez:
a question, quel, qui, est-ce que
b quel, quatre, copine, cartable, curieux, kilo
c Est-ce que mon copain Kevin a quinze cochons d'Inde?

4 Questions et réponses

📖 37

In this three-part activity, students first complete the questions with a part of *avoir*, then complete the answers and finally match up the correct question and answer.

Solution:

a 1 *as*, 2 *as*, 3 *as*, 4 *a*, 5 *as*, 6 *ai*
b a *a*, b *ai*, c *a*, d *ai*, *a*, e *ai*, f *a*
c 1 *f*, 2 *e*, 3 *d*, 4 *a*, 5 *b*, 6 *c*

📖 146 Au choix

5 Chasse à l'intrus

gia 1 p12

Asking questions (3) – using question words

These self-explanatory tasks give further practice in asking questions and would be useful for homework, or could be used later for consolidation.

Worksheet — AfL

Plenaries (pages 36–37)

1 Students work in pairs and explain the ways they know of making a question. This should include adding *Est-ce que …* , and using intonation, but they may be able to talk about inversion and using some question words from *Unités* 1–4. They report back and share any tips on asking questions. This activity is suitable for AfL. Remind students of the spread objectives and agree the criteria for success (perhaps related to how useful the tips are).

2 Students make up a wordsearch (using the 10 x 10 square grid provided on the online worksheet) to include approximately 12 items of vocabulary from the unit so far. They then exchange these and find the words and write them down with their English meaning.

Follow this with reflection and discussion, e.g. did students all choose similar words and if so, why? Which sort of words were chosen (adjectives, nouns) and is this because they are easier to learn? Did certain groups of letters 'pop out' at them from the wordsearch?

4D Tu aimes ça? Et vous aussi?   pages 38–39

- Express opinions

Grammaire	Stratégies	Phonétique
• Use some plural nouns • Understand two ways of saying 'you'	• Adding interest to your writing (2)	• None

Resources

Audio: 1 *Des animaux extraordinaires*; 2a *Tu aimes ça?*, or CD 2, tracks 10 and 11
Copymasters: 4/3 *C'est moi!*, 4/4 *Questions et réponses*, 4/5 *Des conversations au choix*
Worksheets: Starters and plenaries

Interactive activity: *Extraordinaire!*®; Adding interest to your writing (Strat)
Video: *Rue Danton: Alpha adore le foot*
PowerPoint: *Tu ou vous?* (G); Kim's game: *Les animaux*
Grammar in Action: p9

Worksheet

Starters (pages 38–39)

1 *Chasse à l'intrus* (see online worksheet) Display or print out five sets of words from the unit, e.g.

1	2	3	4	5
un cheval	rouge	mignon	aime	as
un oiseau	jaune	petit	déteste	aimes
une souris	orange	gros	beaucoup	es
un jeu	bleu	grande	adore	préfère

Students work in pairs to say which is the odd one out in each set, and why. There could be several reasons for being the odd one out (e.g. 1 – *jeu* is not an animal; *souris* is feminine; *souris* doesn't change for the plural/doesn't have a plural in -*x*). They then try to add one more word to each set which will not alter the odd one out.

2 *Quelle est la question?* On the board, display a number of answers to questions (see online worksheet) – students have to say what the question could be. There will be several possibilities for some of them. Some question beginnings are provided as a stimulus. e.g.

J'habite dans un appartement.
Oui, il s'appelle Ben.
Non, il est bleu.
Elle est noire.
Non, je déteste les chats.
J'ai douze ans.
Je préfère les jeux vidéo.
(list of question beginnings)
Comment …? Qu'est-ce que …?
De quelle couleur …? Quel …?
Est-ce que …? Tu aimes …?
Où …? Tu préfères …?

Tricolore 1 Teacher's Notes

4D Tu aimes ça? Et vous aussi?

The online worksheets can be displayed on the whiteboard or printed out later and set as homework.

🔊 38

1 Des animaux extraordinaires

This recorded passage contains a few new words, of which the most important is *parce que*. Others, probably guessable, are *extraordinaires*, *par exemple* and *naturellement*.

Introducing language which is unfamiliar or more challenging can help students in a number of ways. It is useful for them to understand the gist of a written or spoken sentence without necessarily knowing every word. They should also learn to understand compound sentences, using whatever cues and details are available.

Draw attention to the *Stratégies* on opinions (see below) either before part **a** of the item or before doing part **b**.

Adopt some of the suggested strategies for using recorded text to teach reading. The text is also provided as an online activity (see *kerboodle!* activity (int_04D.1) below), which allows it to be presented in smaller chunks and used for different skills.

Once students are familiar with the text, they can do the *vrai/faux* task in **b**, which focuses on likes and dislikes.

> **Solution:**
> **1** *vrai*, **2** *vrai*, **3** *faux*, **4** *faux*, **5** *vrai*, **6** *faux*, **7** *vrai*, **8** *faux*, **9** *faux*, **10** *faux*

Further questions could also be asked on this passage, e.g.
Est-ce qu'Éric habite dans un appartement?
Est-ce qu'il aime les chiens et les chats?
Comment s'appelle le chien de Marc?
Qu'est-ce qu'il aime? etc.

🔊 CD 2 Track 10

Des animaux extraordinaires

Je m'appelle Éric Garnier. J'habite dans une ferme, près de Toulouse. J'aime beaucoup les animaux, mais à la maison, il y a des animaux extraordinaires … Par exemple, il y a Télé. C'est le petit chien noir de mon frère, Marc. Il s'appelle Télé parce qu'il adore la télévision.
Et il y a aussi Blanco, le petit chat de Maman. Naturellement, il s'appelle Blanco parce qu'il est blanc. Il déteste la télévision, mais il aime beaucoup la radio et il adore la musique.
Eh bien, Télé aime la télévision, mais Blanco préfère la radio … voilà, c'est très bien … mais non! Ce n'est pas très bien parce qu'il y a aussi Jules et quelquefois, il y a Néron. Jules est le perroquet de ma sœur, Claire. Il est petit et très mignon, mais il n'aime pas la télévision, il n'aime pas la radio et il déteste la musique.
Et Néron, qui est-il? Eh bien … Néron est un gros chien noir et blanc. C'est le chien de mon grand-père et il est très méchant. Il déteste les chats, il déteste les perroquets, il déteste la radio, il déteste la musique et il n'aime pas beaucoup le chien de Marc. Alors, qu'est-ce qu'il aime, Néron? Il aime deux choses: mon grand-père et le football … à la télévision, naturellement! Il adore ça!

Interactive activity

Extraordinaire!

38 Dossier-langue

Plural nouns – the x factor!

This covers nouns forming their plural with -x. By this stage, students may want to say they have more than one particular animal or possession. For most nouns this is not a problem, but the few that form their plural with -x are presented here.

Presentation

Jeu de mémoire: Les animaux

38 Stratégies

Adding interest to your writing (2)

This grammar strategy focuses on using connectives to improve fluency when giving opinions and reasons.

🔊 39

2 Tu aimes ça?

a Students listen to the conversations and fill in a grid. They can write the letter or the whole phrase, as appropriate.

b As extension, students create a short illustrated PowerPoint presentation about their real or imaginary likes and dislikes. Encourage them to use previous knowledge and make their presentation fun.

> **Solution:**

	1 Thomas (Exemple:)	2 Camille	3 Maxime	4 Laura
J'adore …		j *la musique classique*		c *le sport*
Je déteste …			g *les ordinateurs*	
J'aime (beaucoup) …	a *la télé*		d *mon lecteur MP3*	i *les animaux*
Je n'aime pas (beaucoup) …		b *le football*		e *la musique pop*
Je préfère …	f *les jeux vidéo*		h *les livres*	

56 Tricolore 1 Teacher's Notes

4D Tu aimes ça? Et vous aussi?

CD 2 Track 11

Tu aimes ça?

1. – Thomas, tu aimes la télé?
   – La télé? Ah oui, j'aime beaucoup la télé, mais je préfère les jeux vidéo.
   – Tu préfères les jeux vidéo, c'est bien, ça.
2. – Et toi, Camille, qu'est-ce que tu aimes?
   – Moi, j'adore la musique classique, surtout Beethoven et Mozart. C'est super!
   – Très bien. Et qu'est-ce que tu n'aimes pas?
   – Alors, le football, je n'aime pas beaucoup le football. C'est nul.
3. – Maxime, tu aimes les ordinateurs?
   – Mais non! Je déteste les ordinateurs. Moi, je préfère les livres.
   – Ah bon, les livres.
   – Oui, et j'aime beaucoup mon lecteur MP3. Quand je lis, j'écoute de la musique.
4. – Alors, Laura, tu aimes la musique pop?
   – Non, pas beaucoup. Je n'aime pas beaucoup la musique pop.
   – Qu'est-ce que tu aimes?
   – Les animaux. J'aime les animaux … et j'adore le sport, c'est cool.

cm 4/3

C'est moi!

147 Au choix

6 Un échange

39

3 Qui dit ça?

Students match the correct captions to the cartoons, choosing mainly on the basis of whether *tu* or *vous* is used. To check answers, ask students to read out the complete captions. Discuss why *tu* or *vous* has been used in each case and refer to the *Dossier-langue* which follows.

Solution:
1 D, 2 G, 3 B, 4 C, 5 E, 6 H, 7 A, 8 F

39   **AfL**

4 Invente des questions

This activity should be used with the *Dossier-langue* to practise the use of *tu* and *vous*. Make sure students understand the rule and work through a few examples as a whole-class activity before students make up questions in pairs. This is an opportunity for AfL. Agree the criteria for success, reminding students of the spread objectives. Finally, collate answers as a class.

39 Dossier-langue

Two ways of saying 'you'

Go through the brief explanation with the students and, to check if they have understood it, ask them to explain the rule to each other in English. The PowerPoint presentation (below) can also be used.

Presentation

Tu ou vous?

Worksheet

S'il vous plaît …?

cm 4/4

Questions et réponses

cm 4/5

Des conversations au choix

gia p9

Using *tu* or *vous*

This page of the Grammar in Action book provides further practice and could be used for homework or later for revision.

Interactive activity

Rue Danton: Alpha adore le foot

Worksheet

Plenaries (pages 38–39)

1. In pairs, students discuss the *tu/vous* rule. What do they think of the rule? Is it better in English, where there's just one word for you? They could then go on to make a list of five people/groups of people/pets, etc. that would be addressed as *tu* or *vous*, writing the appropriate word next to each. They could then change pairs and see whether they agree with each other's answers.
2. In pairs, students tell each other the two most useful, interesting or strange things they have learnt in this unit so far. They then compare with other pairs. This could lead to whole-class comparison/ranking of aspects of the unit so far.

Tricolore 1 Teacher's Notes   **57**

4E Le zoo extraordinaire pages 40–41

- Understand and practise descriptions
- Use some everyday phrases

Grammaire	Stratégies	Phonétique
• None	• Remembering vocabulary (2)	• None

Resources

Audio: 1 *Le zoo extraordinaire*, or CD 2, track 12
Copymasters: 4/6 *Tu comprends?*, 4/7 *Sommaire*
Worksheets: Starters and plenaries; Remembering vocabulary (Strat)
e-book: *Le-sais tu? Les animaux*

Interactive activity: Classroom commands (V)
Grammar in Action: None

Worksheet

Starters (pages 40–41)

1 Reinforce the focus on masculine and feminine. Present an assortment of 12–15 nouns students have learnt so far, without articles (see below and online worksheet). Read out the list of words. Students hold up a blue card if the word is masculine, red if feminine.

   Suggested vocabulary: *livre, maison, souris, chaise, poisson, fenêtre, tarentule, jardin, ordinateur, grand-père, chambre, lapin, cousine, appartement, perruche, fils.*

2 *Loto!* Use items of vocabulary from this unit (see online worksheet).

   Suggested vocabulary: *blanc, un chat, marron, jaune, un chien, vert, gros, un lapin, j'aime, rouge, énorme, un poisson, je déteste, une souris, mignon.*

As an alternative, play 'strip bingo' (see TB page xvi). Students choose any four (or more) items from the list of vocabulary to be used and write the lists quickly themselves.

1 Le zoo extraordinaire

Students listen to the poem and read it aloud. They then read or listen again and put the animals in order.

Remind students about using cognates to help with meaning. The French words for the animals in the poem are all cognates or near-cognates, with just one exception (*ours*). This means that they should be able to work them all out by a process of elimination.

Remind students to be careful when they say the words – they might look like English, but they sound quite different.

Solution:
B, F, D, C, E, A, G, H

CD 2 Track 12

Le zoo extraordinaire

1 Moi, j'adore les animaux –
   Ils sont petits, ils sont très gros,
   Ils sont de toutes les couleurs
   Dans le zoo extraordinaire.
   C'est génial!
2 Un lion rouge et orange!
   Eh bien, c'est très étrange.
   Et un chameau jaune et noir!
   C'est extraordinaire, je crois.
   C'est vrai!
3 Voilà un zèbre vert et blanc.
   Ce n'est pas normal, dis donc!
   Une grande girafe orange et jaune.
   J'aime bien – elle est mignonne.
   Tu trouves?
4 Il y a un gros éléphant ici.
   De quelle couleur? Bleu et gris.
   Voilà un tigre jaune et bleu.
   Est-ce qu'il est dangereux?
   Bien sûr!
5 Voici un ours, il est énorme.
   Tu aimes ses couleurs? Rouge et brun?
   Et le gorille, il n'est pas noir.
   Il est marron et blanc, tu vois?
   Pas mal!
6 Moi, j'adore les animaux –
   Ils sont petits, ils sont très gros,
   Ils sont de toutes les couleurs
   Dans le zoo extraordinaire.
   C'est trop cool!

2 Comment ça se dit?

Students find the French expressions in the poem.

These phrases at the end of each verse are ones students can use in group talk; they are snappy, useful and fun. Encourage students to practise them aloud and use them whenever possible.

Explain also the phrases *dis donc* (I tell you) and *tu vois* (you see).

Tricolore 1 Teacher's Notes

4E Le zoo extraordinaire

Solution:
1 C'est génial! **2** Bien sûr! **3** Pas mal! **4** C'est trop cool! **5** Tu trouves? **6** C'est vrai!

40

3 C'est extraordinaire!

a Students choose a verse of the poem and translate it into English. If necessary, go over some translation strategies with students (e.g. not translating every word, get the sense of a whole phrase, read it back and check whether it sounds English).

b As extension, students make up some weird animals, draw them and describe them – if possible in another verse of the poem. Encourage them to be as creative as possible.

41 Stratégies

Remembering vocabulary (2)

This suggests several memorisation strategies. Point out that not all strategies work for everyone and encourage students to find the method(s) that suit them best. The online worksheet can be used for further reinforcement.

Worksheet

Remembering vocabulary (2)

Interactive activity

Vocabulaire de classe (4)

Presentation

Worksheet

Le sais-tu? Les animaux

cm 4/6

Tu comprends?

41 cm 4/7

Sommaire

A summary of the main language of the unit. This is also provided on copymaster for reference.

Interactive activity

Vocabulaire (4)

Worksheet

Plenaries (pages 40–41)

1 **Think, pair and share.** In pairs, students choose one of the objectives for the unit (these could be allocated so that they are all covered), they discuss it for five minutes in pairs, then they share their findings with the class.

2 Discuss what students have been able to include in their *Dossier personnel* at the end of this unit. Students could assess how far they have come in the first four units and summarise what they now know.

Tricolore 1 Teacher's Notes 59

Unité 4 Consolidation and assessment

Épreuves Unité 4

These worksheets can be used for an informal test of listening, reading and writing or for extra practice, as required. For general notes on the Épreuves, see TB page xv.

🔊 cm 4/8

Écouter 2 tr 13–16

A Les animaux

> **Solution:**
> 1 *b*, 2 *c*, 3 *e*, 4 *d*, 5 *f*, 6 *a*
> mark /5

🔊 CD 2 Track 13

Les animaux

1 Voici mon chien. C'est mon chien.
2 Et voici mon chat. C'est mon chat.
3 Et voilà ma souris, ma souris blanche.
4 J'ai aussi un cochon d'Inde. Mon cochon d'Inde s'appelle Dodu.
5 Puis voici ma perruche. C'est ma perruche bleue.
6 Et voilà mon lapin. Le lapin s'appelle Pierrot.

B Comment ça s'écrit?

> **Solution:**
> as transcript
> mark /5

🔊 CD 2 Track 14

Comment ça s'écrit?

1 V-A-N-I-L-L-E
2 C A R O T T E
3 M I N O U
4 L A R O C H E L L E
5 P A R I S
6 B L A N C O

C C'est quelle image?

> **Solution:**
> 1 *a*, 2 *b*, 3 *a*, 4 *a*, 5 *b*, 6 *b*
> mark /5

🔊 CD 2 Track 15

C'est quelle image?

1 – Est-ce que tu as un animal à la maison?
  – Oui, j'ai un oiseau. C'est une perruche. Regarde, elle est dans sa cage.
2 – Est-ce que tu as un animal, David?
  – Oui, j'ai des poissons. J'ai trois poissons rouges.
3 – Voici mon cheval. Il est super, non?
  – Oui, oui. Il est tout blanc. Il est fantastique, ton cheval!
4 – Regarde! Dans la boîte, il y a deux petits hamsters.
  – Ah oui, ils sont mignons, tes petits hamsters! Tu as des lapins aussi?
  – Non, je n'ai pas de lapins.
5 – Attention! Ton chat est sur la table!
  – Ah non! Maman, Minou est sur la table!
6 – Voici ton prix. C'est un livre sur les animaux.
  – Oh, merci beaucoup. J'aime beaucoup les animaux.

D Un sondage: Aimez-vous les chiens?

> **Solution:**
> 1 *a*, 2 *b*, 3 *c*, 4 *a*, 5 *d*, 6 *a*
> mark /5

🔊 CD 2 Track 16

Un sondage: Aimez-vous les chiens?

1 – Tu aimes les chiens?
  – Oui, j'aime les chiens.
2 – Qu'est-ce que vous préférez, mademoiselle, les chiens ou les chats?
  – J'adore tous les animaux. J'adore les chiens.
3 – Est-ce que vous aimez les chiens, monsieur?
  – Non, pas beaucoup. Enfin, non, je n'aime pas les animaux.
4 – Est-ce que tu aimes les chiens, Linda?
  – Bien sûr. J'ai deux chiens et je les aime.
5 – Tu aimes les chiens, Richard?
  – Ah non. J'aime les chats, mais je déteste les chiens. Ils sont souvent méchants!
6 – Monsieur, on pose des questions sur les chiens. Est-ce que vous aimez les chiens?
  – Euh, les chiens, oui, ça va. Oui, oui, j'aime les chiens, mais je préfère les chats. Les chats sont plus indépendants.

Unité 4 Consolidation and assessment

cm 4/9

Lire

A Les animaux et les couleurs

Pictures to be checked for correct colouring.

mark /7

B C'est quelle description?

Solution:
1 b, 2 a, 3 a, 4 a, 5 a, 6 b
mark /5

C Chez la famille Marchadier

Solution:
1 V, 2 V, 3 V, 4 F, 5 V, 6 F, 7 F, 8 V, 9 F
mark /8

cm 4/10

Écrire et grammaire

A Un serpent

Solution:
1 un chien, 2 une perruche, 3 un chat, 4 un cheval, 5 un poisson, 6 une souris, 7 un perroquet
mark /6

B Masculin ou féminin?

Solution:
1 petit, 2 mignonne, 3 grande, 4 jolie, 5 blanche, 6 grand, 7 gros
mark /6

C Des questions

To be marked by the teacher.
mark /8

Presse-Jeunesse

42–43

Presse-Jeunesse 1

These pages provide material for reading for pleasure and to enhance cultural awareness. The texts and comprehension activities can be used flexibly; by students working alone for extension, for cover lessons, etc. Although they mainly use language previously taught, they may also contain a small amount of additional language.

42–43

1 Bonjour, Mangetout!

Solution:
1 chat, 2 habite, 3 sœurs, 4 aime, 5 poisson, viande, 6 Calinette

2 Le sais-tu?

La France

This is part of a series, some of which appears in other *Presse-Jeunesse* sections and also in online e-books. This item is also linked with the copymaster which is based on the map of France at the beginning of the Student's Book. Students read the article and do the short task. Teachers could, if wished, do a short explanation about the superlative to go with this item.

Solution:
1 la capitale, 2 une montagne, 3 une tour, 4 du parfum, 5 célèbre, 6 une cathédrale, 7 tout le monde, 8 une ville, 9 un pays

3 Chimène!

This can just be read for enjoyment of the story, and perhaps discussed in pairs, or followed by the matching activity.

Solution:
1 f, 2 d, 3 e, 4 b, 5 a, 6 c

4 Crayons de couleur

This poem could perhaps be performed in pairs or groups.

a Students find the French phrases.
b As an **extension activity**, encourage students to make up their own version by replacing the nouns. These would make an excellent classroom display.

Chantal Couliou is a teacher and children's author in Brittany. There are several online resources that French teachers have provided for the poem. A search for the title should provide current links.

Solution:
1 les prairies, 2 le soleil, 3 les fraises, 4 les corbeaux, 5 les nuages, 6 la mer, 7 le ciel, 8 le monde

Au choix

146 Au choix

1 Combien d'animaux?

Students identify the number of different pets in the picture writing the answers as figures or in full.

Solution:
1 trois hamsters, 2 quatre chiens, 3 un oiseau, 4 deux chats, 5 une souris, 6 deux poissons, 7 un lapin

146 Au choix

2 Chat perdu

Teach *perdu* and *trouvé*, demonstrating perhaps by putting a pencil under a book:

J'ai perdu mon crayon, où est mon crayon?
Ah, voilà mon crayon. J'ai trouvé mon crayon.

Unité 4 Consolidation and assessment

It is not necessary to explain the perfect tense other than to give the set phrases *j'ai perdu/trouvé …* = I have lost/ found …. Next talk about the advert and photograph, introducing the expression *Il est comment?*, e.g.

Regardez le chat. Il est comment?

Il est gros ou petit?

De quelle couleur est-il?

Mais le chat dans la photo est perdu, non?

Mais Mme Robert a trouvé le chat? Alors il est à qui?

Écoutez les conversations au téléphone. Est-ce que le chat est à Mme Duval, à Claire Martin ou à François Léon?

Play the three telephone conversations, stopping after each one to let the class compare the details with the photo, perhaps asking some questions, e.g.

Il est comment, le chat de Mme Duval? Il est petit ou gros? Il est blanc?

At the end of the recording, take a vote by show of hands to see who the class thinks owns the cat.

> **Solution:**
> *François*

 CD 2 Track 17

Chat perdu

– Allô. C'est Mme Robert?
– Oui.
– Je m'appelle Mme Marie Duval. J'ai perdu mon chat et …
– Ah bon. Il est comment, votre chat?
– Eh bien, il est noir, tout noir, et il est très gros.

– Allô.
– Allô. Je m'appelle Claire Martin et j'ai perdu mon petit chat, Tigre.
– Bonjour, Claire. Il est comment, ton Tigre?
– Oh, il est adorable! Il est fantastique!
– Oui, oui, mais il est comment? Il est gros ou petit? Il est de quelle couleur?
– Ben, blanc, il est blanc, mais brun aussi, et noir, et jaune aussi. Enfin, il est de toutes les couleurs, mais surtout blanc.
– Et il est gros?
– Oh oui. Il est très, très gros. Il mange beaucoup. Il est énorme!

– Allô. C'est Mme Robert?
– Oui, oui, c'est moi. Je suis Mme Robert.
– Alors, madame, je pense que vous avez trouvé notre chat. Le chat sur la photo, c'est notre chat, Magique!
– Ah bon. Il est comment, Magique?
– Il n'est pas très gros, mais il n'est pas très petit. Il est gris, blanc et noir, avec les pattes blanches.
– Et toi, comment t'appelles-tu?
– Moi, je m'appelle François Léon.

Possibilities for further exploitation of this task:
1 Students could listen again to the recording and try to complete the descriptions of the three cats:
   Le chat de Mme Duval est …
   Le chat de Claire est …
   Le chat de François est …

2 Groups of (able) students could make up similar telephone calls. One student could draw or write a description of a cat and the others could 'phone in' and try to claim it.
3 Students could write descriptions on the computer and import pictures of pets.

 146 Au choix AfL

3 Des animaux

Students write simple descriptions of the animals illustrated. As follow-up, students can draw or use the computer to produce posters with pictures and descriptions of the animals. They can then add text labels to their pictures. Perhaps give the students a time limit and ask them to draw and label an animal in that time – sometimes this produces amusing results! With the most able, this could lead to a game in which one describes the other's animal from memory. Alternatively, someone describes an animal and the other person draws it on the board following instructions. Agree criteria for success, e.g. whether the description matches the picture, and use for AfL. Remind students of the spread objectives.

 146 Au choix

4 Des questions

Students use the substitution table to help them make up six more questions. This can be a speaking or a writing activity.

 147 Au choix

5 Chasse à l'intrus

Use this activity at any point in the unit after teaching *avoir*. In addition to spotting the odd one out, more able students could explain their choice, e.g. 10 – *brun* is masculine, the others are feminine. Encourage them to use phrases like *c'est masculin, c'est féminin, c'est un animal, c'est une couleur*, etc.

This activity could also be used as a starter.

> **Solution:**
> **1** *vingt*, **2** *oui*, **3** *une maison*, **4** *un garçon*, **5** *gros*, **6** *la cuisine*, **7** *un cheval*, **8** *Paris*, **9** *treize*, **10** *brun*, **11** *à**, **12** *très*

* The correct answer is intended to be *à* because it is not part of *avoir*. However, if anyone suggests that *ai* sounds different, this could also be counted as correct as long as the explanation is given.

 147 Au choix

6 Un échange

Students read through the cartoon strip and decide whether the statements are true or false.

> **Solution:**
> **1** *vrai*, **2** *faux*, **3** *faux*, **4** *faux*, **5** *vrai*, **6** *faux*, **7** *faux*, **8** *faux*

Unité 4 Consolidation and assessment

cm 4/1

Les animaux

This is a support worksheet for practising animal vocabulary. Students copy the names of the animals onto the correct square and colour according to the instructions. These could be stuck onto card, cut up and used as mini-flashcards for pair or group practice (see TB pages xix).

cm 4/2

Les animaux de mes amis

This copymaster gives further practice of descriptive vocabulary and some dictionary practice with the names of animals. Some students might need help with the final task.

> **Solution:**
>
> **1** *Où sont les voyelles?*
> **1** *chien,* **2** *poisson,* **3** *souris,* **4** *perroquet,*
> **5** *tarentule,* **6** *oiseau,* **7** *cheval,* **8** *lapin*
>
> **2** *C'est utile, un dictionnaire*
>
> | | |
> |---|---|
> | canard (m) | duck |
> | canari (m) | canary |
> | chameau (m) | camel |
> | chat (m) | cat |
> | chauve-souris (f) | bat |
> | cheval (m) | horse |
> | chien (m) | dog |
> | chimpanzé (m) | chimp |
> | cochon d'Inde (m) | guinea pig |
>
> **3** *Les animaux de mes amis*
> **1** *petite,* **2** *grand,* **3** *blanc,* **4** *noir,* **5** *mignonne,*
> **6** *gris,* **7** *méchant,* **8** *vert*

cm 4/3

C'est moi!

This could be done now, or at the end of the unit as consolidation. Students complete their self-portrait, filling in the blanks to give name, age, address and an account of their possessions and preferences. The corrected version of this sheet could become part of their *Dossier personnel*.

cm 4/4

Questions et réponses

Students compile the complete conversation script, using questions from the box. When they have completed the two conversations, students can read them aloud in pairs, and some could be recorded. The next copymaster provides follow-up speaking practice.

> **Solution:**
> **1 a** 2, **b** 3, **c** 9, **d** 5, **e** 4
> **2 f** 7, **g** 6, **h** 8, **i** 1, **j** 10

cm 4/5

Des conversations au choix

This is a follow-up to cm 4/4. The first activity involves throwing a die or choosing questions in turns and answering from a choice of suggestions or with invented answers. Demonstrate this process first. This is followed by a survey about pets.

cm 4/6

Tu comprends?

1 Ma chambre

Students listen to the recording and colour the picture.

> **CD 2 Track 18**
>
> **Ma chambre**
> 1 Mon lit est bleu.
> 2 Sur mon lit, il y a un classeur jaune et un livre brun.
> 3 Près de mon lit, il y a une chaise rouge.
> 4 Près de la table, il y a une chaise blanche.
> 5 La table est brune.
> 6 Mon ordinateur est sur la table. L'ordinateur est noir.
> 7 Puis il y a la porte. La porte est verte.
> 8 Mon chat est sur le lit, il est gris et blanc.
> 9 Sur la table, il y a deux crayons rouges et un taille-crayon orange.

2 Où sont les animaux?

Students draw a line to show where each animal is in the flat.

> **CD 2 Track 19**
>
> **Où sont les animaux?**
> Aujourd'hui, il y a beaucoup d'animaux dans l'appartement. Le chat est dans la chambre de mes parents. Le poisson rouge est dans la salle de bains. La souris est dans la salle de séjour. Le chien est dans ma chambre. Le perroquet est dans la cuisine et le lapin est dans la salle à manger.

3 Qu'est-ce que c'est?

Students listen and write down the words dictated. They then spot the odd one out.

> **Solution:**
> **4** *calculatrice*

> **CD 2 Track 20**
>
> **Qu'est-ce que c'est?**
> 1 dimanche (spelt out)   4 calculatrice
> 2 mercredi   5 lundi
> 3 vendredi   6 jeudi

cm 4/7

Sommaire

A summary of the main language of the unit on copymaster for reference.

Tricolore 1 Teacher's Notes **63**

Unité 5

Tricolore 1 Unité 5 Des fêtes et des festivals

Pages 44–61

5A L'année en France pages 44–45		
• Ask for and give the date • Learn about saints' days and other festivals		
Grammaire	**Stratégies**	**Phonétique**
• None	• Remembering the months	• None
Resources		
Audio: 1 *Quelle est la date?*; *Les mois*, or CD 2 tracks 21 and 22 **Copymasters:** 5/1 *Des dates* **Worksheets:** Starters and plenaries; *C'est ma fête* (W)		**Interactive activity:** *C'est quelle date?* (R, L) **PowerPoint:** None **Grammar in Action:** None
5B En France, c'est la fête pages 46–47		
• Find out about festivals and events in France • Use correct greetings for special days		
Grammaire	**Stratégies**	**Phonétique**
• The pronoun *on*	• Using clues to work out meaning (3)	• None
Resources		
Audio: 1 *Les fêtes en France*, or CD 2, track 23 **Copymasters:** None **Worksheets:** Starters and plenaries; Using clues to work out meaning (Strat)		**Interactive activity:** None **PowerPoint:** *L'année en France* (V) **Grammar in Action:** None
5C Mardi gras pages 48–49		
• Talk about a fancy dress party		
Grammaire	**Stratégies**	**Phonétique**
• Practise using the verb *être* (to be)	• None	• None
Resources		
Audio: 1 *Mardi gras*, or CD 2, track 24 **Copymasters:** 5/2 *Être* **Worksheets:** Starters and plenaries; Sentences with *être* (G)		**Interactive activity:** None **PowerPoint:** The verb *être* (G) **Grammar in Action:** p13
5D Ton anniversaire, c'est quand? pages 50–51		
• Talk about birthday dates and presents • Use adjectives to add interest		
Grammaire	**Stratégies**	**Phonétique**
• Use adjectives (singular and plural)	• Getting adjectives right	• The letters 'ui'
Resources		
Audio: 1 *L'anniversaire de Marc*, or CD track 25 **Copymasters:** None **Worksheets:** Starters and plenaries		**Interactive activity:** None **Ph** The letters 'ui', or CD 2, track 26 **PowerPoint:** None **Grammar in Action:** p14
5E Des cadeaux pour tout le monde pages 52–53		
• Use wider vocabulary for some more presents • Use some higher numbers and prices		
Grammaire	**Stratégies**	**Phonétique**
• Numbers	• Preparing for listening	• The letters 'ille'
Resources		
Audio: 1 *Vous cherchez un cadeau*; **4a** *La tombola*; *C'est combien?*, or CD 2, tracks 27, 29 and 30 **Copymasters:** 5/3 *Les numéros* **Worksheets:** Starters and plenaries; *C'est combien?* (R, S)		**Interactive activity:** Preparing for listening (Strat) **Ph** The letters 'ille', or CD 2, track 28 **PowerPoint:** None **Grammar in Action:** None

Key language

5F Des vêtements pages 54–55		
• Talk about clothes			
Grammaire	Stratégies	Phonétique
• Use plural nouns	• Recognising three kinds of words	• None
Resources		
Audio: 1 *Lou Leroux. Chic: oui ou non?*, or CD 2, track 31 **Copymasters:** 5/4 *Des vêtements*, 5/5 *Jeux de vocabulaire*, 5/6 *Des cadeaux et des vêtements* **Worksheets:** Starters and plenaries; Recognising three kinds of words (Strat, 1 and 2); *Masculin ou féminin, singulier ou pluriel?* (G)		**Interactive activity:** *On parle des vêtements* (L) **PowerPoint:** *Les vêtements* (V) **Grammar in Action:** None

5G Les descriptions personnelles pages 56–57		
• Describe yourself and other people			
Grammaire	Stratégies	Phonétique
• Use the verb *avoir* (to have)	• Speaking more confidently	• The letters 'eu'
Resources		
Audio: 1 *Des photos d'identité*, or CD 2, track 32 **Copymasters:** 5/7 *Avoir*, 5/8 *Des descriptions* **Worksheets:** Starters and plenaries; *Les descriptions personelles* (W)		**Interactive activity:** *Des jeunes* (L); *Avoir* (G) **Ph** The letters 'eu', or CD 2, track 33 **PowerPoint:** *Ils sont comment?* (V); *Le verbe avoir* (G) **Grammar in Action:** pp15–16

5H Écoutez bien pages 58–59		
• Develop and practise your listening skills			
Grammaire	Stratégies	Phonétique
• None	• Listening with focus	• None
Resources		
Audio: 1 *Trouve le bon mot*; **2** *C'est quelle image?*; **3** *C'est quel mot?*; **4** *Questions ou réponses?*; **5** *L'histoire de Suzanne*, or CD 2, tracks 34, 35, 36, 37 and 38 **Copymasters:** 5/9 *Tu comprends?*, 5/10 *Sommaire* **Worksheets:** Starters and plenaries **e-book:** *Une année de fêtes*		**Interactive activity:** Classroom commands (V) **Video:** *L'anniversaire de Manon* **Grammar in Action:** None

Key language

Months and dates (5A)

janvier
février
mars
avril
mai
juin
juillet
août
septembre
octobre
novembre
décembre
Quelle est la date aujourd'hui?
C'est le …
C'est quand, le concert/le match?
C'est le mardi premier juin.
C'est quand, ton anniversaire?
C'est le dix-neuf juillet.

Special days and greetings (5B and 5C)

le jour de l'An
la fête nationale
Pâques
Noël
mardi gras
Bonne Année!
Joyeuses Pâques!
Joyeux Noël!
Bon anniversaire!
Bonne fête!

Presents (5D and 5E)

Qu'est-ce que tu as reçu comme cadeaux?
J'ai reçu …
un tee-shirt et des chaussures
une carte cadeau
un casque (audio)
des écouteurs

5A L'année en France

Numbers 70–100 (5E)
Clothes (5F)
les vêtements
des baskets
une casquette
des chaussettes
des chaussures
une chemise
une cravate
un jogging
une jupe
un pantalon
un pull
une robe
des sandales
un short
un sweat
un tee-shirt
des tennis

Describing appearance (5G)
J'ai/Il a/Elle a ...
les cheveux longs
les cheveux courts
les cheveux frisés
les cheveux raides
les cheveux noirs
les cheveux blonds
les cheveux roux
les cheveux châtains
les yeux marron/verts
les yeux bleus/gris
Je/Il/Elle porte des lunettes.

5A L'année en France   pages 44–45

- Ask for and give the date
- Learn about saints' days and other festivals

Grammaire	Stratégies	Phonétique
• None	• Remembering the months	• None

Resources

Audio: 1 *Quelle est la date?*; *Les mois*, or CD 2 tracks 21 and 22
Copymasters: 5/1 *Des dates*
Worksheets: Starters and plenaries; *C'est ma fête* (W)

Interactive activity: *C'est quelle date?* (R, L)
PowerPoint: None
Grammar in Action: None

Worksheet

Starters (pages 44–45)

1 Display a selection of numbers from 1–31 for a game of *Effacez!*.
2 **En groupes** Display a list of words in random order or hand this out on paper (see online worksheet). Ask students to put these into four groups, which are:

mardi, jeudi, samedi

je, tu, il

le frère, le père, l'ami

un lapin, un oiseau, une souris

Introduction
Go through the objectives for this spread.

The date
Before using the Student's Book pages, teach the date in oral and written form.

Suggested order:
Numbers
Revise the numbers 1–31 orally, perhaps using some of the number games (see TB page xvi).

Days of the week
a Write some days on the board, missing some out – students read them out and fill in the blanks.
b Play *Loto!* with four days (or four days and four numbers) written on a piece of paper.

Months
Next, teach the months orally, in batches of three months at a time, then write these on the board.

For practice, play games such as *Chef d'orchestre*, *Effacez!*, *Loto!*, *Pelmanism* (see TB pages xvi–xix).

Use a French calendar, if available, for practice, e.g. *C'est* (+ month), *Oui, c'est* (+ month) if correct, or *Non, c'est* (+ correct month). Teach *premier* and *dernier*, e.g. *Le premier mois, c'est …? Le dernier mois, c'est novembre? Non, le dernier mois, c'est décembre.*

The full date
Teach and practise the full date orally and eventually in written form, starting from today's date. Then teach and practise *le premier* before going on to other full dates. Give plenty of practice, e.g. by dictating some to be written down in figures, asking students to supply the date of the days before and after. Play *Effacez!* with the dates written in figures.

5A L'année en France

1 Quelle est la date?

Students should look at the fourteen dates before listening to the recording. They then note down which date is linked with each conversation.

Solution:
1 L, 2 A, 3 I, 4 C, 5 E, 6 G, 7 F, 8 B, 9 H, 10 J

CD 2 Track 21

Quelle est la date?

1 – C'est quand, l'anniversaire de Christophe?
  – C'est le premier novembre.
2 – Salut.
  – Salut. Ça va?
  – Oui, ça va.
  – Tu vas au grand match de foot, Marseille contre Saint-Étienne?
  – C'est quand, le match?
  – C'est le dimanche 20 janvier.
  – Oui, je veux bien.
3 – Hé, Françoise, tu vas au concert?
  – C'est quand, le concert?
  – C'est le dimanche 10 août.
  – Le dix août, hmm … je ne sais pas.
4 – Salut, Pascale. Tu vas à la soirée chez Noah?
  – Non … c'est quand?
  – C'est le jeudi 14 février.
5 – La fête au club des jeunes, c'est quand?
  – C'est le mercredi 2 avril.
6 – La fête de la musique, c'est quand, cette année?
  – C'est le 21 juin. C'est un samedi.
  – Excellent! J'adore ça!
7 – C'est quand, la fête des Mères?
  – C'est dimanche, le 25 mai.
8 – Mardi gras, c'est quand, cette année?
  – C'est le 4 février.
9 – Thomas, c'est quand, le début des vacances d'été?
  – C'est le 3 juillet.
10 – Ingrid, c'est quand, la rentrée scolaire?
   – C'est le 2 septembre.

44

Les mois

This listening discrimination activity focuses on the similarities and differences between the pronunciation of the French and English names of the months.

Solution:
1 F, 2 F, 3 E, 4 F, 5 E, 6 F, 7 E, 8 E, 9 F, 10 F

CD 2 Track 22

Les mois

1 janvier, January – janvier
2 juillet, July – juillet
3 octobre, October – October
4 April, avril – avril
5 décembre, December – December
6 mars, March – mars
7 juin, June – June
8 February, février – February
9 septembre, September – septembre
10 November, novembre – novembre

44 Stratégies

Remembering the months

This memorisation strategy focuses on the similarities and differences between the written forms of the French and English names of the months.

Solution:
1 *all begin with same letter,* 2 *end in -re and décembre has accent,* 3 *février, août, décembre,* 4 *begin with small letter in French*

Interactive activity

C'est quelle date?

44

2 Des dates

Students complete the dates with the correct day and month.

Solution:
1 *quatre février,* 2 *quatorze février,*
3 *deux avril,* 4 *deux septembre,*
5 *vingt janvier,* 6 *vingt-sept mars*

Worksheet

C'est ma fête

45   AfL

3 C'est quand?

One student asks for the date of an event and the other replies by referring to the calendar slips. If preferred, this could be done as a written task.

Solution:
1 *C'est le vingt janvier.*
2 *C'est le quatre février.*
3 *C'est le vingt-et-un juin.*
4 *C'est le six décembre.*
5 *C'est le premier novembre.*
6 *C'est le quatorze février.*
7 *C'est le trente-et-un décembre.*
8 *C'est le dix août.*

5A L'année en France

As follow-up, students could ask each other in turn the date for other events, e.g.

– *La fête des Mères, c'est quand?*

– *C'est le vingt-cinq mai.*

This is an opportunity for peer assessment. Remind students of the spread objectives and agree the criteria for success.

📖 45

4 Bonne fête

This short reading passage gives some background information about the traditional practice of naming French children after saints and celebrating the saint's day as their *fête*. France is a predominantly Catholic country and, in the past, everyone had to be given the name of a saint as a Christian name. Whereas laws still govern what you can call a child, names now often reflect celebrities, popular TV soaps, etc., as elsewhere in the world. If students enquire why *la* is used with the names of masculine saints, point out that *la Saint-Laurent* is short for *la fête de Saint Laurent*.

a When students have read the text, they should find the *fêtes* for the names listed and answer the questions orally and/or in writing.

> **Solution:**
> **1** C'est le 31 décembre, **2** C'est le 6 décembre,
> **3** C'est le 4 février, **4** C'est le 22 octobre,
> **5** C'est le 21 juin, **6** C'est le 2 septembre

b Students write the birthdays of three family members.

c As extension, students write the dates of five festivals during the year.

Students might use the internet to research saints' days (*calendrier des jours saints*). Information can be downloaded for use off-line.

For further research on names, students might like to look on the internet for lists of the most popular names for different years (search for *'prénoms populaires France'* to find a number of useful sites). Refer students also to the *calendrier des jours saints* on *kerboodle!*.

cm 5/1

Des dates

📖 148 Au choix

1 Les mois de l'année

📖 148 Au choix

2 Une année en désordre

Additional activities/Consolidation

Jeu: Rendez-vous?

Students note down two free days in a diary for next week. They then work in pairs to see if they have a free day in common and to see who is first to discover the other person's two free days. They can then play the game again with other partners and continue until they find another person with the same free days as theirs.

Tu es libre le lundi 27 janvier?

Non. Et toi, tu es libre le jeudi 31 janvier?

Oui. Voilà. Alors rendez-vous le jeudi 31 janvier.

Avant/après

This game provides good practice of days and dates. Start by saying, e.g. *C'est le jeudi 15 mars*. Then say, e.g. *Deux jours après* and point to a student (as they don't know who is going to be picked, everyone has to think about the answer). The chosen student should reply *C'est le samedi 17 mars*. Using this date or a new one, point to another student and say, e.g. *Un jour avant*. Keep up a brisk pace. This could also be played in groups.

🔎 Worksheet

Plenaries (pages 44–45)

1 Students should discuss tips for remembering the sound and spelling of the days, months and numbers up to 31. These tips could be collated and assessed by others for their usefulness, perhaps by a show of hands for those who found it helpful.

2 Ask students to look at the objectives for pages 44–45: how well do they think they have done? Can they explain the main points to a partner? What did they find easy or difficult?

Tricolore 1 Teacher's Notes

5B En France, c'est la fête   pages 46–47

- Find out about festivals and events in France
- Use correct greetings for special days

Grammaire	Stratégies	Phonétique
• The pronoun *on*	• Using clues to work out meaning (3)	• None

Resources

Audio: 1 *Les fêtes en France*, or CD 2, track 23
Copymasters: None
Worksheets: Starters and plenaries; Using clues to work out meaning (Strat)

Interactive activity: None
PowerPoint: *L'année en France* (V)
Grammar in Action: None

Worksheet

Starters (pages 46–47)

1 **En ordre** Display the names of the months in random order on the board. Ask students to write these in order using abbreviated spellings (*jan., fév.,* etc.) Ask students randomly for each month in the correct order, e.g. *Le premier mois, c'est quoi? Après janvier, c'est quel mois?* etc.

2 **Chasse à l'intrus** Display or print out the following lists and ask students to write down the odd word out in each list (shown in bold). Students exchange answers for checking. Ask several students for the correct answer before confirming this.

1	2	3	4	5
la chatte	mercredi	**dans**	le salon	noir
la chambre	vendredi	deux	la salle de bains	bleu
le cheval	dimanche	dix	**le classeur**	**sous**
le chien	**difficile**	douze	la cuisine	gris

Presentation

L'année en France

📖 🔊 46

1 Les fêtes en France

Play the complete passage with the class following the text in their books. Use the illustrations to help students understand the information about each event and explain aspects they might not know about, in English if necessary, e.g. *La fête des Rois*. Here are some notes for guidance.

La fête des Rois:

This is a very popular festival. A cardboard crown is supplied with the cake in the shops. The person who gets the lucky charm (*la fève*) is the king or queen and 'rules' for the rest of the day. *Fève* originally means a bean – a white bean was used for the charm, but nowadays this is a Baby Jesus or other plastic or porcelain animal, etc.

Pâques:

At Easter in France, the bells fly back to Rome (in celebration of the Resurrection) and leave chocolate eggs, rabbits, fish, chicks, etc. for the children.

Poisson d'avril:

There are various accounts of this custom. In 1565 Charles IX changed the New Year from 1 April (start of spring) to 1 January (when the days start getting longer). On 1 April, some pranksters gave 'false' New Year presents and played all sorts of tricks. This was also mixed with other customs, e.g. the *Poisson* sign of the zodiac; prolonging Lent when you were only allowed to eat fish instead of meat; confusing simple people by offering them fish at a time of year when fishing was not allowed. For further information about saints' days, there are a number of websites on the subject.

🔊 CD 2 Track 23

Les fêtes en France

1 Le premier janvier, c'est le jour de l'An. On dit «Bonne Année» à ses amis.

2 Le six janvier, c'est la fête des Rois. On mange un gâteau spécial: la galette des Rois. Dans la galette, il y a une fève. La personne qui trouve la fève est le roi ou la reine et porte une couronne.

3 Au mois de février ou mars, il y a mardi gras. On mange des crêpes.

4 En mars ou en avril, il y a Pâques. À Pâques, on mange des œufs en chocolat … et aussi des lapins et des oiseaux en chocolat. On dit «Joyeuses Pâques!».

5 Le premier avril, on fait des poissons d'avril. Ça, c'est amusant!

6 Au mois de mai, il y a la fête des Mères. Les enfants donnent une carte ou des fleurs à leur mère.

7 Le 21 juin, c'est le premier jour de l'été. En France, c'est la fête de la musique.

8 Le 14 juillet, c'est la fête nationale. Il y a un défilé dans les rues. Le soir, il y a un feu d'artifice.

9 À Noël, on chante des chants de Noël. Le père Noël apporte des cadeaux aux petits enfants. On mange un repas délicieux, souvent pendant la nuit du 24 au 25 décembre. On dit «Joyeux Noël» à tout le monde.

10 Le 31 décembre, c'est la Saint-Sylvestre. Le soir, on mange un bon repas. À minuit, on téléphone à ses amis et on dit «Bonne Année» à tout le monde.

11 Il y a aussi d'autres fêtes en France, par exemple la fête de l'Aïd-el-Fitr, pour la religion musulmane, et la fête des lumières à Diwali, pour la religion hindoue.

5B En France, c'est la fête

47 Stratégies

Using clues to work out meaning (3)

This reading strategy focuses on strategies for finding the meaning of new vocabulary. It also encourages students to think about differences and similarities between French and English. The online worksheet can be used for further reinforcement.

Worksheet

Using clues to work out meaning

47

2 Ça veut dire quoi?

This task provides a focus to implement the strategies for finding the meaning of new vocabulary.

> **Solution:**
>
> a 1 *premier*   premier, first
>   2 *délicieux*   delicious
>   3 *une couronne*   crown
>   4 *une carte*   card
>   5 *la religion hindoue* the Hindu religion
> b 1 *le jour de l'An* New Year's Day
>   2 *des crêpes*   pancakes
>   3 *Bonne Année!*   Happy New Year
>   4 *des œufs*   eggs
>   5 *la religion musulmane* the Muslim religion
>   6 *des fleurs*   flowers
>   7 *la nuit*   night
>   8 *un feu d'artifice* fireworks

47 Dossier-langue

The pronoun *on*

The pronoun *on* is used in tasks 1–4. Briefly explain its meaning here. It is taught more fully in Unité 6 (SB page 72).

✚ As extension, some students could translate the sentences into French.

> **Solution:**
>
> 1 À Pâques, on mange des œufs en chocolat.
> 2 À Noël, on chante des chants de Noël. 3 À la Saint-Sylvestre, on dit «Bonne Année» à minuit.
> 4 On mange un gâteau spécial à Noël.

47 AfL

3 C'est quel mois?

Check that students know the greetings for each of the main festivals, e.g.

Qu'est-ce qu'on dit à Noël/Pâques/pour le nouvel an?

On dit «Joyeux Noël/Joyeuses Pâques/Bonne Année».

To give oral practice of saying the greetings and festivals, students work in pairs on this task. In turns, one student reads a statement and the other provides the answer. They can assess each other's performance in terms of pronunciation and the correct answers and give feedback. Agree the criteria before starting and remind students of the spread objectives.

> **Solution:**
>
> **1** *en mars ou en avril,* **2** *en février ou en mars,* **3** *en décembre,* **4** *en janvier,* **5** *en janvier,* **6** *en mai*

47 AfL

4 C'est quelle fête?

In pairs, students read out the short dialogue then, following the example, one student describes an event and the other has to guess the fête. Refer students back to task **3** for models and further ideas for this activity. Review the spread objectives and assessment criteria and use this for peer assessment.

148 Au choix

3 Des annonces

Worksheet

Plenaries (pages 46–47)

1 Students make up a wordsearch (using the 10 x 10 square grid provided on the online worksheet) to include approximately 12 items of vocabulary from the unit so far. They then exchange these and find the words and write them down with their English meaning. Follow this with reflection and discussion, e.g. did students all choose similar words and if so, why? Which sort of words were chosen (adjectives, nouns) and is this because they are easier to learn? Did certain groups of letters 'pop out' at them from the wordsearch?

2 Students could discuss what they have found most useful/difficult so far in the unit.

70 Tricolore 1 Teacher's Notes

5C Mardi gras   pages 48–49

- Talk about a fancy dress party

Grammaire	Stratégies	Phonétique
• Practise using the verb *être* (to be)	• None	• None

Resources
Audio: 1 *Mardi gras*, or CD 2, track 24 **Copymasters:** 5/2 *Être* **Worksheets:** Starters and plenaries; Sentences with *être* (G)	**Interactive activity:** None **PowerPoint:** The verb *être* (G) **Grammar in Action:** p13

Worksheet

Starters (pages 48–49)

1 *Chaque mot à sa place* Display the following task (see online worksheet). Give students a few minutes to read and work out the answers, then ask students collectively or randomly to give the number of the box. Answers are given in brackets.

Quelle est la bonne case pour chaque mot?

mars (2), un cahier (5), vingt (3), brun (4), une fille (1)

1	2	3	4	5
un homme une femme un garçon	février août juillet	neuf seize trente	blanc vert jaune	un livre un crayon un classeur

2 *Trouve les paires* Display the following text on the board, or print it out (see online worksheet). Students match up the two parts of each sentence, writing down each number and the corresponding letter. This can be checked by the teacher randomly selecting students to answer.

Exemple: 1h	
1 J'habite dans	a *télé.*
2 J'aime beaucoup les	b *est un perroquet.*
3 Télé est un	c *et très mignon.*
4 Il aime la	d *la radio.*
5 Blanco est	e *animaux.*
6 Il préfère	f *chien noir.*
7 Jules	g *un chat blanc.*
8 Il est petit	h *une ferme.*

Solution:
1 h, **2** e, **3** f, **4** a, **5** i, **6** d, **7** b, **8** c

Presentation

Le verbe *être*

Paradigm of *être*

Singular paradigm of *être*

Revise the names of rooms in a house taught in *Unité* 3 and use these to revise the singular forms of *être*.

Give printouts of the flashcards (13–17) to individual students and ask *Où es-tu?* for the reply *Je suis dans* (+ room). Next, revise the third person singular by asking the class: *Où est-il/elle? Où est* (name)? for the reply *Il/Elle est dans* (+ room). The singular paradigm could be written on the board for reference. For more practice, see *Touché-coulé* (TB page xvii).

Plural paradigm of *être*

nous form

To present *nous sommes*, say some sentences which relate to the class as a whole, and get students to deduce the meaning, e.g.

Nous sommes dans la salle de classe.

Nous sommes au collège.

Nous sommes à (+ town).

Nous sommes en Angleterre/en Écosse, etc.

Write these on the board for a game of *Effacez!* later (see TB page xvii).

Add *nous sommes* to the paradigm on the board.

vous form

Play a 'mind-reading game' (see TB page xviii). The teacher thinks of a French town from the map (SB page 3). Students guess where the teacher is, using *Vous êtes à* (+ place). Then two students consult together to think of a town and the rest of the class guess where they are. Continue for about six goes. Then write a few example sentences on the board for a game of *Effacez!* (see TB page xvii). Add *vous êtes* to the paradigm.

ils form

Collect together several pencils and revise:

Qu'est-ce que c'est?

C'est un crayon.

Il y a combien de crayons? etc.

Then describe them:

Ils sont verts.

Ils sont sur la table.

Choose two other groups of objects, e.g. pens, books, exercise books, and get the class to think of a few ways to describe them.

Eventually, add *ils sont* to the paradigm.

elles form

The *elles* form can then be presented in a similar way, using *gomme, boîte, règle*, and added to the paradigm.

Tricolore 1 Teacher's Notes

5C Mardi gras

Whole paradigm of *être*

Use the paradigm of *être* built up on the board for a version of *Effacez!* now or after referring to the *Dossier-langue* (SB page 49). Make up sentences, using one of the forms, and choose a student to point to or rub out the form used. After a few parts of the verb have disappeared, replace them, getting members of the class to spell out the missing words to someone else, who writes them in the gap. Where possible, get students to make up further sentences themselves.

🔊 48

1 Mardi gras

This presents examples of all forms of *être* in context. Before listening to the recording, read the brief English introduction to *Mardi gras*, then look at the picture and speech bubbles for task **2** as well as the text for task **1**. Practise some of the strategies mentioned earlier, e.g. ask which words they know. What kind of word is *méchantes*? etc. Elicit the meaning of words like *les deux méchantes sœurs de Cendrillon* and *déguisée*. Write these on the board, e.g.

'Déguisé', qu'est-ce que c'est en anglais?

Et 'les deux méchantes sœurs' de Cendrillon?

Students should then listen to the recording and choose the correct answer, **a** or **b**.

Solution:
1 *a*, 2 *b*, 3 *a*, 4 *a*, 5 *b*, 6 *a*, 7 *b*, 8 *a*

🔊 CD 2 Track 24

Mardi gras

– Bonjour. Je m'appelle Luc. Aujourd'hui, c'est le 5 février.
– Oui, c'est mardi 5 février et c'est mardi gras.
– Nous sommes en boîte pour une grande soirée Carnaval.
– C'est très amusant. Beaucoup de personnes en boîte sont déguisées.
– Regarde le garçon là-bas. Il est déguisé en Dracula.
– Et moi, je suis déguisée en perroquet.
– Voilà les deux méchantes sœurs de Cendrillon. Vous êtes bien déguisées! Qui êtes-vous?
– Tu ne sais pas? Nous sommes Anne-Marie et Suzanne. Nous sommes bien en deux méchantes sœurs, non?
– Oui, vous êtes excellentes.
– Mais regarde le fantôme là-bas. Qui est-ce?
– C'est Sébastien?
– Non, ce n'est pas Sébastien.
– Alors, c'est Olivier. C'est toi, Olivier? Tu es le fantôme?
– Oui, c'est moi, je suis le fantôme.

48

2 C'est qui?

This gives further examples of the verb *être* in use. Students read through the introduction and speech bubbles in order to identify the people in fancy dress.

Solution:
1 *Coralie*, 2 *Luc*, 3 *Sébastien*, 4 *Olivier*,
5 *Roseline*, 6 *Christophe*, 7 *Jean-Pierre*,
8 *Anne-Marie et Suzanne*

49 Dossier-langue

The verb *être* (to be)

This explains the complete paradigm of *être*. If not done earlier, write *être* on the board with some gaps and ask the class to read it out, filling in the gaps.

If not already doing so, start using the terms 1st/2nd/3rd person singular and plural here, in preparation for subsequent work on regular verbs.

cm 5/2

être

Worksheet

Être

49

3 C'est moi!

Students match the subject with the correct part of the verb.

Solution:
1 *g*, 2 *h*, 3 *d*, 4 *c*, 5 *i*, 6 *a*, 7 *f*, 8 *e*, 9 *b*

49 AfL

4 Des photos

a Students complete the comments on the photos with parts of *être*. This can be done orally or by writing the complete part of *être*. Remind students of the spread objective relating to *être* and use this for peer assessment. Agree the criteria for success.

Solution:
1 *Vous êtes*, 2 *je suis*, 3 *Tu es*, 4 *Nous sommes*,
5 *je suis*, 6 *Il est*, 7 *Ils sont*

b As extension, students complete a description of the final picture. Encourage them to give as much information as possible using prior knowledge.

Solution (possible):
Rosaline est Claude le clown. Il est (très) amusant. Coralie est un perroquet. Elle est splendide (et un peu amusante). Les filles sont fantastiques. (Tu trouves?)

For further extension, the most able could imagine that their friends (and family) are going to a fancy dress party. They write four or five sentences to describe what they are wearing and give some opinions, e.g.

Mon ami ... un dragon. Il ... horrible.
Ma copine ...
Les garçons ...
Les filles ... Elles ...

Tricolore 1 Teacher's Notes

5D Ton anniversaire, c'est quand?

149 Au choix

4 Notre famille

gia 1 p13

Using the verb *être* – to be
This provides further practice of *être*.

Worksheet

Plenaries (pages 48–49)

1 In pairs or small groups, students write down as many words as possible with accents on them. They discuss ways of remembering which accent to use and how it affects pronunciation.

2 In pairs or groups, students discuss different techniques they might use for learning verbs, then pool their results and discuss which they find most useful.

5D Ton anniversaire, c'est quand? pages 50–51

- Talk about birthday dates and presents
- Use adjectives to add interest

Grammaire	Stratégies	Phonétique
• Use adjectives (singular and plural)	• Getting adjectives right	• The letters 'ui'

Resources

Audio: 1 *L'anniversaire de Marc*, or CD track 25
Copymasters: None
Worksheets: Starters and plenaries

Interactive activity: None
Ph The letters 'ui', or CD 2, track 26
PowerPoint: None
Grammar in Action: p14

Worksheet

Starters (pages 50–51)

1 **5-4-3-2-1** Display a list of words in random order and ask students to find groups of 5, 4, 3, 2, 1 similar words. Students could record their answers on a pre-printed grid (see online worksheet) and these can then be checked by asking individual students to read out a group of words.

Suggestion:

février, avril, août, octobre, novembre

trois, huit, douze, quinze

mon, ma, mes

lundi, samedi

quand

2 **C'est quel mois?** Display the following text on the board, or print it out (see online worksheet). Students match up the two parts, writing down each number and the corresponding letter. This can be checked by the teacher randomly selecting students to answer.

Exemple: 1f	
1 la rentrée	a *juin*
2 la fête nationale	b *décembre*
3 Noël	c *janvier*
4 la fête des Rois	d *juillet*
5 la fête de la musique	e *mai*
6 la fête des Mères	f *septembre*

Solution:
1 *f*, **2** *d*, **3** *b*, **4** *c*, **5** *a*, **6** *e*

Introduction

C'est quand, ton anniversaire?

First teach orally how to ask and reply about birthday dates. Then ask a few students *C'est quand, ton anniversaire?*

Eventually develop this into a chain game where each person asks someone else the date of their birthday.

🔊 50

1 L'anniversaire de Marc

This conversation is used initially for listening comprehension and then as a model for three dialogues which students practise in pairs. Explain *une raquette de tennis* if necessary.

Solution:
1 *a*, **2** *c*, **3** *b*

🔊 CD 2 Track 25

L'anniversaire de Marc

- Salut, Marc!
- Salut, Claire!
- C'est quand ton anniversaire?
- C'est aujourd'hui, le premier février.
- Ah! Bon anniversaire. Quel âge as-tu?
- Aujourd'hui, j'ai treize ans.
- Qu'est-ce que tu as reçu comme cadeaux?
- J'ai reçu un tee-shirt et une raquette de tennis.
- Il est de quelle couleur, le tee-shirt?
- Il est vert.
- Et la raquette?
- Elle est noire.

Tricolore 1 Teacher's Notes 73

5D Ton anniversaire, c'est quand?

Un sondage

Conduct a birthday survey to see how many students have their birthday in each month and whether any two or more students have a birthday on the same day. Students could work in groups and then report back the results for their group to the class as a whole, e.g.

Dans notre groupe, il y a (number) personnes qui ont un anniversaire au mois de ... , etc.

Or students could work in pairs to find out the date of their partner's birthday and could then report back this information to a group leader or the teacher, e.g.

Robert, c'est quand, ton anniversaire?

C'est le 18 janvier.

Qui a un anniversaire au mois de janvier?

L'anniversaire de Robert est le 18 janvier.

The results could be put on a bar graph or database, showing the distribution of birthdays throughout the 12 months. This could be done using ICT.

J'ai reçu ...

A chain game with an ever-increasing list could be played using vocabulary for presents. These could include classroom items, pets and other vocabulary learnt earlier.

This activity uses the perfect tense, but it can be treated purely as a vocabulary item. Further examples are given in *Unité* 10, but the perfect tense is not taught systematically until Stage 2.

50   AfL

2 Inventez des conversations

Students read the conversation based on the previous activity, then they make up further conversations, changing some details. They can use the suggestions in the coloured boxes or ones of their own choosing. The previous chain game is good preparation for this. These conversations provide a good opportunity for peer assessment. Review the spread objectives and agree assessment criteria.

Interactive activity

Bon anniversaire

50

3 Des cadeaux de Noël

Students match up written descriptions with packages. Remind students about using cognates to work out the meaning of a text.

> **Solution:**
>
> **1** C, **2** A, **3** D, **4** E, **5** B

51

4 Merci pour les cadeaux

a Students choose the appropriate adjective ending.

> **Solution:**
>
> **1** *amusants*, **2** *content*, **3** *intéressant*, **4** *contente*, **5** *petits*, **6** *utiles*, **7** *mignonne*, **8** *nouveau*

b As extension, students write about presents they have received. Encourage them to use previous knowledge and include adjectives and opinions.

As further extension, students could work in pairs and note down the answers they hear.

Student 1: *Comme cadeau de Noël, j'ai reçu (+ noun + adjective). Et toi?*

Student 2: *Moi, j'ai reçu (+ noun + adjective). Et comme cadeau d'anniversaire?*

Student 1: *Comme cadeau d'anniversaire, j'ai reçu (+ noun + adjective). Et toi?*

Student 2: *Moi, j'ai reçu (+ noun + adjective).*

Then change partners and list different presents (a bit like a speed-dating activity).

51 Dossier-langue

Using adjectives (singular and plural)

Briefly revise adjectives previously taught, e.g. colours, *petit*, *grand*. Teach *content* and *nouveau/nouvelle*. This *Dossier-langue* revises and summarises the agreement of adjectives, including some irregulars. Remind students what an adjective is by writing examples on the board and asking *Trouvez des adjectifs*, e.g.

Les perruches sont bleues.

Les chevaux sont grands.

Les souris sont petites.

Students could reply orally or could underline the adjective. Then go through the *Dossier-langue*, pronouncing the examples so that students realise that the final *-s* is not pronounced.

51

5 Cherche des adjectifs

Remind students about the plural endings, e.g.

Quand l'adjectif est au pluriel, il y a un -s ou un -x à la fin du mot.

> **Solution:**
>
> **1** (possible examples on SB page 51) *amusants, blancs, blanches, bons, bonnes, français, françaises, grands, grandes, mignonnes, nouveaux, nouvelles, petits, utiles*
>
> **2** *blanche, bonne, contente, française, grande, intéressante, mignonne, nouvelle, petite, utile*

74   Tricolore 1 Teacher's Notes

5E Des cadeaux pour tout le monde

51 Stratégies

Getting adjectives right

This is a grammar memorisation strategy. Encourage students to learn irregular adjectives in phrases, preferably ones they have invented themselves.

gia 1 p14

Singular and plural – nouns and adjectives

This provides additional practice and consolidation of the singular and plural and could be used by students working independently.

Interactive activity

The letters 'ui'

51 Phonétique

The letters 'ui'

A full explanation of the *'ui'* sound is given on *kerboodle!*, together with interactive practice which includes differentiating between words that are spelt with *'ui'* but do not contain the same sound (e.g. *qui, guitare*).

a Say the word *huit* with the appropriate gesture (drawing a number 8 in the air). Students repeat the word with the same gesture. Then read out the other words with students repeating each one. The words are also included on the recording for optional use (part **a**).

Parts **b** and **c** can be used for further practice.

b Ask students to listen and repeat the words they hear. Then display the words **a** *puis*, **b** *fruit*, **c** *cuisine*, **d** *je suis*, **e** *juillet*, **f** *traduis* for students to match (**b**, **d**, **f**, **e**, **a**, **c**).

c Students listen to the silly sentence and note down how many times they hear the *'ui'* sound (4). They can then repeat the sentence to help them remember this sound.

For further practice, write some additional words on the board to check that students recognise the link between spelling and pronunciation e.g. *nuit, biscuit, lui.*

CD 2 Track 26

The letters 'ui'

Écoutez et répétez:
a huit, cuisine, suis
b fruit, je suis, traduis, juillet, puis, cuisine
c Je suis dans la cuisine avec huit fruits!

Worksheet

Plenaries (pages 50–51)

1 Using a spider diagram with the word *Anniversaire* in the middle (see online worksheet), students note down as many French words as possible to do with birthdays. This could include days, months, dates, presents, people, likes, dislikes, etc.

2 Conduct a mid-unit review. Ask: How's it going so far? What over the first half of the unit has proved most difficult/easiest? Where do you think your personal improvement has been? What is still a problem? What 'repair strategies' need putting in place?

5E Des cadeaux pour tout le monde   pages 52–53

- Use wider vocabulary for some more presents
- Use some higher numbers and prices

Grammaire	Stratégies	Phonétique
• Numbers	• Preparing for listening	• The letters 'ille'

Resources

Audio: 1 *Vous cherchez un cadeaux*; **4a** *La tombola*; *C'est combien?*, or CD 2, tracks 27, 29 and 30
Copymasters: 5/3 *Les numéros*
Worksheets: Starters and plenaries; *C'est combien?* (R, S)

Interactive activity: Preparing for listening (Strat)
Ph The letters 'ille', or CD 2, track 28
PowerPoint: None
Grammar in Action: None

Worksheet

Starters (pages 52–53)

1 *C'est masculin ou féminin?* Display the following words in random order, or say the words and ask students to hold up their *masculin* or *féminin* cards.

Masculin		Féminin	
père	stylo	mère	jupe
frère	livre	sœur	calculatrice
lecteur MP3	cinéma	cuisine	chaussette
lapin	sac	souris	trousse

2 **Revise numbers up to 70.** Play some number games e.g. *Onze*, Fizz-Buzz and Backwards Bingo and/or others from TB page xvi.

Tricolore 1 Teacher's Notes   **75**

5E Des cadeaux pour tout le monde

📖 52

Idées cadeaux

Begin with plenty of oral work based on the items pictured.

📖 🔊 52

1 Vous cherchez un cadeau?

Students listen to the recording and note down the letter for each of the eight items mentioned.

> **Solution:**
> **1** J, **2** A, **3** N, **4** I, **5** C, **6** M, **7** F, **8** O

> 🔊 **CD 2 Track 27**
>
> **Vous cherchez un cadeau?**
> C'est l'anniversaire d'un ami? Vous cherchez un cadeau un peu spécial? Nous avons sélectionné pour vous un grand choix de cadeaux de toutes sortes:
> 1 Pour les enfants, il y a des chaussettes amusantes dans toutes les couleurs.
> 2 Pour les jeunes à l'école, le matériel scolaire est nécessaire et utile mais ça peut être amusant aussi. Nous avons, par exemple, une trousse avec un cahier et un stylo dans des couleurs très jolies.
> 3 Pour les personnes qui aiment le soleil, achetez des lunettes de soleil – très jolies et très utiles aussi.
> 4 Pour les jeunes qui aiment les vêtements, il y a des casquettes de tous les styles.
> 5 Pour les sportifs, il y a une montre sport qui est vraiment fantastique.
> 6 Pour toutes les personnes qui aiment lire, il y a un grand choix de livres de poche.
> 7 Pour les jeunes filles, il y a des bracelets en métal argenté. Très chic, non?
> 8 Et si vous n'avez pas encore trouvé un cadeau, pourquoi ne pas acheter des billets pour le cinéma? Bonne idée, non?

📖 52

2 Les cadeaux

This presents the written form of each gift. Students should note down the letter for each item listed.

> **Solution:**
> **1** P, **2** K, **3** O, **4** F, **5** B, **6** I, **7** G, **8** J, **9** A, **10** L, **11** D, **12** M, **13** N, **14** C, **15** H, **16** E

Interactive activity

The letters 'ille'

📖 🔊 53 Phonétique

The letters 'ille'

A full explanation of the 'ille' sound is given on *kerboodle!*, together with interactive practice which includes recognising words containing the sound.

a Say the word *bille* with the appropriate gesture (flicking a marble). Students repeat the word with the same gesture. Then read out the other words with students repeating each one. Point out the exceptions and practise those, without the gesture. The words are also included on the recording for optional use (part **a**).

Parts **b** and **c** can be used for further practice of the 'ille' sound.

b Ask students to listen and repeat the words they hear. Then display the words **a** *famille*, **b** *juillet*, **c** *Camille*, **d** *gorille*, **e** *billet* for students to match (b, d, e, a, c).

c Students listen to the silly sentence and note down how many times they hear the sound (4). They can then repeat the sentence to help them remember this sound.

> 🔊 **CD 2 Track 28**
>
> **The letters 'ille'**
> Écoutez et répétez:
> a bille, juillet, billet, fille, famille
>   Des exceptions: mille, tranquille, ville
> b juillet, gorille, billet, famille, Camille
> c La jeune fille de la famille Guille mange une glace à la vanille.

📖 53 Dossier-langue

Numbers

This item presents the numbers 70–100 and numbers over 100. If appropriate for the class, explain that there is no -s on *cent* when combined with other numbers (e.g. *deux-cents*, but *deux-cent-cinquante*). There are some questions to help students remember the different combinations of the numbers 70–100.

You could also ask these questions: Which numbers end in *-ante*? (40, 50, 60) What is the equivalent in English? (*-ty*) Which numbers below 100 contain the word *et*? (21, 31, 41, 51, 61, 71)

To provide further practice in working out the meaning of new words, refer students back to the tips on SB page 47, then ask the following questions:

What does the word *poche* mean?

Why does it occur in number 12?

Find any four plural nouns in the list of presents. How can you tell they are plural?

Say them aloud – is the final letter sounded?

> **Solution:**
> **plural nouns:** *billets, bracelets, chaussettes, lunettes, tennis* (NB different from the others because singular also ends in -s)

Finally ask students to look at the list of presents and spot the words which are written the same or almost the same as in English (cognates and near-cognates). Read out the list of words below – students should see how different they sound in each language. The list could be displayed so students can compare the written and spoken word.

ballon, foot, cinéma, bracelets, métal, chic, fantaisie, collection, spécial, danse, jean, sport, parfum, tennis

5E Des cadeaux pour tout le monde

53

3 Un cadeau idéal

a Students choose an appropriate gift for each person. First ask for suggestions and write these on the board. The task could then be completed in writing.

Solution:
1 M, 2 B, 3 L, 4 D, 5 H, 6 N, 7 P (L)

b As extension, students write which present they choose for themselves and why. Encourage them to use previous knowledge of French.

c As further extension, they make up three more sentences like those in part a.

Memory game

At a suitable point, the class could play a memory game. They look at the selection of gifts in *Idées cadeaux*, close their books and try to recall as many items as possible. To help jog memories, write the initial letter of the items on the board.

Numbers 0–100

Use some of the number games to revise numbers 0–70 (see Starters). Teach 71–100 using the *Dossier-langue* item above and practise them using number games, e.g. *Continue!, Comptez comme ça!, Effacez!* (TB page xvii).

53 Stratégies

Preparing for listening

This listening strategy can be presented before doing task 4. Remind students that other clues they could look out for include pictures, titles and the example.

53

4 La tombola

a Check that students can recognise and name the prizes illustrated. They then listen to the recording and match the numbers they hear with each prize.

Solution:
1 une tablette, 2 un stylo, 3 une trousse, 4 des crayons, 5 une carte cadeau, 6 une calculatrice, 7 un poisson rouge, 8 un classeur, 9 un tee-shirt, 10 un sac à dos

CD 2 Track 29

La tombola

1 J'ai le quatre-vingt-seize.
2 J'ai le soixante-sept.
3 J'ai le cinquante.
4 J'ai le trente-huit.
5 J'ai le soixante-treize.
6 J'ai le cent.
7 J'ai le soixante-quinze.
8 J'ai le quatre-vingt-dix.
9 J'ai le quatre-vingts.
10 J'ai le quatre-vingt-un.

b As extension, students work in groups to make a poster. This is a good opportunity for previous learners to include items they know in French.

cm 5/3

Les numéros

53 AfL

C'est combien?

This optional item could be used for practice in recognising numbers in prices. Students refer to the presents on SB page 52. Use this task for peer assessment: review the spread objectives and agree the criteria for success.

Solution:
1 H, 2 G, 3 E, 4 J, 5 K, 6 F, 7 C, 8 M, 9 B, 10 O

CD 2 Track 30

C'est combien?

1 – C'est combien?
  – Ça fait 42 euros, la petite bouteille.
2 – C'est combien?
  – 16 euros 50, s'il vous plaît.
3 – Voilà. C'est combien, s'il vous plaît?
  – C'est 19 euros 45.
4 – J'aime bien les rouges. Et toi?
  – Oui, oui, pour ma petite sœur, c'est très bien.
  – Combien?
  – 2 euros 05.
  – Voilà.
5 – Alors, ça, c'est pour mon frère. C'est combien?
  – 17 euros.
6 – Oh, regarde! Très joli, non?
  – Oui, pas mal. Ça coûte combien?
  – 12 euros les trois, c'est tout!
7 – Regarde! Pour le cadeau de Christophe, c'est idéal.
  – Oui, mais c'est combien?
  – 39 euros 90.
  – 39 euros 90 … hmmm! C'est beaucoup!
8 – Pour Noah, c'est bien. Il adore les livres.
  – C'est combien, alors?
  – C'est 4 euros 99.
9 – C'est combien, ça?
  – 5 euro 30. C'est amusant, non?
10 – C'est combien?
  – 8 euros pour une personne.
  – Alors deux, s'il vous plaît.
  – Deux … ça fait 16 euros.
  – 16 euros. Voilà.

Worksheet

Combien?

Worksheet

Plenaries (pages 52–53)

1 Students summarise the different methods they have found for working out the meaning of unfamiliar words (refer back to SB page 47 if necessary). They could make a list of words which fall into each category.

2 Students discuss in pairs or groups the numbers they have learnt on this spread. Which numbers did they find easy/difficult to remember? Why? What tips can they think of to remember the patterns (especially 70–99)?

Tricolore 1 Teacher's Notes **77**

5F Des vêtements   pages 54–55

- Talk about clothes

Grammaire	Stratégies	Phonétique
• Use plural nouns	• Recognising three kinds of words	• None

Resources

Audio: 1 *Lou Leroux. Chic: oui ou non?*, or CD 2, track 31
Copymasters: 5/4 *Des vêtements*, 5/5 *Jeux de vocabulaire*, 5/6 *Des cadeaux et des vêtements*
Worksheets: Starters and plenaries; Recognising three kinds of words (Strat, 1 and 2); *Masculin ou féminin, singulier ou pluriel?* (G)

Interactive activity: *On parle des vêtements* (L)
PowerPoint: *Les vêtements* (V)
Grammar in Action: None

Worksheet

Starters (pages 54–55)

1 *En groupes* Display a list of words in random order or hand this out on paper (see online worksheet). Ask students to put these into 5 groups.

une maison, un appartement, une ferme; le salon, la chambre, la cuisine; rouge, jaune, vert; nous, vous, ils; grand, petit, long

2 *Trouve les paires* Display the following text on the board (see online worksheet), or print it and hand out for individual work. Students should match up the two parts of the sentence. This can be checked by the teacher randomly selecting students to read out each pair.

1 *Aujourd'hui, c'es*	a *sont déguisées.*
2 *Nous*	b *es un fantôme, non?*
3 *Beaucoup de personnes*	c *est déguisé comme un perroquet.*
4 *Un garçon*	d *suis un chat.*
5 *Anne et Suzanne, vous*	e *mardi gras.*
6 *Et toi, Olivier, tu*	f *sommes au club des jeunes.*
7 *Et moi, je*	g *êtes les deux méchantes sœurs.*

Solution:
1 e, **2** f, **3** a, **4** c, **5** g, **6** b, **7** d

Introduction

Precede work on this spread by revising colours and teaching clothes orally, perhaps using the PowerPoint presentation (below) or actual garments or looking up French websites, e.g. www.promod.com. Other sites can be found on Google. Write new clothing vocabulary on the board for a game of *Effacez!*. Students then copy these into their books. Flashcards for clothing can be made by using pictures from magazines or the internet, particularly of well-known personalities. Distribute visuals to students who then describe one or more item of clothing worn by the person illustrated.

Presentation

Les vêtements

🔊 54

1 Lou Leroux. Chic: oui ou non?

This item introduces items of clothing and adjectives. Students listen to the recording and follow the text.

Remind students of similar phrases to *Tu rigoles!* in the poem *Le zoo extraordinaire* on SB page 40.

🔊 CD 2 Track 31

Lou Leroux. Chic: oui ou non?

Narrator Lou Leroux fait beaucoup d'interviews pour la télé. Cette semaine, sa sœur, Léa, et son amie, Charlotte, sont avec Lou. Il choisit attentivement ses vêtements pour être chic!
Narrator jeudi
Aujourd'hui, il porte une chemise noire, un pantalon blanc, une cravate rouge, des chaussettes noires et des baskets blanches. Sa sœur, Léa, porte un pantalon brun et une chemise jaune et Charlotte, son amie, porte un short noir et un tee-shirt blanc.
Narrator vendredi
Lou Leroux Ça va, Léa? Il est chic, mon pull, non?
Léa Tu rigoles!
Narrator Lou adore son pull vert et jaune et son pantalon vert. Avec ça, il porte des chaussettes jaunes et des chaussures marron. Léa est très chic. Elle porte une chemise blanche, une jupe noire et des chaussures noires.
Narrator samedi
Aujourd'hui, Lou et Léa sont au match de foot. Le joueur de foot porte un maillot rouge et blanc et un short noir. Léa porte une robe bleue et blanche et des sandales blanches. Lou porte un jogging gris, une casquette violette, un sweat orange et des tennis blanches. Est-il chic: oui ou non?
Narrator dimanche
Aujourd'hui, Lou est à la maison. Il porte un tee-shirt et son jean favori.
Léa Très bien, Lou!
Charlotte Aujourd'hui, tu es très chic!

78 Tricolore 1 Teacher's Notes

5F Des vêtements

Interactive activity

On parle des vêtements

📖 54

2 Des vêtements

Students complete the list of clothing, perhaps copying them into their vocabulary books.

📖 55 Stratégies

Recognising three kinds of words

Remind students of the different parts of speech. From Lou's story, they have to find 4 nouns, 4 verbs and 4 adjectives. They could work in pairs and do this against the clock, reporting back their findings to the class. Worksheets ws_05F1.Str and ws_05F2.Str can be used for further reinforcement.

Worksheet

Recognising 3 kinds of words (1)

Worksheet

Recognising 3 kinds of words (2)

📖 55 Dossier-langue

Plural nouns

Several plural words have been introduced earlier, but this table summarises the basic plural forms. After students have read through the explanation, ask them to form plurals orally, using known vocabulary, e.g. *un livre, le garçon, la fille, l'appartement, un tee-shirt, une robe,* etc. Emphasise that the plural does not normally sound any different from the singular in French (unlike in English).

In the final part students look at the Lou Leroux story to find four items of clothing which are plural in English, but singular in French.

> **Solution:**
> *un short, un jean, un pantalon, un jogging* (tracksuit bottoms)

Describing clothing

For further practice of the new vocabulary and colours, play a chain game where each student describes one item of clothing that they are wearing and then names another student, e.g.

Je porte des chaussures noires. Philippe.
Je porte un pantalon gris. Suzanne ... etc.

cm 5/4

Des vêtements

📖 55

3 C'est au pluriel?

Students find five words in the plural.

> **Solution:**
> **2** *mes lunettes,* **3** *les baskets,* **5** *des chaussures,* **6** *des jeux,* **8** *des casquettes*

Worksheet

Au pluriel

📖 55   AfL

4 Vrai ou faux?

a Pairwork practice of items of clothing and adjectives. Review objectives and assessment criteria and use this for peer assessment of pronunciation and intonation.

b For this part of the activity, teachers could provide some magazine photos, preferably slightly zany ones, with people wearing an assortment of clothes. Students describe one of the people and their partner guesses who it is. If preferred, this could be group work.

c As extension, students write down their descriptions. This part also includes an element of peer assessment. Students should be guided to look for accurate adjective endings and spellings as well as the content.

Worksheet

Des adjectifs

📖 149 Au choix

5 Les chaussettes de Jacques

cm 5/5

Jeux de vocabulaire

cm 5/6

Des cadeaux et des vêtements

📖 149 Au choix

6 Une lettre illustrée

Worksheet

Plenaries (pages 54–55)

1 Students discuss different techniques they can use to help remember the items of clothing and how to spell them, e.g. visualising the words spelt out in the shape of the item, identifying an item with a particular colour, etc.

2 In small groups, students think of as many adjectives as possible which they have learnt in French (colours, size, appearance etc.).

Tricolore 1 Teacher's Notes   79

5G Les descriptions personnelles

5G Les descriptions personnelles pages 56–57

- Describe yourself and other people

Grammaire	Stratégies	Phonétique
• Use the verb *avoir* (to have)	• Speaking more confidently	• The letters 'eu'

Resources

Audio: 1 *Des photos d'identité*, or CD 2, track 32
Copymasters: 5/7 *Avoir*, 5/8 *Des descriptions*
Worksheets: Starters and plenaries; *Les descriptions personnelles* (W)

Interactive activity: *Des jeunes* (L); *Avoir* (G)
Ph The letters 'eu', or CD 2, track 33
PowerPoint: *Ils sont comment?* (V); *Le verbe avoir* (G)
Grammar in Action: pp15–16

Worksheet

Starters (pages 56–57)

1 *Chaque mot à sa place* Display the following task (see online worksheet). Give students one minute to read and work out the answers, then ask them collectively or randomly to give the number of the box. Answers are in brackets.

Quelle est la bonne case pour chaque mot?

elles (2), noir (4), grand (1), est (5), un pantalon (3)

1	2	3	4	5
petit	je	un short	bleu	suis
gros	il	un sweat	vert	es
énorme	nous	une jupe	brun	sont

2 *Trouve six noms au pluriel* Display the following list of words (see online worksheet) and ask students to find six nouns in the plural. Answers in bold.

gros, **animaux**, dans, sous, **chevaux**, **lunettes**, suis, **baskets**, mars, **chaussettes**, **chaussures**, faux

Introduction

Les descriptions personnelles

First teach personal descriptions orally in class (just colour of eyes and colour, length and style of hair) and get pupils to deduce that the verb *avoir* is used for these personal descriptions. Then ask general questions such as *Qui a les cheveux châtains/blonds?* getting people to put up hands. A class survey could be undertaken: *x élèves ont les cheveux courts; x élèves ont les yeux bleus*, etc.

Presentation

Ils sont comment?

🔊 56

1 Des photos d'identité

Students listen to descriptions and match to the correct person.

Solution:

1 B *Bruno*, 2 A *Marine*, 3 F *Maxime*, 4 D *Sonia*, 5 E *Zac*, 6 C *Julie*

After they have heard the recording and matched speakers to pictures, play it again and discuss why each description does or does not match, e.g. (C) *Elle a les cheveux assez longs, mais roux, pas blonds*, etc. The table presents the written version of the vocabulary for descriptions, much of which is already familiar. Go through the new words and look for cognates, near cognates and ways of remembering the words (e.g. *frisés* is like 'frizzy'). If necessary, give further examples of the invariable adjective *marron*. Note also that *châtain(s)* is semi-invariable – it agrees in number but not gender.

🔊 CD 2 Track 32

Des photos d'identité

1 J'ai les cheveux châtains et les yeux marron.
2 Moi, j'ai les cheveux longs, très longs, et blonds. Et j'ai les yeux bleus.
3 Alors moi, j'ai les cheveux blonds et les yeux bleus. Mais je n'ai pas les cheveux longs. J'ai les cheveux courts et frisés.
4 J'ai les cheveux très courts, noirs et frisés. J'ai les yeux marron et je porte des lunettes.
5 Je ne porte pas de lunettes, contrairement à ma sœur, mais j'ai les cheveux très courts, noirs et frisés, comme elle. J'ai les yeux marron aussi. Aujourd'hui, je porte mon tee-shirt favori – j'adore le foot!
6 Moi, j'ai les yeux verts et les cheveux roux, frisés et assez longs. Je porte des lunettes.

📖 56

2 Une description personnelle

Prepare this activity by getting individuals to describe themselves orally. They could play a chain game where they describe their hair, then pass on to the next person who describes their own eyes, etc. They should then write their description and keep it in their *Dossier personnel*. For more able students this could be developed to include height, garments worn, even likes and dislikes.

Tricolore 1 Teacher's Notes

5G Les descriptions personnelles

📖 56

3 C'est qui?

a This speaking activity is best done in groups, but it can also be done in pairs or as a whole class game. Make sure students know which verb to use for different aspects of description (*avoir* or *être*). Be aware of the danger of unflattering or insensitive descriptions of some students. Limiting to colour and style of hair and eyes should be fairly safe! Building up the description one characteristic at a time gives extra practice in using these constructions.

b As extension, students write a description.
➕ Encourage them to use prior knowledge and make their description both accurate and interesting.

Worksheet
Des descriptions

Interactive activity
Des jeunes

📖 56 Stratégies
Speaking more confidently

Go over this speaking strategy, explaining that students should concentrate on using and practising structures and vocabulary they have learnt. However, more able students should be encouraged to experiment with those structures and adapt what they know in order to develop their language.

Interactive activity
The letters 'eu'

📖 🔊 56 Phonétique
The letters 'eu'

A full explanation of the *'eu'* sound is given on *kerboodle!*, together with interactive practice which includes recognising words containing the sound.

a Say the word *heureux* with the appropriate gesture (a big smile). Students repeat the word with the same gesture. Then read out the other words with students repeating each one. Point out that the *x* in *-eux* makes no difference to the sound. The words are also included on the recording for optional use (part **a**).

Parts **b** and **c** can be used for further practice.

b Ask students to listen and repeat the words they hear. Then display the words **a** *curieux*, **b** *feu d'artifice*, **c** *deux*, **d** *neuf*, **e** *jeu*, **f** *jeudi* for students to match (d, e, b, a, f, c).

c Students listen to the silly sentence and note down how many times they hear the sound (6). They can then repeat the sentence to help them remember this sound.

For further practice, write some additional words on the board to check that students recognise the link between spelling and pronunciation e.g. *bleu, neveu, heureux, affreux*.

🔊 CD 2 Track 33
The letters 'eu'
Écoutez et répétez:
a heureux, jeu, cheveux, yeux
b neuf, jeu, feu d'artifice, curieux, jeudi, deux
c Jeudi, je veux faire un jeu un peu dangereux avec du beurre.

Presentation
Le verbe avoir

Paradigm of *avoir*

Singular paradigm of *avoir*

Using a collection of classroom objects or clothing, revise the singular paradigm of *avoir*, e.g. *Moi, j'ai une gomme, un livre*, etc. Distribute the objects to students and ask *(Nom), qu'est-ce que tu as?* for the reply *J'ai … (une gomme/un livre)*. Then ask another student *Est-ce que (nom) a … (une gomme/un livre)?* for the reply *Oui/Non, il/elle a …* Write the singular paradigm on the board. Alternatively, ask about personal possessions, perhaps including some ridiculous ones for fun using props or homemade flashcards, e.g. *Est-ce que tu as un portable/un ordinateur/un perroquet/une tarentule/un dragon/un éléphant dans ta chambre?*

Plural paradigm of *avoir*

To present the *nous* and *vous* forms, ask four able students to come to the front, and say they represent *la famille Lafitte*. Give each pupil pictures of two animals. Explain to the rest of the class that the Lafittes have lots of pets, and the class have to ask them questions about them, e.g. *Est-ce que vous avez un chien?* The student with the appropriate picture should reply *Oui, nous avons un chien* and show the picture. Add the *nous* and *vous* forms to the paradigm on the board then make up some sentences about the Lafittes, using the *ils* form, e.g. *Ils ont beaucoup d'animaux. Ils ont un chien, un cheval, un chat, des lapins.* Then complete the paradigm on the board. Make up sentences using the present tense of *avoir* and get students to point to the form used and/or to repeat the sentences. Alternatively, make this into a game of *Effacez!* (TB page xvii).

📖 57 Dossier-langue
The verb *avoir* (to have)

This sets out a gapped version of the full paradigm of *avoir*. Students read the message in task **4** then complete the paradigm in their exercise books.

Tricolore 1 Teacher's Notes **81**

5H Écoutez bien

4 Un message de Léa

This message presents all parts of the verb *avoir* and provides the vocabulary for the task which follows.

> **Solution:**
> **5** *adjectifs:* any five from: *longs, blonds, verts, bruns, petit, mignon, blancs, brun, grand, grise, nouveau*
> **4** *animaux:* any four from: *un hamster, deux lapins, un cochon d'Inde, un chien, une chatte*
> **3** *meubles: un lit, une table, une chaise*
> **2** *membres de la famille: des frères, une sœur*
> **1** *appareil électrique: un ordinateur*

This could be followed by pairwork practice, with students talking about their pets, home and room. Able students could then write a similar message, perhaps to send by e-mail to another class in the UK or in France.

5 Chez nous

Students choose the correct part of the verb *avoir* from three options.

> **Solution:**
> **1** *Nous avons,* **2** *nous avons,* **3** *Nous avons,* **4** *vous avez,* **5** *j'ai,* **6** *ma sœur a,* **7** *mes frères ont,* **8** *tu as*

cm 5/7

avoir

6 Un e-mail

Students write an e-mail describing their house and their room. This revises much of what has been learnt in *Unités* 3–5 and can become part of their *Dossier personnel*. This is a good opportunity for AfL. Remind students of the appropriate objectives in all three units and agree the criteria for success.

7 Une conversation

a   As consolidation of the work on *avoir* and descriptions, students talk in pairs about themselves. Encourage them to use a range of structures and put in adjectives where possible.

b   As extension, students make notes on their partner's description then write a summary.

Review the spread objectives and assessment criteria and use these tasks for peer assessment.

cm 5/8

Des descriptions

gia 1 pp15–16

Using the verb *avoir* – to have

These pages could be used for further practice of *avoir*.

Worksheet

Plenaries (pages 56–57)

1   Display a spider diagram with *MOI* at the centre (see online worksheet). Students fill in as many French words as they can in different categories. This could be done as a team game to see who can get the most entries in a set time.

2   Students should discuss tips for remembering the verb *avoir*, e.g. writing it out in a table and highlighting key differences from other verbs.

5H Écoutez bien   pages 58–59

- Develop and practise your listening skills

Grammaire	Stratégies	Phonétique
• None	• Listening with focus	• None

Resources
Audio: **1** *Trouve le bon mot;* **2** *C'est quelle image?;* **3** *C'est quel mot?;* **4** *Questions ou réponses?;* **5** *L'histoire de Suzanne,* or CD 2, tracks 34, 35, 36, 37 and 38 **Copymasters:** 5/9 *Tu comprends?,* 5/10 *Sommaire* **Worksheets:** Starters and plenaries **e-book:** *Une année de fêtes*	**Interactive activity:** Classroom commands (V) **Video:** *L'anniversaire de Manon* **Grammar in Action:** None

Tricolore 1 Teacher's Notes

5H Écoutez bien

Worksheet

Starters (pages 58–59)

1 *5-4-3-2-1* Display a list of words in random order and ask students to find groups of 5, 4, 3, 2, 1 similar words. Students could record their answers on a pre-printed grid (see online worksheet) and these can then be checked by asking individual students to read out a group of words.

Suggestion: *un pantalon, une chemise, un jean, une jupe, un short; quarante, cinquante, soixante, cent; ton, ta, tes; avons, avez; un lapin*

2 *Trouve les paires* Display the following lists for students to match up, or print these out and give out for individual work (see online worksheet). This can be checked by the teacher randomly selecting students to answer.

Exemple: 1e Un élève,	*c'est … une personne*
1 *un élève*	a *un oiseau*
2 *une souris*	b *une couleur*
3 *mars*	c *un nombre*
4 *blanc*	d *un vêtement*
5 *un perroquet*	e *une personne*
6 *quatre-vingts*	f *un jour*
7 *une cravate*	g *un mois*
8 *dimanche*	h *un animal*

Solution:
1 e, **2** h, **3** g, **4** b, **5** a, **6** c, **7** d, **8** f

🔊 58

1 Trouve le bon mot

This spread concentrates on developing and practising listening skills. Students read through the six words listed, then listen to the recording and write down the letter for each word.

Solution:
1 f, **2** c, **3** a, **4** b, **5** d, **6** e

🔊 CD 2 Track 34

Trouve le bon mot

1 oui, oui
2 livre, livre
3 fille, fille
4 famille, famille
5 ville, ville
6 fils, fils

Ask which letter represents the sound that all these words have in common (*i*). Discuss how this sound is usually spelt in English ('ee' or 'ea').

Refer students also to the phonics items on SB page 12 (*'i', 'y'*), SB page 51 (*'ui'*), SB page 52 (*'ille'*).

🔊 58

2 C'est quelle image?

This task is similar, but uses unfamiliar words. Go through the words and pictures with the students first, perhaps getting them to work out correct pronunciation before you teach it. They should then study the new words and read the listening tip, before listening to the recording.

Solution:
1 D, **2** A, **3** F, **4** B, **5** E, **6** C

🔊 CD 2 Track 35

C'est quelle image?

Exemple – une maison, une maison, un maçon, un maçon
1 un croissant, un croissant
2 la pluie, la pluie
3 un pharmacien, un pharmacien
4 un parapluie, un parapluie
5 une pharmacie, une pharmacie
6 une boisson, une boisson

🔊 58

3 C'est quel mot?

This item demands very careful listening. Two similar words are heard, then one of them is repeated and students have to spot which this is.

Solution:
1 b, **2** b, **3** a, **4** a, **5** b, **6** a

🔊 CD 2 Track 36

C'est quel mot?

1 je, j'ai – j'ai
2 j'ai, j'aime – j'aime
3 je, j'aime – je
4 trois, toi – trois
5 sous, sur – sur
6 sœur, sur – sœur

🔊 58

4 Questions ou réponses?

In this task the emphasis is on tone of voice. Students have to decide if they hear a question or a reply. Some teachers might like to play this item again, this time for dictation.

Solution:
1 Q, **2** Q, **3** R, **4** Q, **5** R, **6** Q, **7** R, **8** Q, **9** R

🔊 CD 2 Track 37

Questions ou réponses?

1 Comment t'appelles-tu?
2 Tu as quel âge?
3 J'ai deux frères.
4 Tu as des frères?
5 Je m'appelle Alex.
6 C'est le quatorze juillet?
7 C'est le quatorze juillet.
8 Le chat est noir?
9 Il est noir et blanc.

Tricolore 1 Teacher's Notes   83

5H Écoutez bien

🔊 58   AfL

5 L'histoire de Suzanne

a Students read through the tips, then listen to the recording three times, each time answering the questions. Any or all of the three stages can be used as peer assessment. After looking again at the spread objective, students should agree the criteria for success (which might be slightly different each time).

b As extension, students write a summary of the story, listening again if necessary.

As an alternative to part **b**, students could listen to the recording and transcribe it. Transcription is not easy, but by now this is familiar vocabulary: *Écoute plusieurs fois et écris l'histoire de Suzanne.*

A further extension task is to give a dictation based on the text.

> **Solution:**
> 1 Suzanne's birthday
> 2 **a** No, **b** All her presents were books about the same group
> 3 **c** 29th January, **d** 14, **e** pop (singing) group

CD 2 Track 38

L'histoire de Suzanne

Le 29 janvier, c'est l'anniversaire de Suzanne. Elle a quatorze ans.
L'après-midi, ses amis et moi, nous arrivons à la maison avec des cadeaux et des cartes. Suzanne aime beaucoup le groupe Citron Pressé. C'est son groupe favori, alors moi, j'ai un nouveau livre sur le groupe pour elle. Mais quel désastre! Les cadeaux de tous ses amis sont aussi des livres sur le groupe. Pauvre Suzanne! Maintenant, elle a beaucoup de livres, mais tous au même sujet!

58 Stratégies

Listening with focus

This listening strategy summarises the tips with each activity on the page.

cm 5/9

Tu comprends?

Interactive activity

Rue Danton: L'anniversaire

Interactive activity

Vocabulaire de classe (5)

Presentation

Une année de fêtes

Worksheet

Une année de fêtes

59 cm 5/10

Sommaire

A summary of the main language and structures of the unit, also provided on copymaster for reference.

Interactive activity

Vocabulaire (5)

Interactive activity

Quiz – Unités 4 et 5

Worksheet

Plenaries (pages 58–59)

1 Students think about how they listen for gist in understanding texts with unfamiliar language. Discuss useful strategies, e.g. similarity to English, context, type of word, need to know, etc.

2 **Think, pair and share.** In pairs, students choose one of the objectives for the unit (these could be allocated so that they are all covered), they discuss it for five minutes in pairs, then they share their findings with the class.

84   Tricolore 1 Teacher's Notes

Unité 5 Consolidation and assessment

Épreuves Unité 5

These worksheets can be used for an informal test of listening, reading and writing or for extra practice, as required. For general notes on the *Épreuves*, see TB page xv.

cm 5/11

Écouter

A Les vêtements

Students listen and write the correct letter.

> Solution:
> **1** e, **2** d, **3** a, **4** f, **5** c, **6** g, **7** b
> (mark /6)

> CD 2 Track 39
> **Les vêtements**
> 1 J'ai un short. Voici mon short.
> 2 Je porte un jogging. J'aime bien ce jogging.
> 3 Sylvie porte une robe. Elle est jolie, la robe.
> 4 Marc a une cravate. La cravate est dans sa poche.
> 5 – Où sont mes baskets?
>   – Tes baskets sont ici.
> 6 Lucie porte une jupe. La jupe est grise.
> 7 – Où sont mes chaussettes?
>   – Voici tes chaussettes.

B C'est quelle date?

Students listen and write the correct letter.

> Solution:
> **1** c, **2** b, **3** g, **4** f, **5** a, **6** d, **7** e
> (mark /6)

> CD 2 Track 40
> 1 – Richard, c'est quand, ta fête?
>   – Ma fête, c'est le trois avril.
>   – Ah bon, la Saint-Richard, c'est le trois avril.
> 2 – Pâques, c'est quand cette année?
>   – Le dimanche de Pâques, c'est le 29 mars.
>   – Alors, c'est le 29 mars.
> 3 – Tu vas au match de football, Lille contre Strasbourg?
>   – Je ne sais pas. C'est quand?
>   – C'est le trois octobre.
>   – Le trois octobre, alors oui, je veux bien.
> 4 – Il y a un bon concert à La Rochelle, tu sais.
>   – Ah bon, c'est quand?
>   – C'est le 13 novembre.
>   – Le 13 novembre? Bon, je vais voir.
> 5 – Isabelle, c'est quand ta fête?
>   – La Sainte-Isabelle, c'est le 22 février.
>   – Ah bon, alors, ta fête, c'est le 22 février.
> 6 – C'est quand, le film sur le Canada?
>   – C'est le cinq juin.
>   – Ah bon, le cinq juin. Et c'est au club des jeunes, non?
>   – Oui, c'est ça.
> 7 – Quelle est la date de ton anniversaire?
>   – Mon anniversaire? C'est le 18 février.
>   – Le 18 février, bon.

C Des cadeaux

Students listen to spot the correct presents and then write the adjective describing each one.

> Solution:
> **1** a *petit*, **2** b *vert*, **3** b *rouge*, **4** b *amusant*,
> **5** a *mignon*
> (mark /8) 1 mark for correct present, 1 mark for adjective; ignore misspellings

> CD 2 Track 41
> **Des cadeaux**
> 1 J'ai reçu un petit lapin. Il est très petit, le lapin.
> 2 Alors moi, j'ai reçu un sac de sport, un sac de sport vert. J'adore le sport et le vert, c'est ma couleur préférée.
> 3 Et moi, j'ai reçu des chaussures, des chaussures rouges. J'aime bien la couleur rouge.
> 4 J'ai reçu une bande dessinée. C'est très amusant. J'adore les bandes dessinées.
> 5 – Alors moi, j'ai reçu un chien. Il est mignon, mon chien. J'adore les chiens.
>   – Oui, il est très mignon.

cm 5/12

Lire

A Pierre

Students read the description and colour the picture.

> Solution:
> *red T-shirt, green jumper, grey trousers, blue socks, black shoes, yellow cap, brown sports bag*
> (mark /6)

B Les fêtes

Students read the sentences and find the pairs.

> Solution:
> **1** b, **2** e, **3** a, **4** d, **5** f, **6** c, **7** g, **8** h
> (mark /7)

C Une conversation

Students match the questions and answers.

> Solution:
> **1** d, **2** g (allow h), **3** h (allow g), **4** f, **5** b, **6** e,
> **7** c, **8** a
> (mark /7)

Unité 5 Consolidation and assessment

cm 5/13

Écrire et grammaire

A C'est quand?
Students complete the date.

Solution:
1 avril, **2** janvier, **3** février, **4** juillet, **5** décembre
(mark /4)

B Une liste de cadeaux
Students choose suitable gifts for everyone.

Solution:
Give one mark each for any five of the following presents that are reasonably appropriate and spelt recognisably:
une cravate, un pull, un livre, des baskets, une raquette de tennis, un tee-shirt, un jeu vidéo, un sac de sport
(mark /5)

C À la maison
Students complete the sentences.

Solution:
1 avons, **2** ont, **3** avez, **4** sont, **5** est, **6** sommes
(mark /5)

D Un message électronique
Students write their own replies.

Solution:
(mark /6) 2 marks for correct date, 2 marks for each present correctly described

Rappel 2

60–61

This section can be used at any point after *Unité* 5 for revision and consolidation. It provides reading and writing activities which are self-instructional and can be used by students working individually for homework or during cover lessons.

60

1 Un jeu 5-4-3-2-1

Solution:
5 blanc, jaune, noir, rouge, vert
4 un cochon d'Inde, un hamster, une souris, un lapin
3 une cravate, une jupe, une robe
2 grand, mignon
1 Pâques

60

2 Chasse à l'intrus

Solution:
1 une carte – les autres sont des choses à manger
2 une chaussure – les autres sont des animaux
3 un lapin – les autres sont des vêtements
4 une cravate – les autres sont des affaires d'école
5 bleu – les autres sont des mois
6 méchant – les autres sont des jours de la semaine
7 mardi – les autres sont des nombres
8 petit – les autres sont des jours de la semaine
9 le perroquet – les autres sont des pièces
10 ma maison – les autres sont des membres de la famille

60

3 Masculin, féminin

Solution:

masculin	féminin
un cadeau	une casquette
un gâteau	une jupe
un oiseau	une gomme
	une salle
	une trousse
	une ville

60

4 Ça commence par un 'c'

Solution:

une calculatrice	des crayons
un cartable	des chaussettes
une carte d'anniversaire	des chaussures
une casquette	un cheval
un CD	un chien
un classeur	une chaise
un cochon d'Inde	une cage

61

5 L'année en France

Solution:
1 janvier, **2** juin, **3** mars, avril, **4** avril, **5** mai, **6** février, mars, **7** juillet, **8** décembre, **9** août, **10** septembre, **11** octobre, **12** novembre

Tricolore 1 Teacher's Notes

Unité 5 Consolidation and assessment

61

6 Beaucoup de cadeaux

Solution:
1 *Le pull est vert.*
2 *Le sac est gris.*
3 *La casquette est rouge.*
4 *Les chaussettes sont jaunes.*
5 *Les baskets sont noires.*
6 *Les chaussures sont blanches.*
7 *Les hamsters sont bruns.*
8 *Le perroquet est bleu, vert et jaune.*
9 *La trousse est bleue.*
10 *Les stylos sont rouges.*

61

7 Questions et réponses

Solution:
a 1 *ton*, 2 *ton*, 3 *ta*, 4 *ta*, 5 *tes*, 6 *tes*
b a *ma*, b *Mes*, c *Mon*, d *mes*, e *Ma*, f *Mon*
c 1 *c*, 2 *f*, 3 *e*, 4 *a*, 5 *b*, 6 *d*

61

8 Charles

Solution:
1 *Je suis*, 2 *Mon père est, ma mère est*, 3 *J'ai*, 4 *J'ai*, 5 *Mon frère a*, 6 *Il est*, 7 *Ma sœur a*, 8 *Elle est*, 9 *Nous avons*, 10 *Ils sont, ils sont*, 11 *Mes amis sont*, 12 *Nous sommes*

Au choix

148 Au choix

1 Les mois de l'année

In this short task, students write out several different months.

Solution:
1 *mars*, 2 *avril*, 3 *août*, 4 *novembre*, 5 *janvier*, 6 *décembre*, 7 *mai*, 8 *septembre*

148 Au choix

2 Une année en désordre

Students unscramble the greetings/festivals and match them to their date.

Solution:
1 *bonne année* – c
2 *la fête des Rois* – f
3 *poisson d'avril* – b
4 *la fête des Mères* – e
5 *la fête nationale* – a
6 *joyeux Noël* – d

148 Au choix

3 Des annonces

Students read material based on events linked to festivals and decide whether the statements are true or false. As an extension activity, students could correct the false sentences.

Solution:
1 *faux. C'est à Pâques.* 2 *vrai*, 3 *faux. C'est vendredi, samedi et lundi.* 4 *faux. C'est le 14 juillet.* 5 *vrai*, 6 *vrai*, 7 *faux. C'est le 17, le 18 et le 19 décembre.*

149 Au choix

4 Notre famille

This task provides further practice of the different parts of *être*.

Solution:
1 *est*, 2 *suis*, 3 *est*, 4 *est*, 5 *est*, 6 *es*, 7 *est*, 8 *est*, 9 *sommes*, 10 *sont*, 11 *sont*

149 Au choix

5 Les chaussettes de Jacques

Students write out the missing words in the picture strip.

Solution:
1 *Bon*, 2 *cadeau*, 3 *merci*, 4 *anniversaire*, 5 *beaucoup*, 6 *gentil*, 7 *rien*, 8 *petit*, 9 *chaussettes*, 10 *rouge*, 11 *aime*

149 Au choix

6 Une lettre illustrée

a Students complete the 'thank you' letter by writing the names of the presents (and colours, if possible).

Solution:
1 *les lunettes de soleil rouges*, 2 *un tee-shirt bleu*, 3 *un short blanc*, 4 *une casquette rouge*, 5 *une raquette de tennis verte*, 6 *des chaussettes bleues*, 7 *deux balles de tennis jaunes*, 8 *une (petite) souris blanche*

b For extension, students write a similar letter, ⊕ describing four presents received.

Copy masters

cm 5/1

Des dates

In this information-gap task, students have to find out details about dates and events.

cm 5/2

être

This provides further practice in using *être* and can be used at any time after the full paradigm has been presented.

Unité 5 Consolidation and assessment

> **Solution:**
> **1** *Où est tout le monde?*
>   **1** *êtes*, **2** *suis*, **3** *est*, **4** *sommes*, **5** *sont*, **6** *est*, **7** *est*
> **2** *Questions*
>   **1** *sommes*, **2** *est*, **3** *es*, **4** *sont*, **5** *Es*, **6** *est*, **7** *êtes*, **8** *est*
> **3** *Réponses*
>   **a** *suis*, **b** *suis*, **c** *est*, **d** *sont*, **e** *est*, **f** *est*, **g** *est*, **h** *sommes*
> **4** *Trouve les paires*
>   **1** *g*, **2** *f*, **3** *b*, **4** *d*, **5** *a*, **6** *e*, **7** *h*, **8** *c*

cm 5/3

Les numéros

These five tasks practise numbers.

1 C'est la loterie

> **Solution:**
> **1** *i*, **2** *f*, **3** *b*, **4** *e*, **5** *l*, **6** *j*, **7** *m*, **8** *a*, **9** *g*, **10** *c*

2 Un message secret

> **Solution:**
> ~~sept~~ *rendez-vous* ~~onze~~ *ce* ~~treize~~ *soir* ~~douze~~ *au* ~~quatorze~~ *café* ~~seize~~

3 Continue comme ça

For an extension activity, students could make up similar sequences.

> **Solution:**
> **1** *huit*, **2** *sept*, **3** *douze*, **4** *quarante*, **5** *cent*, **6** *quatre-vingts*

4 Écris le bon nombre

> **Solution:**
> **1** *soixante-trois*, **2** *quatorze*, **3** *quatre-vingt-huit*, **4** *quinze*, **5** *quarante*

5 Calcule

> **Solution:**
> **1** *neuf*, **2** *quinze*, **3** *treize*, **4** *seize*, **5** *dix-huit*, **6** *onze*, **7** *sept*, **8** *cent*, **9** *douze*, **10** *huit*

cm 5/4

Des vêtements

These mini-flashcards can be used here (to practise clothing) or later (to practise adjectives). See TB page xix for suggestions for use.

cm 5/5

Jeux de vocabulaire

This consists of four vocabulary tasks based on the themes of the unit so far and could be used as an alternative to the other tasks by students who need more support.

> **Solution:**
> **1** *Mots mêlés*
>
> (word search grid)
>
> **2** *Sept vêtements*
>   **1** *chaussettes*, **2** *casquette*, **3** *baskets*, **4** *short*, **5** *jupe*, **6** *pantalon*, **7** *chaussures*
> **3** *Qu'est-ce qu'on dit?*
>   **1** *d*, **2** *a*, **3** *e*, **4** *f*, **5** *b*, **6** *c*
> **4** *Un jour important*
>   **1** *anniversaire*, **2** *cadeau*, **3** *gentil*, **4** *cravate*, **5** *Merci*, **6** *beaucoup*, **7** *rien*

cm 5/6

Des cadeaux et des vêtements

This copymaster provides consolidation for all students.

1 Questions et réponses

This involves matching questions and replies.

> **Solution:**
> **1** *f*, **2** *d*, **3** *a*, **4** *e*, **5** *b*, **6** *c*

2 Conversations au choix

This provides a framework for a short conversation and could be used in pairs in class or written out for homework.

3 Qu'est-ce qu'il y a dans la valise?

This provides practice of the plural forms of clothing and colours.

> **Solution:**
> *Il y a deux tee-shirts, deux pulls, deux pantalons, deux cravates, deux chaussures et deux jupes.*

cm 5/7

avoir

This provides further practice of *avoir*.

1 *avoir* – to have

Students complete the paradigm for future reference.

Tricolore 1 Teacher's Notes

Unité 5 Consolidation and assessment

> **Solution:**
> **2** *En classe*
>   **1** e, **2** f, **3** d, **4** a, **5** c, **6** b
> **3** *Des questions et des réponses*
>   **A 1** *as*, **2** *as*, **3** *ont*, **4** *a*, **5** *avez*, **6** *a*
>   **B a** *ont*, **b** *a*, **c** *a*, **d** *avons*, **e** *ai*, **f** *ai*
>   **C 1** *e*, **2** *f*, **3** *a*, **4** *b*, **5** *d*, **6** *c*
> **4** *Mots croisés*
>   *Horizontalement:* **1** *avons*, **3** *ai*, **5** *tu*, **7** *a*, **8** *elles*
>   *Verticalement:* **1** *avez*, **2** *ont*, **4** *ils*, **6** *il*, **7** *as*

---

cm 5/8   AfL

Des descriptions

This is a writing frame for students to complete and retain as part of their *Dossier personnel*. It would be suitable for peer assessment, students deciding if they think their partner's description of themselves is correct. Review the spread objectives and agree the assessment criteria. As a follow-up students could describe each other.

cm 5/9

Tu comprends?

1 C'est quand?

This worksheet provides independent listening practice. The first task could be used at any time after learning the months and the date.

> **Solution:**
> **1** *août*, **2** *juin*, **3** *avril*, **4** *mai*, **5** *mars*, **6** *octobre*

CD 2 Track 42

C'est quand?

1 – C'est quand le film sur les animaux?
  – C'est le 6 août.
  – Le 6 août, bon.
2 – C'est quand, le concert de musique?
  – C'est le 19 juin.
  – Ah bon, c'est le 19 juin.
3 – C'est quand, la fête d'anniversaire?
  – C'est le 21 avril.
  – Le 21 avril, c'est ça?
  – Oui.
4 – Le match de basket, c'est quand?
  – C'est le 14 mai.
  – Le 14 mai, d'accord.
5 – La soirée carnaval, c'est quand?
  – C'est le 2 mars.
  – Le 2 mars, bon.
6 – Le feu d'artifice, c'est quand?
  – C'est le 28 octobre.
  – Alors, le 28 octobre.

2 Carine et Max

This practises clothing and colours and can be used at any time after SB page 54. Students listen to the recording and colour the pictures of the boy and girl according to the descriptions.

> **Solution:**
> *Carine:* long blond hair, blue eyes, yellow T-shirt, red jumper, blue skirt, grey shoes, black baseball cap
> *Max:* short black curly hair, brown eyes, green shorts, green socks, orange and white shirt, black trainers

CD 2 Track 43

Carine
Je m'appelle Carine. J'ai les cheveux longs et blonds, et les yeux bleus. Aujourd'hui, je porte un tee-shirt jaune avec un pull rouge et une jupe bleue. J'ai des chaussures grises et je porte aussi une casquette noire.

Max
Je m'appelle Max. J'ai les cheveux noirs, courts et bouclés et les yeux marron. Je porte un short vert et des chaussettes vertes avec une chemise orange et blanche. Je porte aussi mes baskets noires. J'aime bien mes baskets noires – elles sont vraiment cool!

3 Des cadeaux de Noël

Students listen to the recording and write the correct letter for each present.

> **Solution:**
> **1** f, **2** d, **3** a, **4** c, **5** h, **6** b, **7** e, **8** g

CD 2 Track 44

1 – Qu'est-ce que c'est? Ah, un DVD. C'est bien; j'adore ce film.
2 – Qu'est-ce que tu as?
  – Une raquette de tennis. C'est fantastique; j'aime bien le tennis.
3 – Et toi?
  – Des baskets! Génial! Elles sont très chic!
4 – Mmm, une boîte de chocolats. Délicieux.
5 – Moi, j'ai des balles de tennis. Ça, c'est toujours utile.
6 – Qu'est-ce que c'est?
  – Un livre, ah! une bande dessinée. J'aime bien ça.
7 – Et toi, qu'est-ce que tu as?
  – Un ballon de football.
8 – Et moi, j'ai un nouveau stylo noir. Regarde, il est très chic.

---

cm 5/10

Sommaire

A summary of the main language and structures of the unit on copymaster for reference.

Unité 6

Tricolore 1 Unité 6 Qu'est-ce que tu fais? Pages 62–77

6A Quel temps fait-il? pages 62–63		
• Talk about the weather • Say what the temperature is		
Grammaire	Stratégies	Phonétique
• None	• Using clues to work out meaning (4)	• The letters 'au', 'aux', 'eau', 'eaux'
Resources		
Audio: 3 *Voici la météo*; **4a** *Écoute la conversation*, or CD 3, tracks 2 and 4 **Copymasters:** 6/1 *Le temps* **Worksheets:** Starters and plenaries; *Est-ce qu'il fait beau?* (W)		**Interactive activity:** *La météo* (L) **Ph** The letters 'au', 'aux', 'eau', 'eaux', or CD 3, track 3 **PowerPoint:** *Le temps qu'il fait* (V) **Grammar in Action:** None
6B Les saisons pages 64–65		
• Talk about months and seasons		
Grammaire	Stratégies	Phonétique
• Use *quand* + a phrase in a sentence	• None	• The letters 'am', 'an', 'em', 'en'
Resources		
Audio: 2 *La chanson des saisons*; **3** *Trouve le mot*, or CD 3, tracks 5, 6 and 7 **Copymasters:** 6/2 *Vocabulaire: La météo et les saisons*, 6/3 *La météo* **Worksheets:** Starters and plenaries; Adding accents (Strat); *En été, il fait beau* (W)		**Interactive activity:** None **Ph** The letters 'am', 'an', 'em', 'en', or CD 3, track 8 **PowerPoint:** *La chanson des saisons* (song) **Grammar in Action:** None
6C Le sport pages 66–67		
• Talk about sport		
Grammaire	Stratégies	Phonétique
• Use the verb *jouer* (to play)	• None	• The letters '-er', '-et', '-ey', '-ez' at the end of a word
Resources		
Audio: 1a *Au club de sports*, or CD 3, track 9 **Copymasters:** None **Worksheets:** Starters and plenaries; *Je joue …* (W)		**Interactive activity:** None **Ph** The letters '-er', '-et', '-ey', '-ez' at the end of a word, or CD 3, track 10 **PowerPoint:** *Les verbes réguliers* (G) **Grammar in Action:** None
6D Des bandes dessinées pages 68–69		
• Find out about *les bandes dessinées* (BD)		
Grammaire	Stratégies	Phonétique
• Use some regular -er verbs	• None	• None
Resources		
Audio: 1 *Tom et Jojo*; **2** *Pendant les vacances*, or CD 3, tracks 11 and 12 **Copymasters:** 6/4 *Tom et Jojo* **Worksheets:** Starters and plenaries		**Interactive activity:** *Les verbes réguliers* (G) ; *Tom et Jojo* (L) **PowerPoint:** *Des activités* (V) **Grammar in Action:** pp17–19, 20–21
6E Des activités en famille pages 70–71		
• Talk about family activities • Say what you do at weekends		
Grammaire	Stratégies	Phonétique
• Use -er verbs	• Keeping your conversation going	• None
Resources		
Audio: 4a *Deux interviews*; **4b** *Deux interviews*; **5a** *Une conversation*, or CD 3, tracks 13 and 14 **Copymasters:** 6/5 *Les verbes*, 6/6 *Des activités* **Worksheets:** Starters and plenaries; *Phrases au choix* (W)		**Interactive activity:** *La vie des Paresseux* (R) ; Keeping your conversation going (Strat) **PowerPoint:** *Les Paresseux* (G) **Grammar in Action:** None

Tricolore 1 Teacher's Notes

Key language

6F On s'amuse pages 72–73		
• Talk about different activities according to the weather		
Grammaire	**Stratégies**	**Phonétique**
• Use *on* + verb	• Translating from French to English	• None
Resources		
Audio: 4a *Au téléphone*; 4b *Au téléphone*, or CD 3, track 15 **Copymasters:** 6/7 *Des cartes postales* **Worksheets:** Starters and plenaries; *Des cartes postales* (W)		**Interactive activity:** None **PowerPoint:** None **Grammar in Action:** None
6G Le weekend pages 74–75		
• Discuss what you do at the weekend • Answer questions about free-time activities		
Grammaire	**Stratégies**	**Phonétique**
• None	• Giving detailed answers	• None
Resources		
Audio: 3 *Deux personnes*, or CD 3, track 16 **Copymasters:** 6/8 *Tu comprends?*, 6/9 *Sommaire* **Worksheets:** Starters and plenaries **e-book:** *Le blog de Sébastien*		**Interactive activity:** Classroom commands (V) **Video :** *Le sport préféré de Manon* **PowerPoint:** None **Grammar in Action:** None

Key language

The weather (6A and 6B)

Quel temps fait-il?

Il fait …

beau

chaud

froid

mauvais

Il pleut.

Il neige.

Il y a …

du brouillard

du soleil

du vent

The seasons (6B)

le printemps

au printemps

l'été

en été

l'automne

en automne

l'hiver

en hiver

regular French –er verbs (6C and 6D)

adorer

aimer

arriver

chercher

cliquer

détester

écouter

entrer

habiter

jouer

penser

regarder

rentrer

rester

surfer

taper

téléphoner

travailler

Time expressions (6B and 6G)

normalement

quelquefois

souvent

Sports (6C and 6E)

Je joue au …

badminton

basket

foot(ball)

golf

hockey

rugby

tennis

tennis de table

volley

Free time activities (6C to 6F)

Qu'est-ce que tu fais?

Qu'est-ce que tu fais le week-end?

Qu'est-ce que tu fais quand il fait mauvais?

Je reste à la maison.

Je regarde …

un film.

la télé.

J'écoute …

de la musique.

la radio.

Je chante.

Je danse.

Je dessine.

Je range ma chambre.

Je joue sur la console de jeux.

Je joue/travaille sur l'ordinateur.

Je surfe sur Internet.

Je regarde mes e-mails/textos.

J'écris des textos/messages.

Je téléphone à un(e) ami(e).

Je retrouve mes amis.

Je discute avec mes amis.

On joue à des jeux vidéo.

On joue aux cartes.

Messages or postcards (6F)

Amitiés

Ton ami(e)

À bientôt

@+ (À plus tard)

Tricolore 1 Teacher's Notes

6A Quel temps fait-il?

6A Quel temps fait-il? pages 62–63

- Talk about the weather
- Say what the temperature is

Grammaire	Stratégies	Phonétique
• None	• Using clues to work out meaning (4)	• The letters 'au', 'aux', 'eau', 'eaux'

Resources

Audio: 3 *Voici la météo*; 4a *Écoute la conversation*, or CD 3, tracks 2 and 4
Copymasters: 6/1 *Le temps*
Worksheets: Starters and plenaries; *Est-ce qu'il fait beau?* (W)

Interactive activity: *La météo* (L)
Ph The letters 'au', 'aux', 'eau', 'eaux', or CD 3, track 3
PowerPoint: *Le temps qu'il fait* (V)
Grammar in Action: None

Worksheet

Starters (pages 62–63)

1 Revise numbers 0–40 orally using *Effacez!* (see TB page xvii).

2 *Où est la ville?* Display the following towns on the board and ask students to match them to the appropriate country/region:

Édimbourg, Dublin, Grenoble, Cardiff, Londres, Paris, Sydney, Belfast

en Écosse, en Angleterre, en France, au pays de Galles, en Irlande, en Australie, en Irlande du Nord, dans les Alpes

Introduction

The weather

Go through the objectives for this spread.

Then start with the PowerPoint presentation (see below) or flashcards (27–33) to teach the following expressions. To help make the meaning clear, mime appropriate gestures, e.g. shivering, wiping brow. Ask which two words appear in many expressions and help students to identify *il fait*.

Quel temps fait-il? Il fait chaud/froid.

For *il fait beau*, use the sunny flashcard.

For *il fait mauvais*, use a combination of two or more of the rain, cold, foggy and windy flashcards.

Il pleut/neige. Il y a du soleil/vent/brouillard.

Use games to practise these expressions, e.g. *Effacez!* (where students point to or take the flashcard) and *Jeu de mémoire* (Kim's game – see below). See TB pages xvii–xviii.

Interactive activity

Le temps qu'il fait

Presentation

Jeu de mémoire: Le temps

62

1 Le temps en France

Introduce the French weather map, checking that the symbols are clearly understood and referring to the *Légende*.

La France est un grand pays. Dans le nord de la France, il fait mauvais. À Lille il pleut. À Dieppe il y a du brouillard. À Strasbourg, il fait froid.

Mais à La Rochelle, il fait beau. Il y a du soleil.

Et dans les Alpes, à Grenoble, quel temps fait-il? Est-ce qu'il pleut? Est-ce qu'il fait chaud?

Et à Nice? Et à Bordeaux? etc.

a Students then complete the *vrai/faux* task. Able students could correct the wrong weather descriptions.

> **Solution:**
>
> **1** faux (*Il fait mauvais.*), **2** vrai, **3** faux (*Il fait chaud.*), **4** vrai, **5** faux (*Il y a du brouillard.*), **6** faux (*Il fait beau.*), **7** vrai, **8** faux (*Il fait froid.*)

b Students refer to the table or the map to complete the weather descriptions.

> **Solution:**
>
> **1** *À Dieppe, il y a du brouillard.*
>
> **2** *À Strasbourg, il fait froid.*
>
> **3** *À Paris, il fait mauvais.*
>
> **4** *À Nice, il fait chaud.*
>
> **5** *À Toulouse, il y a du soleil.*
>
> **6** *À Grenoble, il neige.*
>
> **7** *À Lille, il pleut.*

c As an extension task, students choose three different towns and write a description of the weather in each place.

Weather forecasts

Students could work in groups to give their own weather forecast, using visuals and symbols in the style of a TV presentation. The map on the final copymaster could be used for this.

92 Tricolore 1 Teacher's Notes

6A Quel temps fait-il?

> Worksheet

Est-ce qu'il fait beau?

> 150 Au choix

1 Quel temps fait-il?

> 62

2 Les températures

Look at the thermometer and teach *assez chaud*, *assez froid* and *moins* (+ number). Draw a simplified thermometer on the board, e.g.

Quand il fait 35 degrés, est-ce qu'il fait froid?
Non, il fait chaud.
Est-ce qu'il fait assez chaud?
Non, il fait très chaud.
Et quand il fait moins cinq degrés, est-ce qu'il fait chaud? etc.

Refer students to the table of temperatures and the example. Students could then do the task orally in pairs. For further practice, write a list of towns (perhaps local or well-known ones) on the board, each with a different temperature. Practise giving the temperature in each place with a chain game.

Teacher: *Quelle température fait-il à Strasbourg?*
Student A: *(Il fait) 9 degrés. Et à Paris? …*
Student B: *(Il fait) 18 degrés. Et à Londres? …*

To maintain pace, set a time limit of, say, five seconds for each reply.

> Interactive activity

Quel temps fait-il?

> 62

3 Voici la météo

Teach *parapluie* and write it on the board. The recording could be played with pauses after each town for students to note down their answers – the weather and the temperature for each town. Able students may be able to note both at the same time, or, to make it easier for less able students, students could work in pairs or the class could be divided into two groups, with one group noting the weather, and the other noting the temperatures.

> **Solution:**
> **1a** C, **1b** 7°C, **2a** F, **2b** 12°C, **3a** A, **3b** 13°C,
> **4a** I/G, **4b** 19°C, **5a** G/B, **5b** 21°C, **6a** E, **6b** –4°C,
> **7a** H, **7b** 5°C, **8a** D, **8b** 8°C, **9a** A/F, **9b** 9°C

> CD 3 Track 2

Voici la météo

– Bonjour, mesdames et messieurs.
Aujourd'hui, nous sommes le cinq mars. Est-ce qu'il va faire beau aujourd'hui? Écoutons la météo avec Daniel Dubois.
– Eh bien, voici la météo.
Commençons par la capitale. À Paris, il fait froid pour la saison; la température est de sept degrés.
Dans l'ouest de la France, à Rennes, il pleut. Alors, prenez votre parapluie si vous êtes à Rennes. La température à Rennes est de douze degrés.
À Bordeaux, sur la côte atlantique, il y a du brouillard. Température: treize degrés.
Dans le sud de la France, il fait beau. À Toulouse, il fait beau et la température est de dix-neuf degrés. Alors, du beau temps à Toulouse.
Et à Nice et partout dans la région méditerranéenne, le ciel est bleu. Il y a du soleil et il fait chaud. Température: vingt-et-un degrés.
Par contre, à Grenoble et dans les Alpes, il neige. C'est bien pour les skieurs, mais la température est de moins quatre degrés. À Strasbourg et dans l'est de la France, il y a du vent. Oui, du vent assez fort et la température à Strasbourg est de cinq degrés.
Passons maintenant au nord du pays. À Lille, il fait mauvais en général. Température: huit degrés.
Et à Dieppe, sur la côte nord, il y a du brouillard et il pleut. Température maximum de neuf degrés.

cm 6/1

Le temps

> Interactive activity

The letters 'au', 'aux', 'eau', 'eaux'

> 63 Phonétique

The letters 'au', 'aux', 'eau', 'eaux'

A full explanation of this sound is given on *kerboodle!*, together with interactive practice.

a Say the word *chaud* with an appropriate gesture for hot, e.g. wiping the forehead. Students repeat the word with the same gesture. Then read out the other words, with the students repeating each one: *eau, gâteaux, animaux*. Explain that the letter o and ô in *océan* and *contrôle* is pronounced in the same way. The words are also included on the recording for optional use (part **a**).

Parts **b** and **c** can be used for further practice.

b Ask students to listen and repeat the words they hear. Then display the words **a** *cadeau*, **b** *zéro*, **c** *chaussure*, **d** *tableau*, **e** *oiseaux* for students to match (**b, c, a, e, d**).

c Students listen to the silly sentence and note down how many times they hear the 'au'/'aux'/'eau'/ 'eaux' sound (6). They can then repeat the sentence to help them remember this sound.

For further practice, write some additional words on the board to check that students recognise the link between spelling and pronunciation e.g. *chevaux, côte, drapeaux, Bordeaux*.

Tricolore 1 Teacher's Notes

6A Quel temps fait-il?

> CD 3 Track 3
>
> **The letters 'au', 'aux', 'eau', 'eaux'**
> Écoutez et répétez:
> a chaud, eau, gâteaux, animaux, océan, contrôle
> b zéro, chaussure, cadeau, oiseaux, tableau
> c Il fait beau à Bordeaux, il fait mauvais à Beauvais et aux Maldives il fait chaud.

63   AfL

4 Des conversations

This brings together towns, weather and temperatures and is suitable for peer assessment.

a Students listen to the model conversation first.

> CD 3 Track 4
>
> **Des conversations**
> A: Salut, Paul. C'est Laura.
> B: Bonjour, Laura. Où es-tu?
> A: Je suis à Grenoble.
> B: Quel temps fait-il?
> A: Il neige.
> B: Quelle température fait-il?
> A: Moins cinq.

b They then work in pairs to make up a similar conversation, using the suggestions in the book.

For further practice/peer assessment, consequences could be played in groups.

Each student has a piece of paper and writes the name of the town at the top. The paper is folded over and passed to another student, who adds a weather symbol. The paper is folded again and passed to a third student who writes a number for the temperature.

The next student unfolds the paper and reads the weather forecast according to the prompts.

63

5 La météo aujourd'hui

If not used earlier, the map on copymaster page 128 could be used for revision of places in France and compass points. The map could also be used for follow-up work on the weather – recording weather details for different towns on particular days, perhaps using sticky notes. Teach *nord* and *sud* by referring to towns on the map, e.g.

Lille est dans le nord de la France.

Nice est dans le sud de la France.

Et Dieppe? Et Toulouse?

a Students look at the weather map (SB page 62) and read the incomplete weather description. They choose the correct words to fill the gaps. Explain the noun *pluie*, which is used here (rather than *il pleut*) for the sake of authenticity.

> Solution:
> **1** *fait,* **2** *brouillard,* **3** *soleil,* **4** *beau,* **5** *vent,* **6** *neige*

b Students find the French phrases in the text.

> Solution:
> **1** *dans le nord de la France,* **2** *il ne fait pas mauvais,* **3** *il fait beau,* **4** *en général,* **5** *dans l'ouest de la France,* **6** *il fait froid*

c For extension work, students make up a similar weather description.

63 Stratégies

Using clues to work out meaning (4)

Encourage students to look at prefixes as a clue to meaning, starting with *para-*. Parachute could also be mentioned, with students guessing the meaning of *une chute*. Mention that prefixes can be helpful in decoding meaning and discuss other examples in English or French, e.g. in/im – impossible; un – unsure, unfriendly, unpleasant; dis – displeased, discontent, etc.

Worksheet

Plenaries (pages 62–63)

Students work in pairs to group weather expressions, e.g. *il fait* + adjective, *il y a* + noun, *il* + verb. They see how many weather expressions they can remember and share tips on how to learn them

6B Les saisons pages 64–65

- Talk about months and seasons

Grammaire	Stratégies	Phonétique
• Use *quand* + a phrase in a sentence	• None	• The letters 'am', 'an', 'em', 'en'

Resources

Audio: 2 *La chanson des saisons*; 3 *Trouve le mot*, or CD 3, tracks 5, 6 and 7
Copymasters: 6/2 *Vocabulaire: La météo et les saisons*, 6/3 *La météo*
Worksheets: Starters and plenaries; Adding accents (Strat); *En été, il fait beau* (W)

Interactive activity: None
Ph The letters 'am', 'an', 'em', 'en', or CD 3, track 8
PowerPoint: *La chanson des saisons* (song)
Grammar in Action: None

Worksheet

Starters (pages 64–65)

1 *Complète les mois* Display or give out the following task and ask students to complete the months, by inserting the missing vowels. Ask students randomly for the answers.

 1 s_pt_mbr_   7 m_ _
 2 _vr _ l   8 _ ct_br_
 3 j _ _ ll _ t   9 m_rs
 4 d_c _ mbr _   10 j_ _ n
 5 f_ v r _ _ r   11 n_v_mbr_
 6 j _ nv_ _ r   12 _ _ _ t

2 *Vrai/Faux cards* Make true/false statements about the weather flashcards (27–33) or use a PowerPoint presentation (see 6A) and ask students to indicate whether the statements are true or false by holding up their *vrai* or *faux* card.

Introduction

Seasons

Go through the objectives for this spread. Teach the names of the seasons and practise related weather conditions, using the flashcards 27–33 or the picture in the Student's Book (SB page 64), e.g.

Il y a quatre saisons dans l'année: le printemps, l'été, l'automne et l'hiver.
Le printemps commence le 21 mars.
Quel sont les mois de printemps? (mars, avril, mai)
Au printemps, quel temps fait-il?
Normalement il fait beau et il y a du soleil.
En été, il fait chaud et le ciel est bleu.
En automne, il y a du vent et quelquefois, il y a du brouillard.
Et en hiver, quel temps fait-il en hiver?
Il fait froid et quelquefois il neige.

1 Les quatre saisons

This presents the names of the seasons and some related vocabulary, e.g. *le ciel, la pluie, quelquefois*. Ask how the French say 'in summer', 'in autumn', 'in winter', 'in spring'? Why do students think there is a different word for 'in' with one season?

Explain that all the words are masculine, but *en* is used before a vowel or silent '*h*'.

a Students relate months, events, etc. to specific seasons.

> **Solution:**
>
> 1 *le printemps*, 2 *l'automne*, 3 *l'été*, 4 *l'hiver*,
> 5 *l'automne*, 6 *l'été*, 7 *le printemps*, 8 *l'hiver*

b Students complete the sentences describing typical weather for each season.

> **Solution:**
>
> 1 *beau*, 2 *soleil*, 3 *pleut*, 4 *chaud*, 5 *bleu*, 6 *vent*,
> 7 *brouillard*, 8 *froid*, 9 *mauvais*, 10 *neige*

c Students write sentences about each season, using *souvent, quelquefois* or *normalement*.

Invite suggestions from the class or display suitable sentences around the classroom.

e.g. *En hiver, il fait souvent froid. En Angleterre il pleut souvent.*
Au printemps, normalement il fait beau.
En été il y a souvent du soleil.
En automne, il y a quelquefois du brouillard.

Time expressions

Discuss with students other contexts where *souvent, quelquefois* or *normalement* could be used and mention that these are useful 'high frequency words'.

Tricolore 1 Teacher's Notes

6B Les saisons

Weather chain game

One student says a season and a weather condition and the next student repeats this and adds another appropriate weather condition up to a maximum of three or four, e.g.

En hiver/automne, il pleut et il y a du brouillard … et il y a du vent … et il fait froid.

En été, il fait chaud et il y a du soleil … et le ciel est bleu … et il fait beau.

For variation, towns and countries could be changed, e.g.

À Glasgow il fait froid, mais à Nice …

For practice of seasons, countries in northern and southern hemispheres could be contrasted, e.g.

En Angleterre, c'est l'hiver, mais en Australie …

cm 6/2

Vocabulaire: la météo et les saisons

cm 6/3

La météo

150 Au choix

2 La météo

64 and 77

2 La chanson des saisons

Students listen to the song. It could also be used with a 'gapped' copy of the song words, which students complete when they have listened to the song.

The song is recorded in two versions, first with words, then as an instrumental only version. For further notes on the songs, see TB page xxi.

CD 3 Tracks 5–6

La chanson des saisons

1. Le premier mois, c'est janvier.
   Nous sommes en hiver.
   Il neige beaucoup en février,
   En mars, il fait mauvais.

2. Au mois d'avril, il pleut, il pleut.
   Nous sommes au printemps.
   Il fait très beau au mois de mai,
   La météo dit: beau temps!

3. Et puis c'est juin, et juillet, août.
   Nous sommes en été.
   Il fait très chaud pour les vacances,
   Ma saison préférée.

4. Au mois de septembre la rentrée.
   Octobre, c'est l'automne.
   Du brouillard pendant novembre.
   Oh! Qu'est-ce qu'il fait du vent!

5. Le dernier mois, on fête Noël.
   Nous sommes en décembre.
   Il fait très froid, mais moi, j'ai chaud.
   Je reste dans ma chambre!

Presentation

Chantez! La chanson des saisons

64

3 Trouve le mot

Students listen to the spelling of each word, write it down and identify it.

Solution:
As transcript

CD 3 Track 7

Trouve le mot

1. l-à
2. l-e-ç-o-n
3. é-t-é
4. a-o-û-t
5. o-ù
6. h-ô-p-i-t-a-l
7. î-l-e
8. n-o-ë-l

64

Accents

This extends the work on accents, covering grave and circumflex accents on other vowels, c cedilla and the trema.

Students could look for examples of words with accents on the spread and these can be written on the board.

Worksheet

Les accents

65

4 Le climat en France

This could be introduced by referring to a map of France and talking briefly about the climate (in English, if necessary), mentioning such things as:

- the Mediterranean climate, with hot summers and mild winters, fruit such as peaches and grapes growing outside and people eating outdoors a lot;
- the Alps, where there is often snow for five months of the year, making skiing a popular sport;
- the Mistral, and how houses are built with no windows on the side it blows from;
- the effect of the warmer climate on people's homes – houses have shutters to keep out the strong sunlight, tiled floors in the kitchen to keep the house cool, fitted carpets are generally less common.

Students match each photo with the text.

Solution:
1 d, 2 c, 3 a, 4 b

6B Les saisons

Weather idioms
Students might be interested in learning a few idioms in French, e.g. *il pleut des cordes; il fait un temps de chien*. These sometimes give an insight into the culture.

English is particularly rich in idioms, so if there is time for cross-curricular work, there could be more discussion about idioms in English.

> Worksheet

En été, il fait beau

> 65 Dossier-langue

Using *quand* (when) as a conjunction
This covers clauses with *quand*. Able students could create longer sentences linking weather conditions and activities.

> 65   AfL

5 Dossier personnel
The work on weather should be completed with students writing a few sentences describing the weather in their area.

If used for assessment, review the spread objectives and assessment criteria first. Share with students how work can be improved.

> Interactive activity

The letters 'am', 'an', 'em', 'en'

> 65 Phonétique

The letters 'am', 'an', 'em', 'en'
A full explanation of this sound is given on *kerboodle!*, together with interactive practice.

a Explain that when 'a' or 'e' are followed by 'n' or 'm' they are often nasal vowels and pronounced through the nose. There is no equivalent sound in English. When learning a nasal sound, it can help to say the sound when holding your nose first, and then try to make the same sound without holding your nose. Demonstrate this and say the word *vent* with an appropriate gesture, e.g. sweeping the hand across the body. Students repeat the word with the same gesture. Then read out the other words, with the students repeating each one: *enfant*, *quand*, *temps*. The words are also included on the recording for optional use (part **a**).

Explain that if the letters, 'am', 'an', 'em', 'en', are followed by another vowel or a second *m* or *n*, then they are **not** nasal vowels and they are pronounced differently.

To demonstrate these exceptions, say the following words: *animal*, *anniversaire*, *fenêtre*, without the gesture. Again, these exceptions are given on the recording (part **a**).

Parts **b** and **c** can be used for further pronunciation practice.

b Ask students to listen and repeat the words they hear. Then display the words **a** *ambulance*, **b** *dans*, **c** *appartement*, **d** *Irlande*, **e** *quand* for students to match (**b, d, a, e, c**).

c Students listen to the silly sentence and note down how many times they hear the 'am'/'an'/'em'/'en', sound (8). They can then repeat the sentence to help them remember this sound.

For further practice, write some additional words on the board to check that students recognise the link between spelling and related pronunciation, e.g. *France, en, Angleterre, maman*.

> CD 3 Track 8

The letters 'am', 'an', 'em', 'en'
Écoutez et répétez:
a vent, enfant, quand, temps
   Des exceptions: animal, anniversaire, fenêtre
b dans, Irlande, ambulance, quand, appartement
c Cent éléphants blancs dansent dans le vent en même temps.

> 65

6 C'est quel mot?
a Students work in pairs taking it in turns to ask and answer questions.

> **Solution (suggestions):**
> **1** avril, **2** automne, **3** beau, brouillard, **4** chaud, **5** décembre, **6** été, **7** octobre, **8** hiver

b For extension work, students could make up additional questions for use in a pair or team game. They could refer to the *Sommaire* pages of earlier units for suitable words. If necessary, suggest some of the categories of words, used in 6C Starter 2, *Ça commence par ...*

> Worksheet

Plenaries (pages 64–65)
1 Ask students to think about words with accents and work in pairs to see how many they can recall of the different types mentioned. Ask whether they think the accent helps them with pronunciation. Students who have studied other languages could comment on whether there are accents in other languages and whether they think they would be useful in English.

2 If possible display a large map of France (ICT resource, CM p128) and ask students what they have learnt about the climate in France.

6C Le sport   pages 66–67

- Talk about sport

Grammaire	Stratégies	Phonétique
• Use the verb *jouer* (to play)	• None	• The letters '-er', '-et', '-ey', '-ez' at the end of a word

Resources

Audio: 1a *Au club de sports*, or CD 3, track 9
Copymasters: 6/4 *Tom et Jojo*
Worksheets: Starters and plenaries; *Je joue …* (W)

Interactive activity: None
Ph The letters '-er', '-et', '-ey', '-ez' at the end of a word, or CD 3, track 10
PowerPoint: *Les verbes réguliers* (G)
Grammar in Action: None

Worksheet

Starters (pages 66–67)

1 **Chasse à l'intrus** Display or print out the following lists. Students identify the odd word out in each list (shown in bold). Ask students collectively or randomly to give the 'intrus'. Several students could be asked for their answer before the teacher gives the correct one. Ask for volunteers to explain why.

A	B	C	D	E	F
dimanche	suis	du papier	je	nous	deux
vendredi	êtes	du brouillard	**est**	ils	treize
froid	sont	du vent	tu	**avons**	vingt
samedi	**chaud**	du soleil	elle	vous	**mauvais**

2 **Ça commence par …** Display or print the words in brackets below. Students have to recognise and write down the word which fits each category. Ask students randomly or collectively for the correct answers.

Ça commence par un **c**
1 *un vêtement (une chaussette)*
2 *un animal (un chien)*
3 *une pièce à la maison (une cuisine)*
4 *un verbe (chanter)*
5 *quelque chose dans la salle de classe (un cahier)*
6 *une expression qui décrit le temps (chaud)*
7 *un nombre (cinquante)*

Ça commence par un **p**
1 *une saison (le printemps)*
2 *un oiseau (un perroquet)*
3 *un adjectif (petit)*
4 *un verbe (préférer)*
5 *une fête (Pâques)*
6 *un vêtement (un pantalon)*
7 *un prénom (Pierre)*

Introduction

Les sports

Go through the objectives for this spread. List the names of sports, which are the same in English and French, e.g. *le badminton, le football, le golf, le hockey, le rugby, le tennis,* and read them out so students hear the correct pronunciation. Then teach *le tennis de table, le basket* and *le volley* using the flashcards 38–40. Practise the words orally e.g. through a chain question game:

– *Un sport qui commence par un b?*
– *le badminton*
– *Très bien. Pose une question.*
– *Un sport qui commence par un h,* etc.

Introduce the photographs on SB page 66 orally first, e.g.

Voilà un groupe de jeunes.
On fait beaucoup de sports.
Claire et Thomas jouent au volley. Le volley, qu'est-ce que c'est en anglais? C'est 'volleyball'.
On joue beaucoup au volley en France, et ici?
Est-ce que Claire et Thomas jouent au tennis?
Non, ils jouent au …
Et Sophie, elle joue au volley?
Paul et Yannick jouent à quel sport?
Qui joue au basket? etc.

🔊 66

1 Au club de sports

This task brings together the eight sports and the different forms of *jouer* which are explained and practised later.

a Students note down the correct photo for each speaker.

Solution:
1 A, **2** D, **3** B, **4** F, **5** H, **6** G, **7** E, **8** C

6C Le sport

CD 3 Track 9

Au club de sports

1 – Bonjour Claire, bonjour Thomas. Qu'est-ce que vous faites aujourd'hui?
  – Bonjour. Aujourd'hui, nous jouons au volley.
2 – Et Marc, est-ce qu'il joue avec vous?
  – Non, Marc joue au basket.
3 – Et toi, Simon, tu joues au tennis, non?
  – Oui, moi, je joue au tennis.
4 – Tu aimes le sport, Ibrahim?
  – Oui, j'adore le sport, je joue aujourd'hui au hockey.
5 – Est-ce que Jonathan et Nicole jouent aussi au hockey?
  – Non, ils jouent au badminton.
6 – Et vous, Daniel et Luc, vous jouez au tennis de table, non?
  – Oui, nous jouons au tennis de table.
7 – Et Sophie, elle joue avec vous?
  – Non, Sophie joue au golf.
8 – Et Paul et Yannick, ils jouent au football, je suppose?
  – Oui, ils jouent au football.

b Students correct the mistakes in each sentence. The task presents the third person, singular and plural, and should be done orally first. Point out that the third person singular and plural forms sound identical, although they are spelt differently.

Solution:
1 *Marc joue au basket.*
2 *Claire et Thomas jouent au volley.*
3 *Ibrahim joue au hockey.*
4 *Paul et Yannick jouent au football.*
5 *Simon joue au tennis.*
6 *Sophie joue au golf.*
7 *Daniel et Luc jouent au tennis de table.*
8 *Jonathan et Nicole jouent au badminton.*

Chain game

Play a quick class game, such as a cumulative list of sports or a game where each person has to mention a different sport, referring to the list on the board if necessary, e.g.

Je joue au tennis, et toi, (student A)?
Je joue au tennis et au football, et toi, (student B)? etc.

For other vocabulary games, see TB page xvii.

66

2 Inventez des conversations

Students practise in pairs making up short conversations about sport. This could be done as an information gap activity in pairs, with each student first writing down the names of three sports. They take it in turns to guess the three sports listed by their partner, asking:

- *Tu joues au football?*
- *Non, alors, c'est à moi. Tu joues au golf?*
- *Oui.*
- *Alors je continue. Tu joues au volley?*
- *Non,* etc.

66 Dossier-langue

jouer à + sport/game

Ask: *les noms de ces sports sont-ils masculins ou féminins?* This explains the use of *jouer au* + masculine sport and *jouer aux* + plural game. This point is covered in more detail in Unité 10.

Interactive activity

The letters '-er', '-et', '-ey', '-ez' at the end of a word

66 Phonétique

The letters '-er', '-et', '-ey', '-ez' at the end of a word

A full explanation of this sound is given on kerboodle!, together with interactive practice.

a Say the word *aimer* with an appropriate gesture for 'to love', e.g. hands across heart. Students repeat the word with the same gesture. Then read out the other words, with the students repeating each one: *jouez, juillet, regarder, hockey.*

Remind students that this is the same sound as 'é', as in *éléphant* (taught in 2C). The words are also included on the recording for optional use (part **a**).

Explain that there are some exceptions, often words borrowed from other languages, and read these out, with students repeating each word, without the gesture: *basket, hamster, hiver, internet.* Again, these exceptions are given on the recording (part **a**).

Parts **b** and **c** can be used for further pronunciation practice.

b Ask students to listen and repeat the words they hear. Then display the words **a** *lisez*, **b** *jouet*, **c** *cahier*, **d** *écouter*, **e** *poulet*, for students to match (**c**, **d**, **b**, **a**, **e**).

c Students listen to the silly sentence and note down how many times they hear the sound (12). They can then repeat the sentence to help them remember this sound.

For further practice, write some additional words on the board to check that students recognise the link between spelling and related pronunciation, e.g. *écoutez, regarder, perroquet.*

CD 3 Track 10

The letters '-er', '-et', '-ey', '-ez' at the end of a word

Écoutez et répétez:
a aimer, jouez, juillet, regarder, hockey
  Des exceptions: basket, internet, hiver, hamster
b cahier, écouter, jouet, lisez, poulet
c En janvier et février vous regardez la télé, mais en juillet vous préférez jouer au volley.

Tricolore 1 Teacher's Notes 99

6C Le sport

> **Presentation**

Les verbes réguliers

> **67 Dossier-langue**

jouer (to play) – a regular *-er* verb

This sets out the present tense of *jouer*, with key points that apply to all verbs. More work is done on *-er* verbs later.

Build on students' knowledge of the standard paradigm (following earlier work on *avoir* and *être*) and build up the pattern for a regular *-er* verb.

Write the verb on the board and give plenty of practice, by deleting a few endings at a time or removing the stem or the pronoun from some parts and asking students to replace them. This could be played in teams, with students taking turns to delete or fill in missing parts.

> **67**

3 Ils jouent bien?

Practice in selecting the correct part of the verb from three options.

> **Solution:**
> 1 *Je joue*, 2 *Tu joues*, 3 *Ma fille joue*,
> 4 *Nous jouons*, 5 *Vous jouez*, 6 *Ils jouent*

> **67** AfL

4 Du sport pour tous

Students complete each sentence with the correct part of the verb and the illustrated sport. This could be used for assessment. Revise the spread learning objectives with students and relate success criteria to these objectives.

> **Solution:**
> 1 *(vous) jouez au volley*
> 2 *(nous) jouons au basket*
> 3 **a** *(tu) joues au badminton*, **b** *(je) joue au badminton*
> 4 *(il) joue au hockey*
> 5 **a** *(tes parents) jouent au tennis*, **b** *(ils) jouent au tennis*
> 6 *(mon grand-père) joue au golf*

> FC 37, 41, 42

Vous n'aimez pas le sport?

Present the words for a few activities (with *jouer*) for non-sporty people, e.g.

Moi, je ne suis pas sportif/sportive, je joue aux cartes.
Mon frère n'est pas sportif, il joue aux jeux vidéo.
Mes parents ne sont pas sportifs. Quelquefois, nous jouons tous au Monopoly.

> **67**

5 Dossier personnel

a Prepare this in class with volunteers writing suggestions on the board to help students who need more support.
b For extension, students write a paragraph about sport and games. It can reflect their own interests, or they can imagine what a famous personality might write.

> **Worksheet**

Je joue ...

> **Worksheet**

Plenaries (pages 66–67)

1 Students should discuss tips for remembering regular verb endings; for instance writing out a verb in a table and using colour to distinguish the stem and the ending. They could then use the find and replace function to change the stem of the verb. This could be tried using *jouer* and replacing *jou-* with *aim-* of *aimer*. Applying the paradigm to other regular *-er* verbs is covered fully in the next area.
2 Students (perhaps in pairs) could think of a way to teach someone else the present tense of *jouer* and invent a suitable activity.

6D Des bandes dessinées   pages 68–69

- Find out about *les bandes dessinées (BD)*

Grammaire	Stratégies	Phonétique
• Use some regular -er verbs	• None	• None

Resources

Audio: 1 *Tom et Jojo*; 2 *Pendant les vacances*, or CD 3, tracks 11 and 12
Copymasters: None
Worksheets: Starters and plenaries

Interactive activity: *Les verbes réguliers* (G) ; *Tom et Jojo* (L)
PowerPoint: *Des activités* (V)
Grammar in Action: pp17–19, 20–21

Worksheet

Starters (pages 68–69)

1 *En groupes* Display or print out a list of words in random order and ask students to put these into five groups. Ask for volunteers to read out three words which form a group.

je, tu, elle

Écoute, Regarde, Complète

nous, vous, ils

trouver, jouer, copier

inventez, chantez, travaillez

2 *Trouve les paires* Display or print out the following table. Students match up the two parts and note the pairs. Check these by asking the class collectively to read out the correct sentences.

1 Tu	a *regarde un film.*
2 Est-ce qu'il	b *jouons au golf.*
3 Marie	c *détestent les devoirs.*
4 Nous	d *aimez les animaux?*
5 Vous	e *aimes le football?*
6 Elles	f *joue au tennis?*

Solution:
1 e, 2 f, 3 a, 4 b, 5 d, 6 c

Introduction

Go through the objectives for this spread. Teach *Qu'est-ce que tu fais?* and use this to ask for answers in the first person, e.g.

Je regarde la télé.

J'écoute la radio/de la musique.

Je travaille.

Then play some miming or flashcard games using different persons of the verb (see TB page xx). The flashcards using *jouer* (38–42) can also be used for further practice.

Presentation

Les verbes réguliers

Interactive activity

Des activités

1 Tom et Jojo

This presents several examples of verbs of action.

a Students listen to the recording and follow the text.

CD 1 Track 11

Tom et Jojo

Jojo est une souris. Elle pense à quelque chose. C'est le fromage.
Tom est un chat. Il pense à quelque chose. C'est Jojo.
Voilà le fromage. Voilà Jojo.
Jojo mange le fromage.
Voilà Tom. Tom entre dans la cuisine.
Tom chasse Jojo. Est-ce qu'il mange Jojo? Jojo entre dans le salon.
Tom saute sur Jojo. Il attrape Jojo?
Aïe!! Non, il n'attrape pas Jojo.
Tom chasse Jojo dans la salle de bains. Il saute …
Pouf! Non! Il n'attrape pas Jojo dans la salle de bains.
Jojo rentre dans la cuisine. Voilà le fromage! Mais voilà Tom!
Et voilà Butch! Butch arrive. Butch n'aime pas Tom.
Il chasse Tom … et Jojo mange le fromage.

b Students read the sentences individually or in pairs and decide whether they are true or false.

Solution:
1 *vrai*, 2 *faux*, 3 *vrai*, 4 *vrai*, 5 *faux*, 6 *vrai*, 7 *faux*, 8 *vrai*, 9 *vrai*, 10 *faux*

c For extension, students correct the sentences which are not true.

Solution:
2 *Elle trouve du fromage dans la cuisine.*
5 *Le chat chasse la souris dans la salle de bains.*
7 *Jojo entre dans le salon; Tom aussi.*
10 *Jojo, la souris, mange le fromage.*

Tricolore 1 Teacher's Notes

6D Des bandes dessinées

> Interactive activity

Tom et Jojo

> 69 Dossier-langue

Regular -er verbs

First revise how to recognise a verb and ask students to find some examples in the *Tom et Jojo* activity.

The pattern of regular -er verbs is applied here to other verbs. Use the example of the flower – the stem remains the same whilst the flower has different petals – just like the stem of a verb, which doesn't change whilst the endings do.

To reinforce the importance of learning the endings, explain to students that they can use these to form the present tense of all verbs in French which end in -er (except *aller*). Demonstrate it by giving them one or two verbs they have never used before, to conjugate e.g. *fabriquer, téléphoner, surfer, cliquer, danser*.

Stress that, whilst the spelling changes for some endings, the pronunciation of all the parts is the same except for the *nous* and *vous* forms.

If students created a verb table with *jouer*, they can now add other verbs.

Practice of verbs

There are a number of tasks to practise verbs and the teacher can select those that are most appropriate for the class. It is not necessary to do them all and some could be used later for revision. See also *Games for practising verbs* (TB page xx).

> cm 6/4

Tom et Jojo

> gia 1 pp17–19

Regular -er verbs – singular (1), (2), (3)

Further practice of the singular forms of regular -er verbs.

> 69 AfL

2 Pendant les vacances

Introduce this item by referring to the speech bubbles, e.g.

On va écouter des personnes qui parlent des vacances.

Par exemple, voici François. Il aime les vacances et il adore le camping.

Discuss possible answers first and why – linking the subjects and appropriate endings.

Maintenant écoutez les conversations et trouvez les paires.

Play the conversations, pausing after each one for students to match up the two parts of the sentences, or play the whole recording twice, with shorter pauses. If used in a language laboratory, this task could be done on an individual basis. Correct the task as a class activity, with students reading out the complete sentences as well as giving the matching numbers and letters.

The task could be used for assessment.

> **Solution:**
> **1** *b*, **2** *c*, **3** *a*, **4** *e*, **5** *d*, **6** *g*, **7** *j*, **8** *f*, **9** *h*, **10** *i*

> CD 3 Track 12

Pendant les vacances

1 – François, tu aimes les vacances?
 – Bien sûr.
 – Et qu'est-ce que tu fais pendant les vacances?
 – Je fais du camping avec mes amis. J'adore le camping.
2 – Et toi, Christine, qu'est-ce que tu fais?
 – J'habite à La Rochelle avec ma famille et en été, nous passons beaucoup de temps au soleil.
3 – Jean-Marc et Sandrine, qu'est-ce que vous aimez faire pendant les vacances?
 – Ça dépend. En hiver, nous aimons faire du ski.
4 – Et en été, qu'est-ce que vous faites?
 – En été, nous restons à la maison et nous invitons des amis à la maison.
5 – M. et Mme Duval, qu'est-ce que vous faites pendant les vacances?
 – Eh bien, au mois de juin, il y a la fête de la Musique. Alors nous écoutons toutes sortes de musique.
6 – Et votre fille Mathilde chante dans un groupe, non?
 – Oui, c'est ça. Notre fille Mathilde chante dans un groupe ici.
7 – Salut, Nicolas et Isabelle. Qu'est-ce que vous faites pendant les vacances?
 – Comme nous habitons à la ferme, nous restons ici, normalement. Ma sœur, Isabelle, et moi, nous travaillons à la ferme avec mon père.
8 – Tu aimes les animaux, Isabelle?
 – Ah oui, j'aime beaucoup les animaux.
9 – Et qu'est-ce que tu fais, le soir, Nicolas?
 – Le soir, je joue au football avec mes amis.
10 – Et quand il pleut?
 – Quand il pleut, je joue sur l'ordinateur.

> 150 Au choix

3 Devant la télé

> gia 1 pp20–21

Regular -er verbs – singular (1), (2)

Further practice of the full paradigm of regular -er verbs.

102 Tricolore 1 Teacher's Notes

6E Des activités en famille

📖 69

3 Les bandes dessinées (BD)

Introduce the subject on the following lines.

Comic strip books, like Tintin and Astérix, are very popular in France and Belgium. There is a *Festival de la bande dessinée* held every year in Angoulême, France, where awards are given to the best books. There are also theme parks and museums, based on the most popular characters.

Tintin first appeared in a Belgian newspaper, nearly 100 years ago. He was created by the Belgian writer and illustrator, Georges Rémi, who always signed the books as Hergé (his initials GR in reverse order, so RG).

The adventures of Astérix were first published in 1956 by René Goscinny (who wrote the text) and Albert Uderzo (who did the drawings). Millions of copies of the books have been sold and they have been translated into about 80 languages and dialects. There are more than 30 Astérix books. One recent book, *Astérix chez les pictes*, takes place in Scotland. *Le parc Astérix* is covered in *Unité* 10.

a Students work out the equivalent titles in English of some Tintin and Astérix books. The actual titles for the English language versions are given below, which may not always be a literal translation.

Solution:
1 *Astérix the gladiator*
2 *Astérix at the Olympic Games*
3 *Astérix and Caesar's gift*
4 *Astérix in Belgium*
5 *Tintin in America*
6 *The Black Island*
7 *The Seven Crystal Balls*
8 *Prisoners of the Sun*

b ➕ As an extension activity students could work in pairs or in groups to invent a comic strip character and write a short comic strip story. The example features a rat called *Rangetout* who likes housework.

Worksheet

Plenaries (pages 68–69)

1 Students practise several different techniques for learning verbs in pairs or groups, e.g. paradigm circle practice, chain verb game and then discuss which they find most useful.

2 Students work individually or in pairs to design a framework for learning verbs, e.g. flower with petals, Ollie the Octopus with 8 tentacles, chest of drawers, house with different person of the verb in each room.

6E Des activités en famille   pages 70–71

- Talk about family activities
- Say what you do at weekends

Grammaire	Stratégies	Phonétique
• Use -er verbs	• Keeping your conversation going	• None

Resources

Audio: 4a *Deux interviews*; 4b *Deux interviews*; 5a *Une conversation*, or CD 3, tracks 13 and 14
Copymasters: 6/4 *Tom et Jojo*, 6/5 *Les verbes*, 6/6 *Des activités*
Worksheets: Starters and plenaries; *Phrases au choix* (W)

Interactive activity: *La vie des Paresseux* (R) ; Keeping your conversation going (Strat)
PowerPoint: *Les Paresseux* (G)
Grammar in Action: None

Worksheet

Starters (pages 70–71)

1 *Chasse à l'intrus* Display or print out the following lists. Students identify the odd word out in each list (shown in bold). Ask students collectively or randomly to give the *'intrus'*. Several students could be asked for their answer before the teacher gives the correct one.

A	B	C	D	E	F
un frère	**février**	quatre	chantons	méchant	un lit
une sœur	préparer	onze	cherchons	petit	**un cahier**
une chambre	détester	**range**	**parlent**	**saute**	une table
un cousin	écouter	douze	parlons	grand	une chaise

2 *Chaque mot à sa place* Display the following task. Give students one minute to read and work out the answers, then ask students collectively or randomly to give the number of the box. Several students could be asked, before confirming the correct answer.

Quelle est la bonne boîte pour chaque mot?

quinze (C), *regardons* (D), *bon* (E), *téléphoner* (B), *cahier* (F), *cousin* (A)

A	B	C	D	E	F
frère	préparer	quatre	chantons	méchant	crayon
cousine	détester	onze	cherchons	petit	stylo
sœur	écouter	douze	parlons	grand	classeur

Tricolore 1 Teacher's Notes   103

6E Des activités en famille

Introduction

Go through the objectives for this spread.

📖 **70**

1 Les frères, c'est difficile!

Check that students have understood the main points by asking a few questions, e.g.
Comment s'appelle le frère de Nathan? (Léo)
Léo, quel âge a-t-il? (4 ans)
Léo, est-il méchant ou mignon?
Nathan, qu'est-ce qu'il pense?
Et sa mère?
Et vous, que pensez-vous/Et toi, que penses-tu?

a This could be prepared orally and the missing words written on the board in random order.

Solution:
1 frère, 2 chambre, 3 méchant, 4 saute, 5 dessine, 6 mange, 7 joue, 8 travaille, 9 chante, 10 danse

b This task involves recognition of a range of verbs, including parts of *avoir* and *être*.

Solution:
Any ten verbs from the following:
J'ai, Il s'appelle, Il a, il partage, Il est, Il saute, il dessine, il joue, il mange, je travaille, il chante, il danse, je raconte, elle dit, il est, il est, pensez-vous

📖 **151 Au choix**

Une petite sœur difficile

▸ **Presentation**

Les Paresseux

📖 **70**

2 Les Paresseux

This gives practice of the *nous* and *ils* forms of regular *-er* verbs.

Solution:
1 nous organisons, 2 les Paresseux surfent, 3 nous jouons, 4 les Paresseux regardent, 5 nous dansons, 6 ils écoutent, 7 nous travaillons, 8 ils restent, ils consultent, 9 nous chantons, 10 ils écoutent, 11 nous fêtons

For follow-up ask some questions, e.g.
Est-ce que les Paresseux jouent au tennis?
Et les Actives, est-ce qu'ils jouent?
Et dans ta famille, vous jouez au tennis ou vous regardez le tennis à la télé?

Extra practice

Students work in groups of six, with each person making up a sentence for one person of a different *-er* verb.

▸ **Interactive activity**

La vie des Paresseux

📖 **71**

3 Le weekend

Practice of all forms of the present tense with a range of *-er* verbs.

Solution:
1 Je prépare, 2 Tu chantes, 3 Il déteste, 4 Elle travaille, 5 Nous surfons, 6 Vous travaillez, 7 Ils aiment, 8 Elles regardent

cm 6/5

Les verbes

📖 🔊 **71**

4 Deux interviews

This listening task provides some examples for students to use in their own conversations in task 5.

a Students listen to Anne and choose the correct sentence of two.

Solution:
1 b, 2 a, 3 b, 4 a, 5 a, 6 b

b Students listen to Marc and choose the correct answer from three options.

Solution:
1 c, 2 b, 3 a, 4 a, 5 c

▸ 🔊 CD 3 Track 13

Deux interviews

Anne
– Bonjour. Comment t'appelles-tu?
– Je m'appelle Anne.
– Est-ce que tu aimes le sport, Anne?
– Non, je n'aime pas le sport.
– Qu'est-ce que tu fais, normalement, le weekend?
– Ça dépend. Quelquefois, je retrouve des amis. Nous discutons ensemble. Nous écoutons de la musique.
– Et quand tu n'es pas avec tes amis, qu'est-ce que tu fais?
– Alors, je joue à la console ou je regarde une vidéo.

Marc
– Et toi, comment t'appelles-tu?
– Je m'appelle Marc.
– Et qu'est-ce que tu fais, normalement, le weekend, Marc?
– Eh bien, moi, j'adore le sport. Alors, je joue au football avec des amis. Quelquefois, je joue au tennis dans le parc.
– Et quand il fait mauvais, qu'est-ce que tu fais?
– Quand il fait mauvais, je regarde du sport à la télé.
– Est-ce que tu aimes la musique?
– Non, je n'aime pas beaucoup la musique.

Tricolore 1 Teacher's Notes

6F On s'amuse

🔊 71   AfL

5 Une conversation

a Students listen to the conversation and follow the text.

> 🔊 **CD 3 Track 14**
>
> **Une conversation**
> A: Qu'est-ce que tu fais normalement, le weekend?
> B: Je joue souvent au foot. J'adore ça. Et toi?
> A: Moi, je joue au tennis. Et quand il pleut?
> B: Je surfe sur Internet. Et toi?
> A: Je regarde un film. Tu retrouves des amis?
> B: Oui, quelquefois. Tu aimes le sport à la télé?
> A: Non, je déteste ça.

b Students adapt the conversation by changing the highlighted words.

c For extension, students should develop the ➕ conversation for as long as possible.

Review the spread objectives and assessment criteria, then use this task for peer assessment. A successful conversation could be shared with the class as a model answer.

71 Stratégies

Keeping your conversation going

This mentions the need to ask questions to keep a conversation going. There could be a brainstorming session with useful questions written on the board.

150 Au choix

4 Des phrases au choix

Worksheet

Phrases au choix

cm 6/6

Des activités

Worksheet

Plenaries (pages 70–71)

1 Students could reflect on techniques for developing speaking skills, such as the ways they used to keep the conversation going in the earlier task.

2 Students could discuss what they have found most useful/difficult so far in the unit.

6F On s'amuse   pages 72–73

- Talk about different activities according to the weather

Grammaire	Stratégies	Phonétique
• Use *on* + verb	• Translating from French to English	• None

Resources

Audio: 4a *Au téléphone*; 4b *Au téléphone*, or CD 3, track 15
Copymasters: 6/7 *Des cartes postales*
Worksheets: Starters and plenaries; *Des cartes postales* (W)

Interactive activity: None
PowerPoint: None
Grammar in Action: None

Worksheet

Starters (pages 72–73)

1 *En groupes* Display or print out a list of words in random order and ask students to put these into 5 groups. Ask volunteers to read out three words in a group or circle them on the board.

chanter, danser, écouter
hiver, printemps, automne
juin, janvier, juillet
Pâques, Noël, Eid
beau, mauvais, chaud

2 *Vrai ou faux* cards Make true/false statements, using the weather/activity flashcards and ask students to hold up a *vrai* or *faux* card.

Introduction

Go through the objectives for this spread.

72

1 La fête de la science

La fête (Faites) de la science is a programme of free scientific events for the general public. It is part of the Europe-wide Festival of Science, which aims to increase the links between professional scientists, researchers and the public.

It usually takes place in October/November and comprises workshops, exhibitions, visits to laboratories and industrial organisations, etc. Some towns set up a marquee to house a *village de science* during the fête.

Tricolore 1 Teacher's Notes   **105**

6F On s'amuse

For further details, see the website:
www.fetedelascience.fr

> Solution:
> 1 *October*
> 2 *exhibitions, visits to laboratories, industrial and natural sites, lectures, films, shows*
> 3 *No, it's free to the public.*
> 4 *More than 1 million*

72 Dossier-langue

Using *on* + verb

Explain that *on* is used a lot in French and can be translated in different ways (one, they, we, you, people in general, etc.).

72 Stratégies

Translating from French to English

This gives some tips about translating from one language to another. For further examples, students might like to find out how the titles of well-known books in English are translated into French.

72

2 Comment ça se dit en anglais?

Students translate sentences with *on* into English. There may be several possible versions.

> Solution:
> 1 *Shall we watch the film on TV?*
> 2 *It's raining so shall we surf the net?*
> 3 *At Easter, people eat Easter eggs.*
> 4 *At Eid, people organise a big meal.*
> 5 *At Diwali, we light lamps.*
> 6 *You don't play football in the kitchen.*
> 7 *The weather's good; shall we play tennis?*
> 8 *They don't speak English in France.*

72

3 Qu'est-ce qu'on fait?

a Students work in pairs using *on* to make suggestions depending on the weather.

b For extension, students complete sentences about different leisure activities.

73

4 Au téléphone

These two conversations bring together the themes of weather and leisure activities.

a Discuss possible answers with students before they listen to the recording. They could also guess the answers first then listen to check.

> Solution:
> 1 *Bordeaux*, 2 *basket*, 3 *beau*, 4 *La Rochelle*, 5 *mauvais*, 6 *chambre*

b In this task, students have to answer questions in French.

> Solution:
> 1 *Max*, 2 *Nicole*, 3 *Max*, 4 *Nicole*, 5 *Il fait très froid.*

CD 3 Track 15

Au téléphone

a **Suzanne et Luc**
  – Allô?
  – Salut, Suzanne. C'est Luc à l'appareil.
  – Ah bonjour, Luc. Ça va?
  – Oui, ça va bien. Je suis à Bordeaux.
  – Ah bon, et qu'est-ce que tu fais là-bas?
  – Je suis avec l'équipe de basket. Nous jouons un match aujourd'hui.
  – Et est-ce qu'il fait beau?
  – Oui, il fait beau, mais pas très chaud. C'est bien. Et toi, qu'est-ce que tu fais aujourd'hui?
  – Ben, ici à La Rochelle, il fait très mauvais. Alors, je reste à la maison et je range ma chambre.

b **Nicole et Max**
  – Allô?
  – Bonjour, Nicole. C'est Max à l'appareil.
  – Ah, bonjour, Max. Ça va?
  – Oui, merci. Et toi?
  – Oui, ça va bien.
  – Qu'est-ce que tu fais aujourd'hui?
  – Je travaille sur l'ordinateur. Je regarde mes emails et je tape des messages.
  – Mais on joue au tennis dans le parc. Tu aimes le tennis? Viens jouer avec nous.
  – Merci, mais il fait très froid aujourd'hui. Je préfère rester à la maison.

73

5 Inventez des conversations

Students practise conversations about the weather and related activities.

73 AfL

6 Des cartes postales

a Students choose the appropriate word for each gap.

> Solution:
> 1 *janvier*, 2 *passe*, 3 *mauvais*, 4 *il*, 5 *On*, 6 *jouent*, 7 *regarde*, 8 *prépare*

b Students write their own postcard using the suggestions and tips given. They could refer back to the earlier stratégies for making written work interesting (SB 35, 38). The task could be prepared orally first, with suggestions written on the board.

Review the objectives and assessment criteria for the spread, then use this task for assessment.

Tricolore 1 Teacher's Notes

6G Le weekend

73
Writing a postcard
Tips for writing cards and messages.

Worksheet
Des cartes postales

cm 6/7
Des cartes postales

151 Au choix
6 Ça dépend du temps

151 Au choix
7 Mon blog des vacances

Worksheet
Plenary (pages 72–73)
Students could reflect on writing French; what they find easy and difficult, whether they find writing words and phrases helps to reinforce learning

6G Le weekend   pages 74–75

- Discuss what you do at the weekend
- Answer questions about free-time activities

Grammaire	Stratégies	Phonétique
• None	• Giving detailed answers	• None

Resources

Audio: 3 *Deux personnes*, or CD 3, track 16
Copymasters: 6/8 *Tu comprends?*, 6/9 *Sommaire*
Worksheets: Starters and plenaries
e-book: *Le blog de Sébastien*

Interactive activity: Classroom commands (V)
Video : *Le sport préféré de Manon*
PowerPoint: None
Grammar in Action: None

Worksheet

Starters (pages 74–75)

1 *5-4-3-2-1* Display a list of words and students find groups of 5,4,3,2,1 similar words.
   e.g. *aimer, chercher, écouter, regarder, travailler*
   froid, chaud, beau, mauvais
   printemps, hiver, été
   volley, tennis de table
   souvent

   A sheet with a printed grid for this could be distributed for students to record their answers.

2 *C'est comme l'anglais mais le son est différent*
   Give out a list of cognates or near cognates.
   a *animal*   e *juin*
   b *automne*   f *message*
   c *chocolat*   g *région*
   d *iPod*   h *rugby*
   Read them out in a different order, as below. Students note the number by the word they hear. When checking, ask for volunteers to say the words in French.
   1 *animal*   5 *juin*
   2 *iPod*   6 *message*
   3 *rugby*   7 *chocolat*
   4 *automne*   8 *région*

Introduction
Go through the objectives for this spread. The sequence of tasks should help students to have a conversation with at least three exchanges.

74
1 Des questions
Students write any three questions, using three different structures.

74
2 Des réponses
Working individually, students write answers for their three questions. Alternatively they could work in pairs, asking a partner a question and responding in turn.

74 Stratégies
Giving detailed answers
Explain how students can extend their answers by giving more detail, e.g. covering, who, what, why, when etc.

Tricolore 1 Teacher's Notes 107

6G Le weekend

🔊 74

3 Deux personnes

Students listen to two people in conversation using similar questions and answers and complete the gaps in their text.

Solution:
1 le weekend, **2** amis, **3** mauvais, **4** badminton, **5** basket, **6** télé, **7** musique

> 🔊 CD 3 Track 16
>
> **Deux personnes**
> – Qu'est-ce que tu fais le weekend?
> – Je joue souvent au foot avec mes amis. Quand il fait mauvais, je surfe sur Internet. Est-ce que tu joues au foot?
> – Non, je ne joue pas au foot, mais quelquefois, je joue au badminton avec ma sœur. Tu aimes le sport?
> – Oui, j'adore le sport. Je joue au foot et au basket et je regarde souvent des matchs à la télé. Et toi?
> – Le sport, ça va, mais je préfère écouter de la musique ou surfer sur Internet.

| Interactive activity |

On discute des vacances

74   AfL

4 Une conversation

a Working in pairs, students make up a conversation with at least three exchanges.

b For extension, students could make up a longer ➕ conversation.

This task can be used for peer assessment. Relate success criteria to the spread objectives and encourage students to demonstrate their skills.

74

5 Des photos

Students choose one of the photos and write a short text about it, using the questions as a framework.

cm 6/8

Tu comprends?

75 cm 6/9

Sommaire

A summary of the main vocabulary and structures in the unit.

| Interactive activity |

Rue Danton: Le sport préféré de Manon

| Interactive activity |

Vocabulaire de classe (6)

| Worksheet |

| Presentation |

Le blog de Sébastien

| Interactive activity |

Vocabulaire (6)

| Worksheet |

Plenaries (pages 74–75)

Reflect on the importance of correct pronunciation when speaking French. Give students some cognates to practise saying in French. See if students are beginning to grasp spelling and pronunciation patterns.

e.g. **1** *danger*   **5** *nature*
      2 *excellent*   **6** *table*
      3 *intelligent* **7** *imagination*
      4 *incident*   **8** *important*

Use the *Sommaire* to review the objectives of the unit and what has been learnt. Discuss how the language learnt could be useful in other contexts.

Unité 6 Consolidation and assessment

Épreuves Unité 6

🔊 cm 6/10

Écouter

A Le temps et les saisons

Solution:
1 f, **2** d, **3** i, **4** h, **5** e, **6** g, **7** b, **8** a, **9** c
(mark /4) ½ mark per correct item

🔊 CD 3 Track 17

Le temps et les saisons

1 – Il neige.
  – Ah oui, il neige.
2 – Il fait chaud.
  – Pff, comme il fait chaud.
3 – Il y a du vent.
  – Oui, quel vent.
4 – Il pleut.
  – Oui, il pleut beaucoup.
5 – Il fait froid.
  – Oui, il fait très froid.
6 – Il y a du brouillard.
  – Oui, il y a du brouillard.
7 – C'est l'hiver.
  – On est en hiver.
8 – Moi, je préfère le printemps. Le printemps, c'est ma saison préférée.
9 – Il y a du soleil.
  – Oui, j'adore le soleil.

B À la maison

Solution:

	Musique	ord'teur	cartes	dessiner	télé	console
1 Sanjay			✓			
2 Claire				✓		
3 Jonathan						✓
4 Magali					✓	
5 Daniel	✓					
6 Sika		✓				

(mark /5)

🔊 CD 3 Track 18

À la maison

1 – Qu'est-ce que tu fais quand il fait mauvais, Sanjay?
  – Moi, je joue aux cartes avec mes amis.
  – Tu joues aux cartes. C'est bien.
2 – Et toi, Claire, qu'est-ce que tu fais?
  – Moi, je dessine. J'aime beaucoup dessiner.
3 – Jonathan, qu'est-ce que tu fais, normalement, quand tu es à la maison?
  – Je joue à la console. J'adore les jeux vidéo.
  – Alors, toi, tu joues à la console.
4 – Et toi, Magali, qu'est-ce que tu fais?
  – Moi, je regarde la télévision.
  – Tu regardes la télévision.
5 – Et toi, Daniel, qu'est-ce que tu fais quand il fait mauvais?
  – J'écoute de la musique sur mon baladeur. J'adore la musique.
6 – Et toi, Sika, qu'est-ce que tu fais à la maison?
  – Je travaille sur l'ordinateur. J'écris des messages électroniques à mes amis.
  – Alors, toi, tu travailles sur l'ordinateur.

C Une interview

Solution:
Nom: *Hériot* (1 mark)
Prénom: *Claire*
Adresse: *81 rue Saint-Pierre* (1 mark)
Numéro de téléphone: *13 67 90 75 42* (5 marks)
Sports préférés: *hockey* ✓; *volley* ✓ (2 marks)
Autres loisirs: *drawing* ✓; *listening to music* ✓ (2 marks)
(mark /11) the name Claire is given and is not awarded a mark

🔊 CD 3 Track 19

Une interview

– Bonjour. Comment t'appelles-tu?
– Je m'appelle Claire Hériot.
– Hériot. Comment ça s'écrit?
– H–É–R–I–O–T.
– Alors, c'est H–É–R–I–O–T.
– C'est exact.
– Et ton adresse, Claire?
– Alors, mon adresse, c'est quatre-vingt-un, rue Saint-Pierre.
– Quatre-vingt-un, rue Saint-Pierre. Très bien. Et ton numéro de téléphone?
– Mon numéro de téléphone c'est le 13, 67, 90, 75, 42.
– Alors, je répète, c'est le 13, 67, 90, 75, 42. Et quels sont tes sports favoris?
– Mes sports favoris sont le hockey et le volley.
– Alors, tes sports favoris sont le hockey et le volley. Très bien. Et est-ce que tu as d'autres loisirs, à part le sport?
– Oui, j'écoute souvent de la musique et je dessine.
– Bon, tu écoutes de la musique et tu dessines. Très bien. Merci, Claire.

cm 6/11

Lire

A Des activités

Solution:
1 f, **2** e, **3** h, **4** b, **5** c, **6** g, **7** d, **8** a
(mark /7)

B Samedi

Solution:
1 c, **2** g, **3** d, **4** e, **5** a, **6** b, **7** f
(mark /6)

C Une lettre de Bordeaux

Solution:
1 *faux*, **2** *vrai*, **3** *vrai*, **4** *faux*, **5** *vrai*, **6** *vrai*, **7** *vrai*, **8** *faux*
(mark /7)

Tricolore 1 Teacher's Notes 109

Unité 6 Consolidation and assessment

cm 6/12

Écrire et grammaire W

A Le temps

> **Solution:**
> **1** *mauvais,* **2** *beau,* **3** *chaud,* **4** *froid*
> **(mark /3)**

B Quel temps fait-il?

> **Solution:**
> **1** *Il neige.* **2** *Il pleut.* **3** *Il y a du soleil.* **4** *Il y a du vent.* **5** *Il y a du brouillard.*
> **(mark /4)**

C À Dieppe

> **Solution:**
> **1** *passe,* **2** *habitent,* **3** *travaille,* **4** *jouons,* **5** *aimes,* **6** *chantent,* **7** *rentrez*
> **(marks/6)**

D Une carte postale

> **Solution:**
> **(mark /7)** 1 mark for each meaningful sentence + 2 marks for style/accuracy

Presse-Jeunesse

76–77

Presse-Jeunesse 2

This magazine-style section provides material for reading for pleasure. The items can be used flexibly at any appropriate time, by students working alone.

76–77

1 Le nouvel élève

Students answer the questions in English.

> **Solution:**
> 1 He seems nice.
> 2 He lives in a village.
> 3 He has one brother.
> 4 He's invited to go to a café.
> 5 He's invited to play in a football team.
> 6 He's excused a detention when the rest of the class have to stay behind.
> 7 He has to look after his younger brother while his mother is working.
> 8 His classmates understand the situation and invite his brother to come and watch the football match.

77

La chanson des saisons

Students listen or sing along to the song, (see TB page 96 for transcript).

77

2 Tom et Jojo – Jojo gagne le fromage

Students read the cartoon and find the French for phrases 1–6.

> **Solution:**
> 1 *aujourd'hui*
> 2 *dans la cuisine*
> 3 *aussi*
> 4 *soudain*
> 5 *Il saute sur une chaise.*
> 6 *Le fromage roule.*

Au choix

150 Au choix

1 Quel temps fait-il?

Further practice of writing weather descriptions.

> **Solution:**
> 1 *À Brighton, il fait mauvais.*
> 2 *À Exeter, il fait chaud.*
> 3 *À Bristol, il y a du soleil.*
> 4 *À Bangor, il pleut.*
> 5 *À Dublin, il y a du vent.*
> 6 *À Belfast, il fait beau.*
> 7 *À Glasgow, il fait froid.*
> 8 *À Aberdeen, il neige.*
> 9 *À Leeds, il y a du brouillard.*
> 10 *À Ipswich, il fait beau.*

150 Au choix

2 La météo

To extend their listening skills, students listen to a radio broadcast about events and weather in the UK and note down the details.

> **Solution:**
> **a** *il fait froid,* **b** *6°,* **c** *rugby,* **d** *(il y a du) vent,* **e** *10°,* **f** *football,* **g** *il fait beau,* **h** *12°,* **i** *hockey*

110 Tricolore 1 Teacher's Notes

Unité 6 Consolidation and assessment

🖱️ 🔊 CD 3 Track 20

La météo

– Ce weekend, il y a des matchs importants en Angleterre, en Écosse et au pays de Galles. Alors, quel temps fait-il là-bas ce weekend, Robert Legrand?
– Oui, eh bien, ce weekend le temps est assez variable. À Cardiff, par exemple, où il y a un grand match de rugby, la France contre le pays de Galles, il fait froid. La température est de 6 degrés.
– Oh, à Cardiff, il fait froid. Alors, bon courage à tous les supporters de l'équipe de France. Et à Birmingham?
– À Birmingham, il y a du vent assez fort, alors il ne fait pas beau non plus. Oui, à Birmingham, il y a du vent pour le match de football cet après-midi … mais la température est de 10 degrés, une température normale pour la saison.
– Hmm, du vent à Birmingham. Et en Écosse?
– Eh bien, à Édimbourg, pour le grand match international de hockey, il fait beau. Alors, si vous allez à Édimbourg pour le match de hockey, vous avez de la chance, il fait beau. La température est de 12 degrés.
– Très bien, du beau temps à Édimbourg. Merci, Robert.

📖 150 Au choix

3 Devant la télé

This task gives practice in writing out different parts of the verb *regarder* and provides consolidation for all students.

Solution:
1 *regardes*, 2 *regarde*, 3 *regardent*, 4 *regardez*, 5 *regardent*, 6 *regardons*, 7 *regarde*, 8 *regardent*, 9 *regarde*, 10 *regardent*, 11 *regarde*

📖 150 Au choix

4 Des phrases au choix

Students throw a die or write down numbers randomly to create different sentences. This can be done initially as a speaking activity (pair or groupwork), then written. Students could compete to make up the silliest sentence.

📖 151 Au choix

5 Une petite sœur difficile

This letter, in response to the earlier letter from Nathan (SB page 70, 1 *Les frères, c'est difficile!*), provides further practice of verbs in the context of family life.

a *Vrai/faux* task. For extension, students could correct the false statements.

Solution:
1 *vrai*, 2 *faux* (Elle a une sœur.) 3 *vrai*, 4 *faux* (Elle a sept ans.) 5 *vrai*, 6 *faux* (Sophie porte les vêtements de Julie.) 7 *vrai*

b Students complete a summary of the letter. The missing words could be written in jumbled order on the board.

Solution:
1 *sœur*, 2 *Elle*, 3 *chambre*, 4 *pulls, chaussures*, 5 *écoute, danse*, 6 *travaille*, 7 *jouent*

c Students complete sentences about a difficult younger sister.

Solution:
1 *travaille, mange*, 2 *joue*, 3 *dessine*, 4 *regarde*

📖 151 Au choix

6 Ça dépend du temps

An open-ended task in which students complete the sentences with an appropriate activity.

📖 151 Au choix

7 Mon blog des vacances

Students describe the weather and activities for different days.

Copymasters

cm 6/1

Le temps

Students copy the correct caption for each weather picture. The cards can then be cut up and used for speaking or matching activities, e.g.

Tu fais la météo

Students work in pairs. The weather cards are spread out face down. One asks about the weather in a town and the other turns over a weather card and describes the weather.

e.g. *Quel temps fait-il à Reading?*
Il fait beau aujourd'hui.

cm 6/2

Vocabulaire: la météo et les saisons

Further practice of vocabulary linked to spreads 6A and 6B.

Solution:
1 *Des mots en serpent*
   1 *mauvais*, 2 *froid*, 3 *beau*, 4 *chaud*, 5 *le printemps*
2 *Complète les mots*
   Le ciel est bleu. Il fait chaud.
   Il fait beau. Il y a du soleil.
   Il fait mauvais. Il neige. Il pleut.
   Il y a du vent.
3 *Complète les conversations*
   A – Quel 1 *temps* fait-il en général dans les Alpes?
       – En hiver et au 2 *printemps* il 3 *neige*. Les hivers sont longs. Il fait 4 *froid* mais souvent il y a du 5 *soleil*.
   B – Et dans le Midi?
       – Bon, chez nous, à Nice, il fait 1 *beau* toute l'année. En été, il fait très 2 *chaud* et il ne 3 *pleut* pas souvent, mais il y a du 4 *vent*.
4 *Voici la météo*
   1 *juin*, 2 *dix-huit*, 3 *chaud*, 4 *pleut*, 5 *vent*, 6 *température*, 7 *degrés*

Unité 6 Consolidation and assessment

cm 6/3

La météo

In this information-gap activity, students exchange details about the weather in different towns in order to complete a weather map.

cm 6/4

Tom et Jojo

1 Un petit lexique

This gives the vocabulary required for task 2. Students write down the English meanings.

> **Solution:**
> *adorer* — to love
> *aimer* — to like
> *arriver* — to arrive
> *chasser* — to chase
> *chercher* — to look for
> *détester* — to hate
> *entrer* — to come/go in
> *manger* — to eat
> *penser* — to think
> *regarder* — to look at/watch
> *rentrer* — to return
> *sauter* — to jump

2 Tom et Jojo

Practice of the *il* and *je* forms of the *-er* verbs in the previous list.

> **Solution:**
> **1** *cherche*, **2** *pense*, **3** *regarde*, **4** *entre*, **5** *chasse*, **6** *saute*, **7** *rentre*, **8** *arrive, chasse*, **9** *mange*, **10** *déteste*, **11** *aime*, **12** *adore*

cm 6/5

Les verbes

This provides further practice of the present tense of *-er* verbs.

> **Solution:**
> **1 Sept verbes**
> **1** *chantons*, **2** *regardez*, **3** *préparent*, **4** *travaille*, **5** *écoutes*, **6** *dansent*, **7** *travaillent*
> **2 Qu'est-ce qu'on dit?**
> **1** *joue*, **2** *travailles*, **3** *prépare*, **4** *joue*, **5** *dansons*, **6** *aimez*, **7** *regardent*

cm 6/6

Des activités

Further practice of sport, *-er* verbs and adverbs of time.

1 J'adore le sport

> **Solution:**

b	h	m	r	u	g	b	y	l
a	a	e	h	m	s	t	g	h
s	l	d	i	o	w	u	o	o
k	e	t	m	c	s	a	l	c
e	p	r	a	i	o	t	f	k
t	m	t	e	n	n	i	s	e
k	l	i	o	v	s	t	r	y
c	v	o	l	l	e	y	o	a
f	o	o	t	b	a	l	l	n

2 Chaque jour, un sport différent.

Various answers are possible.

3 Un acrostiche

> **Solution:**
> **1** *téléphonent*, **2** *retrouve*, **3** *cliques*, **4** *préfère*, **5** *écoutez*, **6** *tapent*, **7** *restons*

4 Les verbes

> **Solution:**
> Students complete the table as follows:

anglais	français	phrases
1 to draw	dessiner	dessine
2 to sing	chanter	chantes
3 to listen to	écouter	écoute
4 to dance	danser	danse
5 to play	jouer	jouons
6 to watch	regarder	regardez
7 to type	taper	tapent
8 to prepare	préparer	préparent

cm 6/7

Des cartes postales

This provides further practice of weather, leisure and verbs for use here or later for revision.

1 À lire

> **Solution:**
> **1** ~~un mois~~ – une semaine
> **2** ~~août~~ – octobre
> **3** ~~beau~~ – mauvais
> **4** ~~volley~~ – tennis de table

2 À compléter

> **Solution:**
> Bordeaux, le 12 avril
> Nous passons un weekend ici, dans un hôtel.
> C'est pour fêter l'anniversaire de mon père.
> Il fait chaud. Il y a du soleil. C'est fantastique.
> Aujourd'hui, nous jouons au tennis.
> À bientôt,
> Alex

Unité 6 Consolidation and assessment

3 À écrire

Students can now write their own postcards based on the details given.

🔊 cm 6/8

Tu comprends?

1 Les numéros de téléphone

Solution:
le cinéma Rex: 03.24.13.42.50
le café Robert: 03.15.56.37.60
le collège: 03.39.68.12.41
la famille Laurent: 03.75.80.16.23

🔊 CD 3 Track 21

Les numéros de téléphone

1 – Tu as le numéro de téléphone du cinéma Rex?
  – Oui, le voilà. C'est le zéro trois, vingt-quatre, treize, quarante-deux, cinquante.
  – Alors, je répète: zéro trois, vingt-quatre, treize, quarante-deux, cinquante.
2 – Le numéro du café Robert, qu'est-ce que c'est?
  – C'est le zéro trois, quinze, cinquante-six, trente-sept, soixante. Je répète: zéro trois, quinze, cinquante-six, trente-sept, soixante.
3 – Le numéro du collège, qu'est-ce que c'est?
  – C'est le zéro trois, trente-neuf, soixante-huit, douze, quarante-et-un.
  – Alors, je répète: zéro trois, trente-neuf, soixante-huit, douze, quarante-et-un.
4 – Vous avez le numéro de téléphone de la famille Laurent?
  – Oui, le voilà. C'est le zéro trois, soixante-quinze, quatre-vingts, seize, vingt-trois. Je répète: zéro trois, soixante-quinze, quatre-vingts, seize, vingt-trois.

2 La météo

Solution:
1 b, **2** b, **3** a, **4** a, c, **5** b, a, **6** b, b

🔊 CD 3 Track 22

La météo

– Bonjour mesdames et messieurs. Aujourd'hui, nous sommes le jeudi quinze janvier. Il fait froid. Est-ce que ça va continuer, Claire Artaud?
– Oui, en effet, il fait froid et il va continuer à faire froid dans toute la France. La température est de trois degrés. À Paris, il pleut et il y a du vent.
– Alors de la pluie et du vent à Paris. Et dans les Alpes, est-ce qu'il y a de la neige?
– Oui, dans les Alpes, il y a de la neige et il y a aussi du brouillard. Alors, faites très attention, si vous êtes en montagne.
– Alors, dans les Alpes, de la neige et du brouillard. Et le beau temps, est-ce qu'il y a du beau temps aussi?
– Oui, dans l'ouest, à Bordeaux, il y a du soleil et il fait assez beau, mais il fait toujours froid.
– Alors, voilà, pour trouver le beau temps, il faut aller à Bordeaux. Merci, Claire.

3 Comment ça s'écrit?

Solution:
4 (cahier) is the odd word out.

🔊 CD 3 Track 23

Comment ça s'écrit?

1 c–h–a–n–t–e–r
2 j–o–u–e–r
3 a–i–m–e–r
4 c–a–h–i–e–r
5 é–c–o–u–t–e–r
6 p–r–é–p–a–r–e–r
7 t–r–a–v–a–i–l–l–e–r

4 Un sondage sur le sport

Solution:

	bad-minton	basket	hockey	foot-ball	tennis	volley
1 Anne					✓	✓
2 Marc		✓		✓		
3 Nicole						✓
4 Paul	✓		✓			
5 Lucie	✓				✓	✓
6 Robert				✓		
Total	2	1	1	2	2	3

Le sport le plus populaire est: le volley

🔊 CD 3 Track 24

Un sondage sur le sport

1 – Bonjour, Anne. Est-ce que tu fais du sport?
  – Oui, je fais beaucoup de sport. Je joue au volley et je joue au tennis.
2 – Bonjour, Marc. Est-ce que tu aimes le sport?
  – Oui, j'aime le sport. Je joue au football et au basket.
3 – Bonjour, Nicole. Est-ce que toi aussi tu aimes le sport?
  – Non, pas beaucoup, mais je joue quelquefois au volley.
4 – Tu es Paul, c'est bien ça?
  – Oui, c'est moi.
  – Alors, Paul, est-ce que tu fais du sport?
  – Oui, je fais beaucoup de sport. Je joue au badminton et au hockey. J'aime bien ça.
5 – Lucie, est-ce que tu aimes le sport?
  – Le sport? Oui, j'adore le sport.
  – Qu'est-ce que tu fais comme sports?
  – Je joue au badminton et au tennis et je joue aussi au volley.
6 – Et toi, Robert, est-ce que tu aimes le sport?
  – Un peu. Je joue quelquefois au football, mais c'est tout.

cm 6/9

Sommaire

A summary of the main vocabulary and structures in the unit.

Unité 7

Tricolore 1 Unité 7 En ville pages   Pages 78–93

7A La Rochelle pages 78–79		
• Learn about a town in France • Learn some town vocabulary • Say what happens regularly on a particular day		
Grammaire	Stratégies	Phonétique
• in, an, at + day/time of day	• None	• The letter 'h-' at the beginning of a word
Resources		
Audio: 1a *Voici La Rochelle*, or CD 3, track 25 **Copymasters:** None **Worksheets:** Starters and plenaries		**Interactive activity:** None **Ph** The letter 'h-' at the beginning of a word, or CD 3, track 26 **PowerPoint:** *La Rochelle* (V) **Grammar in Action:** None

7B Qu'est-ce qu'il y a en ville? pages 80–81		
• Understand and give information about a town		
Grammaire	Stratégies	Phonétique
• Learn more about adjectives	• Working out meaning (5)	• None
Resources		
Audio: 1b *En ville*, or CD 3, track 27 **Copymasters:** 7/1 *En ville* **Worksheets:** Starters and plenaries		**Interactive activity:** *Un weekend en ville* (R) **Ph** None **PowerPoint:** *En ville* 1 (V) **Grammar in Action:** None

7C C'est près d'ici? pages 82–83		
• Ask for and understand directions in town • Understand and give directions		
Grammaire	Stratégies	Phonétique
• None	• None	• The letters '-t' or '-te' at the end of a word
Resources		
Audio: 1 *Où vont les touristes?*; 3 *On arrive en ville*; 4 *Dans quelle direction?*; 7a *Conversations en ville*, or CD 3, tracks 28, 29, 30 and 31 **Copymasters:** 7/2 Vocabulaire: *Les endroits*, 7/3 *C'est quelle direction?* **Worksheets:** Starters and plenaries; *À gauche, à droite?* (W)		**Interactive activity:** *Des touristes* (L) **Ph** The letters '-t' or '-te' at the end of a word, or CD 3, track 32 **PowerPoint:** *Trouver son chemin* (V) **Grammar in Action:** None

7D Où exactement? pages 84–85		
• Discuss possible activities in town		
Grammaire	Stratégies	Phonétique
• Use the preposition *à* (*au, à la, à l', aux*) and other prepositions	• Remembering the gender of nouns (3)	• None
Resources		
Audio: 4 *On va où?*, or CD 3, track 33 **Copymasters:** 7/4 *Où va-t-on?*, 7/5 *C'est où?* **Worksheets:** Starters and plenaries; *Trois conversations en ville* (S); *Au / à la / à l'/ aux* (G)		**Interactive activity:** *Dans la rue* (L); *La preposition à* (G); Remembering the gender of nouns (Strat) **PowerPoint:** None **Grammar in Action:** pp22–23, 26–27

7E Elle est comment, ta ville? pages 86–87		
• Talk about the area where you live		
Grammaire	Stratégies	Phonétique
• Use *il y a…* and *il n'y a pas de…*	• Adding interest to your writing (3)	• The letters 'th'
Resources		
Audio: 2 *Mon quartier*, or CD 3, track 34 **Copymasters:** 7/6 *En ville* (2), 7/7 *Ma ville/mon village*, 7/8 *Un plan à compléter* **Worksheets:** Starters and plenaries; *Ma ville et mon quartier* (W); Adding interest to your writing (Strat)		**Interactive activity:** None **Ph** The letters 'th', or CD 3, track 35 **PowerPoint:** Kim's game; *En ville* (2) **Grammar in Action:** None

Key language

7F Allez, on y va pages 72–73		
• Make plans and talk about where you are going		
Grammaire	Stratégies	Phonétique
• Use the verb *aller*	• None	• The letters 'on', 'om'
Resources		
Audio: 2a-b *Coralie est au lit*, or CD 3, track 36 **Copymasters:** 7/9 Aller **Worksheets:** Starters and plenaries; *Le weekend* (W)	**Interactive activity:** None **Ph** The letters 'on', 'om', CD 3, track 37 **PowerPoint:** None **Grammar in Action:** pp24–25	

7G Une ville touristique pages 90–91		
• Understand tourist information		
Grammaire	Stratégies	Phonétique
• None	• Reading and listening to longer passages	• None
Resources		
Audio: 2a *À l'office de tourisme*; Listening to longer passages, or CD 3, track 38 **Copymasters:** 7/10 *Tu comprends?*, 7/11 *Sommaire* **Worksheets:** Starters and plenaries **e-book:** *Bienvenues à La Rochelle*	**Interactive activity:** Classroom commands (V) **PowerPoint:** None **Video:** *En ville* **Grammar in Action:** None	

Key language

Places in a town (7A and 7B)

un aquarium
une auberge de jeunesse
une banque
une bibliothèque
un bowling
un camping
un centre commercial
un centre sportif
un château
une gare
la Grosse-Horloge
un hôpital
un hôtel
un hôtel de ville
un magasin
un marché
un musée
un office de tourisme
un parc
un parking
une patinoire
une piscine
une place
une poste
un restaurant
un terrain de football
un théâtre
une tour
des bâtiments religieux
une cathédrale
une église
une mosquée
une synagogue
un temple

Directions (7C and 7D)

Pardon, monsieur/madame
Pour aller au centre-ville, s'il vous plaît?
Est-ce qu'il y a un café près d'ici?
Où est …?
C'est …
à gauche
à droite
tout droit
Prenez la première (1ère) rue à gauche.
Tournez à droite.
Continuez tout droit.
C'est loin?
C'est tout près.
C'est (assez) loin.
Ce n'est pas loin.
C'est à 50 mètres.

Prepositions (7D)

C'est devant l'église.
C'est derrière l'église.
C'est entre le cinéma et le café.
C'est à côté du cinéma.
C'est à côté de la poste.

Describing places (7E)

Il y a …
Il n'y a pas de …

The present tense of *aller* (7F)

7A La Rochelle

Introduction

La Rochelle

This unit contains information that will be useful when visiting any French town, but La Rochelle was selected as the setting for this unit for a variety of reasons:

- it is an attractive place to visit and a holiday resort, but also very much a working town; a university was opened in 1992.
- it is a major centre for marine and nautical activities (Aquarium opened in 2000).
- it combines old and new areas and has both picturesque buildings and modern developments; it is big enough to contain many interesting features, but not too big to visit on foot.
- it has been at the forefront in developing initiatives to protect the environment and has pioneered recycling schemes, pedestrian zones in the town centre (1975), the municipal bikes scheme (1976) and the use of electric cars. Michel Crépeau was elected mayor in 1971 and later became Minister for the Environment (1981–1983). An earlier councillor was nicknamed *Monsieur Imagination*.
- the festival of French music, *Les Francofolies*, set up in 1984, attracts many musicians in July.
- it is easy to reach by rail, road and air and welcomes school parties!

For more information about La Rochelle, see
http://www.ville-larochelle.fr
http://www.larochelle-tourisme.com.

7A La Rochelle   pages 78–79

- Learn about a town in France
- Learn some town vocabulary
- Say what happens regularly on a particular day

Grammaire	Stratégies	Phonétique
• in, an, at + day/time of day	• None	• The letter 'h-' at the beginning of a word

Resources

Audio: 1a *Voici La Rochelle*, or CD 3, track 25
Copymasters: None
Worksheets: Starters and plenaries

Interactive activity: None
Ph The letter 'h-' at the beginning of a word, or CD 3, track 26
PowerPoint: *La Rochelle* (V)
Grammar in Action: None

Worksheet

Starters (pages 78–79)

1 **5-4-3-2-1** Play in small groups or as a class. Display the following words in random order or partially group them with 1 or 2 word(s) to be added to each group.

5 *bâtiments: une maison, un café, un cinéma, un appartement, un magasin*

4 *points du compas: nord, sud, est, ouest*

3 *saisons: hiver, printemps, été*

2 *prépositions: dans, à*

1 *endroit où se trouvent les bâtiments: une rue*

A sheet with a printed grid could be distributed for students to record their answers. This could then be checked and completed as a class activity.

2 **Use after *Phonétique* has been introduced.** Display the following words and ask students if they can guess/remember how they would be pronounced in French. They could practise in pairs and then volunteers could demonstrate their French pronunciation.

un hôpital, un hôtel, horrible, le horizon, une histoire

Introduction

Go through the objectives for this spread. Mention that the French town of La Rochelle provides the background for the unit. It has been linked with *Tricolore* for over 30 years and has become increasingly popular as a tourist destination (the 3rd most visited town in France); 25% are foreign tourists, of which the majority are English. The town is also known for its many environmental initiatives.

Presentation

La Rochelle

🔊 78

1 La Rochelle

Look at the photos with the class and discuss what they show about the town.

a Students listen to the recording and match the text with the pictures, either individually or in pairs.

Solution:

1 *I*, **2** *B*, **3** *G*, **4** *K*, **5** *A*, **6** *F*, **7** *L*, **8** *H*, **9** *D*, **10** *J*, **11** *C*, **12** *E*

7A La Rochelle

🔊 CD 3 Track 25

La Rochelle

1 – Salut! Je m'appelle Marine, et voici mon frère, Noah.
  – Nous habitons à La Rochelle. C'est une ville dans l'ouest de la France.
2 – La Rochelle est au bord de la mer, alors on fait beaucoup de sports nautiques,
3 – Dans le centre-ville, il y a beaucoup de magasins et de cafés. Il y a un marché dans les rues le mercredi et le samedi.
4 – Et pour se connecter à l'internet, il y a un hotspot wifi, près du parking Saint-Nicolas.
5 – En été, il fait très beau ici et beaucoup de touristes visitent la ville. Ils vont au Vieux-Port et ses trois tours. Quelquefois, il y a des acrobates et des clowns, c'est amusant.
6 – Moi, je vais souvent à la piscine.
7 – Pour aider les touristes, il y a un office de tourisme. Il y a des touristes français, mais aussi beaucoup de touristes britanniques.
8 – Les touristes logent à l'hôtel, au camping ou à l'auberge de jeunesse.
9 – Voici l'hôtel de ville avec son drapeau tricolore.
10 – En ville, il y a des jardins et des parcs.
11 – Il y a aussi des musées et un aquarium. Moi, j'aime bien le musée maritime. On monte à bord de différents bateaux. C'est très sympa.
12 – Et, en été, au mois de juillet, il y a un grand festival de musique avec beaucoup de concerts. Ça s'appelle les Francofolies.

b Students find the French for town vocabulary.

> **Solution:**
> **1** *le centre-ville*, **2** *beaucoup de magasins*, **3** *un marché*, **4** *une piscine*, **5** *un office de tourisme*, **6** *l'auberge de jeunesse*, **7** *l'hôtel de ville*, **8** *le musée*

C'est quelle image?

The class could be divided into two teams. Someone from each team in turn says something about one of the pictures and the other team has to identify the appropriate picture, e.g.
– Ça, c'est le vieux port.
– C'est l'image A. Voici l'hôtel de ville. C'est joli, non?
– C'est l'image D. Ça, c'est le parc.

c As extension, students could research another town in France and write about it. This could be done individually or as a group task.

Interactive activity

The letter 'h-' at the beginning of a word

🔊 79 Phonétique

The letter 'h-' at the beginning of a word

A full explanation of this sound is given on *kerboodle!*, together with interactive practice.

Explain that the letter *h-* at the beginning of a word is usually silent, as if the word begins with a vowel. For these words, the article changes to *l'*, *je* changes to *j'* etc.

a Say the word *l'homme* with an appropriate gesture. Students repeat the word with the same gesture. Then read out the other words, with the students repeating each one: *j'habite, l'hôpital, en hiver*. The words are also included on the recording for optional use.

If helpful at this stage, explain the use of aspirate h, i.e. that for some words beginning with h, the *'h-'* is not pronounced, but acts like a consonant, so there is a pause (for a breath) before the word is pronounced. With these words, the full article is used as though the word begins with a consonant and not a vowel.

To demonstrate this, write and pronounce the following words: *le hamster, Le Havre, le hockey*. Again, these variations are also given on the recording.

Parts **b** and **c** can be used for further pronunciation practice.

b Ask students to listen and repeat the words they hear. Then display the words **a** *l'histoire*, **b** *la Hongrie*, **c** *le héros*, **d** *l'hôtel*, **e** *l'horloge* for students to match (**d, a, e, c, b**).

c Students listen to the silly sentence and note down how many times they hear the sound (7). They can then repeat the sentence to help them remember this sound.

For further practice, write some additional words on the board to check that students recognise the link between spelling and related pronunciation, e.g. *Hélène, habitant, huit, historique*.

🔊 CD 3 Track 26

The letter 'h-' at the beginning of a word

Écoutez et répétez:
a l'homme, j'habite, l'hôpital, en hiver
  Des exceptions: le hamster, Le Havre, le hockey, les haricots verts
b l'hôtel, l'histoire, l'horloge, le héros, la Hongrie
c En hiver Henri et ses huit hamsters habitent à l'hôpital au Havre.

79 Dossier-langue

Say what happens regularly on a particular day

Encourage students to deduce the rule about using *le* with a day of the week to mean 'on' or 'every'. Students then translate the four sentences. For extension, students could make up two or more additional sentences based on the examples given.

> **Solution:**
> **1** I go to the swimming pool on Fridays.
> **2** There's a market in town every Thursday.
> **3** The castle is open on Tuesdays.
> **4** The restaurant is closed on Sundays.

Tricolore 1 Teacher's Notes 117

7B Qu'est-ce qu'il y a en ville?

Worksheet

Plenaries (pages 78–79)

1 Develop the discussion about learning about words, spelling, gender and meaning. Discuss useful tips for remembering these, such as colour-coding, writing masculine words and feminine words in clearly different lists or in a different place (either right/left or opposite sides of the page), learning with a phrase or adjective which clearly denotes feminine gender e.g. *grande/petite*.

2 Practise some of these ideas with a brainstorming session in which one half of the class thinks of masculine town vocabulary and the other half thinks of feminine words. These are then listed on the board in two sections, using blue and red to denote gender.

7B Qu'est-ce qu'il y a en ville? pages 80–81

- Understand and give information about a town

Grammaire	Stratégies	Phonétique
• Learn more about adjectives	• Working out meaning (5)	• None

Resources

Audio: 1b *En ville*, or CD 3, track 27
Copymasters: 7/1 *En ville*
Worksheets: Starters and plenaries

Interactive activity: *Un weekend en ville* (R)
Ph None
PowerPoint: *En ville* 1 (V)
Grammar in Action: None

Worksheet

Starters (pages 80–81)

1 Display the following words and ask students for the English meaning and for volunteers to pronounce the words in French. After several suggestions, give the correct pronunciation for repetition by the whole class.

une banque, la poste, un centre sportif, un supermarché, un centre commercial, le théâtre, un parking, le château, un bowling

2 **Nouns and adjectives** To practise nouns and adjectives, display the following table and ask one half of the class to make up 5 phrases using an adjective which goes before the noun and the other half to make up 5 phrases with an adjective which follows the noun. After a few minutes, ask each team in turn for a phrase and award one point for each correct phrase. If preferred, students could do this in pairs, with one person using the adjectives which precede and the other using adjectives which follow the noun.

avant le nom	les noms	après le nom
exemple: un grand parking		exemple: une maison moderne
grand petit nouveau (nouvel, nouvelle) bon (bonne)	un hôpital un hôtel un parking un supermarché un musée une piscine	moderne énorme historique horrible rouge (autres couleurs) etc.

Introduction

Go through the objectives for this spread. For revision of town vocabulary, play a memory game. Students look back at the photos of La Rochelle for a few minutes, then close their books and try to recall as many different places as possible (individually, in pairs or in groups). This can then be built up as a cumulative list on the board. Prompt as necessary or give initial letters, e.g. *des m..., le p..., des r...*, etc.

Presentation

En ville

🔊 80

1 En ville

a Students match the correct text to each symbol referring to the box of words for help. The box includes three words not needed for this task, but useful for later tasks: *la banque, le centre commercial, le port*.

Solution:

A *un théâtre*   F *un supermarché*
B *un centre sportif* G *un bowling*
C *un hôpital*   H *un château*
D *un parking*   I *une piscine*
E *une poste*   J *la plage*

b Students listen to the eight items and write the letter by the matching symbol.

Solution:
1 *E*, **2** *F*, **3** *D*, **4** *C*, **5** *J*, **6** *H*, **7** *B*, **8** *G*

118 Tricolore 1 Teacher's Notes

7B Qu'est-ce qu'il y a en ville?

CD 3 Track 27

En ville

1 Pardon, madame, est-ce que la poste est près d'ici?
2 Je vais au supermarché pour acheter des provisions pour un pique-nique.
3 Les touristes cherchent un parking au centre-ville.
4 Est-ce qu'il y a un hôpital en ville?
5 Nous allons à la plage. La plage, c'est loin?
6 Il y a un château historique dans la ville. Où est le château exactement?
7 Mes amis vont au centre sportif pour un cours de judo.
8 C'est bien, il y a un bowling en ville. On va au bowling samedi.

c For further practice of reading and new vocabulary, students complete the sentences with appropriate nouns, referring to the box of words for help with spelling. When checking, ask students to read the full sentence aloud to practise pronunciation.

Solution:

1 Pour les touristes, il y a des **hôtels**, une **auberge** de jeunesse et un **camping**.
2 Si vous aimez le shopping, allez aux **magasins** au **centre commercial**.
3 Pour acheter des provisions, allez au **supermarché**.
4 Il y a beaucoup de bateaux au **port**.
5 Il y a des **musées** intéressants et un vieux **château**.
6 Pour les sportifs, il y a une **piscine** et un **centre sportif**.
7 Pour les personnes en voiture, il y a un grand **parking** près du centre-ville.
8 C'est amusant d'aller au **bowling** et au **théâtre**.

cm 7/1

En ville (1) – mini-flashcards

80 Dossier-langue

More about adjectives

Read the caption to the photo and ask students if they can pick out some adjectives (*grosse*, *ancienne*, *vieux*, *vieille*).

Revise adjective forms and explain that *vieux* is irregular but has some features of regular adjectives (feminine ends in –e, plural ends in –x). Do some oral work to practise the pronunciation of *vieux/vieille*, e.g. *vieux: c'est le contraire de moderne, mon père a un vieux vélo et ma mère a une vieille voiture. Dis le contraire: C'est une maison moderne? Non, c'est une vieille maison. C'est un appartement moderne? C'est une voiture moderne?*

Ask students whether *vieux* precedes or follows the noun and revise other adjectives which precede the noun, e.g. *grand*, *petit*, *gros*, *bon*.

80 Stratégies

Working out meaning (5)

Students could read through these suggestions before working on the text, *La Rochelle – ville du vélo*.

81

2 La Rochelle – ville du vélo

This introduces some additional vocabulary for talking about towns, *une zone piétonne*, *circuler*, etc. and describes the municipal bike scheme, which is now a feature of many other cities.

a Students answer comprehension questions in English.

Solution:

1 It's historical with many old buildings and houses and is now a pedestrian zone. There are no cars, but bikes (and pedestrians) are permitted.
2 yellow
3 to reduce pollution

b Student find the French for key phrases.

1 *beaucoup de vieux bâtiments*
2 *maintenant*
3 *une zone piétonne*
4 *la vieille ville*
5 *depuis longtemps*
6 *(c'est) gratuit*
7 *pendant deux heures*
8 *C'est une bonne idée, non?*

81

3 Des cartes postales

In part **a**, students choose the correct words to complete the two postcards.

Solution:

A 1 *l'auberge de jeunesse*, 2 *ville*, 3 *port*, 4 *tours*, 5 *musées*, 6 *chaud*, 7 *piscine*

B 1 *passons*, 2 *camping*, 3 *touristes*, 4 *beau*, 5 *marché*, 6 *parc*, 7 *restaurant*

b Students write their own postcard on similar lines.

c For extension, students add at least three extra sentences. More able students could also invent a gapped task for others to complete.

Une carte postale virtuelle

Many websites offer the chance of selecting and e-mailing a 'virtual' postcard. Students could look at various websites and choose a photo to send as a virtual postcard to a friend.

Possible websites:

http://www.ville-larochelle.fr
http://www.charente-maritime.org

Tricolore 1 Teacher's Notes **119**

7C C'est près d'ici?

AfL

Oral practice

Summarise all the town vocabulary taught so far with a class game, e.g. a chain game listing places that may be found in any town. *En ville, il y a un cinéma et …*

Link this activity with the spread objective and use for assessment. Afterwards discuss what has been achieved and what needs more practice.

Interactive activity

Un weekend en ville

152 Au choix

1 La Rochelle – ville touristique

Worksheet

Plenaries (pages 80–81)

1 **Think, pair and share**

Students discuss in pairs which three town words they find most difficult and consider ways for learning them. They share their ideas with another pair and then a spokesperson relays the findings to the rest of the class.

2 Students brainstorm tips for reading strategies.

7C C'est près d'ici? pages 82–83

- Ask for and understand directions in town
- Understand and give directions

Grammaire	Stratégies	Phonétique
• None	• None	• The letters '-t' or '-te' at the end of a word

Resources

Audio: 1 *Où vont les touristes?*; **3** *On arrive en ville*; **4** *Dans quelle direction?*; **7a** *Conversations en ville*, or CD 3, tracks 28, 29, 30 and 31
Copymasters: 7/2 Vocabulaire: *Les endroits*, 7/3 *C'est quelle direction?*
Worksheets: Starters and plenaries; *À gauche, à droite?* (W)

Interactive activity: *Des touristes* (L)
Ph The letters '-t' or '-te' at the end of a word, or CD 3, track 32
PowerPoint: *Trouver son chemin* (V)
Grammar in Action: None

Worksheet

Starters (pages 82–83)

1 *Quelle est la question?* Display the following incomplete questions and answers and ask students to note down the correct question word.

1 – … est la Rochelle?
 – C'est dans l'ouest de la France, au bord de la mer.
2 – … temps fait-il?
 – Il fait beau.
3 – … de touristes visitent La Rochelle par an?
 – Plus de 3 millions – c'est beaucoup!
4 – … habite à La Rochelle?
 – Marine et Noah habitent là.
5 – … il y a au centre-ville?
 – Il y a le port, des musées et un aquarium.
6 – … un théâtre?
 – Oui, il y a un théâtre et des cinémas.

Solution:
1 *Où*, **2** *Quel*, **3** *Combien*, **4** *Qui*, **5** *Qu'est-ce qu'*, **6** *Est-ce qu'il y a*

2 **Revise numbers** Ask easy questions or sums for students to write down a number. Check the answers as above, e.g.

Il y a combien de jours dans une semaine?
Il y a combien de mois dans l'année?
Deux plus trois, ça fait combien?

Introduction

Go through the objectives for this spread.

🔊 82

1 Où vont les touristes?

In part **a**, students choose the correct words to complete the two postcards.

Solution:
1 D, **2** F, **3** H, **4** I, **5** E, **6** B, **7** G, **8** J, **9** A, **10** C

120 Tricolore 1 Teacher's Notes

7C C'est près d'ici?

CD 3 Track 28

Où vont les touristes?

1 Pardon, monsieur, pour aller au théâtre, s'il vous plaît?
2 Pardon, madame, est-ce qu'il y a un supermarché près d'ici?
3 Pardon, monsieur, le centre-ville, c'est loin?
4 Pardon, madame, pour aller à l'église Notre Dame, s'il vous plaît?
5 Pardon, madame, est-ce qu'il y a des toilettes près d'ici?
6 Pardon, monsieur, le marché, c'est près d'ici?
7 Pardon, monsieur, pour aller à la gare, s'il vous plaît?
8 Pardon, madame, pour aller aux magasins, s'il vous plaît?
9 Pardon, madame, est-ce qu'il y a une piscine près d'ici?
10 Pardon, monsieur, l'office de tourisme, c'est loin?

Interactive activity

Des touristes

82

2 Excusez-moi

A three part activity where students practise asking questions either in pairs or as a class activity.

> **Solution:**
> a 1 *Pour aller au cinéma, s'il vous plaît?*
>   2 *Pour aller au port, s'il vous plaît?*
>   3 *Pour aller à l'hôpital, s'il vous plaît?*
> b 1 *Est-ce qu'il y a un parking près d'ici?*
>   2 *Est-ce qu'il y a un hôtel près d'ici?*
>   3 *Est-ce qu'il y a un camping près d'ici?*
> c 1 *La plage, c'est loin/c'est près d'ici?*
>   2 *Le parc, c'est loin/c'est près d'ici?*
>   3 *La gare, c'est loin/c'est près d'ici?*

Consolidation	AfL

Chain game

Play a chain question game, with students asking a different question each time, e.g.

Student A: *Le port, c'est loin*, (Student B)?

Student B: *Oui/Non/Je ne sais pas. Est-ce qu'il y a un camping près d'ici*, (Student C)? etc.

This could be done in groups with three students keeping the chain going and a fourth acting as referee and listening to each phrase to make sure it is correct. As it links to the spread objective, it could be used for peer assessment. At the end, discuss what was achieved and what needs extra practice.

Flashcard games

If students need extra practice of these structures, use flashcards to cue further questions or play some games, such as **Flashcard noughts and crosses**. For this, stick nine 'town' flashcards to the board. Students play in two teams, with each team in turn asking the way to a place (*Pour aller au …/Est-ce qu'il y a … près d'ici?*). The card representing the place is then removed and replaced with a cross or a nought. The object of the game is to get three in a row.

82

3 On arrive en ville

a Discuss strategies to help with listening to French, e.g. noting tone of voice, background noise, key words which might give a clue to the gist of the text.

Then play the recording, first without the text, and ask students to find out roughly what it's about. Then go through the text, encouraging students to ask in French if there is anything they don't understand. Students can then practise reading the conversations aloud, in groups of six (three students, three passers-by).

CD 3 Track 29

On arrive en ville

Hassan et ses amis, Claude et Léa, passent les vacances à La Rochelle. Ils arrivent à la gare de La Rochelle. C'est le cinq juillet et il fait très chaud.
– Pardon, madame. Le centre-ville, c'est loin?
– Le centre-ville? Oui, c'est loin!
– Est-ce qu'il y a un bus?
– Oui, prenez le bus numéro 1 devant la gare.
– Merci, madame.
– De rien.
Les trois amis arrivent au centre-ville. Ils descendent place de Verdun.
– Alors, on va à l'office de tourisme?
– Bonne idée!
– Pardon, monsieur, est-ce que l'office de tourisme est près d'ici?
– L'office de tourisme? Oh, c'est loin! C'est sur le quai du Gabut.
– C'est où, ça?
– C'est près de la mer et c'est assez près de la gare.
– C'est près de la gare, oh non! Ça alors!
– Mince alors! L'office de tourisme est très loin!
– Pfff! Il fait très chaud, n'est-ce pas?
– Oui, c'est vrai. Alors, on cherche un café?
– Bonne idée. … Pardon, madame. Est-ce qu'il y a un café près d'ici?
– Bien sûr! Il y a le café de la Paix dans la rue à gauche. Ce n'est pas loin.

b Students say whether the statements are true or false.

c For extension, students correct the errors.

7C C'est près d'ici?

Solution:
1 faux – ~~janvier~~ juillet
2 faux – ~~froid~~ chaud
3 faux – ~~piscine~~ gare
4 faux – numéro 1
5 faux – ~~l'auberge de jeunesse~~ l'office de tourisme
6 vrai
7 faux – ~~marché~~ café
8 vrai

Presentation

Trouver son chemin

À gauche, à droite, tout droit

To introduce the expressions *à gauche*, *à droite* and *tout droit*, draw three arrows on the board pointing to the left, right and straight on. Hold or attach flashcards on the left and right, and talk about them, e.g.

Où est le cinéma?

Le cinéma est à gauche.

La piscine est à droite.

Repeat this, and introduce *tout droit*.

Gradually encourage students to ask and answer the questions and add:

Pour aller au cinéma, s'il vous plaît?

Tournez à gauche, etc.

83

4 Dans quelle direction?

Students write down the numbers 1 to 10 in their books and listen to find out whether the places mentioned are to the right, to the left or straight on. They can write their answers in English or draw arrows.

Solution:
1 left, 2 straight on, 3 right, 4 straight on,
5 left, 6 right, 7 straight on, 8 right, 9 left,
10 straight on

CD 3 Track 30

Dans quelle direction?

1 – Pardon, madame, la piscine, c'est où, s'il vous plaît?
   – C'est à gauche, monsieur.
2 – La cathédrale, c'est où, s'il vous plaît?
   – C'est tout droit.
3 – L'hôtel de ville, c'est loin, monsieur?
   – Non, c'est tout près, c'est à droite.
4 – Pour aller au supermarché, s'il vous plaît?
   – C'est tout droit, madame.
5 – Où est le camping, s'il vous plaît, monsieur?
   – C'est là-bas, à gauche.
6 – Où est l'hôpital, s'il vous plaît, madame?
   – C'est ici, à droite, monsieur.
7 – Le vieux port, c'est loin, madame?
   – Non, c'est tout droit.
8 – Pour aller au marché, s'il vous plaît?
   – C'est là-bas, à droite, madame.
9 – Où est le bowling, s'il vous plaît?
   – Le bowling? C'est tout près, à gauche.
10 – Pardon, je cherche le restaurant, Le Perroquet Vert?
   – Le restaurant, Le Perroquet Vert? Hmm – Ah oui, ce n'est pas loin. Allez tout droit.

Worksheet

À gauche, à droite?

83

5 À gauche, à droite ou tout droit?

Students consult the signposts to find the answers.

Solution:
1 à gauche, 2 à droite, 3 tout droit, 4 à droite,
5 tout droit, 6 tout droit, 7 à droite, 8 à gauche

cm 7/2

Vocabulaire: les endroits

Premier(ère), deuxième, troisième

Introduce the idea of *premier/première*, *deuxième*, *troisième*, by describing where students are sitting in class (*au premier/deuxième rang*, etc.), or draw a simple town plan on the board and describe the turnings in order. (*Voici la première rue à gauche*, etc.).

83

6 Par ici!

First use the map to give directions to students, who follow these and discover where they are going, e.g. *Prenez la première rue à gauche. Puis c'est tout droit. Où êtes-vous? (À la poste.)* Students could also practise giving each other directions in pairs. The task involves matching each question with the correct directions.

Solution:
1 b, 2 d, 3 a, 4 c, 5 e

Tricolore 1 Teacher's Notes

7C C'est près d'ici?

83 Dossier-langue

Giving directions

This introduces the imperative (*vous* form) for giving directions.

83 AfL

7 Conversations en ville

a Students listen to the two conversations.

b They practise the conversation in pairs and invent other conversations by changing the highlighted words.

Explain how the task reflects the spread objectives and demonstrate a successful conversation to indicate assessment criteria. This could then be used for peer assessment with students awarding two stars (for what is done well) and a wish for what could be improved.

CD 3 Track 31

Conversations en ville

1 – On va à la piscine?
– Oui, d'accord.
– Pardon, monsieur, pour aller à la piscine, s'il vous plaît?
– Continuez tout droit, puis prenez la rue à gauche. Descendez la rue et voilà!
– Merci, monsieur. C'est loin?
– Non, c'est tout près.

2 – Pardon, madame, est-ce qu'il y a un supermarché près d'ici?
– Continuez tout droit, puis prenez la première rue à gauche.
– Merci, madame. C'est loin?
– Oui, c'est assez loin.

Interactive activity

The letters '-t' or '-te' at the end of a word

83 Phonétique

The letters '-t' or '-te' at the end of a word

A full explanation of this point is given on *kerboodle!*, together with interactive practice.

a Explain that when a word ends in '-t', the final 't' is not normally sounded. Demonstrate this by pronouncing the French word, *sport*, with an appropriate gesture. Then read out the other words, with the students repeating each one: *port, droit, restaurant*. All the words are included on the recording for optional use (part **a**).

If appropriate, mention that there are a few exceptions to this, where the final 't' is sounded, e.g. *huit, le foot, un sweat, le basket, internet*.
Explain that when a word ends in '-te', the 't' is always sounded.
Demonstrate this by saying *soixante* and making the number 60 with a finger gesture.
Read out the other words: *porte, j'habite, droite*, with students repeating the words.

Parts **b** and **c** can be used for further pronunciation practice.

b Ask students to listen and repeat the words they hear. Then display the words **a** *mot*, **b** *carte*, **c** *vert*, **d** *lit*, **e** *trente* for students to match (**d, a, e, b, c**).

c Students listen to the silly sentence and note down how many times the silent '-t' at the end of a word occurs (4), and how many times they hear the 't' because of the following 'e' (2). They can then repeat the sentence to help them remember these sounds.

For further practice, write some additional words on the board to check that students recognise the link between spelling and pronunciation, e.g. *moment, petit, méchante, enfant, tente*.

CD 3 Track 32

The letters '-t' or '-te' at the end of a word

Écoutez et répétez:
a *words ending in -t*
sport, port, restaurant, droit
Des exceptions: huit, le foot, un sweat, le basket, internet
words ending in -te
soixante, porte, j'habite, droite
b lit, mot, trente, carte, vert
c Le chat est content parce qu'il habite au restaurant près de la poste.

cm 7/3

C'est quelle direction?

Worksheet

Plenaries (pages 82–83)

Conduct a mid-unit review. Ask: How's it going so far? What over the last 2–3 spreads has proved most difficult/ easiest? Where do you think your personal improvement has been? What is still a problem? Students discuss these questions in groups and then a spokesperson gives group feedback to the whole class.

Tricolore 1 Teacher's Notes 123

7D Où exactement?

7D Où exactement? pages 84–85

- Discuss possible activities in town

Grammaire	Stratégies	Phonétique
• Use the preposition à (au, à la, à l', aux) and other prepositions	• Remembering the gender of nouns (3)	• None

Resources

Audio: 4 *On va où?*, or CD 3, track 33
Copymasters: 7/4 *Où va-t-on?*, 7/5 *C'est où?*
Worksheets: Starters and plenaries; *Trois conversations en ville* (S); *Au / à la / à l'/ aux* (G)

Interactive activity: *Dans la rue* (L); *La preposition à* (G); Remembering the gender of nouns (Strat)
PowerPoint: None
Grammar in Action: pp22–23, 26–27

Worksheet

Starters (pages 84–85)

1 *Chasse à l'intrus* Display the following words or print them out so students can circle the odd word out (shown in bold). If using the board, the answers can be checked as a whole class activity. If students are using the printed grid, they can exchange papers with a partner for marking.

un magasin **un vélo** un château un théâtre	**mardi** brouillard soleil vent	aller continuer **janvier** tourner	la plage la mer le port **le chat**	nous ils vous **dans**	cinq **sous** cent soixante

2 *C'est masculin ou féminin?* Display the following words, use flashcards, or say the words and ask students to hold up their *masculin* or *féminin* cards.

masculin: parking, château, musée, marché, magasin, camping, théâtre

féminin: auberge de jeunesse, gare, plage, piscine, poste, banque, église

Introduction

Go through the objectives for this spread.

FC 43–56

Preposition *à/au* etc.

Using the flashcards, demonstrate how to say where you are or where you're going, using *à, au, à la, à l'* and *aux* (which could be written on the board with suitable nouns). Distribute the flashcards to students, saying *Où vas-tu?* They reply *À la piscine* or *J'arrive à la piscine*, then return the flashcard.

84

1 Questions sur la ville

This short quiz includes many examples of the preposition *à* in use. Ask students to spot these and say what they have noticed about how *à* changes form.

Solution:
1 c, 2 b, 3 c, 4 b, 5 a, 6 c

84 AfL

2 On va en ville?

Students read through the dialogue then practise it in pairs, changing the destinations, etc., using the substitution table to help them. Explain how the task reflects the spread objective and demonstrate a successful conversation to indicate assessment criteria. This could then be used for peer assessment.

84 Stratégies

Remembering the gender of nouns (3)

Explain that word endings can sometimes indicate whether a noun is masculine or feminine and that this is a grammar memorisation strategy.

Some examples from spreads 7D and 7E include:

Masc: supermarché, château, magasin, quartier (7E), bowling, tourisme;

Fem: idée, ville, banque

84 Dossier-langue

Saying 'to' and 'at' + place

This summarises the different forms of *à*. Ask students to look out for other examples as they work through the unit.

Worksheet

C'est loin?

84

3 Une semaine de vacances

Students follow the lines to find the destinations and complete the sentences, practising the different forms of *à*.

Solution:
1 au bowling, 2 au musée, 3 à la plage, 4 à l'aquarium, 5 à la piscine, 6 au château

7D Où exactement?

---

cm 7/4

Où va-t-on?

gia 1 pp22–23

Using *au*, *à la*, *à l'*, *aux* (1) and (2)

This provides further practice, if required.

> Interactive activity

Dans la rue

> Worksheet

La ville

> 152 Au choix

2 Attention aux accents!

> 152 Au choix

3 Quelle est la destination?

FC 10–12, 43–56

Presentation and practice of prepositions

Teach *devant*, *derrière*, *à côté de* and *entre* by describing where students are sitting and where things are in the classroom. Use the flashcards for various places in a town. Prop them against the board or hold them one behind another and describe where certain places are located, e.g.

La piscine est derrière le parc.
L'hôtel est entre la poste et le cinéma.

> 85

4 On va où?

Students listen and note the place mentioned and any further details.

Solution:
1 castle, quite far, after supermarket
2 café, nearby, between cinema and supermarket
3 youth hostel, next to campsite, take bus
4 aquarium, not far, near station
5 car park, behind hotel
6 toilets, in the square
7 bike, in front of the swimming pool
8 bowling alley, in the shopping centre, next to cinema

> CD 3 Track 33

On va où?

1 – Pour aller au château, s'il vous plaît?
– Le château? C'est assez loin. Continuez tout droit. C'est après le supermarché.
2 – Est-ce qu'il y a un café près d'ici?
– Oui, il y a un café tout près, entre le cinema et le supermarché.
3 – L'auberge de jeunesse, c'est loin?
– Ah oui, c'est loin. C'est à côté du camping. Prenez le bus là-bas.
4 – Pour aller à l'aquarium, s'il vous plaît?
– Ah, l'aquarium, ce n'est pas loin, c'est près de la gare.
5 – Est-ce qu'il y a un parking à l'hôtel?
– Oui, il y a un parking derrière l'hôtel.
6 – Pardon, madame, est-ce qu'il y a des toilettes près d'ici?
– Oui, il y a des toilettes sur la place.
7 – Où est ton vélo?
– Mon vélo? Il est là-bas, devant la piscine.
8 – Pardon, monsieur, je cherche le bowling. C'est près d'ici?
– Le bowling, c'est dans le centre commercial. C'est à côté du cinéma.

> 85 Dossier-langue

Other prepositions

This summarises other prepositions for place, including *à côté de* and *près de*. The different forms of *de* could be explained here with able students, but are covered in detail in Stage 2.

> 85

5 Dans la rue

Start with some oral work on the illustration, e.g. *Où est le café? Entre le supermarché et …?* Then students can work on the true/false task.

Solution:
1 *faux*, 2 *vrai*, 3 *faux*, 4 *vrai*, 5 *faux*, 6 *faux*, 7 *vrai*, 8 *faux*

> Interactive activity

Des conversations

> 85

6 Où?

This item provides practice of *entre*, *devant* and *derrière* and revision of the prepositions *sur*, *dans* and *sous* learnt earlier.

a Students complete each sentence with the correct preposition.

Solution:
1 *entre*, 2 *derrière*, 3 *sur*, 4 *sous*, 5 *devant*, 6 *sur*, 7 *entre*, 8 *dans*

7E Elle est comment, ta ville?

b For extension, students invent three similar cartoons to illustrate prepositions. They could look for appropriate images in magazines or on the internet.

Extra practice

Students make true/false statements about the location of objects in the classroom. The class have to decide whether it's true or false, e.g. *Il y a des livres sur la table. Il y a un vélo sous la table. Il y a un lion derrière la porte*, etc.

cm 7/5

C'est où?

gia 1 pp26–27

Using prepositions (1) and (2)

These pages provide additional practice of prepositions if required.

Worksheet

Plenaries (pages 84–85)

1 Students could reflect on how prepositions are used in French and English. Do they find the different forms of *à* hard to remember; what might help – learning some key phrases, e.g. *au collège, aux magasins*.

2 How easy do they find the other prepositions? Are there any tips for remembering them, e.g. visualising animals in/behind/on/under a box, etc. and remembering key phrases.

7E Elle est comment, ta ville?   pages 86–87

- Talk about the area where you live

Grammaire	Stratégies	Phonétique
• Use *il y a …* and *il n'y a pas de …*	• Adding interest to your writing (3)	• The letters 'th'

Resources

Audio: 2 *Mon quartier*, or CD 3, track 34
Copymasters: 7/6 *En ville (2)*, 7/7 *Ma ville/mon village*, 7/8 *Un plan à compléter*
Worksheets: Starters and plenaries; *Ma ville et mon quartier* (W); Adding interest to your writing (Strat)

Interactive activity: None
Ph The letters 'th', or CD 3, track 35
PowerPoint: Kim's game; *En ville* (2)
Grammar in Action: None

Worksheet

Starters (pages 86–87)

1 *En groupes* Display a list of words in random order or print these out and ask students to put them into 5 groups. This could be done as a class activity with students taking it in turns to find a group of words – each group could be underlined in a different colour. If students are working on the printed lists, they could do this individually, then exchange lists with a partner for marking.

   sur, sous, dans

   je, tu, il

   un château, un musée, un théâtre

   vieux, petit, jaune

   Prenez, Tournez, Visitez

   une rue, une avenue, une place

2 *Chaque mot à sa place* Display the following lists of words and then, for each individual word, ask: *Quelle est la bonne boîte?*

   derrière (E), *un poisson* (C), *aux* (D), *une piscine* (A), *un vélo* (F), *habiter* (B)

   Students could write down the appropriate letter and display it when asked.

A	B	C	D	E	F
un bowling	visiter	une souris	au	devant	un bus
un centre sportif	chercher	un oiseau	à la	entre	une voiture

Introduction

Go through the objectives for this spread.

FC 57–60

Use the flashcards (57–60) to teach and practise: *une mosquée, une patinoire, un terrain de football, une bibliothèque*.

cm 7/6

En ville (2) – mini-flashcards

86

1 Un jeu 5-4-3-2-1

This is a game to reinforce the new vocabulary.

126 Tricolore 1 Teacher's Notes

7E Elle est comment, ta ville?

Solution:

5 *la religion*
  une cathédrale
  une église
  une mosquée
  une synagogue
  un temple

4 *le sport*
  une patinoire
  un centre sportif
  un terrain de football
  une piscine

3 *le logement*
  un hôtel
  un camping
  une auberge de jeunesse

2 *on mange là*
  un café
  un restaurant

1 *on trouve des livres là*
  une bibliothèque

86

2 Mon quartier

Check that the symbols are clear. Students should listen first for the location and note the appropriate letter. They can then listen again and note any further information in English.

Solution:
1 C, 2 E, 3 I, 4 J, 5 F, 6 A, 7 D, 8 G, 9 B, 10 H

CD 3 Track 34

Mon quartier

1 Dans mon quartier, il y a un grand parc avec un terrain de football. J'aime bien jouer au football au parc.
2 Le mercredi, après l'école, je vais à la bibliothèque. Il y a des ordinateurs et je surfe sur le Net. Je regarde des livres aussi.
3 En ville, il y a un centre sportif. Je vais souvent au centre sportif pour jouer au basket et au badminton. J'adore le sport.
4 Pendant le weekend, je vais quelquefois au bowling avec mes amis.
5 Le dimanche, je vais à l'église avec ma mère.
6 Pour ma fête, je vais à la patinoire. J'aime bien ça.
7 Il y a une piscine dans mon quartier et en été, nous allons à la piscine le samedi.
8 J'aime bien ma ville parce qu'il y a beaucoup de magasins et un grand centre commercial – et moi, j'adore le shopping.
9 Le vendredi, ma famille va à la mosquée.
10 À Diwali, nous allons au temple.

86 Dossier-langue

Il y a and *il n'y a pas de*

This gives examples of the two useful phrases: *Il y a ...* and *Il n'y a pas de ...* Check that students notice that *un/une* change to *de* after *pas*. This is explained more fully in *Unité 9*.

152 Au choix

4 Des endroits en ville

86

3 Qu'est-ce qu'il y a?

Students complete the sentences as indicated, taking care to get the genders correct.

Solution:
1 *Dans le centre-ville, il y a **un centre sportif**.*
2 *Dans ma ville, il y a **une patinoire** et **une bibliothèque**.*
3 *Près d'ici, il y a **un centre commercial** avec beaucoup de magasins.*
4 *J'aime bien mon quartier parce qu'il y a **un bowling** et **un cinéma**.*
5 *Dans mon quartier, il y a **un parc** avec **une piscine** et **un terrain de football**.*

86

4 Et qu'est-ce qu'il n'y a pas?

Practice in using *il n'y a pas de ...*

Solution:
1 *Il n'y a pas de bowling.* 2 *Il n'y a pas de piscine.* 3 *Il n'y a pas de bibliothèque.* 4 *Il n'y a pas de cinéma.* 5 *Il n'y a pas de supermarché.* 6 *Il n'y a pas de parc.* 7 *Il n'y a pas de patinoire.* 8 *Il n'y a pas de centre commercial.*

Presentation

Jeu de mémoire: En ville

Notre ville

Discuss a local town/area, which is familiar to everyone and build up a description on the board. This could lead to further productive work, perhaps creating a mini town guide for French-speaking visitors.

87 AfL

5 Jeu de mémoire

Students work in groups to play a chain game, with each person in turn repeating the suggestions already made and adding an additional place.

a Students describe which places there are in their own, or in an imaginary, town.
b They build up a list of places which are not available in the town.

7E Elle est comment, ta ville?

87

6 Ma ville/mon quartier

Students complete a description of an imaginary town by choosing the appropriate word for each gap.

> **Solution:**
>
> J'habite à Tricville. C'est une **1 ville** moyenne au centre de la France. Mon quartier est assez **2 loin** du centre-ville. Dans mon quartier il y a des **3 magasins**, une église, un café et un parc, mais il n'y a pas de centre sportif. Ce n'est pas intéressant **4 pour** les jeunes. Au **5 contraire**, au centre-ville, il y a un grand centre commercial, une piscine, une **6 bibliothèque** et un bowling mais il n'y a **7 pas** de théâtre. J'aime bien aller en ville **8 parce que** j'adore le shopping.

Interactive activity

The letters 'th'

87 Phonétique

The letters 'th'

A full explanation of this sound is given on *kerboodle!*, together with interactive practice.

a Say the word *thé* with an appropriate gesture. Students repeat the word with the same gesture. Then read out the other words, with the students repeating each one: *théâtre, cathédrale*. Explain that the sound is the same as '*t*' in French and English, e.g. *tigre, toit*. The '*th*' words are also included on the recording for optional use (part **a**).

Parts **b** and **c** can be used for further practice.

b Ask students to listen and repeat the words they hear. Then display the words a *maths*, b *Théo*, c *Mathieu*, d *sympathique*, e *théorie*, for students to match (**b, e, c, a, d**).

c Students listen to the silly sentence and note down how many times they hear the sound (6). They can then repeat the sentence to help them remember this sound.

For further practice, write some additional words on the board to check that students recognise the link between spelling and pronunciation e.g. *Thérèse, thème, température*.

CD 3 Track 35

The letters 'th'

Écoutez et répétez:
a thé, théâtre, cathédrale
b Théo, théorie, Mathieu, maths, sympathique
c Théo et Thomas prennent du thé et regardent le tigre au toit du théâtre.

87 Stratégies

Adding interest to your writing (3)

This summarises different ways of adding interest to writing (and speaking) and encourages students to look for suitable examples which can be noted down and used in their own work.

87 *AfL*

7 Dossier personnel

a Students write four sentences about their town or area referring to the example given.
b As extension, students develop this into two ⊕ paragraphs.

This links well with the spread objective and can be used for self-evaluation. Prepare this by building up a suitable description on the board so students understand the criteria.

Worksheet

Ma ville et mon quartier

cm 7/7

Ma ville/mon village

cm 7/8

Un plan à compléter

153 Au choix

5 Un message

Worksheet

Plenary (pages 86–87)

As there is a large amount of vocabulary in this unit, one plenary should be spent talking about how to memorise genders of words. How do students do this? Have their approaches been successful? Have they noticed any patterns to help, e.g. spelling. If appropriate, refer to the lists of word endings, which often denote a specific gender (SB *La Grammaire*, 1.2).

7F Allez, on y va   pages 88–89

- Make plans and talk about where you are going

Grammaire	Stratégies	Phonétique
• Use the verb *aller*	• None	• The letters 'on', 'om'

Resources

Audio: 2a-b *Coralie est au lit*, or CD 3, track 36
Copymasters: 7/9 *Aller*
Worksheets: Starters and plenaries; *Le weekend* (W)

Interactive activity: None
Ph The letters 'on', 'om', CD 3, track 37
PowerPoint: None
Grammar in Action: pp24–25

Worksheet

Starters (pages 88–89)

1 *Trouve les paires* Display different subjects and verb endings on the board for students to match up, or print these on slips of paper and give out for individual work. This can be checked by the teacher randomly selecting students to answer. Some variations are possible.

1 Tu	a *visite un vieux château.*
2 Sa passion, c'est le sport – elle	b *allons souvent au cinéma.*
3 Pour mon cours d'histoire, je	c *regardent les poissons.*
4 Nous	d *cherches la patinoire?*
5 Vous	e *travaille à la bibliothèque.*
6 Les chats sont méchants, ils	f *jouez au tennis?*
7 Mon ami écossais	g *arrivent à l'école à 8 heures.*
8 Ma mère aime les livres – elle	h *habite à Edimbourg.*
9 Les élèves	i *joue au football ce soir.*

Solution:
1 *d*, 2 *i*, 3 *a*, 4 *b*, 5 *f*, 6 *c*, 7 *h*, 8 *e*, 9 *g*

2 *Complète les phrases* Display the following. Give students a few minutes to read and work out the answers, then ask:
Le verbe numéro un va avec quelle phrase?
les verbes:
1 *aimez*, 2 *cherche*, 3 *continues*, 4 *écoutons*, 5 *habitent*, 6 *passe*

a *Je … le weekend ici.*
b *Tu … tout droit.*
c *Elle … le bowling.*
d *Nous … le CD.*
e *Vous … le camping?*
f *Ils … à La Rochelle.*

Solution:
1 *e*, 2 *c*, 3 *b*, 4 *d*, 5 *f*, 6 *a*

Introduction

Go through the objectives for this spread.

88

1 Où vont-ils?

This revises the correct form of *à* with places in a town and introduces different parts of the present tense of *aller*.

Solution:
1 *au concert*, 2 *à la piscine*, 3 *à la poste*, 4 *à l'église*, 5 *au camping*, 6 *au collège*

88 Dossier-langue

The verb *aller* (to go)

Students have already used several parts of *aller* in the unit. Revise the different pronouns and their meanings (*je, tu, il, elle, nous, vous, ils, elles*).

Encourage the class to produce different parts of *aller* from memory or by looking at earlier pages.

Gradually build up the whole verb on the board, e.g. using the flashcards, ask students:

Où vas-tu? for the reply *Je vais …*

Où va-t-il/elle? (*Il/Elle va …*)

Remind students about the idea of the paradigm, regular and irregular verbs, and that nouns are usually followed by the third person of the verb, etc. Refer to the cartoons to explain this.

88

2 Coralie est au lit

Students practise the third person of *aller* singular and plural.

a Students listen to the recording and note down the letter, indicating who goes where. When checking orally, ask for the full sentences.

Solution:
1 *Sébastien va au cinéma Dragon.* c
2 *Luc va au parc.* f
3 *Anne-Marie va aux magasins.* d
4 *Vincent va au musée Maritime.* a
5 *Stéphanie et Mireille vont au club des jeunes.* e
6 *Christophe et Jean-Pierre vont à la discothèque Plaza.*
Mais le soir, ils vont tous chez Coralie. b

7F Allez, on y va

b For further work, students listen again to the recording and write down with whom each person goes out.

Solution:
1 *Sébastien va en ville avec son cousin.*
2 *Luc va en ville avec son frère.*
3 *Anne-Marie va en ville avec sa mère.*
4 *Vincent va en ville avec ses cousins.*
5 *Stéphanie va en ville avec Mireille.*
6 *Christophe va en ville avec Jean-Pierre.*

CD 3 Track 36

Coralie est au lit

– Allô!
– Salut, Coralie. Ça va?
– Ah, bonjour, Sébastien. Non, ça ne va pas. Je suis au lit. Où vas-tu aujourd'hui?
– Je vais au cinéma avec mon cousin.
– Ah oui. Alors, au revoir.
– Au revoir, Coralie.
…
– Allô, oui?
– Bonjour, Coralie.
– Ah, bonjour, Luc. Qu'est-ce que tu fais ce soir? Tu viens chez moi?
– Euh, Coralie, je suis désolé, mais moi, je vais au parc avec mon frère – il y a un match de football.
– Ah bon. Alors, au revoir, Luc.
– Au revoir.
…
– Salut, Coralie. C'est moi, Anne-Marie.
– Ah, bonjour, Anne-Marie, tu viens me voir?
– Ah … non. Je suis désolée, mais je vais aux magasins avec ma mère. Je vais te téléphoner ce soir, ça va?
– Ah, oui, oui, oui. Ça va!
…
– Bonjour, Coralie. C'est Vincent ici.
– Ah salut, Vincent. Je me suis cassé la jambe, tu sais. Tu viens me voir?
– Non Coralie. Je vais au musée Maritime avec mes cousins. Je suis désolé!
– Moi aussi! Au revoir, Vincent.
…
– Salut, Coralie. C'est Stéphanie ici.
– Bonjour, Stéphanie. Qu'est-ce que tu fais?
– Ben, je suis avec Mireille. Nous allons au club des jeunes. Tu viens?
– Ah non. Je suis au lit. Je me suis cassée la jambe.
– Ça alors! Quel désastre! Alors, au revoir, Coralie.
– Au revoir!
…
– Bonjour, Coralie. C'est Christophe. Je vais à la discothèque avec Jean-Pierre. Nous allons au Plaza. Tu viens?
– Mais non Christophe, je me suis cassée la jambe!
– Oh pardon, Coralie. Je suis désolé!
…
Coralie reste au lit, elle regarde la télé, elle dessine … mais ça ne va pas. Elle n'est pas contente.
– Zut alors! J'ai beaucoup d'amis, ils sont gentils, mais où sont-ils? … Qu'est-ce que c'est?
– Salut, Coralie!
– Surprise, surprise!
– Voilà, c'est nous!
– Oh, salut, bonjour … ça alors, mais c'est fantastique!

89

3 Allez!

Grammar practice in matching correct pronouns with the different parts of *aller*.

Solution:
1 *h*, 2 *e*, 3 *c*, 4 *a*, 5 *b*, 6 *g*, 7 *d*, 8 *f*

Interactive activity

The letters 'on', 'om'

89 Phonétique

The letters 'on', 'om'

A full explanation of this sound is given on *kerboodle!*, together with interactive practice.

a Explain that the when 'o' is followed by 'n' or 'm' it is often a nasal vowel (pronounced through the nose). Remind students of the nasal vowels, *am, an, em, en,* taught in 6B, and the tip of holding the nose, when saying the nasal sound, then trying to make the same sound without holding the nose.

Say the word *citron* with an appropriate gesture, e.g. sucking a lemon. Students repeat the word with the same gesture. Then read out the other words, with the students repeating each one: *combien, vont, oncle*. The words are also included on the recording for optional use (part **a**).

Explain that if the letters are followed by another vowel or a second 'm' or 'n', then they are pronounced differently. Read aloud the exceptions: *tomate, sommes, donne,* with students repeating the words. Again, these are included on the recording

Parts **b** and **c** can be used for further practice.

b Ask students to listen and repeat the words they hear. Then display the words in a different order, e.g. **a** *nom,* **b** *solution,* **c** *non,* **d** *comment,* **e** *confortable* for students to match (**c, a, b, e, d**).

c Students listen to the silly sentence and note down how many times they hear the sound (8). They can then repeat the sentence to help them remember this sound.

For further practice, write some additional words on the board to check that students recognise the link between spelling and pronunciation e.g. *pont, rond, prononciation, comprend, concombre.*

CD 3 Track 37

The letters 'on', 'om'

Écoutez et répétez:
a citron, combien, vont, oncle
  Des exceptions: tomate sommes donne
b non, nom, solution, confortable, comment
c Je compte onze crayons, deux trompettes et mon poisson sur le balcon du salon.

7G Une ville touristique

📖 89 — AfL

4 Ah non!

This links well with the spread objective and can be used for peer assessment.

a Students complete the sentences in the conversation with the correct part of *aller*.

> **Solution:**
> 1 *vais*, 2 *vais*, 3 *allons*, 4 *vais*, 5 *va*, *vas*, 6 *va*, *vais*, 7 *allons*

b For extension, students could invent a similar conversation and practise it in pairs.

📖 89

5 Le weekend

Check the class remember the difference between the two words for 'you' and respective parts of *aller*. Ask questions using *Où vas-tu le samedi?* and also *Où allez-vous?* and help them to make up some answers orally before they write their own six sentences. Students should not feel restricted by the words listed and could invent their own phrases in a more creative way. Students could work in small groups, seeing which group can make the most sentences in, say, ten minutes.

Worksheet

Le weekend

cm 7/9

Aller

gia pp24–25

Using the verb *aller* – to go (1) and (2)

This provides further practice of *aller*.

Worksheet

Plenary (pages 88–89)

Discuss other irregular verbs learnt so far, e.g. *avoir*, *être*, and ask: how do you know verbs are irregular, are they hard to learn, are there patterns you can learn for irregulars too? (There is a regular pattern of endings to most irregulars – s/s/t ons/ez/ent.) Discuss tips to learn irregular verbs, such as learning the most useful parts in key phrases.

7G Une ville touristique   pages 90–91

- Understand tourist information

Grammaire	Stratégies	Phonétique
• None	• Reading and listening to longer passages	• None

Resources

Audio: 2a *À l'office de tourisme*; Listening to longer passages, or CD 3, track 38
Copymasters: 7/10 *Tu comprends?*, 7/11 *Sommaire*
Worksheets: Starters and plenaries
e-book: *Bienvenues à La Rochelle*

Interactive activity: Classroom commands (V)
PowerPoint: None
Video: *En ville*
Grammar in Action: None

Worksheet

Starters (pages 90–91)

1 *Vrai/faux?* Make some true/false statements about La Rochelle. Students respond by showing their *vrai* or *faux* card. e.g.

Il n'y a pas beaucoup de touristes en été.
C'est au bord de la mer.
C'est à la montagne.
Le centre-ville est une zone piétonne.
Les vélos de La Rochelle sont verts.
Il y a des musées mais il n'y a pas d'aquarium.
Il y a trois tours.
Il y a un vieux port intéressant.

2 *C'est masculin ou féminin?* Display the following words, use flashcards, or say the words and ask students to hold up their *masculin* or *féminin* cards.

masculin: hôtel, centre sportif, aquarium, bateau, bowling, cinéma

féminin: mosquée, cathédrale, patinoire, rue, ville, bibliothèque

Introduction

Go through the objectives for this spread.

7G Une ville touristique

90

1 Une fenêtre ouverte sur l'océan

This presents some information about the aquarium in La Rochelle. Ask a few questions, e.g. *Qu'est-ce qu'on trouve dans un aquarium? Des oiseaux? Des souris? Qui a visité un aquarium? Où ça?* Ask for suggestions to explain *un requin, des étoiles de mer, une méduse.* Revise reading strategies and refer to the *Stratégies* box.

a Students reply to questions in English.

> **Solution:**
> **1** a, **2** in the town centre, near the train station, **3** visit the café

b Students decide whether statements are true or false.

> **Solution:**
> **1** faux, **2** faux, **3** vrai, **4** faux

c For extension, students correct the false statements.

> **Solution:**
> **1** *L'aquarium est **près** de la gare,* **2** *Il y a un parking,* **4** *On trouve des requins **dans le grand aquarium**.*

For further work, the photo can be used as a stimulus for a description or a conversation at an aquarium. Students could look at the website and find other photos to describe and/or look for examples of *un requin, des étoiles de mer, une méduse.*

www.aquarium-larochelle.com

90 Stratégies

Reading and listening to longer passages

This gives some tips to help with comprehension. The online worksheet listed below can be used for further reinforcement.

Worksheet

Listening to longer passages

90 AfL

2 À l'office de tourisme

Revise listening strategies before students work on this fairly long text. Students should listen to the recording several times in order to complete the tasks.

> **Solution:**
> **a** c, **b** c, e, f, a, h, b, d, g, **c** various

CD 3 Track 38

À l'office de tourisme

Hasan, Claude et Léa arrivent à l'office de tourisme de La Rochelle.

H – Bonjour, madame. Nous passons quelques jours à La Rochelle. Qu'est-ce qu'il y a à faire ici?

M – À La Rochelle, il y a beaucoup de choses. Il y a le vieux port avec les trois tours. On peut visiter les tours et monter en haut. La tour de la Lanterne, par exemple, était une prison autrefois et on peut voir les graffiti réalisés par les prisonniers. Vous aimez les musées?

A – Ça dépend. Qu'est-ce qu'il y a comme musées ici?

M – Ah... bon, il y a beaucoup de musées différents. Il y a par exemple le musée Maritime, qui est très intéressant. C'est un musée flottant. On embarque sur des bateaux dans le port. Un bateau, ou plutôt un navire, était utilisé autrefois pour les services de la météo. Un autre est un ancien bateau de pêche. La pêche est très importante à La Rochelle. Il y a le port de pêche et un marché aux poissons ici.

C – Ah bon. J'aime bien les poissons.

M – Ah, mais si vous aimez les poissons, allez visiter l'aquarium. C'est vraiment fantastique. Il y a des poissons de toutes sortes.

C – Et l'aquarium est près d'ici?

M – Oui, ce n'est pas loin.

H – Et pour circuler en ville, il y a des vélos?

M – Oui, il y a des vélos jaunes. C'est un très bon système. On trouve des vélos sur la place de Verdun.

H – C'est près d'ici?

M – Non, c'est assez loin, à 30 minutes environ, mais il y a un bus.

A – Est-ce qu'il y a des excursions en bateau?

M – Oui, il y a des excursions en bateau aux îles, par exemple l'Île de Ré. Il y a aussi le bus de mer qui va au port des Minimes, le port de plaisance. Là-bas, il y a beaucoup de bateaux et on fait des sports nautiques.
Voilà de la documentation. Il y a beaucoup à faire. Amusez-vous bien à La Rochelle.

H – Merci, madame.

C – Alors on va visiter d'abord l'aquarium, comme c'est tout près.

A – Et après on va prendre le bus de mer.

H – D'accord. On y va.

153 Au choix

6 Des renseignements touristiques

Interactive activity

Rue Danton: En ville

Interactive activity

Vocabulaire de classe (7)

Worksheet

Presentation

Bienvenues à La Rochelle

132 Tricolore 1 Teacher's Notes

7G Une ville touristique

cm 7/10

Tu comprends?

91 cm 7/11

Sommaire

A summary of the main language and structures of the unit, also on copymaster for ease of reference.

Interactive activity

Vocabulaire (7)

Interactive activity

Quiz – Unités 6–7

Worksheet

Plenaries (pages 90–91)

1 Students think about three things in the unit they have found useful/interesting and compare their choice with others.

2 Use the *Sommaire* to review the objectives of the unit and what has been learnt.

Unité 7 Consolidation and assessment

Épreuves Unité 7

These worksheets can be used for an informal test of listening, reading and writing or for extra practice, as required.

For general notes on the *Épreuves*, see TB page xv.

🔊 cm 7/12

Écouter L

A Voici ma ville

Solution:
1 b, **2** a, **3** f, **4** c, **5** d, **6** e, **7** h, **8** g
(mark /7)

🔊 CD 3 Track 39

Voici ma ville

1 Voici le musée. Le musée est sur la place principale.
2 Et voici la piscine. J'aime bien aller à la piscine.
3 Et ici, c'est un restaurant. C'est un très bon restaurant.
4 Ça, c'est la bibliothèque. La bibliothèque est ouverte le mercredi et le vendredi.
5 Puis il y a un supermarché. Voici le supermarché.
6 Et voici la poste. Là, c'est la poste.
7 Et voilà l'église. C'est l'église St. Pierre.
8 Et la gare est ici. Voici la gare SNCF.

B Qu'est-ce qu'ils cherchent?

Students identify **a)** the correct symbol and **b)** note whether it's *près* (P) or *loin* (L).

Solution:
1 b P, **2** h L, **3** e P, **4** a L, **5** d P, **6** g P, **7** f P, **8** c L
(mark /7)

🔊 CD 3 Track 40

Qu'est-ce qu'ils cherchent?

1 – Est-ce que l'hôtel de ville est près d'ici?
   – Oui, oui, l'hôtel de ville, c'est tout près.
2 – Le bowling, c'est loin?
   – Le bowling? Ah oui, c'est assez loin.
3 – L'auberge de jeunesse c'est près d'ici?
   – L'auberge de jeunesse? Oui, c'est assez près, c'est à dix minutes d'ici.
4 – Je cherche le camping 'Bon séjour'. C'est près d'ici?
   – Le camping? Ah non, il est à cinq ou six kilomètres de la ville. Il est loin, le camping.
5 – Je vais au parc aujourd'hui. Tu viens?
   – Au parc? Oui, je viens. Ce n'est pas loin.
6 – Où est l'hôpital, s'il vous plaît? C'est urgent!
   – C'est tout près. Tournez à gauche et voilà l'hôpital.
7 – Je voudrais un plan de la ville.
   – Alors, allez à l'office de tourisme.
   – À l'office de tourisme. Oui, c'est tout près.
8 – Où allez-vous?
   – Je vais à la mosquée.
   – À la mosquée? Mais c'est très loin!

C Sophie

Solution:
1 V, **2** F, **3** V, **4** F, **5** V, **6** F, **7** V
(mark /6)

🔊 CD 3 Track 41

Sophie

– Où habites-tu, Sophie?
– J'habite dans un village près de Saint-Malo.
– Dans un village? Et qu'est-ce qu'il y a dans le village?
– Bof … Il n'y a pas grand-chose. Il y a deux ou trois magasins, un café … des maisons et une église.
– Alors, pour les jeunes, c'est bien? C'est comment pour les jeunes?
– Moi, je trouve que c'est ennuyeux. Il n'y a pas de piscine, il n'y a pas de cinéma. Oui, c'est vraiment ennuyeux, surtout pendant les vacances.
– Alors, tu vas à Saint-Malo quelquefois?
– Ah oui. Saint-Malo n'est pas loin et je vais quelquefois en ville avec mes parents. Saint-Malo, c'est super. Il y a un grand centre commercial avec beaucoup de magasins, c'est très bien pour le shopping. Il y a aussi un grand centre sportif avec une piscine et il y a une patinoire, des cinémas, etc. C'est vraiment bien. J'aime bien la ville.

cm 7/13

Lire

A C'est où?

Solution:
1 ←, **2** →, **3** ↑, **4** ←, **5** ←, **6** ↑
(mark /5)

B Le jeu des définitions

Solution:
1 g, **2** d, **3** a, **4** f, **5** b, **6** c
(mark /5)

C C'est où, exactement?

Solution:
1 b, **2** c, **3** a, **4** c, **5** b
(mark /4)

D Des vacances de Christelle

Solution:
1 b, **2** a, **3** e, **4** d, **5** f, **6** c, **7** g
(mark /6)

cm 7/14

Écrire et Grammaire W

A En ville

This is an open-ended task.
(mark /4)

134 Tricolore 1 Teacher's Notes

Unité 7 Consolidation and assessment

B Où va-t-on?

Solution:
1 *Je vais à l'église.*
2 *Je vais au collège.*
3 *Nous allons à la piscine.*
4 *Tous mes amis vont au cinéma ce soir.*
5 *Ils vont aux magasins.*

(mark /4)

C Des destinations

This is an open-ended task.
(mark /6)

D Chez moi

This is an open-ended task.
(mark /6)

Rappel 3

92–93

This section can be used at any point after *Unité* 7 for revision and consolidation. It provides reading and writing activities which are self-instructional and can be used by students working individually for homework or during cover lessons.

92

1 Au contraire

Solution:
1 e, **2** g, **3** a, **4** f, **5** h, **6** d, **7** c, **8** b

92

2 Les mots en escargot

Solution:
a *église, gare, hôpital, poste, banque, tour*
b *printemps*

92

3 Chasse à l'intrus

Solution:
a **1** *du sport,* **2** *travailler,* **3** *février,* **4** *un homme,* **5** *derrière,* **6** *méchant,* **7** *l'ami,* **8** *le printemps*
b **1** *Les autres sont des descriptions du temps.*
2 *Les autres sont des nombres.*
3 *Les autres sont des verbes.*
4 *Les autres sont des bâtiments.*
5 *Les autres sont des nombres.*
6 *Les autres sont des prépositions.*
7 *Les autres sont des saisons.*
8 *Les autres sont des sports.*

92

4 Quel temps fait-il?

Solution:
1 *Il y a du soleil.* (C)
2 *Il fait froid.* (A)
3 *Il pleut.* (D)
4 *Il y a du brouillard.* (B)
5 *Il neige.* (E)
6 *Il fait chaud.* (F)

92

5 Masculin, féminin

Solution:

masculin	féminin
un bureau	une brochure
un camping	une chaussette
un bateau	une chaussure
un parking	une calculatrice
un tableau	

92

6 À la maison

Solution:
1 *neige,* **2** *reste,* **3** *téléphone,* **4** *travailles,* **5** *écoute,* **6** *dessine,* **7** *préparons,* **8** *rangez,* **9** *jouent,* **10** *regardent*

93

7 Où est le lapin?

Solution:
1 *Le lapin est entre les livres.*
2 *Le lapin est sur l'ordinateur.*
3 *Le lapin est sous la chaise.*
4 *Le lapin est derrière la radio.*
5 *Le lapin est dans la boîte.*
6 *Le lapin est devant la télé.*

93

8 Le weekend

Solution:
1 c, **2** d, **3** b, **4** e, **5** h, **6** g, **7** a, **8** f

93

9 À toi

This is an open-ended task.

Tricolore 1 Teacher's Notes 135

Unité 7 Consolidation and assessment

93

10 Tom et Jojo en ville

Solution:
1 ville, 2 aux, 3 au, 4 à l', 5 à la, 6 à la, 7 chasse, 8 va, 9 tourne, 10 tout droit, 11 au, 12 tombe

Au choix

152 Au choix

1 La Rochelle – ville touristique

For reading and writing practice, students complete the publicity material.

Solution:
1 ville, 2 port, 3 tours, 4 magasins, 5 restaurants, 6 vélo, 7 musées, 8 aquarium

152 Au choix

2 Attention aux accents!

Practice in completing town vocabulary with vowels and accents.

Solution:
1 une cathédrale   5 un hôpital
2 un bâtiment   6 un musée
3 un château   7 un supermarché
4 une église   8 un théâtre

152 Au choix

3 Quelle est la destination?

Further practice in using the correct form of à.

Solution:
1 Ils vont au terrain de football. B
2 Il va au centre sportif. A
3 Elles vont aux magasins. H
4 Elle va à l'aquarium. G
5 Ils vont à la gare. F
6 L'ambulance va à l'hôpital. D
7 Ils vont à l'office de tourisme. E
8 Ils vont à l'auberge de jeunesse. C

152 Au choix

4 Des endroits en ville

This provides more practice of town vocabulary.

L'A, B, C en ville

As an alternative, students could work in pairs or groups to think of places in a town beginning with as many different letters of the alphabet as possible. They can then check their answers by looking at the *Sommaire*.

Possible solution:

c	h
la cathédrale	l'hôpital
le centre commercial	l'hôtel de ville
le centre sportif	un hôtel
le cinéma	**m**
le château	le musée
le collège	le magasin
un café	le marché
	la mosquée
	une maison
p	**des lettres différentes**
une piscine	une auberge de jeunesse
une patinoire	la gare
un parc	un office de tourisme
la poste	un restaurant
un parking	un théâtre

153 Au choix

5 Un message

This provides more practice of reading and writing about a town.

a Students correct the errors.

Solution:
1 C'est bientôt les vacances de **printemps**.
2 Hugo et Élodie vont souvent à **Saint-Malo** pendant les vacances.
3 Hugo trouve que c'est **super** à Saint-Malo.
4 La sœur de Hugo s'appelle **Élodie**.
5 Élodie **adore** le shopping.
6 En **été** il y a beaucoup de touristes à Saint-Malo.

b Students answer the questions.

Solution:
1 Il va à Saint-Malo.
2 Il pense que c'est super.
3 Il y a un grand centre sportif et une piscine olympique.
4 Élodie aime la ville parce qu'il y a beaucoup de magasins et elle adore le shopping.
5 Several possible answers, e.g. Il y a un château, un fort, des musées et la plage.

c Students write their own message to Hugo, describing a town they like.

153 Au choix

6 Des renseignements touristiques

Students could look at the adverts and spot any cognates or near-cognates, e.g. *une prison, graffiti, un prisonnier, flottant*, etc., then answer the comprehension questions.

Tricolore 1 Teacher's Notes

Unité 7 Consolidation and assessment

Solution:

1 prison, **2** graffiti (made by prisoners), **3** under 18s, **4** place de Verdun, **5** no, **6** either the Vieux-Port (near the tour de la Chaîne) or the port des Minimes, **7** 15–20 mins, **8** because it's on several ships (including a weather ship and a fishing boat).

Copymasters

cm 7/1

En ville (1) – mini-flashcards

Students fill in the words and colour the pictures. The students could then stick them in their books, or the completed sheets could also be mounted on card and used as mini-flashcards for additional practice in pairs or groups. See TB page xix for ideas for using mini-flashcards.

Solution:

1 H, **2** B, **3** F, **4** A, **5** C, **6** D, **7** K, **8** L, **9** J, **10** I, **11** G, **12** E

cm 7/2

Vocabulaire: les endroits

These word games and activities can be used at any convenient point to consolidate vocabulary.

Solution:

1 *Mots mêlés*

  a *Insert wordsearch from previous edition (p135) here - to be supplied*

â	p	é	s	t	u	w	h	l
m	a	r	c	h	é	y	n	p
o	r	l	è	é	d	o	b	i
é	k	c	h	â	t	e	a	u
t	i	d	f	t	g	u	n	s
î	n	d	a	r	j	r	q	p
k	g	f	h	e	i	s	u	o
t	o	i	l	e	t	t	e	s
e	r	s	u	h	c	â	m	t
h	ô	p	i	t	a	l	b	e

  b *Écris le mot*
  1 market *le marché*   **5** bank *la banque*
  2 car park *le parking* **6** post office *la poste*
  3 theatre *le théâtre* **7** hospital *l'hôpital*
  4 castle *le château*   **8** toilets *les toilettes*

2 *Dans l'ordre alphabétique*
  1 auberge de jeunesse = youth hostel
  2 bowling = bowling alley
  3 cinéma = cinema
  4 église = church
  5 hôtel = hotel
  6 magasin = shop
  7 place = square
  8 tour = tower

3 *Un panneau*

  A 1 *Ex. plage* **2** *camping,* **3** *auberge de jeunesse,* **4** *port,* **5** *gare,* **6** *centre sportif,* **7** *piscine,* **8** *bowling,* **9** *centre commercial,* **10** *parc*

  B 1 Le bowling, c'est à droite
   2 La piscine, c'est tout droit
   3 Le camping, c'est à gauche
   4 La plage, c'est à gauche
   5 La gare, c'est tout droit
   6 Le parc, c'est à droite

cm 7/3

C'est quelle direction?

This provides practice of understanding directions using a simple plan.

Solution:

1 *Une petite ville*

  A 1 *vrai,* **2** *faux,* **3** *vrai,* **4** *faux,* **5** *vrai,* **6** *vrai,* **7** *faux,* **8** *vrai*

  B 1 *première,* **2** *première,* **3** *deuxième,* **4** *deuxième,* **5** *troisième,* **6** *troisième,* **7** *gauche,* **8** *droite*

2 *Pour arriver chez moi*

  En sortant de la gare, tourne à gauche, puis prends la deuxième rue à droite et continue tout droit. (c'est la rue de l'Église). Notre maison est à gauche. C'est le numéro 5, près de l'église. Ce n'est pas loin.

cm 7/4

Où va-t-on?

Extra practice of different forms of à.

Solution:

1 *La semaine de Charles*

  1 *au cinéma,* **2** *au parc,* **3** *à la plage,* **4** *à la piscine,* **5** *aux magasins,* **6** *à l'auberge de jeunesse,* **7** *au lit*

2 *Où vont-ils?*

  1 *au camping,* **2** *à la gare,* **3** *à la poste,* **4** *au restaurant,* **5** *à l'hôpital,* **6** *à la plage*

cm 7/5

C'est où?

Further practice of prepositions in the context of animals hiding in a room.

Solution:

1 *Un petit lexique*

  a *dans* – in, **b** *derrière* – behind, **c** *entre* – between, **d** *sur* – on, **e** *sous* – under, **f** *devant* – in front of

2 *Attention! Le vétérinaire arrive!*

  A 1 V, **2** V, **3** F, **4** V, **5** F, **6** F, **7** V, **8** F
  B 1 *devant,* **2** *entre,* **3** *sur,* **4** *sous,* **5** *dans,* **6** *sous*
  C This is an open-ended task.

Tricolore 1 Teacher's Notes

Unité 7 Consolidation and assessment

cm 7/6

En ville (2) – mini-flashcards

Students fill in the words and colour the pictures. The students could then stick them in their books, or the completed sheets could also be mounted on card and used as mini-flashcards for additional practice in pairs or groups. See TB page xix for ideas for using mini-flashcards.

> **Solution:**
> 1 *F la plage*, 2 *C la gare*, 3 *J le supermarché*, 4 *L le théâtre*, 5 *B la cathédrale*, 6 *I le centre sportif*, 7 *A la bibliothèque*, 8 *H le camping*, 9 *K le terrain de football*, 10 *D la mosquée*, 11 *G le bowling*, 12 *E la patinoire*

cm 7/7

Ma ville/mon village

This writing frame provides further support for writing about a town/area.

cm 7/8

Un plan à compléter

This worksheet provides extra oral practice of prepositions and places in a town. Cut the sheet in half so that each partner has a different set of information. Each student asks questions to fill in the missing places on their plan.

cm 7/9

Aller

This provides practice of *aller* in the context of a cartoon strip.

1 *aller* – to go

Check that the paradigm has been correctly completed before students work on the comic strip, or ask students to check it themselves in *Grammaire, 11.13*.

2 *Une erreur*

> **Solution:**
> 1 *vais*, 2 *va*, 3 *va*, 4 *va*, 5 *allons*, 6 *vas*, 7 *vont*, 8 *va*, 9 *allons*, 10 *allez*

cm 7/10

Tu comprends?
1 Qu'est-ce que c'est?

Simple practice, matching town vocabulary with pictures or symbols.

> **Solution:**
> 1 *b*, 2 *j*, 3 *h*, 4 *i*, 5 *e*, 6 *g*, 7 *f*, 8 *d*, 9 *a*, 10 *c*

CD 3 Track 42

Qu'est-ce que c'est?

Nous sommes en ville.
1 – Voici la poste. C'est la poste principale.
2 – Où est l'hôtel de ville?
  – L'hôtel de ville est ici.
3 – Et voilà la cathédrale. Elle est superbe, la cathédrale, non?
4 – Pardon, je cherche l'office de tourisme.
  – L'office de tourisme est par là.
5 – Où est la piscine, s'il vous plaît?
  – La piscine? Là-bas, à droite.
6 – Est-ce qu'il y a des toilettes par ici?
  – Des toilettes? Oui, voilà les toilettes.
7 – Pour aller au centre-ville, c'est par là?
  – Le centre-ville? Oui, c'est par là.
8 – Le camping, c'est loin?
  – Le camping? Non, ce n'est pas loin.
9 – Est-ce que la gare est près d'ici?
  – La gare? Oui, c'est près d'ici.
10 – Est-ce que l'auberge de jeunesse est loin d'ici?
  – L'auberge de jeunesse? Oui, c'est assez loin.

2 C'est dans quelle direction?

Choosing directions to match each conversation.

> **Solution:**
> 1 *b*, 2 *c*, 3 *d*, 4 *a*, 5 *e*, 6 *f*

CD 3 Track 43

C'est dans quelle direction?

1 Tournez à gauche.
2 Continuez tout droit.
3 Prenez la première rue à gauche.
4 Tournez à droite.
5 Prenez la première rue à droite.
6 Prenez la deuxième rue à gauche.

3 Où vas-tu?

Following directions and giving the destinations.

> **Solution:**
> 1c *à l'hôtel Royal*, 2a *au parc*, 3f *aux toilettes*, 4d *au supermarché*, 5b *à la piscine*, 6e *au théâtre*, 7g *à l'auberge de jeunesse*

CD 3 Track 44

Où vas-tu?

1 Allez tout droit et prenez la deuxième rue à droite.
2 Allez tout droit et prenez la deuxième rue à gauche. Puis c'est à gauche.
3 Allez tout droit et tournez à droite. C'est la première rue à droite.
4 Allez tout droit et prenez la première rue à gauche. C'est devant vous.
5 Tout droit, toujours tout droit, puis prenez la troisième rue à droite.
6 Allez tout droit, puis prenez la deuxième rue à gauche et c'est sur votre droite.
7 Allez tout droit, puis prenez la deuxième rue à gauche, puis la première rue à droite.

Unité 7 Consolidation and assessment

4 Ma ville

Solution:
1 V, **2** F, **3** V, **4** F, **5** V, **6** F, **7** V, **8** F

CD 3 Track 45

Ma ville

Salut. Je m'appelle Hugo. J'habite à Boulogne-sur-mer. C'est une ville de taille moyenne dans le nord de la France et c'est un port important. Mon quartier est près de la plage mais c'est assez loin du centre-ville. Dans mon quartier il y a de petits magasins, des maisons et une église. Au centre-ville, il y a une piscine, une bibliothèque, des cinémas, un aquarium et beaucoup de magasins. C'est très bien parce que j'adore le shopping. L'aquarium aussi est très intéressant. Il y a aussi un vieux quartier dans la ville, où il y a un château. J'aime bien ma ville.

cm 7/11

Sommaire

A summary of the main language and structures of the unit.

Unité 8

Tricolore 1 Unité 8 Une journée scolaire   Pages 94–111

8A À quelle heure? pages 94–95		
• Say at what time events take place • Understand and tell the time		
Grammaire	Stratégies	Phonétique
• None	• None	• None
Resources		
Audio: 1 *C'est à quelle heure?*; **4** *Rendez-vous à quelle heure?*, or CD 4, Tracks 2 and 3 **Copymasters:** 8/1 *Quelle heure est-il?* **Flashcards:** 43–60 **Worksheets:** Starters and plenaries; *On va au cinéma?* (S)		**Interactive activity:** *L'heure du rendez-vous* (L) **PowerPoint:** *Quelle heure est-il?* (V) **Grammar in Action:** pp28–29
8B Une journée en semaine pages 96–97		
• Talk about daily routine		
Grammaire	Stratégies	Phonétique
• Recognise some reflexive verbs	• None	• None
Resources		
Audio: 1 *Une journée typique*, or CD 4, track 4 **Copymasters:** 8/2 *Qui est-ce?* **Flashcards:** 81, 90, 95 **Worksheets:** Starters and plenaries, *À quelle heure est-ce que …?* (R)		**Interactive activity:** *Une journée typique* (R) **PowerPoint:** *Attention, c'est l'heure* (song) **Grammar in Action:** None
8C Mon emploi du temps pages 98–99		
• Talk about school subjects • Practise telling the time		
Grammaire	Stratégies	Phonétique
• Use of the definite article	• Using spelling patterns to improve writing	• The letters 'im', 'in'
Resources		
Audio: 1a *Les matières*, **5** *C'est quel jour?*, or CD 4, tracks 5 and 7 **Copymasters:** 8/3 *Jeux de vocabulaire: les matières*, 8/4 *La vie scolaire* **Worksheets:** Starters and plenaries; *Un emploi de temps* (S)		**Interactive activity:** *Le matin, l'après-midi ou le soir?* (L) **Ph** The letters 'im', 'in', or CD 4, track 8 **PowerPoint:** None **Grammar in Action:** None
8D Qu'est-ce que vous faites? pages 100–101		
• Discuss school subjects		
Grammaire	Stratégies	Phonétique
• Use the verb *faire* (to do, to make)	• Adding interest to your writing (4)	• None
Resources		
Key language: See below **Audio: 1** *Conversations au collège*; **3** *Ils aiment ou ils n'aiment pas?*; **4** *Six élèves*, or CD 4, tracks 11, 12 and 13 **Copymasters:** 8/5 *On fait beaucoup de choses* **Worksheets:** Starters and plenaries		**Interactive activity:** *On fait ça* (R) **PowerPoint:** None **Grammar in Action:** None
8E Ma matière préférée pages 102–103		
• Ask questions to get to know someone • Talk about your favourite things		
Grammaire	Stratégies	Phonétique
• Say 'his', 'her' and 'its' • 'which … ?', 'what … ?'	• Improving your speaking skills	• None
Resources		
Audio: 1 *Un nouvel élève*, or CD 4, track 14 **Copymasters:** 8/6 *Mon, ton, son* **Worksheets:** Starters and plenaries; *Des phrases au choix* (W)		**Interactive activity:** *Son, sa, ses* (G) **PowerPoint:** None **Grammar in Action:** pp30–31, p32

Tricolore 1 Teacher's Notes

8F Notre collège pages 104–105		
• Talk about your school			
Grammaire	Stratégies	Phonétique
• Say 'our', 'your' and 'their'	• Translating from French to English (2)	• None
Resources			
Audio: 1 *Au collège*, or CD 4, track 15 Copymasters: 8/7 *Des questions et des réponses (notre/nos, votre/vos)* Worksheets: Starters and plenaries; Possessive adjectives (G)	Interactive activity: None PowerPoint: None Grammar in Action: pp33–34	

8G Au Sénégal pages 106–107		
• Find out about a French-speaking country • Understand a longer text			
Grammaire	Stratégies	Phonétique
• None	• None	• The letter 'r'
Resources			
Audio: 1 *Notre pays – le Sénégal*, or CD 4, track 16 Copymasters: None Worksheets: Starters and plenaries e-book: *La Polynésie française*	Interactive activity: None Ph The letter 'r', or CD 4, track 17 PowerPoint: None Grammar in Action: None	

8H Une présentation pages 108–109		
• Learn more about a French school • Prepare a presentation about your school			
Grammaire	Stratégies	Phonétique
• None	• Preparing a presentation	• None
Resources			
Audio: 1 *Le collège Missy*, or CD 4, track 18 Copymasters: 8/8 *Tu comprends?*, 8/9 *Sommaire* Worksheets: Starters and plenaries; Preparing a good presentation (Strat)	Interactive activity: Classroom commands (V) Video: *Les profs du collège* PowerPoint: *Le Collège Missy* (R) Grammar in Action: None	

Key language

Telling the time (8A)
Quelle heure est-il?
Il est une heure …
cinq
dix
et quart
vingt
vingt-cinq
et demie
moins vingt-cinq
moins vingt
moins le quart
moins dix
moins cinq
Il est midi.
Il est midi et demi.
Il est minuit.
Il est minuit et demi.

Daily routine (8B)
le matin
l'après-midi
le soir
la nuit
Le matin, je prends mon petit déjeuner à …
J'arrive au collège à …
Les cours commencent à …
À midi, …
je mange à la cantine.
je mange des sandwichs.
Je rentre à la maison à …
Je commence mes devoirs à …
Le soir, on mange à …
Je vais au lit à … / Je me couche à …

8A À quelle heure?

Meals (8B)
un repas
le petit déjeuner
le déjeuner
le goûter
le dîner

Reflexive verbs (8B)
Je me lève …
Je me couche …
Je m'appelle …

School subjects (8C and 8D)
l'allemand
l'anglais
le dessin
l'EPS (éducation physique et sportive)
l'éducation civique
l'espagnol
le français
la géographie
l'histoire
l'informatique
les maths
la musique
les sciences
les SVT (Sciences de la Vie et de la Terre)
le sport
la technologie

Subject preferences (8D and 8E)
Qu'est-ce que tu aimes comme matire?
J'aime / Je n'aime pas …
Ma matière préférée, c'est …
Pourquoi?
Parce que c'est …
amusant
difficile
ennuyeux
facile
génial
intéressant
nul
super
sympa
utile

Qualifiers (8D and 8E)
très
assez
un peu
vraiment

8A À quelle heure? pages 94–95

- Say at what time events take place
- Understand and tell the time

Grammaire	Stratégies	Phonétique
• None	• None	• None

Resources

Audio: 1 *C'est à quelle heure?*; **4** *Rendez-vous à quelle heure?*, or CD 4, Tracks 2 and 3
Copymasters: 8/1 *Quelle heure est-il?*
Flashcards: 43–60
Worksheets: Starters and plenaries; *On va au cinéma?* (S)

Interactive activity: *L'heure du rendez-vous* (L)
PowerPoint: *Quelle heure est-il?* (V)
Grammar in Action: pp28–29

Worksheet

Starters (pages 94–95)

1 **Numbers** Revise numbers 0–60 using a number game, e.g. *Effacez!*
2 *Vrai ou faux/Masculin ou féminin* + places in a town
   a Display a selection of flashcards from 43–60. Say the correct or incorrect name and ask students to respond with their *vrai/faux* cards.
   b Display the following words or read them randomly and ask *C'est masculin ou féminin?* Students respond by showing a *masculin* or *féminin* card.
   A (masc): collège, marché, parc, parking, supermarché
   B (fém): piscine, gare, poste, église, plage

Introduction

Teaching the time

Go through the objectives for this spread.

Tricolore 1 Teacher's Notes

8A À quelle heure?

It is useful to space out the teaching of the time, giving practice at each stage, as this helps to avoid confusion later on.

All times are presented in this section but practice can take place at various points in the unit so full competence can be built up gradually.

In order to keep things simple, in *Unité* 8 most items use the 12 hour clock, although the 24 hour clock is increasingly common in France. The 24 hour clock is mentioned in 8C and taught and practised in *Unité* 10 (10E).

Once the time has been taught, remember to ask two or three students the time at some point in each lesson.

Presentation

L'heure

Using the presentation or a clock with movable hands, start by teaching the hours involving numbers that do not change in pronunciation, i.e. 4, 5, 7, 8 and 11. Then add 2, 3, 6 and 10. Ask the class to listen for the *z* sound before *heures*. If appropriate, explain that this is called elision and occurs before a vowel – here the *h* acts like a vowel, so it is as if the word begins with *e*.

Next, teach 9 and 1, *midi* and *minuit* and then put them all together.

94

1 C'est à quelle heure?

Students listen to the recording and write down, in figures, the time mentioned in each conversation.

Solution:
1 3h00, 2 8h00, 3 2h00, 4 9h00, 5 10h00,
6 11h00, 7 midi, 8 minuit

CD 4 Track 2

C'est à quelle heure?

1 – Salut, Guy!
   – Salut, Jean-Claude. Tu vas au match de football?
   – Oui.
   – C'est à quelle heure?
   – Le match commence à trois heures.
2 – Qu'est-ce que tu fais ce soir, Monique?
   – Je vais au cinéma. Il y a un bon film.
   – Ça commence à quelle heure?
   – À huit heures.
3 – Christophe, à quelle heure est-ce que tu joues au tennis avec Marc?
   – À deux heures.
4 – Bonjour, Anne-Marie. C'est Jean-Claude à l'appareil. Écoute, il y a une surprise-partie chez Robert samedi soir.
   – Ah, chouette! C'est à quelle heure?
   – Ça commence à neuf heures.
5 – Maman, tu vas en ville ce matin?
   – Oui, j'y vais à dix heures.
6 – Quand est-ce que papa va en ville?
   – Il va aux magasins à onze heures, puis il va jouer au golf.
7 – Vous allez en ville ce matin?
   – Oui, nous allons en ville, et à midi, nous allons au restaurant. Tu viens avec nous au restaurant?
   – Oui, je veux bien. À midi, alors.
8 – Le supermarché est ouvert jusqu'à quelle heure, le vendredi?
   – Le vendredi, c'est ouvert jusqu'à minuit.

94

2 Le weekend

Revise the places illustrated then work through this task orally. Students can then complete it for homework.

Solution:
1 *à midi*, 2 *à onze heures*, 3 *à quatre heures*,
4 *à sept heures*, 5 *à deux heures*, 6 *à minuit*

94 Dossier-langue

The time

This summarises phrases linked to telling the time for future reference.

94

3 Français/Anglais

Students work out the English for useful questions and phrases linked to the time. Explain that the 24 hour clock is used widely in France, particularly for official and business information. This is taught and practised more fully in *Unité* 10.

Solution:
1 What time does it start?
2 It's at 10 o'clock.
3 What time is it?
4 It's midday.
5 What time is the shop open until?
6 It's open until 7 o'clock / 7pm.

Presentation

L'heure

Use the presentation to introduce quarter past, half past and quarter to.

Dictate some times to students, who write them down as Xh15, Xh30, etc. Students then read them back.

Write some times on the board for a game of *Effacez!*

94

4 Rendez-vous à quelle heure?

The times in the recording are given using the 12 hour clock, although the 24 hour clock is increasingly common in France.

Explain *une horloge* (large clock or clock tower). *La grosse horloge* is a well-known site in La Rochelle.

Students could note down their answers in English or in any helpful way (symbols, abbreviations in French, etc.), so they can read them back correctly. If noting in French for part **b**, students could refer to the *Sommaire* for *Unité* 7 for spellings of places in a town.

Tricolore 1 Teacher's Notes 143

8A À quelle heure?

a Students listen to the conversations and write down the time (in figures) of each meeting.

> **Solution:**
> **1** à 2h30, **2** à 11h, **3** à 3h15, **4** à 4h45, **5** à 7h30, **6** à 1h30, **7** à 8h15, **8** à 8h, **9** à 10h15, **10** à 10h30

b They listen again and write down the meeting place.

> **Solution:**
> **1** under the large clock tower, **2** in front of the museum, **3** behind the cathedral, **4** at the café, **5** in front of the cinema, **6** in the park, **7** at the station, **8** in front of the restaurant, **9** in front of the swimming pool, **10** at the supermarket

CD 4 Track 3

Rendez-vous à quelle heure?

1. – On va en ville samedi?
   – Oui, je veux bien, À quelle heure?
   – À deux heures et demie?
   – D'accord. Alors rendez-vous sous la grosse horloge à deux heures et demie.
2. – Tu es libre ce matin? On va au musée?
   – Oui, d'accord. À onze heures?
   – Oui, d'accord. Alors, rendez-vous devant le musée à onze heures.
3. – On va au marché cet après-midi?
   – Oui, d'accord.
   – Alors, rendez-vous derrière la cathédrale à trois heures et quart.
   – À trois heures et quart, d'accord.
4. – On va au café après?
   – Oui, d'accord.
   – Alors, rendez-vous au café à cinq heures moins le quart.
   – À cinq heures moins le quart, d'accord.
5. – On va au cinéma ce soir?
   – Oui, je veux bien. À quelle heure?
   – À sept heures et demie?
   – D'accord. Alors, rendez-vous devant le cinéma à sept heures et demie.
6. – On joue au tennis cet après-midi?
   – Oui, je veux bien.
   – Alors, rendez-vous dans le parc à une heure et demie.
   – D'accord, à une heure et demie dans le parc.
7. – Tu es libre vendredi? On va à Bordeaux?
   – À Bordeaux? Oui, je veux bien.
   – Alors, rendez-vous à la gare à huit heures et quart.
   – Bon, à huit heures et quart à la gare.
   – C'est ça. À vendredi alors.
8. – On va au restaurant ce soir?
   – Oui, bonne idée. À quelle heure?
   – À huit heures.
   – Alors rendez-vous devant le restaurant à huit heures.
   – C'est ça. À ce soir.
9. – On va à la piscine ce matin?
   – Oui, d'accord.
   – Alors, rendez-vous devant la piscine à dix heures et quart.
   – D'accord, à bientôt.
10. – Tu vas au supermarché, ce matin?
    – Oui, à dix heures et demie.
    – Alors, rendez-vous au supermarché à dix heures et demie.

Interactive activity

L'heure du rendez-vous

Presentation

L'heure

Use the presentation to introduce the remaining times past and to.

cm 8/1

Quelle heure est-il? – mini-flashcards

95

5 Quelle journée!

This provides practice of all forms of the time linked with places in a town.

a Students match the picture and text with the correct clock.

> **Solution:**
> **1** C, **2** F, **3** A, **4** H, **5** B, **6** E, **7** G, **8** D

b For extension, students write a description of a similar day, changing the places and times, and with a girl in charge of the children.

95   AfL

6 Conversations aux nombres

Students make up conversations in pairs to arrange a meeting place and time.

Review the spread objectives and assessment criteria, then use this for peer assessment. Ask successful students to demonstrate their conversation to the class.

Worksheet

Inventez des conversations

154 Au choix

1 Mlle Dupont

Further practice in using the correct form of à.

gia 1 pp28–29

Telling the time (1) and (2)

This provides graded practice of all times.

144   Tricolore 1 Teacher's Notes

8B Une journée en semaine

Regular practice

From now on, spend a short time in each lesson of this unit, dictating some times which students take down in figures and then read back. This can gradually be taken over by the students themselves or developed as a pairwork or group activity. When asking the time, use *Quelle heure est-il?* and *Il est quelle heure?* to familiarise students with both expressions.

Further revision of time

Time and the 24-hour clock is revised in *Unité* 10.

Worksheet

Plenaries (pages 94–95)

1 Students work in pairs or groups to discuss what they find the easiest and the most difficult points to remember about telling the time in French and to share any tips for learning the time. This can be discussed first in pairs or groups and then shared with the class.

2 A similar discussion can take place about numbers.

8B Une journée en semaine   pages 96–97

- Talk about daily routine

Grammaire	Stratégies	Phonétique
• Recognise some reflexive verbs	• None	• None

Resources

Audio: 1 *Une journée typique*, or CD 4, track 4
Copymasters: 8/2 *Qui est-ce?*
Flashcards: 81, 90, 95
Worksheets: Starters and plenaries, *À quelle heure est-ce que …?* (R)

Interactive activity: *Une journée typique* (R)
PowerPoint: *Attention, c'est l'heure* (song)
Grammar in Action: None

Worksheet

Starters (pages 96–97)

1 *Chaque mot à sa place* Display the following task. Give students one minute to read and work out the answers, then ask students collectively or randomly to give the number of the box.

Quelle est la bonne boîte pour chaque mot?
l'église (2), noir (4), le volley (5), entre (1), vingt (3)

1	2	3	4	5
devant	le temple	huit	blanc	le judo
derrière	la mosquée	quinze	vert	le hockey
sur	le synagogue	soixante	jaune	le basket

2 *Quel verbe?* Display the following:
  a *Je … à une amie.*
  b *Tu … au football?*
  c *Nous … en ville.*
  d *Vous … à la maison après l'école?*
  e *Ils … un sandwich à midi.*
  1 rentrez **2** parle **3** mangent **4** allons **5** joues

Give students one minute to read and work out the answers. Then ask students collectively or randomly for the answers.

Solution:
a *2*, b *5*, c *4*, d *1*, e *3*

Introduction

Go through the objectives for this spread.

Time of day

Revise *la journée, le matin, l'après-midi, le soir* and teach *la nuit* perhaps by drawing a diagram on the board, representing *la journée*, and dividing it into parts shown by time ranges, e.g. 7h00–12h00, 12h01–18h00, 18h01–23h00, 23h01–6h59.

Les repas

Teach and practise *le repas, le petit déjeuner, le déjeuner, le goûter, le dîner*, e.g. *Le matin, on prend le petit déjeuner; à midi, on prend le déjeuner; l'après-midi, on prend le goûter et le soir, on prend le dîner.* Write the new vocabulary on the board for reference and/or for a game of *Effacez!* (TB page xvii).

Food

Flashcards (81, 90, 95) can be used to present and practise *du pain, du jus d'orange, un chocolat chaud.* These are used in the following item, but are not taught for active use until Unité 9.

🔊 96

1 Une journée typique

Students listen to the recording and follow the text in their books.

Ask some questions to check comprehension, e.g.
C'est la journée d'un élève français, non?
Comment s'appelle-t-il?

Tricolore 1 Teacher's Notes   **145**

8B Une journée en semaine

C'est une journée scolaire ou c'est dimanche?
Qu'est-ce qu'il fait à midi? (Teach and practise *le déjeuner*)
Qu'est-ce qu'il fait pendant la journée? Il va au parc? Il va au collège?
Et quand il rentre à la maison, qu'est-ce qu'il fait?
Il joue au football? Il travaille? Il joue sur l'ordinateur? etc.

Remind students about hard and soft c and g and point out the use of ç in *nous commençons* and the extra e after g in *nous mangeons* to soften the sound.

CD 4 Track 4

Une journée typique

Olivier parle d'une journée scolaire.
Le matin, je me lève à sept heures.
Je prends mon petit déjeuner à sept heures et demie. Je mange du pain avec du beurre et de la confiture et je bois du jus d'orange.
Je quitte la maison à huit heures et j'arrive au collège à huit heures vingt.
Les cours commencent à huit heures et demie. J'ai quatre cours le matin.
À dix heures et demie, il y a la récréation du matin. Ça dure dix minutes.
À midi, je mange à la cantine. Puis je vais dans la cour avec mes copains. Quelquefois, nous jouons au football.
L'après-midi, nous commençons à deux heures. J'ai cours jusqu'à quatre heures moins dix. Puis je rentre à la maison.
Pour mon goûter, je mange un sandwich et je bois un chocolat chaud.
À six heures, je commence mes devoirs.
Le soir, nous mangeons à sept heures. Après le dîner, je continue à travailler.
Puis je regarde la télé, j'écoute de la musique ou je joue sur l'ordinateur.
Et à neuf heures, je me couche.

Interactive activity

Une journée typique

97

2 La journée d'Olivier

Three short follow-up tasks provide more vocabulary practice.

> **Solution:**
> a *La journée: le matin, l'après-midi, le soir, la nuit*
> *Les repas: le petit déjeuner, le déjeuner, le goûter, le dîner*
> b 4 *nombres:* various, e.g. *sept, huit, quatre, dix, deux, six, neuf*
> 3 *verbes:* various e.g. (-er verbs) *mange, quitte, arrive, commencent, dure, jouons, rentre, regarde, écoute*
> 2 *bâtiments: la maison, le collège*
> 1 *chose à manger:* various, e.g. *du pain, du beurre, de la confiture, un sandwich*
> c 1 f, 2 a, 3 e, 4 b, 5 i, 6 g, 7 h, 8 c, 9 j, 10 d

79 Dossier-langue

Reflexive verbs

Reflexive verbs are briefly mentioned in connection with *je me lève* and *je me couche*. They are covered in more detail in Stage 2. Other examples used in Stage 1 which could be mentioned are: *je m'appelle, tu t'appelles, il/elle s'appelle; asseyez-vous, levez-vous*.

97

3 Ma journée

This task practises mealtimes and time of day. The times relate to a typical day in the UK rather than France.

> **Solution:**
> 1 *matin,* 2 *petit déjeuner,* 3 *cours,* 4 *déjeuner,* 5 *après-midi,* 6 *goûter,* 7 *devoirs,* 8 *soir*

Worksheet

À quelle heure est-ce que ...?

97

4 Un questionnaire

Before interviewing their partner, students should jot down the times for themselves. Some questions could be asked of the whole class, e.g. *Combien de personnes quittent la maison à sept heures du matin? Qui arrive au collège à huit heures?* etc.

154 Au choix

2 Notre journée au collège

97 AfL

5 Dossier personnel

a In order to build up a description of their own typical day, students write replies in full sentences to the questions of the questionnaire, but combining their answers, where appropriate, using connectives.

b For extension, students write a longer description based on *Une journée typique*.

This task relates closely to the spread objective. Discuss assessment criteria by giving examples of successful language, and use this for self-assessment.

cm 8/2

Qui est-ce?

8C Mon emploi du temps

> **Worksheet**

Plenaries (pages 96–97)

1 **Learning nouns** Discuss what students find most difficult about learning nouns (gender, spellings, etc). Share useful tips, such as Look, say, copy, spell, hide and repeat or similar. With gender, ask how students are learning this and whether their strategies are successful. Has anyone worked out any patterns that might help? Perhaps suggest some word endings which normally denote a specific gender (see SB page 158).

2 **Using the *Sommaire*** Suggest students find five words that they have difficulty remembering in this area which are listed in the *Sommaire*. They should discuss in pairs how they can remember them. They should share ideas with another pair and a spokesperson then reports back to the class.

8C Mon emploi du temps   pages 98–99

- Talk about school subjects
- Practise telling the time

Grammaire	Stratégies	Phonétique
• Use of the definite article	• Using spelling patterns to improve writing	• The letters 'im', 'in'

Resources

Audio: 1a *Les matières*, 5 *C'est quel jour?*, or CD 4, tracks 5 and 7
Copymasters: 8/3 *Jeux de vocabulaire: les matières*, 8/4 *La vie scolaire*
Worksheets: Starters and plenaries; *Un emploi de temps* (S)

Interactive activity: *Le matin, l'après-midi ou le soir?* (L)
Ph The letters 'im', 'in', or CD 4, track 8
PowerPoint: None
Grammar in Action: None

> **Worksheet**

Starters (pages 98–99)

1 **Times** Display a selection of times for students to write down in figures on mini-whiteboards or paper.

huit heures, neuf heures, midi, sept heures vingt, cinq heures moins le quart, six heures cinq, onze heures dix, dix heures vingt-cinq, trois heures et demie, une heure et quart.

Point to a time and ask students to say it in chorus and hold up their mini-whiteboard or paper.

2 **Cognates** Hand out a list of the following cognates in random order. Read them out and students mark 1, 2, 3, 4, etc. by the side of the word as they recognise it. Volunteers then read out the words. In this way, students can work privately, change their minds and be passive and still learn.

géographie, musique, biologie, art, maths, histoire, technologie, double, éducation, fruit

Introduction

Go through the objectives for this spread.

Ask students if they have a text book for different subjects, e.g.

(Name), *tu as ton livre d'anglais?* (Name) *tu as ton livre de maths?* etc.

Use these to teach the names for different subjects.

Write a list on the board for a game of *Effacez!*, then write some initial letters on the board and ask volunteers to complete the words, thereby recreating the list.

🔊 98

1 Les matières

a Students listen to the recording and write the appropriate letter.

Solution:

1 G, **2** C, **3** A, **4** E, **5** H, **6** F, **7** B, **8** I, **9** K, **10** D, **11** J, **12** M, **13** N, **14** L

> 🔊 CD 4 Track 5

Les matières

1	la technologie	8	les sciences
2	l'anglais	9	l'informatique
3	la géographie	10	le français
4	les maths	11	le dessin
5	le sport	12	l'allemand
6	l'histoire	13	l'espagnol
7	la musique	14	l'éducation civique

b Students then go through the symbols in order, giving the French for the subject. These can be written out, perhaps with the English equivalent.

8C Mon emploi du temps

Solution:
A *la géographie*, **B** *la musique*, **C** *l'anglais*, **D** *le français*, **E** *les maths*, **F** *l'histoire*, **G** *la technologie*, **H** *le sport*, **I** *les sciences*, **J** *le dessin*, **K** *l'informatique*, **L** *l'éducation civique*, **M** *l'allemand*, **N** *l'espagnol*

98

2 Une journée au collège

Revision of times, subjects and daily school events. Teach *la pause-déjeuner*. Students match the sentences to the digital clocks, which include some examples using the 24-hour clock as it is widely used on school timetables.

Solution:
1 G, **2** D, **3** F, **4** B, **5** E, **6** H, **7** A, **8** C

98

3 Dans la cour

This provides further practice of times and subjects. Explain *EPS* (*éducation physique et sportive*) which is used in item 4. Students note the subject and the time of the lesson.

Solution:
1 *anglais 8h30*, **2** *technologie 10h10*, **3** *histoire 11h05*, **4** *EPS 14h00*, **5** *géographie 09h15*, **6** *maths 15h00*, **7** *sciences 13h25*, **8** *dessin 16h20*

CD 4 Track 6

Dans la cour

1 – Quel est ton premier cours aujourd'hui?
 – On a anglais à huit heures et demie.
 – Alors, anglais à huit heures et demie.
2 – Tu as technologie ce matin?
 – Oui, un cours de deux heures de technologie à dix heures dix.
3 – Tu as histoire mercredi?
 – Oui, on a histoire à 11h05.
4 – C'est bien, on a EPS cet après-midi.
 – Oui, EPS à deux heures.
5 – C'est quand, le cours de géographie?
 – On a géographie à neuf heures et quart.
6 – Les maths, c'est à quelle heure?
 – On a maths à trois heures.
7 – Tu as sciences à quelle heure?
 – Nous avons sciences à une heure vingt-cinq.
8 – Nous avons dessin cet après-midi.
 – Oui, nous avons dessin à quatre heures vingt. C'est le dernier cours.

98 Stratégies

Using spelling patterns to improve writing

This covers some common spelling patterns of French and English words: French words ending in *-ie* often ending in *-y* in English; French words ending in *-que* often ending in *-c* in English.

99

4 Un emploi du temps

Teach *un emploi du temps* and then use this for oral work, pointing out some of the differences of a French school, e.g.

Regardez l'emploi du temps.

Est-ce qu'on a cours tous les jours de la semaine?

Et vous, vous avez cours le samedi aussi?

Et le mercredi? Souvent il n'y a pas cours le mercredi en France.

Qu'est-ce qu'on a comme cours, lundi à 8h30? Est-ce qu'on a sciences, lundi? Est-ce qu'on a histoire? etc.

The 24-hour clock is normally used on French timetables. This is taught for active use in *Unité* 10.

Worksheet

Un emploi du temps

99

5 C'est quel jour?

Students listen to the recording and decide which day is being referred to.

Solution:
1 *samedi matin*, **2** *lundi après-midi*, **3** *jeudi matin*, **4** *mardi matin*, **5** *mardi après-midi*, **6** *lundi matin*, **7** *vendredi matin*, **8** *vendredi après-midi*

CD 4 Track 7

C'est quel jour?

1 Alors, je commence avec un cours de français, puis j'ai anglais. À dix heures vingt, c'est la récréation, et après la récré, j'ai musique.
2 Après le déjeuner, nous avons technologie. Ça c'est bien, c'est ma matière préférée.
3 Eh bien, nous commençons avec un cours de maths. Après on a anglais. Puis c'est la récré, et après la récré, on a français et informatique.
4 Je commence à huit heures et demie avec un cours de français, après ça c'est la géographie. Après la récré, nous avons maths, et puis dessin.
5 Après le déjeuner, nous avons un cours de deux heures, on a sciences, puis c'est la récré et après la récré, on a EPS (éducation physique et sportive).
6 On commence à huit heures et demie avec un cours d'anglais, puis on a histoire. Après la récréation, on a français et puis maths.
7 D'abord, on a éducation civique. Puis le deuxième cours, c'est français. Après la récréation, on a un cours de deux heures de maths.
8 Après le déjeuner, nous avons EPS de deux heures dix jusqu'à quatre heures. Et cette semaine, nous allons à la piscine. Ça, c'est bien.

Interactive activity

Le matin ou l'après-midi?

Tricolore 1 Teacher's Notes

8C Mon emploi du temps

99

6 On a quelle matière?

Students make up their own conversations with partners, based on the timetable. There could be a class brainstorming session to build up words for positive and negative opinions, to be used here.

99 Dossier-langue

When to use the definite article (le/la/les)

This explains the use of avoir + subject without the use of le/la/les and the use of aimer/détester with le/la/les + noun.

Interactive activity

The letters 'im', 'in'

99 Phonétique

The letters 'im', 'in'

A full explanation of this sound is given on kerboodle!, together with interactive practice.

a Explain that when 'i' is followed by 'n' or 'm' it is often a nasal vowel (pronounced through the nose). Remind students of other nasal vowels, 'am', 'an', 'em', 'en', 'on', 'om', and the tip of holding the nose when saying the nasal sound, then trying to make the same sound without holding the nose.

Say the word vingt with an appropriate gesture with both hands twice. Students repeat the word with the same gesture. Then read out the other words, with the students repeating each one: informatique, impossible, matin. The words are also included on the recording for optional use (part a).

Explain that if the letters are followed by another vowel or a second 'm' or 'n', then they are pronounced differently. Read aloud the exceptions: image, inutile, innocent, immédiatement, with students repeating the words, without the gesture. Again, these are included on the recording.

Parts b and c can be used for further practice.

b Ask students to listen and repeat the words they hear. Then display the words in a different order, e.g. a important, b interview, c Inde, d imperméable, e intéressant, for students to match (b, c, a, e, d).

c Students listen to the silly sentence and note down how many times they hear the sound (7). They can then repeat the sentence to help them remember this sound.

For further practice, write some additional words on the board to check that students recognise the link between spelling and pronunciation e.g. impossible, vin, main, soudain.

CD 4 Track 8

The letters 'im', 'in'

Écoutez et répétez:
a vingt, informatique, impossible, matin
  Des exceptions: image, inutile, innocent, immédiatement
b interview, Inde, important, intéressant, imperméable
c Ce matin cinq trains américains transportent des ingrédients importants en Inde.

99 AfL

7 Dossier personnel

a This could be done initially as a class activity with students volunteering information to build up their school timetable for a favourite day.

b For extension, students describe why it's a ⊕ favourite day.

c Students describe a day they dislike with reasons. ⊕

Then review the spread objectives and discuss assessment criteria.

Presentation

Chantez! Attention, c'est l'heure!

Chanson

Chantez! Attention, c'est l'heure!

This rap can be used at any appropriate point. The words also appear on kerboodle!. Further notes for using this and other songs appear on TB page xxi.

CD 4 Tracks 9–10

Chantez! Attention, c'est l'heure!

Attention c'est l'heure!
Déjà sept heures moins dix, dix, dix,
Vite, vite, je vais être en retard.
Sept heures et quart je me prépare,
Je quitte la maison, enfin je pars.
Attention, c'est l'heure!
Ça y est, huit heures du mat, matin,
On entre en gare, j'arrive en train.
La cloche sonne à huit heures vingt,
Je suis au collège, tout va bien.
Attention, c'est l'heure!
Enfin midi, j'ai faim, faim, faim,
On va manger à la cantine.
Il est cinq heures, viens Géraldine,
La fin des cours, vive les copines.
Attention, c'est l'heure!
Il est six heures du soir, soir, soir,
Je fais mes devoirs, ouf, ça y est!
Huit heures, on prend tous le dîner,
Et puis, on regarde la télé.
Attention, c'est l'heure!
Besoin d'un bon dodo, dodo,
Très fatigué, je vais au lit.
Eh oui, il est dix heures et demie,
Alors à bientôt, bonne nuit.
Attention, c'est l'heure!

Tricolore 1 Teacher's Notes **149**

8D Qu'est-ce que vous faites?

cm 8/3

Jeux de vocabulaire: les matières

cm 8/4

La vie scolaire

> **Worksheet**

Plenary (pages 98–99)

Think, pair and share Students think about the topic of school life in France for a few minutes. Working in pairs, they have two minutes to come up with two differences between French and British schooling. They then report back to the class. Then they have one minute to come up with two things which are the same, before reporting back. Ask for any further comments about school life in France.

8D Qu'est-ce que vous faites?   pages 100–101

- Discuss school subjects

Grammaire	Stratégies	Phonétique
• Use the verb *faire* (to do, to make)	• Adding interest to your writing (4)	• None

Resources

Key language: See below **Audio:** 1 *Conversations au collège*; 3 *Ils aiment ou ils n'aiment pas?*; 4 *Six élèves*, or CD 4, tracks 11, 12 and 13 **Copymasters:** 8/5 *On fait beaucoup de choses* **Worksheets:** Starters and plenaries	**Interactive activity:** *On fait ça* (R) **PowerPoint:** None **Grammar in Action:** None

> **Worksheet**

Starters (pages 100–101)

1 *En groupes* Display a list of words in random order or hand this out on slips of paper. Ask students to put these into 5 groups:

le déjeuner, le dîner, le goûter

les maths, l'histoire, le dessin

la chaussette, la jupe, le pantalon

as, ont, avons

grand, petit, long

2 *Quel verbe?* Display the following:

a *Je … à la bibliothèque.*

b *Tu … à la cantine?*

c *Nous … dans la salle d'informatique.*

d *Vous … au gymnase pour EPS?*

e *Elles … à la piscine ce matin.*

1 *allons*, **2** *vas*, **3** *vont*, **4** *vais*, **5** *allez*

Give students one minute to read and work out the answers, then ask students collectively or randomly to read the sentence with the correct verb.

> **Solution:**
> **a** 4, **b** 2, **c** 1, **d** 5, **e** 3

Introduction

Go through the objectives for this spread.

> 📖 ◀)) 100

1 Conversations au collège

Before listening to this, recap the listening strategies covered so far. Then read through the conversation and ask the class to think about what kind of word is missing in each case. Students could try to guess the missing words first. Some clues could be given e.g. (1) *c'est le nom d'une matière/d'un sport/d'une couleur/d'une saison.*

> **Solution:**
>
> **1** EPS, **2** sport, **3** basket, **4** la piscine, **5** été, **6** judo, **7** le français, **8** l'informatique, **9** Le français, **10** L'informatique

> ◀)) CD 4 Track 11

Conversations au collège

– Qu'est-ce que tu aimes comme matières?
– Ma matière préférée est l'EPS. J'adore le sport.
– Qu'est-ce que vous faites comme sport au collège?
– En hiver, nous faisons de la gymnastique, du volley et du basket. On fait aussi de la natation. Nous allons à la piscine en ville le jeudi après-midi. Et en été, nous faisons de l'athlétisme.
– Est-ce qu'il y a des clubs de sports?
– Oui, il y a un club de judo. J'ai des amis qui font du judo, mais pas moi. Et toi, quelles sont tes matières préférées?
– Mes matières préférées sont le français et l'informatique.
– Pourquoi?
– Le français parce que j'adore la lecture et nous faisons aussi du théâtre. C'est amusant. Et j'aime l'informatique, parce que nous faisons des choses intéressantes.

150 Tricolore 1 Teacher's Notes

8D Qu'est-ce que vous faites?

100 Dossier-langue

The verb *faire* (to do, to make)

Students have been using parts of the singular of *faire* for some time. This brings together the complete present tense. It is further practised in *Unité* 10. Discuss other irregular verbs taught and see if students can see any similarities with any parts, e.g. *ils font (ils vont/ils sont/ils ont)*. Mention that *faire* is used in many useful expressions, as listed in the box.

100

2 Fais des phrases

Practice in writing the correct part of *faire* with each subject. Students can refer to the box to help with the phrases for the activities.

> Solution:
> 1 *Je fais du théâtre.*
> 2 *Moi, je fais du dessin.*
> 3 *Tu fais de la natation.*
> 4 *Il fait des photos.*
> 5 *Elle fait de la gymnastique.*
> 6 *Nous faisons du vélo.*
> 7 *Vous faites du judo.*
> 8 *Ils font de l'athlétisme.*

Interactive activity

On fait ça

cm 8/5

On fait beaucoup de choses

100

3 Ils aiment ou ils n'aiment pas?

a Students listen and note down whether the person likes ♥, loves ♥♥, dislikes ✗ or hates ✗✗ each subject and the names of the subject.

> Solution:
> 1 ✗ *(l'histoire)*, 2 ♥♥ *(les sciences)*,
> 3 ♥ *(l'anglais)*, 4 ✗✗ *(les maths)*,
> 5 ♥♥ *(la technologie)*, 6 ♥ *(l'éducation physique)*, 7 ♥ *(le dessin)*, 8 ✗✗ *(la géographie)*

CD 4 Track 12

Ils aiment ou ils n'aiment pas?

1 – Je n'aime pas l'histoire.
 – Pourquoi?
 – Parce que c'est ennuyeux.
2 – J'adore les sciences.
 – Pourquoi?
 – J'adore les sciences parce que je trouve ça très intéressant.
3 – Tu aimes l'anglais?
 – Oui, j'aime beaucoup l'anglais.
 – Pourquoi?
 – L'anglais, c'est super et c'est assez facile.
4 – Moi, je déteste les maths.
 – Pourquoi?
 – Parce que c'est difficile. Oh, les maths, je trouve ça très difficile.
5 – Tu aimes la technologie?
 – Oui, j'adore la technologie. La technologie, c'est utile et amusant.
6 – Tu aimes l'éducation physique?
 – Oui, j'aime ça.
 – Pourquoi?
 – J'aime l'éducation physique parce que je trouve ça amusant.
7 – Moi, j'aime beaucoup le dessin.
 – Ah bon? Pourquoi?
 – Le dessin, c'est génial.
8 – Tu aimes la géographie?
 – Non je déteste la géographie, c'est nul.

b Students listen again and write down the adjectives under the correct heading: *des opinions positives*, *des opinions négatives*.

c They guess the meaning, and then check the English translation and add that to the list.

> Solution:
>
> | des opinions positives | des opinions négatives |
> | --- | --- |
> | *amusant* – fun | *difficile* – difficult |
> | *super* – great | *nul* – rubbish |
> | *facile* – easy | *ennuyeux* – boring |
> | *intéressant* – interesting | |
> | *utile* – useful | |
> | *sympa* – nice | |
> | *génial* – brilliant | |

101

4 Six élèves

Start by doing some oral work, using *Qui aime le sport? Qui n'aime pas la géographie?* etc. Students could spend some time studying the preferences of the six young people before listening to the recording.

a They note down who is speaking.

> Solution:
> 1 E Sylvie, 2 D Thomas, 3 A Sika, 4 C Marion, 5 F Tchang, 6 B Philippe

b They listen again and note down details of the subjects mentioned and any adjectives used (none in 5).

Tricolore 1 Teacher's Notes **151**

8D Qu'est-ce que vous faites?

Solution:
1 les maths – très utile; le dessin – ennuyeux
2 les maths – très difficile; le sport – super
3 l'anglais – nul; les sciences – amusant
4 le français – intéressant et facile; l'histoire – pas intéressant
5 la musique; la technologie
6 l'informatique – super; la géographie – ennuyeux

🔊 CD 4 Track 13

Six élèves

1 – Quelle est ta matière préférée?
  – Les maths, j'adore les maths. C'est très utile et notre prof de maths est très gentil. Il explique tout très bien.
  – Est-ce qu'il y a des matières que tu n'aimes pas?
  – Oui, je déteste le dessin. C'est ennuyeux.
2 – Et toi?
  – Moi, je n'aime pas les maths. Ça, c'est très difficile, mais j'aime le sport. Le sport, c'est super.
3 – Est-ce que tu aimes l'anglais?
  – Ah non, je déteste ça. L'anglais, c'est nul.
  – Alors, qu'est-ce que tu aimes, comme matières?
  – J'aime les sciences. Les sciences, c'est amusant.
4 – Quelle est ta matière préférée?
  – Le français, j'adore le français. Je trouve ça très intéressant et c'est facile.
  – Est-ce qu'il y a des matières que tu n'aimes pas?
  – Oui, je n'aime pas l'histoire. Ce n'est pas intéressant.
5 – Et toi, qu'est-ce que tu aimes comme matières?
  – Moi, j'aime la musique. Oui, la musique, c'est ma matière préférée.
  – Et qu'est-ce que tu n'aimes pas?
  – Je n'aime pas la technologie.
6 – Et toi, quelle est ta matière préférée?
  – L'informatique, j'adore l'informatique. C'est super.
  – Et est-ce qu'il y a des matières que tu n'aimes pas?
  – Oui, je n'aime pas la géographie. C'est ennuyeux.

📖 101   AfL

5 Inventez des conversations

a Students, in pairs, read and then adapt a conversation about school subjects.

Review the spread objectives and assessment criteria. Ask volunteers to demonstrate a suitable conversation. Students could discuss how they could make their conversations more interesting by using qualifiers, e.g. *très, assez, un peu, vraiment* and connectives. This can then be used for peer assessment.

b For extension, students could write a paragraph about school subjects, using some of the strategies suggested.

📖 101 Stratégies

Adding interest to your writing (4)

This suggests how students could enrich their use of language by using connectives (*mais, et, parce que*) and qualifiers such as *très, assez, vraiment*.

Ask students to practise in pairs adding more detail and complexity to a sentence. Give them a simple sentence, e.g. *J'aime le sport*, and challenge them to make it more interesting.

The online worksheet can be used for further reinforcement.

Worksheet

Adding interest to your writing

Worksheet

Plenary (pages 100–101)

Irregular verbs Have a general discussion about the use of irregular verbs and mention that of the twenty most commonly-used French verbs, seventeen are irregular. Five of these are taught in Stage 1 (*être, avoir, faire, aller, prendre*). Discuss how many irregular verbs have been learnt so far. How do you know when verbs are irregular? Are they hard to learn? Is it useful to learn irregulars in set phrases? Are there patterns you can learn for irregulars too – e.g. endings?

(There is a regular pattern of endings to most irregulars – *s/s/t ons/ez/ent* or *ont* – most irregulars share some of these endings, but not all.)

8E Ma matière préférée   pages 102–103

- Ask questions to get to know someone
- Talk about your favourite things

Grammaire	Stratégies	Phonétique
• Say 'his', 'her' and 'its' • 'which ...?', 'what ...?'	• Improving your speaking skills	• None

Resources

Audio: 1 *Un nouvel élève*, or CD 4, track 14
Copymasters: 8/6 *Mon, ton, son*
Worksheets: Starters and plenaries; *Des phrases au choix* (W)

Interactive activity: *Son, sa, ses* (G)
PowerPoint: None
Grammar in Action: pp30–31, p32

Worksheet

Starters (pages 102–103)

1 **C'est masculin ou féminin?** Display the following list or hand it out on slips of paper. Ask students to work out whether each word is masculine or féminin. Students reply by holding up a *masculin* or *féminin* card or in chorus.

lecteur MP3 m	jeu m
cadeau m	raquette f
cahier m	souris f
casquette f	stylo m
chambre f	trousse f

2 **Quel mot?** Display the following. Give students one minute to read and work out the answers, then ask for them randomly or collectively.

a ... s'appelle le nouveau prof de dessin?
b Tu n'aimes pas l'anglais – mais ...?
c C'est ..., le match de tennis?
d ... va au club d'informatique ce soir?
e ... est la bibliothèque?
1 Qui 2 quand 3 Où 4 Comment 5 pourquoi

Solution:
a *4*, b *5*, c *2*, d *1*, e *3*

Introduction

Go through the objectives for this spread.

📖 🔊 102

1 Un nouvel élève

This three-part task presents examples of different question forms, including *quel*, as well as examples of *ton, ta, tes* and *mon, ma, mes*. Read through the questions and check that students understand them, then play the recording.

Solution:
a La question qu'on ne pose pas est la question 6.
b a le basket, b le sport et l'informatique, c douze ans, d l'histoire, e le 8 juillet
c 1 *c*, 2 *e*, 3 *d*, 4 *b*, 5 *a*

CD 4 Track 14

1 Un nouvel élève

– Karim, quel âge as-tu?
– J'ai douze ans.
– Et quelle est la date de ton anniversaire?
– C'est en juillet, le huit juillet.
– Quelle est ta matière préférée?
– Ma matière préférée? Bon, l'anglais, c'est utile, mais ce n'est pas ma matière préférée. Ma matière préférée, c'est l'histoire.
– Et quels sont tes passe-temps préférés?
– Mes passe-temps préférés sont le sport et l'informatique. J'adore faire du sport.
– Quel est ton sport préféré?
– Mon sport préféré est le basket.

📖 102 Dossier-langue

'which...?'/'what...?'

Using *quel* to ask questions.

📖 102

2 Des questions utiles

This gives practice in using the correct spelling of *quel*.

Solution:
1 Quel, 2 Quelle, 3 Quelle, 4 Quels, 5 Quels, 6 Quel, 7 Quel

📖 102

3 Mes choses préférées

Before students work in pairs on this task, ask how they can work out the gender of the noun in each question (by looking at the spelling of *quel/quelle* and *préféré/e*).

a One student asks the question, supplying *ton/ta*, the other responds using *mon/ma*. After three questions, they could change roles.

Tricolore 1 Teacher's Notes **153**

8E Ma matière préférée

Solution:
1 *ton* sport préféré/*mon* sport préféré,
2 *ta* couleur préférée/*ma* couleur préférée,
3 *ton* jour préféré/*mon* jour préféré,
4 *ton* animal préféré/*mon* animal préféré
5 *ta* saison préférée/ *ma* saison préférée,
6 *ta* matière préférée/*ma* matière préférée.

b The questions are repeated, but students reply with their own personal preferences. The answers to part **b** could be written and added to the *Dossier personnel*.

Worksheet

Mes préférences

102 Stratégies

Improving your speaking skills

This gives some tips for adapting questions to keep a conversation going.

103

4 Inventez des conversations

Students practise in pairs asking and answering questions.

gia 1 pp30–31

More practice of *mon, ma, mes*/*ton, ta, tes* (1) and (2).

Further practice of these possessive adjectives, if required.

155 Au choix

4 As-tu une bonne mémoire?

103

5 Mes amis

This description of two friends presents examples of *son*, *sa*, *ses* meaning his or her.

a Students read through the text and then correct the statements.

Solution:
1 Camille est **française**.
2 Son sport préféré est la **gymnastique**.
3 Elle aime **les maths**.
4 Ses grands-parents habitent **au Sénégal**.
5 Son frère s'appelle **Noah**.
6 Son anniversaire est le 15 **avril**.
7 Sa souris s'appelle **Minnie**.
8 Ses passe-temps préférés sont **la natation** et **le football**.

b For extension, students could write a similar description of a friend (four sentences or more).

103 Dossier-langue

son, sa, ses (his, her, its)

Remind students of the earlier work on *mon*, *ma*, *mes* and *ton*, *ta*, *tes* and get them to work out the rule for *son*, *sa*, *ses*. Emphasise the importance of the adjective agreeing with the object, not the owner.

103

6 Comment ça se dit en français?

Practice in linking the use of *son* and *sa* with the correct meaning.

Solution:
1 *son* anniversaire, 2 *son* anniversaire, 3 *sa* sœur, 4 *sa* sœur, 5 *son* chat, 6 *son* dîner, 7 *son* chien, 8 *son* ami/*son* amie

Worksheet

Des phrases au choix

103 AfL

7 Jeu d'identité

Students could interview one another, then write a description or make up descriptions of famous people for a 'guess the identity' game.
Review the spread objectives and assessment criteria. This can then be used for peer assessment.

cm 8/6

Mon, ton, son

154 Au choix

3 Luc et Louise

gia 1 p32

The possessive adjectives *son*/*sa*/*ses*

This provides further practice of the third person singular possessive adjectives, if required.

Worksheet

Plenaries (pages 102–103)

Have a brainstorming session to see how many question words students remember. Do students find it easy or hard to make up questions in French? Students work in pairs, then join a second pair to share findings, then one spokesperson from the foursome reports on the most common findings.
Mid unit review: Ask students how it's going so far and suggest they discuss the following in pairs/ groups and then get a spokesperson to relay the most common answers back to the whole class.

- What over the last 2–3 spreads has proved most difficult/easiest?
- Where do you think your personal improvement has been?
- What is still a problem?

Use the discussion as an opportunity to discuss the spread objectives and assess what has been achieved.

8F Notre collège   pages 104–105

- Talk about your school

Grammaire	Stratégies	Phonétique
• Say 'our', 'your' and 'their'	• Translating from French to English (2)	• None

Resources

Audio: 1 *Au collège*, or CD 4, track 15
Copymasters: 8/7 *Des questions et des réponses (notre/nos, votre/vos)*
Worksheets: Starters and plenaries; Possessive adjectives (G)

Interactive activity: None
PowerPoint: None
Grammar in Action: pp33–34

Worksheet

Starter (pages 104–105)

Chasse à l'intrus Display or print out the following lists and ask students to write down the odd word out in each list (shown in bold). Students exchange answers for checking. Ask several students for the correct answer before confirming this.

1	2	3	4	5
le chat	lundi	treize	la salle	quand
le château	dimanche	**faites**	la bibliothèque	facile
le cheval	**difficile**	quinze	la cuisine	sympa
le chien	vendredi	cinq	**la nuit**	utile

Introduction

Go through the objectives for this spread.

🔊 104

1 Au collège

Mention that students won't understand all of the words in the interview, but can use skills previously learnt to work out the gist. Students could listen for *notre* and *votre* in the passage and suggest what they could mean.

After a second listening, students should note down the missing words. Use the pause button as required.

> **Solution:**
> **1** *Jules Verne*, **2** *trente-huit*, **3** *la biologie*, **4** *le dessin*, **5** *maths*, **6** *technologie*, **7** *huit heures et demie*, **8** *mercredi*, **9** *samedi*

🔊 CD 4 Track 15

Au collège

Nos jeunes reporters, Robert et Cécile, visitent un collège et parlent à deux élèves, Marc et Anne.
- Bonjour, Anne et Marc, comment s'appelle votre collège?
- Notre collège s'appelle le collège Jules Verne.
- Et vous êtes en quelle classe?
- Nous sommes en Sixième B.
- Il y a combien d'élèves dans votre classe?
- Il y a trente-huit élèves. C'est beaucoup.
- Oui, c'est vrai. Quelles sont vos matières préférées?
- Moi, j'aime beaucoup la biologie. Notre prof est très sympa.
- Moi, je préfère le dessin. Notre prof de dessin est très amusant.
- En général, est-ce que vos profs sont gentils?
- Oui, en général, ils sont assez gentils. Notre prof de maths, par exemple, est super. Il organise bien ses cours et il explique tout très bien.
- Oui, mais notre prof de technologie est un peu sévère.
- Vos cours commencent à quelle heure, le matin?
- À huit heures et demie, mais on n'a pas cours le mercredi, et le samedi, on finit à midi.

104 Dossier-langue

'our' and 'your'

This sets out the different forms of *notre* and *votre*. Ask students how these possessive adjectives differ from *mon*, *ma*, *mes*, etc. Students could work in pairs and see how many examples they can find in the interview in a given time, e.g. 5 minutes.

104

2 Notre voyage scolaire

Students practise using *notre* and *nos*.

> **Solution:**
> **1** *notre*, **2** *Notre*, **3** *notre*, **4** *nos*, **5** *notre*, **6** *nos*, **7** *nos*, **8** *notre*

Tricolore 1 Teacher's Notes   155

8F Notre collège

📖 104

3 Vos affaires d'école

Students practise using *votre* and *vos*.

> **Solution:**
> **1** votre clé USB, **2** votre gomme, **3** vos crayons, **4** votre calculatrice, **5** vos classeurs, **6** votre trousse, **7** vos surligneurs, **8** vos bics/stylos

cm 8/7

Des questions et des réponses

📖 105

4 Notre collège

a Students complete sentences about their school, using *notre* and *nos*.

b For extension, students could write a paragraph about their school. This could be added to the *Dossier personnel*. Suitable articles could be displayed in the classroom or posted on the school network/website.

Interactive activity

Une interview

📖 105

5 Le blog de Julien

This letter about French school life includes examples of *leur* and *leurs* in context. Students read the blog and correct mistakes in the sentences which follow it.

> **Solution:**
> **1** Lucie et Théo vont **au collège** aujourd'hui.
> **2** Leur collège est **assez loin**.
> **3** Leur premier cours est **anglais**.
> **4** C'est assez **intéressant**.
> **5** Leur prof d'anglais est très **sympa**.
> **6** Ils ont des cours de **sciences** et de **géographie**.
> **7** À midi, ils mangent à la **cantine**.
> **8** L'après-midi, ils ont **technologie** et EPS.
> **9** Julien **adore** le sport.

📖 105 Dossier-langue

'their'

This sets out the different forms of *leur*. Ask students to spot similarities with *notre/nos*. They then find some examples in Julien's blog.

> **Solution:**
> *Leur collège est assez loin; Nous retrouvons leurs amis; Leur premier cours est anglais; Leur prof d'anglais; Leur livre de géographie*

📖 105 Stratégies

Translating from French to English (2)

This covers differences in French and English regarding word order and the use of *de* and *d'* in French phrases.

Students look for the French for six phrases in *Le blog de Julien*. Ask students if they can think of other examples of phrases where the word order is different, e.g. physical education = *éducation physique*.

> **Solution:**
> **1** Leur prof d'anglais
> **2** des cours de sciences et de géographie
> **3** Leur livre de géographie
> **4** Le prof de maths
> **5** un cours de français
> **6** leur livre d'histoire

📖 155 Au choix

5 Une conversation

📖 105 AfL

6 Une interview

Students work in pairs and take it in turns to interview one another asking two questions each time.

Review the spread objectives and use this for peer assessment.

gia 1 pp33–34

Using *notre/nos*, *votre/vos*, *leur/leurs* (1) and (2)

This provides further practice of the plural possessive adjectives.

Worksheet

La famille d'Enzo

Worksheet

Plenary (pages 104–105)

Think, pair and share What do students find to be the main grammatical differences between French and English? (Gender, different word order, prepositions, e.g. *à* changing form) Which present the most difficulties?

Tricolore 1 Teacher's Notes

8G Au Sénégal   pages 106–107

- Find out about a French-speaking country
- Understand a longer text

Grammaire	Stratégies	Phonétique
• None	• None	• The letter 'r'

Resources

Audio: 1 *Notre pays – le Sénégal*, or CD 4, track 16
Copymasters: None
Worksheets: Starters and plenaries
e-book: *La Polynésie française*

Interactive activity: None
Ph The letter 'r', or CD 4, track 17
PowerPoint: None
Grammar in Action: None

Worksheet

Starter (pages 106–107)

5-4-3-2-1 Display a list of words and ask students to find groups of 5,4,3,2,1 similar words, e.g.

ennuyeux, facile, génial, intéressant, nul

fais, faisons, faites, font

matin, soir, nuit

lapin, souris

élève

Students could record their answers on a pre-printed grid and these can then be checked in the usual way.

Introduction

Go through the objectives for this spread.

106

1 Notre pays – le Sénégal

This presents information about the French-speaking African country, Senegal. Students should look through the photos and captions to aid comprehension before listening to the recording.

CD 4 Track 16

Notre pays – le Sénégal

Jabu et Pirane habitent au Sénégal, en Afrique. Elles parlent de leur pays.

– Notre pays se trouve en Afrique de l'ouest.
  La capitale s'appelle Dakar. C'est une grande ville au bord de la mer.
– De juin à octobre, il fait très chaud (30°C) et il pleut souvent. C'est la saison des pluies.
  De novembre à mai, il fait moins chaud (17 à 27°C) et il pleut moins. C'est la saison sèche.
  À Dakar il fait un peu moins chaud parce que la ville est sur la côte.
– Nous allons à l'école à Dakar. À l'école on parle français (c'est la langue officielle), mais à la maison on parle wolof.
– Ma matière préférée est les sciences parce que c'est très intéressant. En plus, notre prof de sciences est très sympa.
– Et moi, j'aime beaucoup la musique.
– Comme sports, nous faisons du basket et du hand. Le football est un sport très populaire au Sénégal.
– Voici une photo de mardi gras à Dakar.
  Sur la photo, il y a une mosquée. Nous sommes catholiques mais beaucoup de personnes sont musulmanes.
– Voici le marché de Sandaga au centre-ville. Moi, j'adore faire du shopping ici.
  Quelquefois, il y a des touristes au Sénégal. Ils vont à la plage et ils visitent des parcs et des réserves. Ils aiment voir les hippopotames, les crocodiles et les dauphins.
  À la campagne, il y a des serpents, comme des pythons, des cobras et des mambas, mais ils sont assez rares.

107

2 Tu comprends?

Ask the class about the various reading comprehension strategies they have learnt. They can then put them into practice with this task. Check they understand the terms cognate and near cognate.

8G Au Sénégal

Solution:

a Some possibilities include: *Afrique, capitale, côte* (remind students that the circumflex often indicates the letter 's' in English), *officielle, sport, musique, photo, touristes, les hippopotames, des crocodiles, des pythons*

b 1 *v*, 2 *a*, 3 *v*, 4 *n*, 5 *n*

c There are other possibilities for 1 and 4.

1 *De novembre à mai, il fait moins chaud (17 à 27°C) et il pleut moins.* (less)

2 *À Dakar il fait un peu moins chaud parce que la ville est sur la côte.* (because)

3 *En plus, notre prof de sciences est très sympa.* (in addition, what's more)

4 *À la campagne, il y a des serpents, comme des pythons, des cobras et des mambas, mais ils sont assez rares.* (but)

107

3 Une journée à Dakar

Students complete the summary using words from the box. Display a model answer for constructive feedback.

Solution:

1 *collège*, 2 *cours*, 3 *parle*, 4 *récréation*, 5 *cantine*, 6 *quatre heures*, 7 *rentrent*, 8 *dîner*, 9 *mange*

107 AfL

4 Que sais-tu du Sénégal?

a The questions about *Sénégal* could be answered in a few words or able students could reply in a full sentence.

Solution:

1 *En Afrique (de l'ouest)*
2 *Dakar*
3 *Il fait très chaud et il pleut souvent. C'est la saison des pluies.*
4 *le français*
5 *des hippopotames, des crocodiles et des dauphins.*

b For extension, students can expand their answers to write a short paragraph about Senegal, e.g. *Le Sénégal se trouve en Afrique de l'ouest.*

Review the spread objectives with the class and use this for assessment.

Worksheet

La Polynésie française

Presentation

La Polynésie française

Interactive activity

The letter 'r'

158 Tricolore 1 Teacher's Notes

107 Phonétique

The letter 'r'

A full explanation of this sound is given on *kerboodle!*, together with interactive practice.

a Explain that the letter 'r', both at the beginning and in the middle of a word, is pronounced much more strongly in French and students should try to exaggerate it. Say the word *rat* with an appropriate gesture. Students repeat the word with the same gesture. Then read out the other words, with the students repeating each one: *repas, terrible, écris*. The words are also included on the recording for optional use (part **a**).

Parts **b** and **c** can be used for further practice.

b Ask students to listen and repeat the words they hear. Then display the words in a different order, e.g. **a** *rue*, **b** *règle*, **c** *raquette*, **d** *riche*, **e** *robe* for students to match (c, b, d, e, a).

c Students listen to the silly sentence and note down how many times they hear the sound (9). They can then repeat the sentence to help them remember this sound.

For further practice, write some additional words on the board to check that students recognise the link between spelling and pronunciation e.g. *rugby, radio, restaurant, résultats, rose.*

CD 4 Track 17

The letter 'r'

Écoutez et répétez:
a rat, repas, terrible, écris
b raquette, règle, riche, robe, rue
c Rangetout le rat range régulièrement le garage car il a horreur du désordre.

107

5 Faites des recherches

Students could work in pairs or groups to find out the names of two other francophone countries in Africa and find out (or write) a few facts about them. The following are all members of *L'Afrique francophone*:

Bénin, Burkina Faso, Burundi, Cameroun, Congo (Brazzaville), Congo, République Démocratique (Kinshasa) (RDC), Côte d'Ivoire, Djibouti, Gabon, Guinée, Mali, La Mauritanie, Niger, République Centrafricaine, Rwanda, Sénégal, Tchad, Togo, Liban, Algérie, Maroc, Tunisie.

Worksheet

Plenary (pages 106–107)

Cognates Students brainstorm cognates, trying to find 3 for each topic: school subjects, animals, verbs.

Working in pairs, students use their knowledge of French pronunciation to work out how the following cognates are pronounced:

une girafe, un tigre, un éléphant, un lion, un crocodile, une gorille, un zébra

8H Une présentation   pages 108–109

- Learn more about a French school
- Prepare a presentation about your school

Grammaire	Stratégies	Phonétique
• None	• Preparing a presentation	• None

Resources

Audio: 1 *Le collège Missy*, or CD 4, track 18
Copymasters: 8/8 *Tu comprends?*, 8/9 *Sommaire*
Worksheets: Starters and plenaries; Preparing a good presentation (Strat)

Interactive activity: Classroom commands (V)
Video: *Les profs du collège*
PowerPoint: *Le Collège Missy* (R)
Grammar in Action: None

Worksheet (ws_08G.S)

Starter (pages 108–109)

En groupes Display a list of words in random order or hand this out on slips of paper. Ask students to put these into 5 groups.

cinq, huit, onze

l'anglais, la géographie, la technologie

l'athlétisme, le basket, le badminton

fais, font, fait

vraiment, très, assez

Introduction

Go through the objectives for this spread.

Presentation

Le Collège Missy

📖 108

1 Le Collège Missy

Students should watch the presentation (see above) and find out the gist and any information they can. Then they read through the text, perhaps with different students reading each caption aloud to practise pronunciation.

CD 4 Track 18

Le Collège Missy

Le Collège Missy est un collège mixte pour les élèves de onze à quinze ans.
Voici le logo du collège. C'est un arbre aux feuilles colorées. C'est une élève du collège qui a dessiné le logo.
Le collège est dans la rue Missy à La Rochelle en France.
Il y a environ 500 élèves.
Les élèves de onze ans sont en classe de sixième. Je suis en 6ème B.
Comme matières, nous faisons histoire-géo, maths, français, SVT, technologie et arts plastiques.
Comme langues, on fait anglais ou espagnol. Les élèves de 4ème, qui ont treize ou quatorze ans, font aussi latin ou grec.
En EPS, on fait de l'athlétisme, du hand, du basket et du badminton. On fait aussi de la natation.
Les élèves de 6ème font un stage de voile. Ça dure une semaine. On va à l'Île de Ré. C'est vraiment bien.
Il y a des ordinateurs qui sont reliés au réseau du collège et à Internet. Chaque personne a un code d'accès personnel.
Voici la cantine. On mange ici le lundi, le mardi, le jeudi et le vendredi.
La journée scolaire commence à huit heures vingt et finit à cinq heures de l'après-midi.

📖 108   AfL

2 Une présentation

Students prepare a similar presentation about their own school, perhaps working in groups, with each group taking a different theme, referring to the *Stratégies* for tips.

a Students give at least one sentence about each point.

b For extension, students add further details, ⊕ including opinions.

Some students could give their presentation to the class. This can be used for peer assessment.

Tricolore 1 Teacher's Notes   **159**

8H Une présentation

108 Stratégies

Preparing a presentation
This gives some suggestions for preparing a presentation.

The online worksheet can be used for further reinforcement.

Worksheet

Preparing a good presentation

Interactive activity

Rue Danton: Les profs du collège

155 Au choix

6 Une belle journée

cm 8/8

Tu comprends?

109 cm 8/9

Sommaire
A summary of the main vocabulary and structures of the unit.

Interactive activity

Vocabulaire de classe (8)

Worksheet

Plenaries (pages 108–109)
Improving use of spoken and written French
1. Start with a very simple phrase and challenge students to suggest at least three ways it could be improved/made more interesting or complex.
2. Use the *Sommaire* to review the objectives of the unit and what has been learnt. Discuss how the language could be used in different contexts.

Unité 8 Consolidation and assessment

Épreuves Unité 8

🔊 cm 8/10

Écouter
A Quelle heure est-il?

Solution:
1 d, 2 c, 3 b, 4 g, 5 e, 6 a, 7 f (mark /6)

🔊 CD 4 Track 19

Quelle heure est-il?

1 – On va au cinéma cet après-midi?
   – Oui, bonne idée.
   – Alors, rendez-vous à deux heures moins le quart?
   – À deux heures moins le quart. D'accord.
2 – Quelle heure est-il, s'il vous plaît?
   – Il est dix heures et demie.
   – Dix heures et demie, merci.
3 – Quand est-ce que Marc et Sophie arrivent à la gare?
   – Ils arrivent à trois heures et quart.
   – À trois heures et quart, bon.
4 – Quand est-ce que le film commence?
   – Il commence à huit heures moins le quart.
   – À huit heures moins le quart. Bon.
5 – Le concert commence à quelle heure?
   – Il commence à neuf heures et quart.
   – À neuf heures et quart. Bon, merci.
6 – Les cours se terminent à quelle heure le mercredi?
   – Ils se terminent à onze heures.
   – À onze heures?
   – Oui, c'est ça.
7 – Papa rentre à quelle heure ce soir, maman?
   – Il rentre très tard, à minuit.
   – À minuit, ah bon.

B On parle des matières

Solution:
1 a *difficile*, 2 a *facile*, 3 b *intéressant*,
4 c *ennuyeux*, 5 c *amusant*
(mark /8)

🔊 CD 4 Track 20

On parle des matières

1 – Est-ce que tu aimes la géographie?
   – Non, je n'aime pas la géographie.
   – Pourquoi?
   – Parce que c'est difficile.
2 – Quelle est ta matière préférée?
   – La technologie. J'adore la technologie.
   – Pourquoi?
   – C'est facile.
3 – Tu aimes l'anglais?
   – Oui, j'aime beaucoup l'anglais. L'anglais, c'est très intéressant.
4 – Est-ce qu'il y a une matière que tu n'aimes pas?
   – Les maths. Je déteste les maths.
   – Pourquoi?
   – Parce que c'est ennuyeux. Oh, les maths, je trouve ça ennuyeux.
5 – Tu aimes le dessin?
   – Oui, j'adore le dessin. Le dessin, c'est amusant.

C Un jour de la semaine scolaire

Solution:
1 6h50, 2 6h55, 3 7h40, 4 8h20, 5 10h25, 6 5h10,
7 7h00
(mark /6)

🔊 CD 4 Track 21

Un jour de la semaine scolaire

1 – Quand est-ce que tu te lèves, le matin?
   – Je me lève à sept heures moins dix.
   – À sept heures moins dix.
2 – Et tu prends ton petit déjeuner à quelle heure?
   – Je prends mon petit déjeuner à sept heures moins cinq.
   – Ah bon, tu prends le petit déjeuner à sept heures moins cinq.
3 – À quelle heure est-ce que tu quittes la maison?
   – Je quitte la maison à huit heures moins vingt.
   – Alors, à huit heures moins vingt, tu quittes la maison.
4 – Quand est-ce que les cours commencent?
   – Les cours commencent à huit heures vingt.
5 – La récréation est à quelle heure?
   – À dix heures vingt-cinq.
   – La récréation est à dix heures vingt-cinq.
6 – Quand est-ce que tu rentres à la maison?
   – Normalement, je rentre à la maison à cinq heures dix.
   – Alors, tu rentres à la maison à cinq heures dix.
7 – Et le soir, vous mangez à quelle heure?
   – Nous mangeons à sept heures, normalement.
   – Alors, vous mangez à sept heures.

Unité 8 Consolidation and assessment

cm 8/11

Lire

A La journée

> Solution:
> **1** b, **2** c, **3** e, **4** a, **5** d
> (mark /4)

B Les matières préférées

> Solution:

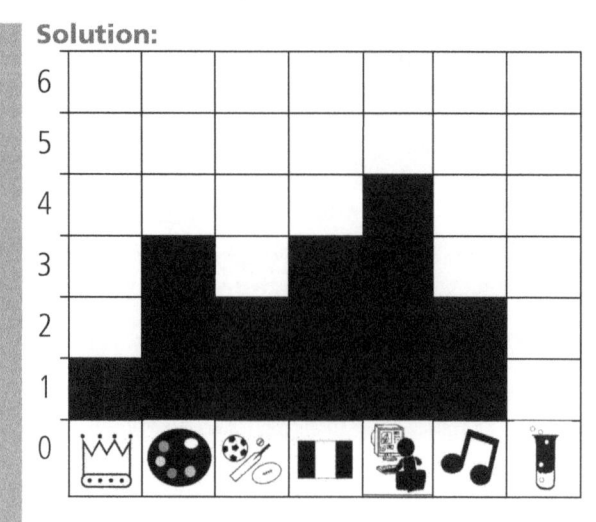

La matière préférée de la classe est l'informatique.

(mark /6) 5 for correct graph, 1 for correct statement

C Questions et réponses

> Solution:
> **1** e, **2** d, **3** a, **4** c, **5** b
> (mark /4)

D Une interview

> Solution:
> **1** V, **2** F, **3** F, **4** V, **5** F, **6** F, **7** V
> (mark /6)

cm 8/12

Écrire et grammaire

A Les matières

For more able students, the words in the box could be blanked out. This is an open-ended task.
(mark /6)

B Des questions

Students complete the questions with the correct form of *quel*.

> Solution:
> **1** Quel, **2** Quel, **3** Quelles, **4** Quelle, **5** Quels
> (mark /4)

C Des conversations

> Solution:
> **a** **3** votre, **4** Notre, **5** Vos, **6** Nos
> **b** **3** sa, son, **4** leurs, **5** leur
> (mark /4) ½ mark for each correct word

D Des questions

This is an open-ended task.
(mark /6) 2 marks per correct answer

Presse-Jeunesse

110–111

Presse-Jeunesse 3

These magazine-style pages provide material for reading for pleasure and to enhance cultural awareness. The texts and comprehension activities can be used flexibly; by students working alone for extension, for cover lessons, etc. Although they mainly use language previously taught, they may also contain a small amount of additional language.

110

Tout est bien qui finit bien!

Students read the story, then do the Find the French and *Vrai ou faux* tasks.

> Solution:
> **a** **1** tard, **2** après, **3** pendant, **4** (je suis) désolée, **5** triste, **6** sans payer
> **b** **1** V, **2** V, **3** F, **4** V, **5** V, **6** V

111

Infos France

This presents information about French culture, including the French flag, Marianne, the Eiffel tower and the euro. Students match the text with the pictures.

> Solution:
> **1** C, **2** D, **3** A, **4** E, **5** B

111

Jeu-test

Es-tu un(e) élève modèle?

a Students choose the appropriate word to fill the gaps in the personality quiz.
b They do the quiz and read the results for fun.

> Solution:
> **1** pas, **2** as, **3** mais, **4** on, **5** au, **6** premier, **7** écoutes, **8** tu, **9** fais, **10** après

Tricolore 1 Teacher's Notes

Unité 8 Consolidation and assessment

Au-choix

154 Au choix

1 Mlle Dupont

This task provides revision of times and *à* with places in a town.

Solution:

1. À six heures, elle va à la poste.
2. À sept heures et demie, elle va au collège.
3. À huit heures et quart, elle va à la piscine.
4. À neuf heures vingt, elle va au café.
5. À dix heures moins cinq, elle va au parc.
6. À dix heures vingt-cinq, elle va à la gare.
7. À midi moins vingt, elle va à l'hôtel.
8. À midi, elle va au cinéma.
9. À une heure et demie, elle va au restaurant.
10. À dix heures et quart, elle va au lit.

154 Au choix

2 Notre journée au collège

For additional reading practice, students put the sentences in the correct order.

Solution:

Le matin: d, b, f, a, e, c
L'après-midi et le soir: j, g, i, h, k, l

154 Au choix

3 Luc et Louise

a Students complete sentences using *son, sa, ses* to mean 'his' or 'her'.

Solution:

1 *ses, sa,* 2 *Ses, sa,* 3 *son, ses, son,* 4 *son, ses,* 5 *son, ses,* 6 *son, son, ses,* 7 *son, son,* 8 *ses, sa, son*

b They decide which sentences describe Louise.

Solution:
Louise: 3, 5, 8

For extension, students could translate some or all of the sentences into English.

155 Au choix

4 As-tu une bonne mémoire?

This optional task based on *Un nouvel élève* (SB page 102) presents examples of *son, sa, ses* meaning 'his'.

Solution:

1. Non, son sport préféré est le basket.
2. Non, ses passe-temps préférés sont le sport et l'informatique.
3. Non, sa matière préférée est l'histoire.
4. Non, son anniversaire est le 8 juillet.

155 Au choix

5 Une conversation

This task brings together practice of all the plural possessive adjectives.

Solution:

1 *nos grands-parents,* 2 *notre grand-mère,* 3 *vos cousins,* 4 *nos grands-parents,* 5 *Leur maison,* 6 *Leurs chiens,* 7 *leur cheval*

155 Au choix

6 Une belle journée

a For consolidation of time and daily routine, students answer questions about a typical day for the cat, *Mangetout*.

Solution:

A *dans la cuisine, il mange.*
B *il est midi, le déjeuner,*
C *l'après-midi, il dort dans son panier,*
D *le soir, il est sept heures et demie, il mange, 1*
E *il est minuit, il dort et il rêve.*

b Creative students could make up a similar description for a rat, *Rangetout*, who likes tidying up.

Copymasters

cm 8/1

Quelle heure est-il? – mini-flashcards

Students draw in the hands so the clock face shows the correct time. When completed, the worksheet can be stuck on to card, cut up and used as a set of mini-flashcards. With two or more sets, various games can be played in pairs, e.g. dominos and Pelmanism (see TB page xix). Students have to give the correct time on a matching pair of cards before they can keep them.

cm 8/2

Qui est-ce?

Able students could work in pairs on this information gap activity to find out details about a person's day in order to identify the person. Additional forms of the reflexive verb *se coucher* are used (*tu te couches, il/elle se couche*). Perhaps two able students could demonstrate how this works, so everyone understands what is entailed.

cm 8/3

Jeux de vocabulaire: les matières

Some students could work on this worksheet, while others do CM 8/4. (See TB page 64.)

Tricolore 1 Teacher's Notes   163

Unité 8 Consolidation and assessment

Solution:
1 *Mots mêlés*
Correct answers to be circled.

a	p	r	è	s	-	m	i	d	i
é	t	e	-	o	b	a	l	é	r
r	c	p	ê	i	a	t	à	j	o
n	o	a	t	r	t	i	p	e	s
u	u	s	-	m	o	n	f	u	t
i	r	l	c	a	n	t	i	n	e
t	s	c	o	l	l	è	g	e	r
c	a	l	d	e	v	o	i	r	s

1 school *collège* **6** lesson *cours*
2 morning *matin* **7** meal *repas*
3 afternoon *après-midi* **8** lunch *déjeuner*
4 evening *soir* **9** canteen *cantine*
5 night *nuit* **10** homework *devoirs*

2 *Où sont les voyelles?*
1 l'informatique, **2** la musique, **3** l'éducation physique, **4** le dessin, **5** l'histoire, **6** la géographie

3 *Un serpent*
Des opinions positives: utile, amusant, facile.
Des opinions négatives: difficile, nul, ennuyeux.
Le repas est dîner.

4 *Un acrostiche*
1 technologie, **2** histoire, **3** sciences, **4** français, **5** anglais, **6** géographie, **7** dessin

cm 8/4

La vie scolaire

More able students could work on this worksheet or it could be used later for revision.

1 Mots croisés

Solution:
Horizontalement:
2 de, **3** maths, **4** tu, **7** histoire, **8** la, **9** je, **10** son, **12** géographie, **14** repas
Verticalement:
1 technologie, **2** dessin, **3** musique, **5** temps, **6** sciences, **11** jour, **13** pas

2 Un jeu

Students invent an acrostic puzzle, using school subjects. This is a possible solution. Clues should be given in English.

Solution:
1 sciences, **2** français, **3** géographie, **4** maths, **5** histoire, **6** musique, **7** informatique

cm 8/5

On fait beaucoup de choses

Solution:
1 *Un acrostiche*
1 faisons, **2** faites, **3** fait, **4** font, **5** fais
2 *Samedi après-midi*
1 elle fait **5** Nous faisons
2 Vous faites **6** (Théo) fait
3 Tu fais **7** Elles font
4 Je fais **8** (Les chats) font

cm 8/6

Mon, ton, son

Further practice of the singular possessive adjectives.

Solution:
1 *Fais des listes*
Mots masculins: jour, livre, film
Mots féminins: matière, saison, ville
Mots féminins (avec voyelle): affiche, amie, équipe
Mots au pluriel: animaux, couleurs, sports
2 *Remplis les blancs*
1 livre, **2** ville, **3** équipe, **4** sports, **5** film, **6** matière, **7** couleurs, **8** animaux, **9** jour, **10** saison
3 *Un questionnaire*
This can be discussed in class and some suggestions written on the board.

cm 8/7

Des questions et des réponses

Practice of *notre/nos* and *votre/vos*.

Solution:
1 *Dans le bon ordre*
Students write out the sentences in the correct order.
1 Comment s'appelle votre collège?
2 Il y a combien d'élèves dans votre classe?
3 Comment s'appelle votre prof de français?
4 Votre uniforme scolaire est de quelle couleur?
5 Vos cours commencent à quelle heure, le matin?
6 Quel est votre premier cours le lundi?
7 Quel est votre dernier cours le vendredi?
2 *Complète les réponses avec* **notre** *ou* **nos**
a Notre, **b** notre, **c** nos, **d** Notre, **e** Notre, **f** notre, **g** Notre
3 *Trouve les paires*
Students match the completed answers to the questions in the correct order.
1 e, **2** b, **3** g, **4** a, **5** c, **6** f, **7** d
4 *Un peu différent*
a Students practise changing one detail in any three questions.
b Students respond to any three questions on the worksheet.

Tricolore 1 Teacher's Notes

Unité 8 Consolidation and assessment

cm 8/8

Tu comprends

1 Quelle heure est-il?

Solution:
1 9h00, **2** 8h00, **3** 12h00, **4** 11h30, **5** 2h15, **6** 2h45, **7** 1h30, **8** 5h15

CD 4 Track 22

Quelle heure est-il?
1. Il est neuf heures.
2. Il est huit heures.
3. Il est midi.
4. Il est onze heures et demie.
5. Il est deux heures et quart.
6. Il est trois heures moins le quart.
7. Il est une heure et demie.
8. Il est cinq heures et quart.

2 Samedi

The language needed for the speaking task in CM 8/8 is incorporated in this dialogue for practice.

Solution:
1 7h15, **2** a, **3** 8h20, **4** 11h00, **5** c, **6** b, **7** 9h30

CD 4 Track 23

Samedi
- Tu prends le petit déjeuner à quelle heure le samedi?
- Normalement, je prends le petit déjeuner à sept heures et quart.
- À sept heures et quart? Et qu'est-ce que tu fais le matin?
- Eh bien, le matin, je vais au collège. J'ai cours le samedi matin.
- Ah bon, tu as cours le samedi matin? Les cours commencent à quelle heure?
- À huit heures vingt, comme les autres jours.
- Bon, le collège commence à huit heures vingt. Et les cours se terminent à quelle heure?
- À onze heures. Donc je rentre à la maison à midi.
- Et l'après-midi, qu'est-ce que tu fais?
- Pas grand-chose … je joue sur l'ordinateur, par exemple.
- Et le soir, qu'est-ce que tu fais le soir?
- Le samedi soir, je regarde la télévision.
- Et le soir, tu te couches à quelle heure?
- À neuf heures et demie, normalement.

3 Comment ça s'écrit?

Solution:
Le mot qui ne va pas avec les autres est déjeuner (2).

CD 4 Track 24

Comment ça s'écrit?
1 d–e–s–s–i–n
2 d–é–j–e–u–n–e–r
3 m–u–s–i–q–u–e
4 h–i–s–t–o–i–r–e
5 a–n–g–l–a–i–s
6 m–a–t–h–s
7 g–é–o–g–r–a–p–h–i–e

4 L'emploi du temps

Solution:

8h	maths	déjeuner	
9h	sciences	14h	français
récréation		15h	technologie
10h10	histoire	16h	EPS
11h10	anglais		

CD 4 Track 25

L'emploi du temps
- Qu'est-ce que tu as comme cours le lundi?
- Le lundi? Bon, le matin on a quatre cours. On commence avec maths.
- Alors, maths comme premier cours.
- Ensuite, nous avons sciences.
- Alors sciences, puis …
- Puis il y a la récréation.
- Et après la récréation?
- Nous avons histoire.
- Alors, histoire.
- Et ensuite, nous avons anglais.
- Alors, anglais, et puis c'est l'heure du déjeuner, je suppose.
- Oui, alors l'après-midi, on a trois cours. Pour commencer, il y a français.
- Alors, français.
- Puis nous avons technologie.
- Ensuite, technologie, et puis?
- Et puis nous avons EPS, c'est à dire éducation physique et sportive.
- Alors, EPS. Et ça, c'est le dernier cours?
- Oui, c'est ça.
- Alors, le lundi, tu as maths, sciences, histoire, anglais, français, technologie et EPS.
- Exactement.

cm 8/9

Sommaire

A summary of the main vocabulary and structures of the unit.

Tricolore 1 Teacher's Notes **165**

Unité 9

Tricolore 1 Unité 9 C'est bon ça!   Pages 112–125

9A Les repas en France   pages 112–113

- Find out about meals in France
- Learn the words for things to eat and drink

Grammaire	Stratégies	Phonétique
• Use the words for 'some'	• Tackling a gapfill text	• The circumflex accent

Resources

Audio: 2 *Trois familles*; 3 *Mon repas idéal*, or CD 4, tracks 26 and 28
Copymasters: 9/1 *On mange et on boit*
Flashcards: 61–88
Worksheets: Starters and plenaries; *Un repas typique* (V)

Interactive activity: None
Ph The circumflex accent, or CD 4, track 27
PowerPoint: None
Grammar in Action: None

9B Qu'est-ce que tu prends?   pages 114–115

- Understand more about meals in France

Grammaire	Stratégies	Phonétique
• Use the partitive article (du, de la, de l', des) • Use the verbs manger and prendre	• Recognising false friends	• None

Resources

Audio: 1 *Le petit déjeuner*, or CD 4, track 29
Copymasters: 9/2 *C'est quel mot?*
Worksheets: Starters and plenaries; *Du / de la / de l' / des* (G)

Interactive activity: *Du / de la / de l' / des* (grammar); *Je prends* (L)
PowerPoint: None
Grammar in Action: pp35–36, pp37–38, p39

9C On mange sainement   pages 116–117

- Use words for fruit and vegetables
- Discuss healthy eating
- Say what you have eaten

Grammaire	Stratégies	Phonétique
• Introduction to the perfect tense of *manger*	• Developing your written work	• The letters 'gn'

Resources

Audio: 1 *Les fruits et les légumes*; *Ils mangent sainement?*; 4 *Lou Leroux et la bonne alimentation*, or CD 4, tracks 31, 33 and 34
Copymasters: 9/3 *Des jeux de vocabulaire*
Flashcards: 56–80
Worksheets: Starters and plenaries; *C'est bon* (G, V)

Interactive activity: *Les fruits et les légumes* (V)
Ph The letters 'gn' or CD 4, track 32
PowerPoint: None
Grammar in Action: None

9D Un repas en famille   pages 118–119

- Discuss what you like to eat and drink
- Use phrases when dining with French people

Grammaire	Stratégies	Phonétique
• Use the negative and say 'not any'	• None	• The letters 'c', 'k', 'qu'

Resources

Audio: 4 *À table*, or CD 4, track 36
Copymasters: 9/4 *La forme négative*, 9/5 *À table*
Worksheets: Starters and plenaries; *Deux réponses possibles* (R)

Interactive activity: *Qu'est-ce qu'ils mangent?* (L)
Ph The letters 'c', 'k', 'qu', or CD 4, track 35
PowerPoint: Kim's game: *La nourriture*
Grammar in Action: pp40-41

9E Des projets   pages 120–121

- Plan some meals and some picnics

Grammaire	Stratégies	Phonétique
• Discuss what you are going to do (using *aller* + infinitive)	• None	• None

Resources

Audio: 2 *Un pique-nique un peu special!*; 3b *Le concours "c'est bon pour la santé"*; 4a *Faites des projets*; *Pique-nique à la plage* or CD 4, tracks 37 and 38, Student CD track 35
Copymasters: 9/6 *Qu'est-ce qu'on va faire?*
Worksheets: Starters and plenaries

Interactive activity: None
PowerPoint: *Aller* + infinitif (G); *Pique-nique à la plage* (song)
Grammar in Action: p42

166   Tricolore 1 Teacher's Notes

Key language

9F La fête autour du monde pages 122–123		
• Practise reading longer passages • Learn more about festival foods		
Grammaire	Stratégies	Phonétique
• None	• Reading for gist and detail • Using clues to work out meaning (5)	• None
Resources		
Audio: None **Copymasters:** 9/7 *Tu comprends?*, 9/8 *Sommaire* **Worksheets:** Starters and plenaries; Reading for gist and detail (Strat); *Autour du monde* (R) **e-book:** *Métallo*		**Interactive activity:** Classroom commands (V) **PowerPoint:** None **Grammar in Action:** None

Key language

Food and meals (9A to 9D)

un repas
un hors-d'œuvre
le plat principal
du fromage
du jambon
de l'omelette
du pâté
de la pizza
du poisson
du potage
du poulet
du riz
de la viande
des légumes
des brocolis
des carottes
un chou
un chou-fleur
des frites
des chips
des haricots verts
un oignon
des petits pois
des pommes de terre
de la salade
une tomate
des fruits
un ananas
une banane
une fraise
une framboise
un melon
une orange
une pêche
une poire
une pomme
des raisins
des desserts
un gâteau
une glace
une tarte aux pommes
un yaourt

Breakfast items (9B)

des croissants
du beurre
des céréales
de la confiture
de la confiture d'oranges
un œuf (à la coque)
des œufs au bacon
du pain
du sucre
des tartines
des toasts
du pain grillé
croustillant

Drinks (9A to 9D)

des boissons froides
du coca cola
de l'eau (minérale)
de la limonade
du jus de fruit
du lait
du vin rouge/blanc
des boissons chaudes
du café
du thé
un chocolat chaud

Healthy eating (9C)

bon pour la santé
des bonbons
le sel
des sucreries
surtout
un peu
pas trop

Mealtime etiquette and food preferences (9D)

Oui, s'il vous plaît.
Oui, je veux bien.
Non, merci.
C'est (très) bon/délicieux.
Encore du/de la/de l'/des …?
Merci, j'ai assez mangé.
J'aime (beaucoup) le/la/les …
Désolé(e), mais je n'aime pas beaucoup ça.

9A Les repas en France

9A Les repas en France   pages 112–113

- Find out about meals in France
- Learn the words for things to eat and drink

Grammaire	Stratégies	Phonétique
• Use the words for 'some'	• Tackling a gapfill text	• The circumflex accent

Resources

Audio: 2 *Trois familles*; 3 *Mon repas idéal*, or CD 4, tracks 26 and 28
Copymasters: 9/1 *On mange et on boit*
Flashcards: 61–88
Worksheets: Starters and plenaries; *Un repas typique* (V)

Interactive activity: None
Ph The circumflex accent, or CD 4, track 27
PowerPoint: None
Grammar in Action: None

Worksheet

Starters (pages 112–113)

1 *C'est masculin ou féminin?* Reinforce the focus on masculine and feminine in preparation for the use of *du/de la/des*. Display the following words (see online worksheet), use flashcards (e.g. of places in town), or say the words and ask students to hold up their *masculin* or *féminin* cards.
masculin: bowling, château, cinéma, français, hôpital, magasin, marché, matin, restaurant, soir, sport
féminin: banque, église, musique, nuit, patinoire, plage, poste, sciences, technologie

2 Dictate a selection of times for students to write down in figures. As you check the answers, display them and use them for a game of *Effacez!* for reinforcement.
Suggestion: 7h00, 12h00 (*midi*), 3h45, 5h30, 7h40, 9h20, 10h05, 3h25, 2h15, 1h10
This will prepare students to talk about times of meals later.

Introduction

Food

Use flashcards 61–88 to introduce and practise the new vocabulary for food and meals. Ensure plenty of oral practice before students look at the printed text.

With food, use the correct word for 'some', as this will familiarise the class with the different forms of the partitive article. This is explained fully later and practised throughout the unit.

Ask questions, such as *Qu'est-ce que c'est? Qu'est-ce que tu manges? Et comme boisson?* and prompt replies with the flashcards.

After plenty of oral practice, write some of the words on the board for a game of *Effacez!* later.

The words fall naturally into groups, such as the separate courses (as presented in SB page 112–113).

At this stage, students can absorb a lot of vocabulary at once so long as they use it in plenty of enjoyable activities, e.g. *Jeu de mémoire, Morpion,* etc. (TB page xviii).

Ongoing activities

Wall Display

Students, perhaps working in pairs or small groups, could cut out pictures of food and drink from magazines. At the appropriate point, they could label them in French, using the words for 'some'.

They could make these into collages or simple wall displays, each featuring a particular meal or category of food, or their own favourite meal. As they learn more vocabulary, they can add to their displays. Several groups could combine to make their display into a complete meal, e.g.
Comme hors-d'œuvre, il y a/je préfère …
Comme plat principal, il y a …
Comme légumes, il y a …
Comme dessert, il y a …
Comme boisson, il y a …

Labels, short sentences in French, artwork, etc. could be prepared on the computer and used in these displays.

French food tasting

Brave teachers, or a school French club, could organise a French food-tasting session or a French meal with French bread, cheeses and pâté, etc.

French culture

During the following activities, encourage students to spot differences between French and British meals (e.g. cheese before or after dessert, vegetables with or after meat, etc.) and tell them about the general importance of food in French culture.

Mealtime arrangements are changing in France, e.g. the main meal is often not at lunchtime but in the evening, and the practice of two big meals daily is no longer the norm. Similarly, the habit of eating the vegetables separately from the meat or fish seems to be changing. However, practice varies and some agricultural areas may still have a long break at midday.

Students could also be given information on typical school dinners in France (how long students get, example of a menu).

Students could work in pairs/groups and report back what they have found out about meals in France. Some students could prepare visuals to describe different meals using the new vocabulary.

9A Les repas en France

112–113

1 Un repas typique

A lot of vocabulary is introduced in the first item, which is re-used and practised throughout the unit.

a Discuss the photos, and introduce and practise the vocabulary, e.g.
  Le numéro neuf, qu'est-ce que c'est? (Des frites.)
  Qu'est-ce qu'il y a comme hors-d'œuvre/desserts/boissons?
  Le poulet, c'est un légume?
  Explain the meaning of *prendre*, which is taught fully on pages 114–115.

b The simple matching activity reinforces the vocabulary for the different categories of food and drink.

> **Solution:**
> **b 1** *b*, **2** *e*, **3** *a*, **4** *d*, **5** *f*, **6** *c*

For some groups, point out that most of the captions with the food pictures include one of these words for 'some': *du/de la/de l'/des*. Can they work out the pattern for which one to use? They will find out more about the partitive article on page 114.

113   AfL

2 Trois familles

Students listen to the recording, in which three families discuss what they are eating for their main meal, and then note down the number for each item mentioned. This can be used as an assessment task. Remind students of the spread objectives, and encourage them to self-evaluate their skills.

As follow-up, students can listen for and identify sequencers (*ensuite, puis, alors, pour commencer*). They can then use these in their own work.

> **Solution:**
> *les Dubois:* 2, 4, 11, 14, 15, 18, 19
> *les Martin:* 1, 7, 9, 12, 16
> *les Lacan:* 3, 6, 8, 10, 13, 17, 18, 20

CD 4 Track 26
Trois familles

La famille Dubois
– Chez la famille Dubois, on mange du pâté, comme hors-d'œuvre. Ensuite, comme plat principal, il y a du poulet avec des petits pois. Puis il y a des yaourts et des fruits. Comme boisson, il y a du vin et de l'eau.

La famille Martin
– La famille Martin est végétarienne. Alors, pour commencer, ils vont manger du melon. Puis, comme plat principal, ils vont manger de l'omelette avec des frites. Toute la famille aime ça. Puis ils vont prendre de la salade. Et comme dessert, ils vont manger un gâteau.

La famille Lacan
– Mme Lacan, qu'est-ce que vous mangez aujourd'hui pour le déjeuner?
– Comme hors-d'œuvre, nous mangeons du jambon. Puis comme plat principal, nous mangeons du poisson, avec, comme légumes, des pommes de terre et des carottes. Ensuite, on va prendre du fromage. Et comme dessert, il y a une tarte aux pommes.
– Et qu'est-ce que vous prenez comme boisson?
– Alors, comme boisson, il y a du vin et, pour les enfants, il y a de la limonade.

156 Au choix

1 Qu'est-ce que c'est?

Worksheet

On prend …

Interactive activity

The circumflex accent

113 Phonétique

The circumflex accent

A full explanation of the use of the circumflex accent (*accent circonflexe*) is given on *kerboodle!*, together with interactive practice of transcribing words with the correct accented vowels.

a Say the word *gâteau* with the appropriate gesture (eating a piece of delicious cake). Students repeat the word with the same gesture. Then read out the other words with students repeating each one. The words are also included on the recording for optional use (part **a**). Point out that the accent does not affect the pronunciation of the vowel.

Parts **b** and **c** can be used to practise pronunciation of the accented vowels.

b Ask students to listen and repeat the words they hear. Then display the words **a** *château*, **b** *forêt*, **c** *dîner*, **d** *côté*, **e** *flûte* for students to match (**d**, **b**, **e**, **a**, **c**).

c Students listen to and repeat the silly sentence to help them remember words that include the accent.

For further practice write some additional words on the board to check that students recognise the link between spelling and related pronunciation, e.g. *être, fête, s'il vous plaît, rôti*.

CD 4 Track 27
The circumflex accent

Écoutez et répétez:
a gâteau, fenêtre, dîner, bientôt, août
b côté, forêt, flûte, château, dîner
c Au château dans la forêt il y a une boîte avec du pâté pour le dîner.

113 Stratégies

Tackling a gapfill text

This listening strategy focuses on anticipating what might be needed to complete a gapped text, what words to expect and using clues within the text.

9B Qu'est-ce que tu prends?

📖 🔊 113

3 Mon repas idéal

a Students listen to and read the text then write the missing words.

> **Solution:**
> **1** pâté, **2** salade, **3** principal, **4** poulet, **5** légumes, **6** frites, **7** pommes, **8** boisson

🔊 **CD 4 Track 28**

Mon repas idéal

Mon repas idéal, c'est un repas de trois plats. Comme hors-d'œuvre, il y a du pâté – mmm, j'adore ça avec du pain croustillant et de la salade. Délicieux! Puis comme plat principal, on mange du poulet rôti et comme légumes il y a des carottes et des frites. Ensuite, comme dessert, il y a une tarte aux pommes. Et comme boisson, il y a tout simplement de l'eau. Ça, c'est idéal!

b Students find French words and phrases in the text.

> **Solution:**
> **1** un repas de trois plats, **2** du pain croustillant, **3** délicieux, **4** rôti, **5** puis / ensuite, **6** tout simplement

Worksheet

Un repas typique

📖 113

4 Une présentation

a Students prepare an illustrated PowerPoint presentation of a three-course meal, writing a simple sentence for each course and one for the drinks. Provide online flashcard images or other images for inclusion in the presentations. Students could record their description and add it to their presentation.

b As extension, students describe two more meals.
➕ Encourage them to look up any further items of food and drink they want to use but to check carefully that they have the right words and can pronounce them properly. They could be referred to the *Phonétique* items they have practised and to online dictionaries which have examples of the pronunciation.

cm 9/1

On mange et on boit

Worksheet

Plenaries (pages 112–113)

1 **Think, pair and share** Students think about the topic of meals in France for a few minutes. They then discuss it in pairs for five minutes, then share what they know with the class.

2 **Pronunciation** Students discuss which sounds they find most difficult (with particular regard to the vocabulary of this spread) and share ideas about how they can practise them.

9B Qu'est-ce que tu prends?   pages 114–115

- Understand more about meals in France

Grammaire	Stratégies	Phonétique
• Use the partitive article (du, de la, de l', des) • Use the verbs manger and prendre	• Recognising false friends	• None

Resources

Audio: 1 *Le petit déjeuner*, or CD 4, track 29
Copymasters: 9/2 *C'est quel mot?*
Worksheets: Starters and plenaries; *Du / de la / de l' / des* (G)

Interactive activity: *Du / de la / de l' / des* (grammar); *Je prends* (L)
PowerPoint: None
Grammar in Action: pp35–36, pp37–38, p39

Worksheet

Starters (pages 114–115)

1 *En groupes* Display a list of words in random order or hand this out on paper (see online worksheet). Ask students to put these into four groups.

goûter, déjeuner, petit déjeuner; mange, est, avons; pomme, banane, melon; hors-d'œuvre, plat principal, dessert

2 *Chaque mot à sa place* Hand out the table below to students and display the following words on the board (see online worksheet):
cent, sont, grand, commencer, thé
Students write the correct word in each column. This can be done as a game to see who is fastest.

> **Solution:**
>
> | A | B | C | D | E |
> |---|---|---|---|---|
> | eau | manger | quinze | suis | bon |
> | café | aimer | soixante | sommes | vert |
> | limonade | détester | trois | est | petit |
> | thé | commencer | cent | ont | grand |

170 Tricolore 1 Teacher's Notes

9B Qu'est-ce que tu prends?

Introduction

Breakfast food and drink

Introduce this topic by saying what you (and other members of the family) eat for breakfast and display an image each time one of the items of food and drink is mentioned, e.g.

À sept heures et demie, je prends le petit déjeuner. Je mange du pain avec du beurre et de la confiture. Quelquefois, je mange un fruit, par exemple une banane. Je bois du jus de fruit et un café au lait.

114

1 Le petit déjeuner

a Students listen to the recording and look at the list of breakfast food and drink. They repeat each item and note down the appropriate letter. This could be done in two stages: listen and repeat; listen again and note down the letter.

Solution:
1 c, **2** o, **3** l, **4** e, **5** q, **6** h, **7** a, **8** n, **9** i, **10** p, **11** k, **12** r, **13** m, **14** f, **15** b, **16** j, **17** g, **18** d

CD 4 Track 29

Le petit déjeuner

1	du jus de fruit	10	des fruits
2	des croissants	11	un yaourt
3	de la confiture	12	des tartines
4	du Nutella®	13	de la confiture d'oranges
5	des toasts	14	du pain
6	du thé	15	du beurre
7	du café	16	un œuf à la coque
8	des céréales	17	du sucre
9	un chocolat chaud	18	du lait

b Go through the illustrations, asking students to repeat the names of the items illustrated. They then match the numbered items to the list of words in part **a**.

Solution:
1 n, **2** p, **3** a, **4** o, **5** e, **6** f, **7** l, **8** m, **9** c, **10** d, **11** k, **12** r, **13** g, **14** i, **15** j, **16** h, **17** q, **18** b

If not covered earlier, explain *des tartines*, *des croissants*, *Nutella®* and the custom of drinking hot chocolate, coffee, etc. from a *bol*. Encourage students to deduce the meanings by using reading strategies.

114

2 Qu'est-ce qu'ils prennent?

Next, students listen to the recording of what people have for breakfast. They note down the letters (from task 1a) to indicate each item mentioned after the appropriate name.

Solution:
Nicole – f, b, l (or m), i
Marc – n, q, c
Claire – r (or f, b), e, h
Luc – o, f, b, l (or m), a (+ d), g
Des touristes – n, k, p, j, f, o, a, h

CD 4 Track 30

Qu'est-ce qu'ils prennent?

Nicole
– Normalement, je prends le petit déjeuner à sept heures du matin. Je prends du pain avec du beurre et de la confiture. Comme boisson, je prends un chocolat chaud.

Marc
– Moi, je prends le petit déjeuner à sept heures et quart. Je mange des céréales, par exemple des Corn Flakes, et des toasts et je bois du jus de fruit.

Claire
– Pendant la semaine, je prends le petit déjeuner à huit heures moins le quart. Je mange des tartines, c'est à dire, du pain avec du beurre. Quelquefois, je me fais des tartines avec du Nutella®. J'aime bien ça. Comme boisson, je prends du thé.

Luc
– Le dimanche, nous prenons le petit déjeuner plus tard, vers huit heures et demie. Nous mangeons souvent des croissants ou du pain avec du beurre et de la confiture. Moi, je bois du café au lait avec du sucre.

Des touristes
– Mes parents travaillent dans un grand hôtel. À l'hôtel, on prépare un petit déjeuner sous forme de buffet pour les touristes. Souvent, des touristes mangent des céréales ou des yaourts ou des fruits. Puis ils mangent un œuf à la coque avec du pain ou des croissants. Comme boissons, ils prennent du café ou du thé.

Au petit déjeuner, je prends…

Play a chain breakfast game with an ever-increasing list. This could be done as a whole-class activity or in groups.

Interactive activity

Je prends …

114 Stratégies

Recognising false friends

This reading strategy focuses on cognates and false friends.

114 Dossier-langue

'some' (*du, de la, de l', des*)

Go through the explanation and encourage students to find other examples for 'some' from earlier in the unit. Emphasise the link between the correct word for 'some' and the gender of the noun.

If appropriate, explain that, in French, the word for 'some' is always used, whereas in English it is sometimes omitted, e.g. *Au petit déjeuner, je prends du pain et du beurre.* (For breakfast I have bread and butter.)

114

3 On mange

This gap-fill activity provides a useful summary of the partitive article.

Tricolore 1 Teacher's Notes **171**

9B Qu'est-ce que tu prends?

> **Solution:**
> **1** du, **2** du, **3** de la, **4** de la, **5** de l', **6** des

156 Au choix

2 Un mélange

cm 9/2

C'est quel mot?

gia 1 pp35–36

Using *du, de la, de l', des* (1) and (2)

This provides practice of the partitive but would be best used later in the unit, when more food and drink vocabulary has been taught.

114 Dossier-langue

The verb *manger* (to eat)

This looks at the slight difference in the *nous* form of *manger* (and other verbs ending in *-ger*).

156 Au choix

3 Le plat favori

115

4 Un quiz: les repas en France

Revise the names of all meals, e.g. *Le matin, on prend quel repas? Et à midi, et le soir? Quand les enfants rentrent à la maison, ils prennent souvent quelque chose à manger et à boire, ça s'appelle …?*

This short quiz presents most parts of the verb *prendre*.

> **Solution:**
> **1** c, **2** b, **3** c, **4** a, **5** c

gia 1 p39

The verbs *manger* and *commencer*

Further practice of *manger*, and introduction of the similar pattern of *commencer*.

115 Dossier-langue

The verb *prendre* (to take)

Check that students understand the more common meaning of *prendre* – to take. If students have compiled an individual verb table using a table facility on the computer, *prendre* could be added at this point.

If necessary, explain that an irregular verb is one which does not follow the normal, regular pattern.

115

5 Questions et réponses

a Using the verb *prendre*, students have to complete first questions, then replies, then match them up.

> **Solution:**
> **1** prenez, **f** prenons, **2** prend, **d** prend, **3** prend, **e** prenons, **4** prends, **a** prends, **5** prennent, **b** prennent, **6** prends, **c** prends

b As extension, students work in pairs to make up a conversation based on the questions and answers in part **a**, using the table to help them. Go over the example and some sample questions and answers so students are aware what they can change from the original question, e.g. meals or the verbs (*tu* instead of *vous*, etc.).

157 Au choix   AfL

5 Mes repas

gia 1 pp37–38

Using the verb *prendre* – to take (1) & (2)

Further practice of *prendre*, if required.

Worksheet

Plenaries (pages 114–115)

1 Discuss what students find most difficult about learning nouns (gender, spellings, etc.). Share useful tips, such as 'Look, say, copy, spell, hide and repeat', or similar. With gender, ask how students are learning this and whether their approach has been successful and whether anyone has worked out any patterns.

2 Students think about three things in the unit so far that they have found useful/interesting and compare their choice with that of others.

9C On mange sainement   pages 116–117

- Use words for fruit and vegetables
- Discuss healthy eating
- Say what you have eaten

Grammaire	Stratégies	Phonétique
• Introduction to the perfect tense of *manger*	• Developing your written work	• The letters 'gn'

Resources

Audio: 1 *Les fruits et les légumes; Ils mangent sainement?;* 4 *Lou Leroux et la bonne alimentation,* or CD 4, tracks 31, 33 and 34
Copymasters: 9/3 *Des jeux de vocabulaire*
Flashcards: 56–80
Worksheets: Starters and plenaries; *C'est bon* (G, V)

Interactive activity: *Les fruits et les légumes* (V)
Ph The letters 'gn' or CD 4, track 32
PowerPoint: None
Grammar in Action: None

Worksheet

Starters (pages 116–117)

1 *Chasse à l'intrus* Students are given the six sets of words (see online worksheet) and have to find the odd one out, giving a reason for their choice. This could be done individually or in groups.
If required, give the first one as an example. For extra support, the 'reasons' could be written in jumbled order on the board (see Solution).

Solution:

1 *le dîner, le déjeuner, le marché, le goûter (le marché – les autres sont des repas)*
2 *des carottes, des petits pois, des pommes de terre, des oranges (des oranges – les autres sont des légumes)*
3 *de la limonade, de l'eau, du vin, de la salade (de la salade – les autres sont des boissons)*
4 *du lait, de la viande, du poisson, de l'omelette (du lait – les autres sont des plats)*
5 *du melon, du jambon, des pommes, des bananes (du jambon – les autres sont des fruits)*
6 *des frites, une tarte aux pommes, des fruits, un gâteau (des frites – les autres sont des desserts)*

2 *Quel mot?* Students read the definitions and find the correct word in the box to complete each one. If required, give the first one as an example.
(in the box) *omelette, pommes, melon, carottes, vin, viande*

a C'est une boisson alcoolisée. C'est rouge ou blanc. C'est du …
b C'est un fruit. Quelquefois, on mange ce fruit comme hors-d'œuvre. C'est du …
c C'est souvent un plat principal. Les végétariens ne mangent pas ça. C'est de la …
d C'est un plat de couleur jaune. C'est fait avec des œufs. C'est de l'…
e Ce sont des légumes. Ils sont oranges. Ce sont des …
f Ce sont des fruits. Ils sont verts, rouges ou jaunes. Ce sont des …

Solution:

a *vin,* b *melon,* c *viande,* d *omelette,* e *carottes,* f *pommes*

116 FC 66–80

1 Les fruits et les légumes

Teach the vocabulary orally first, using flashcards 66–80 and/or actual/plastic fruit and vegetables before commencing this task. Many students could already be familiar with fruit and vegetable language from primary French. Students match the text and pictures and then listen to check their answers.

Alternatively, get students (perhaps as a pairwork activity) to try to work out which item of fruit or vegetable is which, as follows:

- Start with the ones they know – *carottes, petits pois, melon, pomme, pommes de terre* (point out the link between these last two items).
- Next use similarity with English – *banane, orange, pêche, raisins* (dried grapes), *brocolis, courgette, oignons, radis.*
- They are then left with *ananas, fraises, framboises, poire* (which they might guess from the sound), *chou, chou-fleur, haricots verts* (might guess if they have heard of haricot beans). They will probably need to look these up in a dictionary/the glossary.

Students then list the fruit and the vegetables and listen to the recording to check. The recording can also be used for recognition and repetition practice. Once the lists have been checked, they can be copied into vocab books.

Solution:

Les fruits: *un ananas, une banane, des fraises, des framboises, du melon, une orange, une pêche, une poire, une pomme, des raisins*

Les légumes: *des brocolis, une carotte, un chou, une courgette, un chou-fleur, des haricots verts, un oignon, des petits pois, des pommes de terre, des radis*

Tricolore 1 Teacher's Notes

9C On mange sainement

CD 4 Track 31

1 Les fruits et les légumes

Voici les fruits: un ananas, une banane, des fraises, des framboises, du melon, une orange, une pêche, une poire, une pomme, des raisins.
Et voici les légumes: des brocolis, une carotte, un chou, une courgette, un chou-fleur, des haricots verts, un oignon, des petits pois, des pommes de terre, des radis.

Worksheet

C'est bon

Jeu

1 Qu'est-ce que c'est?

One student picks up a card, not showing it to the rest of the class. They can ask up to five 'yes/no' type questions to guess what it is, e.g.

C'est un fruit/un légume? C'est grand/petit? C'est rouge/vert/orange/jaune/blanc?

2 J'adore les fruits et les légumes

A chain game in which one person says a fruit or vegetable that they eat and the next person adds another one, e.g.

Je mange une pêche.
Je mange une pêche et deux bananes.
Je mange une pêche, deux bananes et trois oignons, etc.

This can be played in various ways, e.g. alternating fruit and vegetables, with different subjects, e.g. *Mon chat mange …* etc.

3 Feely bag

Put items of fruit and veg (real or plastic, or both) in a bag. Students feel inside and guess what is in the bag.

cm 9/3

Des jeux de vocabulaire

Interactive activity

The letters 'gn'

116 Phonétique

The letters 'gn'

A full explanation of the 'gn' sound is given on *kerboodle!*, together with interactive practice which includes recognising words that include the sound.

a Say the word *oignon* with the appropriate gesture (wiping tears from eyes). Students repeat the word with the same gesture. Then read out the other words with students repeating each one. The words are also included on the recording for optional use (part a).

Parts **b** and **c** can be used to practise pronunciation of the *'gn'* sound.

b Ask students to listen and repeat the words they hear. Then display the words **a** *Bretagne*, **b** *gagner*, **c** *Allemagne*, **d** *surligneur*, **e** *magnifique* for students to match (**e, a, b, d, c**).

c Students listen to the silly sentence and note down how many times they hear the sound (4). They can then repeat the sentence to help them remember this sound.

For further practice write some additional words on the board to check that students recognise the link between spelling and related pronunciation, e.g. *champagne, mignon, signature, agneau*.

CD 4 Track 32

The letters 'gn'

Écoutez et répétez:
a oignon, magnifique, Espagne, gagner
b magnifique, Bretagne, gagner, surligneur, Allemagne
c En Espagne, on gagne des oignons – c'est magnifique!

116 — AfL

2 L'alimentation

The exercises with this reading text take students through it in four stages:

1 Look at the text title with the teacher and predict what kind of advice they are going to get before doing more focused reading, e.g. they could find three pieces of advice and check what they found with a partner.

Solution:
a fruit, vegetables, **b** sugar and salt, **c** exercise

2 Work out the meaning of specific French words and expressions.

Solution:
a it's obvious/evident, **b** it's necessary, **c** to be fit, **d** sugary things

3 From the article, find the French for the English expressions.

Solution:
a *être en forme*, **b** *faites de l'exercice tous les jours*, **c** *L'important*, **d** *un peu de variété*, **e** *mais pas trop*

4 Complete sentences using information from the text. The last stage can be used as an AfL task: students have to explain why/how they made their choices, thus showing evidence of reading and understanding.

With words like *sucreries* the teacher can do work on word families (e.g. we know that *sucre* means sugar…). There is also the opportunity to reinforce time phrases learnt in *Unité* 6 (*quelquefois, souvent, normalement*).

If support for part 4 is needed, display the following words:

riz	sucreries	sel
légumes	fruit	chocolat
chips	gâteaux	frites
bonbons	glaces	pommes
yaourt	desserts	poisson

9C On mange sainement

116 Stratégies

Developing your written work

This writing strategy focuses on adapting texts to what students want to write.

116

3 Ils mangent sainement?

This listening activity provides practice of the phrases needed to talk about healthy eating.

Solution:
1 *Karine – oui,* 2 *Noah – pas mal,* 3 *Nicolas – oui,* 4 *Valérie – non*

CD 4 Track 33
Ils mangent sainement?

1 – Karine qu'est-ce que tu manges au petit déjeuner?
 – Alors, pour le petit déjeuner, je mange des fruits et une tartine avec de la confiture d'oranges et, comme boisson, je prends un jus de fruits.
2 – Noah, tu déjeunes à la maison, non? Qu'est-ce que tu manges, d'habitude?
 – Au déjeuner, je mange un hors-d'œuvre – par exemple, du melon avec du jambon. Puis de la viande avec des légumes comme des haricots verts, mais comme dessert, du gâteau ou une glace – j'adore ça!
3 – Nicolas, tu aimes être en forme, non, et tu manges bien?
 – Bien sûr. Aujourd'hui, on fait un pique-nique avec de la salade, des tomates et du fromage, puis après, du yaourt et un fruit.
4 – Valérie, c'est ton anniversaire aujourd'hui. Qu'est-ce que tu vas manger pour le goûter?
 – Euh, je ... alors, j'invite des amies à la maison et on va manger une grande glace au chocolat. Moi, je vais manger deux morceaux de mon gâteau favori. C'est mon anniversaire après tout!!

117

4 Lou Leroux et la bonne alimentation

a Play the recording while students read the text.
b Students then answer some general questions about the text. These provide a model for the next speaking activity.

The expressions with *manger* in the perfect tense should be treated as vocabulary items here. In *Unité* 10 there is an optional section on the perfect tense for teachers to use if they wish.

Point out a common *faux ami* (*les chips*). The phrase *une pomme d'amour* (toffee apple) in the text could also provide scope for discussion.

Solution:
1 *Elle mange une banane ou une poire.*
2 *Thierry mange du gâteau au déjeuner.*
3 *Non, ce n'est pas bon pour la santé.*
4 *Non, il ne mange pas sainement.*

CD 4 Track 34
Lou Leroux et la bonne alimentation

– Alors, Sophie, qu'est-ce que tu manges au goûter?
– Au goûter, je mange une banane ou une poire, et quelquefois du chocolat aussi.
– Et toi, Thierry, qu'est-ce que tu prends normalement au déjeuner?
– Au déjeuner, je mange un sandwich au fromage ou au jambon, avec beaucoup de chips et une tomate, puis un gâteau au chocolat.
– Alors, les enfants, ce n'est pas très bien. Pour être en forme, mangez cinq portions de fruits et légumes par jour. Manger des chips et des gâteaux, ce n'est pas bon pour la santé.
– Monsieur! Hier j'ai mangé cinq portions de fruits et légumes.
– Excellent, Sébastien! Qu'est-ce que tu as mangé?
– Au goûter, j'ai mangé une pomme, et le soir, au dîner, j'ai mangé des pommes de terre et des oignons. Puis comme dessert, j'ai mangé des fraises et des pêches.
– Fantastique!
– Votre fils a mangé cinq portions de fruits et légumes hier, c'est excellent!
– Voilà ce qu'il a mangé: une pomme d'amour ... un hamburger aux oignons et des frites ... et des fraises et des pêches avec beaucoup de crème.
– Zut alors, Sébastien! La bonne alimentation, ce n'est pas ça!

117 Dossier-langue

The perfect tense (*manger*)

This provides a brief introduction to the perfect tense of *manger*. Some teachers might prefer to avoid teaching the perfect tense at this stage and introduce it fully in Stage 2. The phrases introduced here could be treated as purely lexical items.

Interactive activity

Tu manges sainement?

117 AfL

5 C'est bon pour la santé?

a This pairwork activity draws together the discussion about healthy eating and food vocabulary. Some of the conversations could be recorded or presented to the class, with students giving feedback on the quality of the content and the accuracy of pronunciation. Remind them of the spread objectives and agree the criteria for success.

As follow-up, students could say whether their partner eats healthily or not, e.g.

Teacher: *Décide si ton/ta partenaire mange sainement.*

Student: *Bravo! Tu manges sainement! / C'est bon pour la santé. / Ah non, tu ne manges pas sainement!*

b As extension, students give an account of their meals for four days, including an opinion. This could be a speaking or writing activity.

Tricolore 1 Teacher's Notes 175

9D Un repas en famille

> **Worksheet**

Plenaries (pages 116–117)

1 Students write down two sentences summarising the lesson, then share these with the class. Discuss the key points to remember and what aspects might cause difficulties.

2 Students agree on (for instance) 10 words that they are going to find more difficult to remember from this unit so far. They then suggest and discuss things they are going to do to remember them.

9D Un repas en famille   pages 118–119

- Discuss what you like to eat and drink
- Use phrases when dining with French people

Grammaire	Stratégies	Phonétique
• Use the negative and say 'not any'	• None	• The letters 'c', 'k', 'qu'

Resources

Audio: 4 *À table*, or CD 4, track 36
Copymasters: 9/4 *La forme négative*, 9/5 *À table*
Worksheets: Starters and plenaries; *Deux réponses possibles* (R)

Interactive activity: *Qu'est-ce qu'ils mangent?* (L)
Ph The letters 'c', 'k', 'qu', or CD 4, track 35
PowerPoint: Kim's game: *La nourriture*
Grammar in Action: pp40-41

> **Worksheet**

Starters (pages 118–119)

1 *Qu'est que ça va être?* Display a random list of vocabulary items (food, drink, items from previous units such as animals, rooms, furniture – see online worksheet for suggestions). Begin to draw any one of the items. Students tell you as soon as they know what it is. Bad drawing makes this activity even more effective! Students can then continue in pairs.

2 **5-4-3-2-1** Display the grid and a list of words in random order (see online worksheet). Students find groups of similar words.
   5 **fruits/légumes:** pêche, carotte, oignon, chou-fleur, fraise
   4 **adjectifs:** petit, jaune, bonne, délicieux
   3 **boissons:** café, eau, limonade
   2 **repas:** goûter, déjeuner
   1 **verbe:** mangeons

118

1 Tu aimes ça?

a Students read the posts on the forum and decide which sentences are true.

> **Solution:**
> *vrai* = 1, 3, 4, 8

b As extension, students correct the false sentences. ✚ Revise question forms if necessary and see how many different questions students can ask about the posts.

Remind students of words like *surtout* and as follow-up get them to make up sentences saying what they particularly like or dislike, e.g. *j'adore/j'aime/je déteste (les fruits), surtout (l'ananas)*.

> **Solution (possible answers):**
> 2 *nourris-moi-99 n'est pas végétarienne.*
> 5 *mmmathilde_24 aime le poulet.*
> 6 *mmmathilde_24 déteste le chou-fleur, mais elle mange d'autres légumes.* 7 *hamster-heureux mange des œufs parce qu'il aime les omelettes.*

118 Dossier-langue

The negative

Before looking for examples in the forum posts, remind students, if necessary, about negatives they have been using since *Unité* 4, e.g. *Je n'aime pas …, Je n'ai pas de …, Il n'y a pas …* and summarise the key points on the board, e.g.

In English, the word ……… is used to make a sentence negative.

In French two words are used: …… and …………
(Use …… before a vowel.)

These two words go before and after the ………… in a sentence.

118

2 Je n'aime pas ça!

This short activity practises using the negative to say what students do not like (especially food, drink and activities).

176 Tricolore 1 Teacher's Notes

9D Un repas en famille

Interactive activity
Qu'est-ce qu'ils mangent?

Interactive activity
The letters 'c', 'k', 'qu'

116 Phonétique

The letters 'c', 'k', 'qu'

A full explanation of the hard *'k'* sound is given on *kerboodle!*, together with interactive practice which includes recognising words that contain the sound.

a Say the word *carotte* with the appropriate gesture (eating a carrot like a rabbit). Students repeat the word with the same gesture. Then read out the other words with students repeating each one. The words are also included on the recording for optional use (part **a**). Remind students that *'qu'*, *'k'* (not very common) and hard *'c'* (*ca, co, cu*) all produce the same sound.

Parts **b** and **c** can be used to practise pronunciation of the hard *'k'* sound.

b Ask students to listen and repeat the words they hear. Then display the words **a** *curieuse*, **b** *quoi*, **c** *cartable*, **d** *quatorze*, **e** *kilomètre*, **f** *comment* for students to match (**f**, **e**, **b**, **d**, **a**, **c**).

c Students listen to the silly sentence and note down how many times they hear the sound (6). They can then repeat the sentence to help them remember this sound.

CD 4 Track 35

The letters 'c', 'k', 'qu'
Écoutez et répétez:
a carotte, content, kilo, que
b comment, kilomètre, quoi, quatorze, curieuse, cartable
c Un kangourou qui mange quinze kilos de carottes coûte cher.

119 Dossier-langue

pas de – not any

This explains the use of *de* instead of *du/de la/de l'/des* in the negative. The *Mangetout* cartoon on SB page 118 presents several examples of *pas de/d'*. Do some oral work by displaying an item on the board and saying, e.g. *Il y a du fromage*. Then remove it and ask *Et maintenant? Il n'y a pas de fromage*. Gradually hand the activity over to students.

For further practice, display several items (this could be the online version of Kim's game below) then remove one or two items and ask *Qu'est-ce qu'il n'y a pas?*

Presentation
Jeu de mémoire: Il y a des frites?

cm 9/4
La forme négative

119

3 Une recette
This activity provides further practice of the negative.

> **Solution:**
> *Il n'y a pas de sucre.*
> *Il n'y a pas de farine.*
> *Il n'y a pas de margarine et il n'y a pas d'œufs.*

gia 1 pp40–41

The negative (1) and (2)
Further practice of the negative.

156 Au choix

4 Le jeu de la carotte

157 Au choix

6 Les chiens et les chats

119

4 À table
This item contains some key phrases and vocabulary, which are practised in part **b** and should be learnt by heart by the majority of students.

a Students listen to the recording without looking at the text. Ask a few general questions, e.g. *C'est quel repas? Est-ce qu'on prend un dessert?* Then students listen with the text. To check understanding, ask what they would say (in French) in the following situations:
- say you'll have some water
- accept something you are offered
- say something is good
- say something is delicious
- say you don't like something very much
- say you've eaten enough of something
- say 'No thank you'
- say you'd like a banana.

b Students vary the core conversation, which should help them to learn the key phrases and vocabulary.

Tricolore 1 Teacher's Notes **177**

9E Des projets

CD 4 Track 36
À table

Alex dîne chez une famille française.
- Assieds-toi là, Alex, à côté de Laurent.
- Oui, madame.
- Qu'est-ce que tu prends comme boisson? Il y a de l'eau minérale et de la limonade.
- De l'eau, s'il vous plaît.

- Pour commencer, il y a du potage aux légumes.
- Bon appétit, tout le monde.
- Mmm! C'est bon, ça.
- Tu veux encore du potage?
- Oui, je veux bien.

- Voilà. Maintenant, il y a du poisson. Et comme légumes, il y a des pommes de terre et du chou-fleur.
- C'est délicieux, madame.
- Tu veux encore du poisson?
- Non, merci, j'ai assez mangé.
- Tu prends de la salade?
- Non, merci, je n'aime pas beaucoup ça.
- Comme dessert, il y a des fruits. Qu'est-ce que tu prends?
- Je voudrais une banane, s'il vous plaît. Merci.

119
French manners

This information box refers to some cultural differences in the use of 'please' and 'thank you'. Ask students if they are familiar with the letters RSVP at the bottom of an invitation and encourage them to work out the French words represented (*Répondez s'il vous plaît.*).

Worksheet
Deux réponses possibles

cm 9/5

À table

Worksheet
Plenaries (pages 118–119)

1 Find out from students how they remember the gender, spelling and pronunciation of the items of food and drink. They work in pairs then report back to the whole class. If necessary, provide some ideas to start them off, e.g. *du chou* – both end in *u* – and cabbage can be tough/tasty as a 'shoe'?; *omelette* – spell it rhythmically O–M–E … L–E … T–T–E.

2 Mid-unit review: This is a suitable point for a Unit Review. Students shut their books and take stock of what they have learnt so far in this unit: vocabulary for food and meals, differences between *du/de la/de l'/ des*, using the negative, discussing healthy eating.

9E Des projets   pages 120–121

- Plan some meals and some picnics

Grammaire	Stratégies	Phonétique
• Discuss what you are going to do (using *aller* + infinitive)	• None	• None

Resources

Audio: 2 *Un pique-nique un peu special!*; **3b** *Le concours "c'est bon pour la santé"*; **4a** *Faites des projets*; *Pique-nique à la plage* or CD 4, tracks 37 and 38, Student CD track 35
Copymasters: 9/6 *Qu'est-ce qu'on va faire?*
Worksheets: Starters and plenaries

Interactive activity: None
PowerPoint: *Aller* + infinitif (G); *Pique-nique à la plage* (song)
Grammar in Action: p42

Worksheet

Starters (pages 120–121)

1 *En groupes* Display a list of words in random order or hand this out on slips of paper (see online worksheet). Ask students to put these into five groups:

   le français, les mathématiques, la technologie; le déjeuner, le goûter, le dîner; des chaussures, une chemise, une veste; aime, adore, préfère; vert, petit, intéressant

2 *Complète les phrases* Display the following (see online worksheet). Give students a few minutes to read and work out the answers, then ask: *Le verbe numéro un va avec quelle phrase?* etc.

les verbes	les phrases
1 allons	a *Je … à Paris ce weekend.*
2 allez	b *Tu … au cinéma ce soir?*
3 vais	c *Mon frère … au bowling.*
4 vas	d *Nous … à la plage s'il fait beau.*
5 vont	e *Vous … aux magasins?*
6 va	f *Elles … au centre sportif.*

Solution:
1 *d,* **2** *e,* **3** *a,* **4** *b,* **5** *f,* **6** *c*

178   Tricolore 1 Teacher's Notes

9E Des projets

120

1 Réseau Tricolore

These messages on *Réseau Tricolore*, an imaginary social media network, contain several examples of the future using *aller* + infinitive. Students should first read through the messages for gist and say what they think they are about. The online worksheet below can be used to display the text initially and can accompany the *Dossier-langue* to highlight words like the infinitives and parts of *aller*.

Go through the true/false activity orally. To make it more interesting and involve all students, they could hold up a green card for *vrai* and a red one for *faux*. This also makes it easy to assess at a glance who has understood the text.

Solution:
1 *faux*, **2** *vrai*, **3** *vrai*, **4** *vrai*, **5** *faux*, **6** *faux*

Worksheet
Réseau Tricolore

120 Dossier-langue

The future – *aller* + infinitive

Go through this, helping students to work out the structure and meaning of *aller* + infinitive. Check that they remember how to recognise an infinitive.

Presentation
aller + infinitif

120

2 Un pique-nique un peu spécial!

Go through the introductory text and make sure all students know what the conversations will cover. Ask questions such as *Est-ce qu'il va faire beau samedi prochain? Quel temps va-t-il faire dimanche?* etc.

Ask a few quick questions about the pictures, e.g. *Le jambon, c'est quel numéro? Le numéro 6, c'est quoi?* etc. Students then listen to the recording and note down the items each person brings.

Solution:
Léa 3, 5 *(jambon + ananas)*; **Dominique** 7 *(poulet)*; **Chloé** 2, 6 *(tomates + oignons)*; **Vivienne** 1 *(fromage)*; **Hugo** 8 *(poisson/sardines)*; **Noah** 4 *(petits pois)*

CD 4 Track 37
Un pique-nique un peu spécial!

Chloé	Allô, c'est toi, Léa?
Léa	Oui, c'est moi. Salut, Chloé!
Chloé	Tu vas venir au pique-nique 'pizza'?
Léa	Oui, je vais venir. C'est une bonne idée.
Chloé	Qu'est-ce que tu vas apporter?
Léa	Euh, du jambon et de l'ananas pour une pizza hawaïenne. Ça va?
Chloé	Très bien! À samedi, alors.
……	
Chloé	Allô! C'est toi, Dominique?
Dom.	Oui, c'est moi, Chloé. Ça va?
Chloé	Oui, oui. Très bien. Dis-moi, Dominique, qu'est-ce que tu vas apporter pour le pique-nique?
Dom.	Ben, du poulet. Ça va, des morceaux de poulet?
Chloé	Des morceaux de poulet? C'est idéal!
Dom.	Et toi, Chloé? Qu'est-ce que tu vas mettre sur la pizza?
Chloé	Alors, moi, des tomates … et aussi des oignons.
Dom.	Ah bon! J'adore les oignons!
……	
Chloé	Salut! C'est Chloé à l'appareil. C'est Vivienne?
Viv.	Oui, oui, c'est moi, Vivienne. Tout va bien pour la pique-nique pizza?
Chloé	Oui, très bien.
Viv.	Moi, je vais apporter du fromage et Hugo va apporter du poisson.
Chloé	Ah, Hugo est là aussi! Génial! Alors toi, tu vas apporter du fromage, et Hugo du poisson. Quelle sorte de poisson?
Viv.	Je ne sais pas exactement. Des sardines, peut-être.
Chloé	Et ton frère, Noah, il vient aussi? Il va apporter quelque chose?
Viv.	Euh, oui. Il va venir! Mais il va apporter des petits pois!
Chloé	Des petits pois? C'est bon, sur les pizzas?
Viv.	Je ne sais pas. Mais Noah adore les petits pois, alors il pense que tout le monde les adore aussi.
Chloé	Ça va. À samedi, alors! Et bon appétit!
Viv.	Au revoir, Chloé. À samedi!

AfL

Follow-up for this activity could involve planning pizzas for different people, e.g. *une pizza pour les végétariens/ carnivores …* Students work in pairs or groups and present their planned pizza to the class. This can be used as an opportunity for peer assessment, with students agreeing the criteria first (e.g. range of vocabulary, accuracy of French, use of future, suitability of content) then giving a score. This makes them listen carefully and critically to each presentation.

This could be followed by a pair work discussion planning what to put in a lunch box (*panier-repas*).

9E Des projets

121

3 Le concours «c'est bon pour la santé»

This activity provides further practice of the future in the context of preparing healthy meals.

a Students read the text and answer structured questions using the future with *aller*.

Solution:
1 *Comme hors-d'œuvre, elle va manger du potage aux légumes.*
2 *Comme légumes, elle va prendre des carottes et des oignons.*
3 *Comme plat principal, Julien va préparer une grosse omelette avec du jambon et des petits pois.*
4 *Ses frères vont manger des frites avec l'omelette.*
5 *Ils vont manger du fromage avant le dessert.*
6 *Ses frères vont probablement manger du gâteau.*
7 *Oui, Marine va manger sainement.*
8 *Non, ses frères ne vont pas manger sainement.*

b Students look at an example of a healthy meal. Ask students questions similar to the ones in part **a** and discuss with them whether they think this is a healthy meal. *La salade, c'est bon pour la santé? Tu aimes les fruits? Est-ce que Max et sa sœur vont manger du fromage? Et de la viande?* etc. *Alors, le repas, c'est bon pour la santé?* Take a vote in the class. Students then listen to the recording and complete the sentences.

Solution:
1 *de la salade*, **2** *des carottes, du chou et des brocolis*, **3** *des pommes ou des poires et peut-être du raisin*, **4** *viande/poisson*, **5** *des lapins*

CD 4 Track 38
Le concours «c'est bon pour la santé»

– Alors Clémentine, félicitations! Ton repas, c'est vraiment très bon pour la santé. Tu vas préparer beaucoup de légumes, n'est-ce pas?
– Oui, c'est ça. Pour commencer, je vais préparer de la salade. Max adore ça.
– Oui, et comme plat principal?
– Alors, comme plat principal, Max et sa sœur vont manger des carottes, du chou et des brocolis.
– Mais il n'y a pas de viande et il n'y a pas de poisson?
– Ah non, ils n'aiment pas ça.
– Ah bon. Et comme dessert, ils vont manger des fruits, non?
– Oui. Je vais préparer une grande sélection de fruits: des pommes ou des poires et peut-être du raisin.
– Mais, dis-moi, Clémentine. Tu es sûre qu'ils vont manger tout ça, tous ces fruits et légumes?
– Oui, oui. Ils vont adorer tout ça.
– C'est qui, Max? C'est ton ami?
– Ah non. Max et sa sœur, ce sont mes deux lapins. Ils sont mignons!

121

4 Faites des projets

a In this activity students discuss a meal they would make for the person described.

Read through the text and explain any new vocabulary. They then work in pairs (or small groups) to discuss what they would offer for each course. Brainstorm suitable questions and display them as a reminder, e.g. *Qu'est-ce qu'on va manger comme hors-d'œuvre? Il/Elle va aimer le fromage? Le poisson, c'est bon pour la santé?*

Remind students that the answer to the question *Est-ce qu'il/elle va manger du fromage?* will require *de* rather than *du* if it is negative: *Non, il/elle ne va pas manger de fromage.*

b As extension, students discuss a weekend menu for family or friends, then they write out the menu.

Students could refer to *Au choix* exercise 7 (SB page 157) for ideas. They could also look back at the writing strategy on SB page 116 to use texts to develop their own writing and adapt a text to their own needs.

cm 9/6   AfL

Qu'est-ce qu'on va faire?

> Interactive activity

On va manger

gia 1 p42

Verbs followed by an infinitive

Further practice of *aller* + infinitive.

> Worksheet

Plenaries (pages 120–121)

1 Show visuals of some of the items of vocabulary that students have met in this unit (and also from earlier units). Which, if any, do students find hard to remember? Is it easy to remember the gender? Discuss as a class ways of memorising the more difficult words.

2 Discuss what students have been able to include in their *Dossier personnel* at this stage of the unit. Students could assess how far they have come in the last 3 units (before moving on to the final *Rappel* section of the book) and summarise what they now know.

9F La fête autour du monde   pages 122–123

- Practise reading longer passages
- Learn more about festival foods

Grammaire	Stratégies	Phonétique
• None	• Reading for gist and detail • Using clues to work out meaning (5)	• None

Resources

Audio: None
Copymasters: 9/7 *Tu comprends?*, 9/8 *Sommaire*
Worksheets: Starters and plenaries; Reading for gist and detail (Strat); *Autour du monde* (R)
e-book: *Métallo*

Interactive activity: Classroom commands (V)
PowerPoint: None
Grammar in Action: None

Worksheet

Starters (pages 122–123)

1 *Vrai ou faux?* Display a series of statements (see online worksheet). When you read out each statement, students have to hold up a green card if it is true and a red card if it is false.

Statements:

Le chou est un fruit. [F]

Les carottes sont des légumes. [V]

Normalement, on mange le petit déjeuner l'après-midi, à cinq heures. [F]

Il n'y a pas de fruit dans une tarte aux pommes. [F]

La limonade est une boisson froide. [V]

Les lapins sont des légumes. [F]

Normalement, on prend le déjeuner à midi. [V]

Les végétariens mangent beaucoup de poulet. [F]

Manger beaucoup de chips, c'est bon pour la santé. [F]

Les Français prennent le dîner entre sept et huit heures du soir. [V]

2 *En groupes* Display a list of words (see online worksheet) in random order and ask students to put these into six groups:

un peu, beaucoup, pas trop; écris, lis, choisis; de l'eau, du jus, du lait; aller, manger, prendre; inventez, chantez, travaillez; des tartines, des croissants, des toasts

122

1 On parle des fêtes

This page practises reading harder texts and provides tips on how to approach longer texts. The descriptions cover three different festivals in the francophone world. Work through the various hints and strategies before students tackle each text and answer the questions.

Students who are familiar with Eid, Thanksgiving and Diwali could give more information. The Islamic and Hindu calendars are different from the Gregorian calendar used in Europe, so the months do not entirely correspond. Ramadan can occur at various times of the year. Diwali is in October or November.

a Students answer comprehension questions in English.

Solution:

1 new clothes, **2** a year, **3** work, **4** rice, milk, sugar, almonds, pistachio nuts and sultanas, **5** They use sticks and the music gets faster and faster.

b As extension, they find the French for key expressions in the texts.

As follow-up, they could read straight through all the texts, or take it in turns to read a paragraph aloud.

Solution:

1 *pendant trente jours*, **2** *pendant la journée*, **3** *à la fin*, **4** *du curry d'agneau*, **5** *la première récolte*, **6** *avec de la dinde*, **7** *de la tarte à la citrouille*, **8** *au milieu de*, **9** *fait avec du riz*, **10** *de plus en plus vite*

Worksheet

Autour du monde

122 Stratégies

Reading for gist and detail

This reading strategy focuses on the first two stages of tackling a longer text – reading for gist, then reading for more detail. The online worksheet can be used for further reinforcement.

Worksheet

Reading for gist and detail

9F La fête autour du monde

122 Stratégies

Using clues to work out meaning (5)

Encourage students to try to work out meaning from clues such as cognates and context, then refer them to the *Glossaire* and/or dictionaries to find or check the meaning of any words they need to know.

As a memorisation strategy and a way of building up vocabulary, they could write down five new key words or phrases which they think would be useful, then try to use them in future.

157 Au choix

7 On déjeune au collège Missy

Presentation

Chantez! Pique-nique à la plage

cm 9/7

Tu comprends?

Interactive activity

Rue Danton: Les courses à l'hypermarché

Interactive activity

Vocabulaire de classe (9)

Worksheet

Presentation

Métallo

12 cm 9/8

Sommaire

A summary of the main language and structures of the unit, also provided on copymaster for reference.

Interactive activity

Vocabulaire (9)

Interactive activity

Quiz – Unités 8 et 9

Worksheet

Plenaries (pages 122–123)

1 Students think about how they read for gist in understanding texts with unfamiliar language, e.g. *La fête autour du monde.* Discuss useful strategies, e.g. similarity to English, context, type of word, need to know, etc.

2 Students produce a spider diagram of everything learnt in the unit. This could be in groups or as a whole-class activity with students contributing to the spider diagram on the board.

Unité 9 Consolidation and assessment

Épreuves Unité 9

These worksheets can be used for an informal test of listening, reading and writing or for extra practice. For general notes on the *Épreuves*, see TB page xv.

cm 9/9

Écouter L

A Le pique-nique

Solution:
1 f, **2** j, **3** b, **4** a, **5** h, **6** g, **7** c, **8** e
(mark /7)

CD 4 Track 39

Le pique-nique
Qu'est-ce qu'il y a pour le pique-nique?
1 Il y a du pain, du pain,
2 du jambon, du jambon,
3 du fromage, du fromage,
4 des tomates, des tomates,
5 des œufs, des œufs,
6 des pommes, des pommes,
7 des raisins, des raisins.
8 Et comme boisson? Comme boisson, il y a de la limonade. Ah bon, j'aime bien la limonade.

B Le petit déjeuner

Solution:

	bread etc.	cereal	juice	coffee	milk	choc	tea
1	✓			✓			
2	✓						✓
3	✓	✓	✓				
4		✓				✓	
5	✓				✓		
6	✓	✓		✓			

(mark /6) 1/2 mark per correct tick

CD 4 Track 40

Le petit déjeuner
1 – Au petit déjeuner, je prends du café au lait et des tartines avec du beurre.
– Alors, tu prends du café comme boisson et du pain avec du beurre, c'est tout?
– Oui, c'est tout.
2 – Le matin, je prends des tartines avec du beurre et de la confiture et un bol de thé.
– Tu prends du thé comme boisson et du pain avec du beurre et de la confiture, c'est ça?
– Oui, c'est ça.
3 – Au petit déjeuner, je prends du jus de fruit et des céréales. Et je prends aussi des tartines beurrées.
– Comme boisson, tu prends un jus de fruit, et avec ça tu prends des céréales et des tartines avec du beurre.
4 – Et moi, je prends un chocolat chaud comme boisson et je mange des céréales.
– Alors, tu prends un chocolat chaud et des céréales, c'est tout?
– Oui, c'est tout.
5 – Le matin, je prends des tartines avec du beurre et de la confiture et je bois du lait.
– Bon, tu prends du lait comme boisson et tu manges du pain avec du beurre et de la confiture, c'est ça?
– Oui, c'est ça.
6 – Au petit déjeuner, je mange des céréales et des tartines avec du beurre et je bois du café.
– Alors, comme boisson, tu prends un café, et avec ça tu prends des céréales et des tartines avec du beurre.
– Oui, c'est ça.

C À table

Solution:
1 a, **2** c, **3** b, **4** a, **5** b, **6** a, **7** b, **8** a
(mark /7)

CD 4 Track 41

À table
– Assieds-toi là, Claire, à côté de Sophie.
– Oui, madame.
– Qu'est-ce que tu prends comme boisson? Il y a de la limonade et de l'eau.
– De la limonade, s'il vous plaît.
– Pour commencer, il y a de la salade aux tomates.
– Bon appétit, tout le monde.
– Mmm! C'est bon, ça.
...
– Voilà, maintenant, il y a de l'omelette au fromage. Et comme légumes, il y a des pommes de terre et du chou.
– C'est délicieux, madame.
– Tu veux encore de l'omelette?
– Non, merci, j'ai assez mangé.
...
– Tu veux de la salade?
– Oui, s'il vous plaît.
– Et comme fromage, il y a du Camembert. Tu veux du fromage, Claire?
– Non, merci, désolée mais je n'aime pas beaucoup ça.
– Comme dessert, il y a des fruits. Qu'est-ce que tu prends?
– Je voudrais une pêche, s'il vous plaît. Merci.

Tricolore 1 Teacher's Notes

Unité 9 Consolidation and assessment

cm 9/10

Lire R

A Le déjeuner

> **Solution:**
> **1** a, **2** f, **3** b, **4** d, **5** c, **6** h, **7** g, **8** e
> **(mark /7)**

B Mon repas idéal

> **Solution:**
> **1** F, **2** V, **3** F, **4** F, **5** F, **6** F, **7** F
> **(mark /6)**

C Une conversation

> **Solution:**
> **1** d, **2** h, **3** a (accept e), **4** f, **5** b (accept e), **6** e (accept b), **7** c, **8** g
> **(mark /7)**

cm 9/11

Écrire et grammaire W

A Une liste

> **Solution:**
> **1** du pain, **2** du beurre, **3** de la confiture, **4** des carottes, **5** de l'eau (minérale), **6** des pommes
> **(mark /5)** ½ mark for correct partitive, ½ mark for correct noun

B Qu'est-ce qu'on prend?

> **Solution:**
> **1** prenez, **2** prenons, **3** prennent, **4** prend, **5** prends, **6** prends
> **(mark /5)** 1 mark per correct answer

C Ça ne va pas!

> **Solution:**
> **1** Il ne fait pas beau. **2** Nous ne mangeons pas de viande. **3** Mes amis n'ont pas d'animaux à la maison. **4** Je ne suis pas content.
> **(mark /6)** 1 for correct verb, 1 for correct ne ... pas

D Mon repas idéal

> **Solution:**
> This is an open-ended task.
> **(mark /4)** give 1 mark for each item listed

Rappel 4

124–125

This section can be used at any point after *Unité* 9 for revision and consolidation. It provides reading and writing activities which are self-instructional and can be used by students working individually for homework or during cover lessons.

124

1 Où sont les voyelles?

> **Solution:**
> **1** juillet July, **2** novembre November, **3** septembre September, **4** avril April **5** mai May, **6** l'anglais English, **7** l'histoire history, **8** la géographie geography, **9** la musique music, **10** la technologie technology, **11** vert green, **12** rouge red, **13** jaune yellow, **14** noir black, **15** blanc white, **16** le jogging tracksuit bottoms, **17** la chemise shirt, **18** le pantalon trousers, **19** les chaussettes socks, **20** la cravate tie

124

2 Des listes

> **Solution:**
> **1** mercredi, **2** le soir, **3** il est une heure et quart, **4** troisième, **5** l'hiver, **6** le déjeuner

124

3 Masculin, féminin

> **Solution:**
>
> | masculin | féminin |
> |---|---|
> | le matin | une carotte |
> | le fromage | une omelette |
> | le dessin | une heure |
> | un lapin | une pomme |
> | le potage | la confiture |
> | un village | la salade |
> | | la limonade |
> | | une galette |

124

4 C'est quel verbe?

> **Solution:**
> **1** J'ai, **2** j'aime, **3** Je vais, **4** je prends, **5** je suis, **6** j'aime, je vais, **7** je prends, je suis, **8** j'ai

124

5 Un e-mail

> **Solution:**
> **1** mon, **2** mes, **3** ma, **4** mes, **5** leur, **6** leurs, **7** nos, **8** ton

Unité 9 Consolidation and assessment

125

6 Un repas en morceaux

Solution:
1 *jambon*, 2 *poisson*, 3 *carottes*, 4 *salade*, 5 *fromage*, 6 *gâteau*, 7 *limonade*

125

7 La journée de Mangetout

Solution:
a a *entre*, b *reste*, c *commence*, d *mange*, e *retourne*, f *cherche*, g *pense*, h *chasse*
b 1 b, 2 a, 3 f, 4 c, 5 h, 6 g, 7 d, 8 e

125

8 Questions et réponses

Solution:
1 c, 2 g, 3 e, 4 b, 5 a, 6 j, 7 d, 8 f, 9 h, 10 i

125

9 À toi!

This is an open-ended task.

Au choix

156 Au choix

1 Qu'est-ce que c'est?

Students supply the vowels to identify items of food and drink. This could be done orally first.

Solution:
1 *de la viande*, 2 *de l'omelette*, 3 *du poulet*, 4 *des petits pois*, 5 *des pommes de terre*, 6 *une banane*, 7 *un yaourt*, 8 *de l'eau*, 9 *du melon*

156 Au choix

2 Un mélange

Students write the names of food and drink for different courses, with the partitive article.

Solution:
1 *du jambon, du pâté*, 2 *de la viande, de l'omelette*, 3 *des carottes, des oignons*, 4 *des tartes aux fruits, des yaourts*, 5 *de l'eau, du vin*, 6 *des bananes, des oranges*

156 Au choix

3 Le plat favori

This activity provides revision of animals and practice of the partitive article.

Solution:
1 *La souris mange du fromage.*
2 *L'oiseau mange du pain.*
3 *Le cheval mange du sucre.*
4 *Le chien mange de la viande.*
5 *Le perroquet mange une tomate.*
6 *Le cochon d'Inde mange une pomme.*
7 *Le chat mange du poisson.*
8 *Le lapin mange des carottes.*

156 Au choix

4 Le jeu de la carotte

First check that students recognise and remember the words for all the items illustrated. The clues to the correct answers are in the negative. If some students need help, write the two alternatives on the board and work out one or two answers with them, letting them finish alone.

Solution:
1 *sucre*, 2 *fromage*, 3 *beurre*, 4 *poisson*, 5 *chocolats*, 6 *carotte*, 7 *viande*

157 Au choix   AfL

5 Mes repas

This pairwork game could be used to practise meals and food. It is suitable as an assessment task. Discuss spread 9B objectives with students and emphasise that this task will allow them to demonstrate their skills.

a Each student writes down (secretly) three things to eat and one thing to drink for each meal, e.g. *Au petit déjeuner, je prends du lait, un croissant, du beurre et de la confiture.*

b Students take turns to ask each other questions to find out what they have chosen for one of their meals (see example). This could be done as a game to see who is first to discover their partner's choices.

Students who are not good at writing could draw pictures of the food and drink they choose or use some of the mini-flashcards made from CM 9/1.

157 Au choix

6 Les chiens et les chats

This sequencing task provides practice of the formation of negative sentences. If help is needed, suggest that students pick out the verb and then 'surround' it by *ne ... pas*. The rest of the sentence should then be easily guessable.

Tricolore 1 Teacher's Notes 185

Unité 9 Consolidation and assessment

Solution:

a 1 *Les chats ne jouent pas avec les enfants.*
2 *Les chats ne sont pas intelligents.*
3 *Les chats ne mangent pas bien.*
4 *Les chats ne restent pas à la maison.*
5 *Les chats n'aiment pas les enfants.*

b 1 *Les chiens ne sont pas indépendants.*
2 *Les chiens ne sont pas intelligents.*
3 *Les chiens ne mangent pas bien.*
4 *Les chiens ne respectent pas les jardins.*
5 *Les chiens n'aiment pas les autres animaux.*

157 Au choix

7 On déjeune au collège Missy

This item is based on authentic school dinner menus from the *Collège Missy* in La Rochelle. Besides doing the linked tasks, pupils could discuss these menus, asking each other which they would choose.

a Students look at the menus and pick out the information listed.

Solution:

1 4, 2 starter, main course, cheese, dessert,
3 1, 4 4, 5 Wednesday (no school that day)

b Students complete the sentences referring to the menus.

Solution:

1 *une salade composée,* 2 *haricots (au beurre),*
3 *poisson, lentilles,* 4 *mardi,* 5 *potage (aux légumes),* 6 *mardi,* 7 *fruits,* 8 *jambon*

c Students listen to the short dialogues and decide which day's menu is being discussed.

Solution:

1 *jeudi,* 2 *jeudi,* 3 *lundi,* 4 *vendredi,* 5 *mardi,*
6 *vendredi,* 7 *vendredi,* 8 *jeudi*

CD 4 Track 42

On déjeune au collège Missy

1 – Qu'est-ce qu'on va manger aujourd'hui?
– Alors, de l'agneau comme plat principal – un kebab d'agneau. Et puis du fromage.
2 – On va manger un dessert aujourd'hui?
– Bien sûr! On va manger de la mousse au chocolat.
– Mmm! J'aime beaucoup ça!
3 – Qu'est-ce qu'on va manger comme plat principal?
– Du poulet. Tu aimes ça?
– Oui, j'aime beaucoup le poulet.
4 – Il fait froid ce matin. On va manger une entrée chaude?
– Oui, il y a du potage au menu, du potage aux légumes.
– Fantastique!
5 – Nous allons manger du poisson aujourd'hui?
– Oui, c'est ça.
– Avec des frites?
– Ah non! Avec des lentilles.
6 – Ah bon! On va manger du steak aujourd'hui. J'adore ça.
– Oui, oui, mais c'est du steak haché.
– Oui, je sais. C'est avec quoi?
– Avec des pommes de terre.
7 – J'adore les fruits. On va manger un fruit comme dessert aujourd'hui?
– Regardons le menu … Ah oui, il y a des fruits. Moi, je vais choisir une banane. J'adore les bananes.
– Excellent!
8 – On va nous servir de la charcuterie cette semaine?
– Oui, regarde. Voilà!
– Ah bon! Et des petits pois avec de la viande comme plat principal. Délicieux!

d Students make up a school lunch menu for two days.

Copymasters

cm 9/1

On mange et on boit

The mini-flashcards can be used for a number of games,

e.g. *Le jeu des sept familles, Je pense à quelque chose,* etc. (see TB page xix).

cm 9/2

C'est quel mot?

This copymaster provides practice of genders and the partitive with a slightly wider range of food and drink vocabulary.

1 Masculin/féminin

Practice in identifying genders.

Solution:

a m: *un repas, un yaourt, le petit déjeuner, le dîner, le goûter, le poisson*

f: *une tarte, la pomme, la salade, une banane, la viande, une poire*

b *une boisson (f), le petit pois (m), le légume (m), une banane (f), une carotte (f), un croissant (m), le sandwich (m), le gâteau (m)*

Tricolore 1 Teacher's Notes

Unité 9 Consolidation and assessment

2 Un tableau

Students identify the gender, then complete a grid with the appropriate articles and possessive adjective.

3 Mon repas favori

Productive practice of the above language.

> **Solution:**
> 1 *Mon repas favori est le goûter. Je mange du pain avec de la confiture ou un fruit et je bois un chocolat chaud ou un jus de fruit.*
> 2 *Mon repas favori est le dîner. Je prends du pâté et comme plat principal, du poisson avec des petits pois. Mon dessert favori est la tarte aux pommes et ma boisson favorite est le jus d'orange.*

cm 9/3

Des jeux de vocabulaire

This copymaster provides a range of activities practising food and drink vocabulary. There is an incline of difficulty.

> **Solution:**
> 1 *Mots mêlés*

o	p	ê	c	h	e	r	a
i	o	e	l	o	ç	b	i
g	i	e	a	u	v	a	m
n	r	a	i	s	i	n	è
o	e	u	t	ê	n	a	h
n	p	a	s	r	u	n	g
c	a	r	o	t	t	e	j
d	é	j	e	u	n	e	r

> 2 *Un serpent*
>   a *potage, viande, pommes de terre, salade, yaourt*
>   b *limonade*
> 3 *Mots croisés*
> **Horizontalement:**
> 1 *délicieux,* 6 *le,* 8 *va,* 9 *eau,* 11 *viande,* 12 *sucre,* 14 *sel,* 16 *beurre,* 17 *un*
> **Verticalement:**
> 1 *déjeuner,* 2 *légumes,* 3 *café,* 4 *un,* 5 *de,* 6 *la,* 7 *frites,* 8 *vin,* 10 *melon,* 13 *chou,* 15 *du*

cm 9/4

forme négative

s copymaster practises the negative.

> **Solution:**
> 1 *Des expressions utiles*
>   1 *e,* 2 *a,* 3 *d,* 4 *c,* 5 *b*

> 2 *À la cantine*
>   1 *e,* 2 *d,* 3 *c,* 4 *a,* 5 *f,* 6 *g,* 7 *b*
> 3 *Luc et Lucie*
>   1 *d,* 2 *f,* 3 *h,* 4 *a,* 5 *b,* 6 *e,* 7 *c,* 8 *g*
> 4 *Des phrases*
> In this open-ended task, students make up their own sentences using some negative expressions.

cm 9/5

À table

This provides further practice of what to say when having a meal with a family.

1 Questions et réponses

In task 1, students match the questions to the answers.

> **Solution:**
> 1 *g,* 2 *e,* 3 *c,* 4 *d,* 5 *f,* 6 *a,* 7 *b*

2 On déjeune

In task 2, students practise a dialogue with different variations.

cm 9/6   AfL

Qu'est-ce qu'on va faire?

1 *aller* to go/to be going to

Students revise the verb *aller* and complete the paradigm.

2 Chez la diseuse de bonne aventure

a They then read the fortune teller's predictions and complete the *vrai ou faux* section.

> **Solution:**
> 1 *vrai,* 2 *vrai,* 3 *faux,* 4 *vrai,* 5 *faux,* 6 *faux*

b This time students complete the sentences about the future and underline the infinitives.

> **Solution:**
> 1 *va vivre,* 2 *vont aller,* 3 *va perdre,* 4 *vont avoir,* 5 *va gagner,* 6 *va arriver*

cm 9/7

Tu comprends?

Students work alone on these listening activities.

1 Le déjeuner

> **Solution:**
> 1 *c,* 2 *b,* 3 *c,* 4 *b,* 5 *c,* 6 *b*

Tricolore 1 Teacher's Notes **187**

Unité 9 Consolidation and assessment

🔊 CD 4 Track 43

Le déjeuner
– Qu'est-ce qu'on mange aujourd'hui au déjeuner?
– Pour commencer, il y a du jambon.
– Alors comme entrée, il y a du jambon.
– Oui, et comme plat principal, il y a du poisson.
– Mmm, j'aime bien le poisson. Et comme légumes?
– Comme légumes, il y a des petits pois.
– Des petits pois, oui.
– Et ensuite, il y a du fromage.
– Ah, j'aime bien le fromage. Et comme dessert?
– Comme dessert, il y a un gâteau au chocolat.
– Un gâteau au chocolat, chouette!
– Et comme boisson, il y a de l'eau minérale.
– De l'eau minérale, bien.

2 Qu'est-ce qu'ils prennent?

Solution:
A 1 b, **2** a, **3** g, **4** h, **5** d, **6** e
B 1 f, **2** d, **3** g, **4** b, **5** a, **6** c

🔊 CD 4 Track 44–45

Qu'est-ce qu'ils prennent?
A Des boissons
1 – Qu'est-ce que vous prenez, comme boisson?
 – Je prends un café, s'il te plaît.
2 – Pour moi, un thé.
 – Un thé, oui.
3 – Et Thomas, qu'est-ce qu'il prend?
 – Alors pour Thomas, du lait, s'il te plaît.
 – Un verre de lait, oui.
4 – Et toi, Nicole?
 – Pour moi, un Coca, s'il te plaît.
 – Un Coca, d'accord.
5 – Et toi, Luc?
 – Un jus d'orange, s'il te plaît.
6 – Très bien, et pour moi, un chocolat chaud.

B Des fruits
 – Comme dessert, il y a des fruits, alors qu'est-ce que vous prenez?
1 – Pour moi, des raisins, s'il vous plaît.
2 – Moi, je prends une pêche.
3 – Mmm, moi j'adore les fraises, alors je prends des fraises.
4 – Moi, je voudrais une poire.
5 – Pour moi, une pomme, s'il vous plaît.
6 – Et moi, je prends une banane.

3 Réponse positive ou négative?

Solution:
1 ✓, **2** ✗, **3** ✗, **4** ✗, **5** ✓, **6** ✗, **7** ✗, **8** ✗

cm 9/8

Sommaire
A summary of the main language and structures of the unit on copymaster for reference.

Unité 10

Tricolore 1 Unité 10 Amuse-toi bien!   Pages 126–141

10A On fait du sport? pages 126–127		
• Talk about different sports		
Grammaire	**Stratégies**	**Phonétique**
• Revise the verb *faire*	• Translating from French to English	• None
Resources		
Audio: 1a *Qu'est-ce qu'on fait?*, or CD 5, track 2 **Copymasters:** 10/1 *Faire* **Worksheets:** Starters and plenaries; The present tense of *faire* (G)		**Interactive activity:** *Faire* (G) **PowerPoint:** None **Grammar in Action:** p43

10B Tu aimes la musique? pages 128–129		
• Talk about music		
Grammaire	**Stratégies**	**Phonétique**
• Use *jouer de* + instrument	• None	• None
Resources		
Audio: 2a *La musique, c'est ma passion*, or CD 5, track 3 **Copymasters:** 10/2 *Grands mots croisés: la musique* **Worksheets:** Starters and plenaries; *Faites de la musique* (R)		**Interactive activity:** *Les loisirs* (L) **PowerPoint:** None **Grammar in Action:** None

10C Mes passe-temps pages 130–131		
• Talk about leisure activities • Read and write messages about leisure		
Grammaire	**Stratégies**	**Phonétique**
• Use *jouer à* + sport/games	• Adding interest to your writing	• The letters 'un', 'um'
Resources		
Audio: 3a *Des interviews*, or CD 5, track 5 **Copymasters:** 10/3 *Les loisirs*, 10/4 *Manon et Clément* **Worksheets:** Starters and plenaries; *Mes loisirs* (W)		**Interactive activity:** *Le mail de Sylvain* (R) **Ph** The letters 'un', 'um', or CD 5, track 4 **PowerPoint:** Kim's game: *Les loisirs* **Grammar in Action:** pp44–45

10D La semaine dernière pages 132–133		
• Talk about some recent activities		
Grammaire	**Stratégies**	**Phonétique**
• Nouns and adjectives • Recognise and use some phrases about the past	• None	• None
Resources		
Audio: 1 *Samedi dernier*; 5 *La semaine dernière*, or CD 5, tracks 6 and 7 **Copymasters:** 10/5 *La semaine dernière* **Worksheets:** Starters and plenaries; The present and perfect tenses (G)		**Interactive activity:** None **PowerPoint:** *Présent et passé* (G) **Grammar in Action:** pp48–49

10E Au parc d'attractions pages 134–135		
• Find out about Astérix and the Parc Astérix • Use the 24-hour clock		
Grammaire	**Stratégies**	**Phonétique**
• None	• Translating from French to English	• The letter 'x'
Resources		
Audio: 3 *24 heures*, or CD 5, track 9 **Copymasters:** 10/6 *24 heures* **Worksheets:** Starters and plenaries		**Interactive activity:** *C'est quand?* (L) **Ph** The letter 'x', or CD 5, track 8 **PowerPoint:** None **Grammar in Action:** p46

Key language

10F Une journée exceptionnelle pages 136–137		
• Describe a special day		
Grammaire	Stratégies	Phonétique
• Learn how to say 'I went'	• Planning your writing	• None
Resources		

Audio: 4 *Tu as passé un bon weekend?*; 6 *Une journée à Paris*, or CD 5, tracks 10 and 11
Copymasters: 10/7 *Qu'est-ce que tu as fait?*
Worksheets: Starters and plenaries; Translating from French to English (Strat); *Une carte postale* (G); *Ma journée idéale* (W)

Interactive activity: *Une journée un peu différente* (R)
PowerPoint: None
Grammar in Action: p47

10G Les loisirs pages 136–137		
• Talk about leisure in general		
Grammaire	Stratégies	Phonétique
• None	• Learning and revising vocabulary	• The letters '-sion', '-tion'
Resources		

Audio: *Samedi, on part en vacances*, or CD 5, track 17
Copymasters: 10/8 *Tu comprends?*, 10/9 *Sommaire*
Worksheets: Starters and plenaries
e-book: *Les vacances de Margot*

Interactive activity: Classroom commands (V)
Ph The letters '-sion', '-tion', or CD 5, track 12
Video: *En musique*
PowerPoint: *Samedi, on part en vacances* (song)
Grammar in Action: None

Key language

Sports (10A)

Est-ce que tu aimes le sport?
Je fais …
du cyclisme/du vélo.
du roller.
du skate.
du ski.
du VTT.
de la danse.
de la gymnastique.
de la natation.
de la planche à voile.
de la voile.
de l'équitation.
des promenades.
Je joue …
au basket.
au volley.

Music (10B)

Est-ce que tu aimes la musique?
Je joue …
du clavier.
du piano.
du violon.
de la batterie.
de la flute (à bec).
de la guitare.
de la trompette.
du violoncelle.
du saxophone.
J'aime la musique, mais je ne joue pas d'un instrument.

Other free time activities (10C)

Est-ce que tu fais autre chose?
Je fais …
du dessin.
de la peinture.
du théâtre.
de la photo.
Je joue …
sur l'ordinateur.
à des jeux vidéo.
aux cartes.
aux échecs.
J'aime lire.

Time expressions (10D to 10G)

samedi dernier
le weekend dernier
la semaine dernière
le matin
l'après-midi
le soir
d'abord
puis
ensuite
plus tard

24-hour clock (10E)

Visiting a theme park (10E)

un parc d'attractions
C'est situé près de …
C'est pour … (les enfants et les adultes).
C'est ouvert … (tous les jours en été).
L'entrée coûte … (35 euros).
C'est gratuit …

Perfect tense expressions (10F)

Tu as passé un bon weekend?
J'ai fait … (de la natation).
J'ai joué … (au football).
Je suis allé(e) … (au cinéma).

10A On fait du sport? pages 126–127

- Talk about different sports

Grammaire	Stratégies	Phonétique
• Revise the verb *faire*	• Translating from French to English (4)	• None

Resources

Audio: 1a *Qu'est-ce qu'on fait?*, or CD 5, track 2 **Copymasters:** 10/1 *Faire* **Worksheets:** Starters and plenaries; The present tense of *faire* (G)	**Interactive activity:** *Faire* (G) **PowerPoint:** None **Grammar in Action:** p43

Worksheet

Starters (pages 126–127)

1 *Chaque mot à sa place* Display the following task. Give students one minute to read and work out the answers, then ask several students to give the number of the box before confirming the correct answer.
Quelle est la bonne boîte pour chaque mot?
le jour (4), juin (5), jouez (2), jeudi (1), jaune (3)

1	2	3	4	5
dimanche	joues	vert	le mois	janvier
lundi	jouent	rouge	la semaine	juillet

2 *Quel verbe?* Display the following:
a *Je … mes devoirs.*
b *Il … beau aujourd'hui.*
c *Nous … de l'informatique.*
d *Vous … du shopping?*
e *Ils … du sport.*
1 faisons **2** fait **3** font **4** fais **5** faites
Give students one minute to read and work out the answers, then ask for them collectively or randomly, e.g.
– *Le verbe numéro un va avec quelle phrase?*
– *Nous faisons de l'informatique.*
– *Oui, c'est ça. C'est la phrase 'c'.*

Solution:
1 c, **2** b, **3** e, **4** a, **5** d

Introduction
Go through the objectives for this spread.

Interactive activity

Les loisirs

🔊 126

1 Qu'est-ce qu'on fait?

Go through the article, reading the captions and teaching the new words (*faire de la voile/de la planche à voile/du VTT/des promenades*) and asking questions, e.g.
Qu'est-ce qu'on fait comme sport dans la photo D?

Ask volunteers to read out different captions and ask a question of the class. For reinforcement, play a game such as *Jeu de mémoire* (this could be a group activity, each group being asked in turn to name one of the activities described until all have been mentioned), *Effacez!* or *Le jeu des mimes* (see TB page xvii).

a Students listen and write down the letter of the photo illustrating the sport mentioned.

Solution:
1 G, **2** F, **3** C, **4** A, **5** H, **6** E, **7** D, **8** B

🔊 CD 5 Track 2

Qu'est-ce qu'on fait?

1 – Qu'est-ce que vous faites comme sport, monsieur?
   – Moi, je fais des promenades, euh, des promenades avec mon chien.
2 – Qu'est-ce que vous faites comme sport, mademoiselle?
   – Je fais de l'équitation. J'adore les chevaux, mais je ne suis pas très sportive!
3 – Et toi, Christine, toi et ton frère, vous faites du sport?
   – Oui, oui. En été, nous faisons de la planche à voile.
   – Il y a un grand lac près d'ici où on fait de la planche à voile.
4 – Est-ce que vous faites du sport, mademoiselle?
   – Oui, je fais de la natation. Je vais à la piscine tous les samedis.
5 – Est-ce que vous faites du sport, les garçons?
   – Oui, nous faisons du skate.
   – Du skate. Où faites-vous ça?
   – Au centre sportif, c'est très populaire.
6 – Qu'est-ce que tu fais comme sports, Lucie?
   – Je fais du roller avec mes copines.
   – Ah, le patin à roulettes, tu aimes ça?
   – J'adore ça. On va très vite, c'est fantastique!
7 – Est-ce que vous faites du sport en famille, madame?
   – Nous faisons du vélo. Ça, c'est un sport qu'on fait ensemble. C'est bien.
8 – Quel est ton sport préféré, Richard?
   – Pour moi, c'est la voile. J'aime beaucoup faire de la voile avec mes cousins. C'est amusant!

b For extension, students choose one photo and write three sentences about it.

Tricolore 1 Teacher's Notes

10B Tu aimes la musique?

📖 127   **AfL**

2 Qu'est-ce qu'ils font?

Students match up captions and pictures. Check the answers orally to give practice of the different parts of *faire* as well as names of sports. As it links with the spread objectives, it could be used for assessment. Discuss with students how they can achieve the learning objectives.

Solution:
1 c, **2** b, **3** f, **4** e, **5** a, **6** d

📖 127 Stratégies

Translating from French to English (4)

Students will be familiar with using parts of the verb *faire* (presented in full in *Unité* 8). This focuses on the many expressions using *faire* and how these are best translated into English.

📖 127

3 Français/Anglais

Students match French and English meanings.

Solution:
1 b, **2** d, **3** f, **4** c, **5** a, **6** e

📖 127   **AfL**

4 On fait de la voile

a Students supply the missing parts of *faire*. This activity could be used for assessment after a review of the spread objectives.

Solution:
1 fais, **2** fais, **3** fait, **4** font, **5** fait, **6** fait, **7** faisons, **8** faites, **9** faisons, **10** fais, **11** faites

b Students read the text aloud in groups of three; they could act it out like a short sketch.

c ➕ For extension, students find the French for sentences used in the text.

Solution:
1 *Qu'est-ce que tu fais aujourd'hui?*
2 *Je fais des courses.*
3 *Il fait beau.*
4 *Mes amis font de la voile.*
5 *Elle fait ses devoirs.*
6 *On fait de la voile.*

📖 158 Au choix

1 Qu'est-ce qu'on fait?

🖱 Worksheet

Questions et réponses

cm 10/1

faire

gia 1 p43

Using the verb *faire* – to do, to make

This provides further practice of *faire*, if required.

🖱 Worksheet

Plenaries (pages 126–127)

1 Students could have a brainstorming session to think of the many contexts in which the verb *faire* is used.
2 There could also be a short discussion about how meaning is expressed in different languages and the challenge of translation. Mention that the way foreigners construct sentences in English often indicates the way the same meanings are expressed in their own language, such as Yoda in *Star Wars*.

10B Tu aimes la musique?   pages 128–129

- Talk about music

Grammaire	Stratégies	Phonétique
• Use *jouer de* + instrument	• None	• None

Resources
Audio: 2a *La musique, c'est ma passion*, or CD 5, track 3   **Interactive activity:** *Les loisirs* (L)
Copymasters: 10/2 *Grands mots croisés: la musique*   **PowerPoint:** None
Worksheets: Starters and plenaries; *Faites de la musique* (R)   **Grammar in Action:** None

192   Tricolore 1 Teacher's Notes

10B Tu aimes la musique?

Worksheet

Starters (pages 128–129)

1 **Understanding cognates** Display visuals for the following instruments and say the names in French. As these are *vrais amis*, students need to listen to the pronunciation and then call out the number of the correct visual.

le piano, la flûte, le violon, la guitare, la trompette, la clarinette, le trombone, le saxophone.

Remind students that *le trombone* has an alternative meaning and ask them what it is.

2 *Quel verbe?* Display the following:

a *Je ... du piano*
b *Tu ... de la guitare?*
c *Nous ... de la flûte.*
d *Vous ... du trombone?*
e *Ils ... du violon.*

1 jouez **2** joue **3** jouent **4** jouons **5** joues

Give students one minute to read and work out the answers, then ask for them collectively or randomly.

Solution:
a 2, **b** 5, **c** 4, **d** 1, **e** 3

Interactive activity

Les loisirs

Introduction

Teaching musical instruments

Go through the objectives for the spread. There are activities requiring productive use of all instruments in this area, but some teachers may prefer to adopt a modified approach as follows.

Students should be able to recognise all pronunciations and meanings, so the main emphasis should be on those, which do not look like English, e.g. *la flute à bec, le clavier, la batterie*. For some students, production could be limited to those instruments that are personal to them for use in personal conversation and their *Dossier personnel*.

128

1 Les instruments de musique

Teach or practise the new vocabulary using flashcards, actual instruments or the photos. Teach the six masculine words, then the six feminine ones. Revise *jouer* (*Unité* 6) and introduce *jouer de* + instrument with questions, e.g.

Regardez la photo. C'est quel instrument? Qui joue d'un instrument de musique? (Student A), *tu joues de quel instrument?* etc.

Teach the names of any additional instruments that students actually play, e.g. double bass – *une contrebasse*.

Solution:
1 *D*, **2** *H*, **3** *J*, **4** *C*, **5** *F*, **6** *E*, **7** *G*, **8** *L*, **9** *A*, **10** *I*, **11** *B*, **12** *K*

128

2 La musique, c'est ma passion

a Students listen and note the letter corresponding to each instrument mentioned.

Solution:
1 *F*, **2** *G*, **3** *B*, **4** *K*, **5** *I*, **6** *D*, **7** *H*, **8** *L*

CD 5 Track 3

La musique, c'est ma passion

1 – J'aime beaucoup la musique et je joue du violon dans l'orchestre du collège.
2 – Je joue de la batterie dans un groupe. Nous jouons le samedi après-midi.
3 – J'adore la musique et je joue de la guitare.
4 – Moi, j'aime bien écouter de la musique, mais je ne joue pas d'un instrument. Mon ami joue de la trompette.
5 – Je joue de la flûte à bec. Beaucoup d'élèves apprennent la flûte à bec dans ma classe.
6 – Moi, j'aime beaucoup la musique, surtout le jazz. Je joue du clavier. Le clavier, c'est mon instrument préféré.
7 – Je joue du piano. C'est très bien parce que nous avons un piano à la maison. Ma sœur aussi apprend le piano et quelquefois nous jouons ensemble.
8 – Moi, je ne joue pas d'un instrument mais mon frère joue de la clarinette. Je vais aussi apprendre à jouer de la clarinette un jour.

b Students complete the sentences with the correct form of *de*, referring to the *Dossier-langue*.

Solution:
1 *du violon*
2 *de la batterie*
3 *de la guitare*
4 *de la trompette*
5 *de la flûte à bec*
6 *du clavier*
7 *du piano*
8 *de la clarinette*

c For extension, students make up similar sentences but changing the instrument.

128 Dossier-langue

jouer de + musical instrument

Students work out the rule for the correct form of *de* by referring to the table.

Solution:
1 masculine, **2** feminine, **3** *pas*

129 AfL

3 Les jeunes musiciens

Students complete the text with the correct preposition and instrument.

After reviewing the spread objectives and assessment criteria, this activity could be used for assessment.

Tricolore 1 Teacher's Notes 193

10C Mes passe-temps

> **Solution:**
> 1 *de la flûte à bec,* 2 *du piano,* 3 *du violon,* 4 *de la batterie,* 5 *de la guitare,* 6 *d'un instrument*

📖 **129**

4 Fête de la musique (Faites de la musique)

This musical festival is a great event in France and in other cities around the world. It was started in 1982 by Maurice Fleuret to encourage young musicians to perform. Students should read the article, using reading strategies to work out the gist and new language.

a Students could work on this in pairs and read out the French phrases to one another for checking.

> **Solution:**
> 1 *la journée la plus longue*
> 2 *une très grande manifestation culturelle*
> 3 *On fait de la musique partout*
> 4 *tous les concerts sont gratuits*

b Students answer comprehension questions in English.

> **Solution:**
> 1 21st June, summer solstice/longest day
> 2 Any of streets, parks, gardens, squares; cafés, theatres, schools, churches, prisons, hospitals
> 3 more than one hundred
> 4 All events are free to the public.

c For extension, students could prepare a poster or an advert for the fête, perhaps referring to the website for ideas and further information.

Worksheet

Faites de la musique …

cm 10/2

Grands mots croisés: la musique

Worksheet

Plenary (pages 128–129)

Think, pair and share Students think about how they can practise pronouncing cognates so they sound French. Have they noticed any spelling patterns which help with pronunciation, e.g. *…ette (clarinette, trompette), …on (violon, ballon)*? They could discuss this in pairs, then share what they know with the class.

10C Mes passe-temps   pages 130–131

- Talk about leisure activities
- Read and write messages about leisure

Grammaire	Stratégies	Phonétique
• Use *jouer* à + sport/games	• Adding interest to your writing (4)	• The letters 'un', 'um'

Resources
Audio: 3a *Des interviews,* or CD 5, track 5 **Copymasters:** 10/3 *Les loisirs,* 10/4 *Manon et Clément* **Worksheets:** Starters and plenaries; *Mes loisirs* (W)	**Interactive activity:** *Le mail de Sylvain* (R) **Ph** The letters 'un', 'um', or CD 5, track 4 **PowerPoint:** Kim's game: *Les loisirs* **Grammar in Action:** pp44–45

Worksheet

Starter (pages 130–131)

1 *Chasse à l'intrus* Display or print out the following lists. Students should write down the odd word out in each list. Ask several students for the answers, before confirming the correct one, then ask if anyone can explain why.

1	2	3	4	5
la natation	fais	le clavier	mais	les baskets
l'équitation	**fête**	la batterie	rouge	les chaussures
le violon	fait	**le vélo**	noir	les chaussettes
la voile	faites	la trompette	blanc	**les lunettes**

Introduction

Go through the objectives for this spread.

Other activities

Teach the words for other activities, not previously taught: *jouer aux jeux vidéo/aux cartes/aux échecs/sur l'ordinateur, faire de la peinture/du dessin/des photos/du théâtre/de la lecture/de la cuisine.*

Practise with oral question and answer work.

Interactive activity

Les loisirs

194   Tricolore 1 Teacher's Notes

10C Mes passe-temps

1 On s'amuse

Read the introductory text, then students match the text and photos. Check this orally asking for complete sentences. Develop a wider discussion by asking who in the class does/likes/dislikes the activities shown here.

Solution:
1 D, 2 B, 3 A, 4 C, 5 E, 6 F

130 Dossier-langue

jouer de … /jouer à … /faire de

This summarises the use of prepositions after *faire* and *jouer* with music, sport and other activities.

2 C'est quelle activité?

Prepare this orally, then students write captions for the pictures. When checking this, ask students to read out their answers to practise pronunciation.

If appropriate, for further practice students could work in pairs to mime and guess the activities covered here.

Solution:
1 *Il joue de la trompette.*
2 *Elles jouent de la flûte.*
3 *Ils jouent de la guitare.*
4 *Elle joue de la batterie.*
5 *Elles jouent au football.*
6 *Ils jouent aux échecs.*

Interactive activity

L'interview d'Éloïse

Interactive activity

The letters 'un', 'um'

130 Phonétique

The letters 'un', 'um'

A full explanation of this sound is given on *kerboodle!*, together with interactive practice.

a Explain that when 'u' is followed by 'n' or 'm' it is often a nasal vowel (pronounced through the nose). Remind students of the other nasal vowels already taught, and the tip of holding the nose, when saying the nasal sound, then trying to make the same sound without holding the nose. This nasal vowel is not common; there are few examples and this sound seems to be disappearing and merging with 'in'/'im'.

Say the word *parfum* with an appropriate gesture. Students repeat the word with the same gesture. Then read out the other words, with the students repeating each one: *lundi, brun, un*. The words are included on the recording for optional use (part **a**).

Explain that if the letters are followed by another vowel or a second 'm' or 'n', then they are pronounced differently. Read aloud the exceptions: *une, lumière, jaune*, with students repeating the words without the gesture. Again, these are included on the recording.

b Students listen to the silly sentence and note down how many times they hear the sound (4). They can then repeat the sentence to help them remember this sound.

For further practice, write some additional words on the board to check that students recognise the link between spelling and pronunciation e.g. *quelqu'un, chacun.*

CD 5 Track 4

The letters 'un', 'um'

Écoutez et répétez:
a parfum, lundi, brun, un
   Des exceptions: une lumière jaune
b Quelqu'un de Verdun trouve du parfum brun.

130

3 Des interviews

a Students read the questions then listen to the short interviews and note the question asked and the response.

Solution:
1 e *du sport – football, natation*
2 b *préfère la musique*
3 c *du clavier – cours le mercredi*
4 d *du théâtre – club au collège*
5 a *(s'il fait beau) promenade, (s'il pleut) jouer aux échecs/à des jeux vidéo*

CD 5 Track 5

Des interviews

1 – Tu as des passe-temps?
  – Oui, j'adore le sport. Je fais beaucoup de sport le weekend, surtout du football et de la natation. La natation, c'est super.
2 – Et toi, qu'est-ce que tu fais comme sport?
  – Pas grand-chose. Je ne suis vraiment pas sportive. Je préfère la musique.
3 – Est-ce que tu joues d'un instrument de musique?
  – Oui, je joue du clavier. J'ai un cours de clavier le mercredi après l'école.
4 – Et toi, est-ce que tu fais d'autres activités?
  – Oui, quelquefois je fais du théâtre. Il y a un club de théâtre au collège et j'aime bien ça.
5 – Et le weekend, qu'est-ce que tu fais le weekend normalement?
  – Ça dépend. S'il fait beau, j'aime faire une promenade avec mes amis. S'il pleut, j'aime jouer aux échecs ou à des jeux vidéo sur l'ordinateur.

b Students choose three questions and write personal responses.

c Students interview one another in pairs.

Tricolore 1 Teacher's Notes   **195**

10C Mes passe-temps

Group identity game

Able students could write up the interview in the third person and this could be collected in and used for a group identity game, if the replies are sufficiently different, e.g. *Il adore le sport. Il fait beaucoup de sport le weekend, surtout le football et la natation. Qui est-ce?* No names are given and the descriptions for each group are handed out to that group. Students have to interview other people in the group to identify the person fitting each description.

📖 **131**

4 Forum des jeunes

To practise pronunciation, ask for volunteers to read each message aloud.

a Students read through the messages and identify the person.

> **Solution:**
> 1 *Sportif+++*, 2 *Rienafaire*, 3 *Sportif+++*,
> 4 *FanadeBD*, 5 *FanadeBD*, 6 *Mélomane_99*

b Students look at the messages again and note any useful phrases they could use themselves in their own work. These could be later collected in a class feedback session. They should also look at the nicknames and work out what they would be in English.

c For extension, students invent a suitable message and nickname for a person who likes music and sport.

📖 **131**   **AfL**

5 Un message

Students write a short message about leisure activities, adding extra detail such as opinions, friends and asking some questions. They could refer to the info box and the *Stratégies* for help.

Review the spread objectives and discuss how this task could be used for assessment of progress. Perhaps give a model answer to demonstrate what is required.

When the task has been done, ask for volunteers to present their work. Finish with a general discussion about what was well done and what could be improved.

📖 **131 Stratégies**

Adding interest to your writing (4)

This explains how students can make sentences more interesting by adding extra detail. They could practise with a different short sentence, eg. *Je joue au tennis* and expand it to a longer sentence in the same way.

🖱 **Interactive activity**

Le mail de Sylvain

🖱 **Worksheet**

Mes loisirs

🖱 **Presentation**

Jeu de mémoire: Les activités

📖 **158 Au choix**

2 Mes loisirs

cm 10/3

Les loisirs

cm 10/4

Manon et Clément

gia 1 pp44–45

Using *jouer à* and *jouer de* – to play (1) and (2)

🖱 **Worksheet**

Plenary (pages 130–131)

Using the *Sommaire*, suggest students find five words related to leisure that they have difficulty remembering. They should focus on each of the five words, and collect suggestions from round the class as to how to remember them. If few ideas are forthcoming, suggest perhaps linking each word to a finger, practise each word during the day and seeing if they can recall them in the next lesson.

196   Tricolore 1 Teacher's Notes

10D La semaine dernière   pages 132–133

- Talk about some recent activities

Grammaire	Stratégies	Phonétique
• Nouns and adjectives • Recognise and use some phrases about the past	• None	• None

Resources

Audio: 1 *Samedi dernier*; 5 *La semaine dernière*, or CD 5, tracks 6 and 7
Copymasters: 10/5 *La semaine dernière*
Worksheets: Starters and plenaries; The present and perfect tenses (G)

Interactive activity: None
PowerPoint: *Présent et passé* (G)
Grammar in Action: pp48–49

This optional spread introduces some examples of the perfect tense with *avoir* to enable students to understand and talk about events in the past, using the *je* and *tu* forms.

Very little new vocabulary is introduced and the spread can be omitted if preferred. The perfect tense is taught systematically in Stage 2.

Worksheet

Starters (pages 132–133)

1 *Chaque mot à sa place* Display the following task. Give students one minute to read and work out the answers, then ask several individual students to give the number of the box, before confirming the correct answer.

Quelle est la bonne boîte pour chaque mot?

mardi (2), la casquette (5), le dessin (4), la planche à voile (1), intéressant (3)

1	2	3	4	5
le ski la natation le roller	lundi mercredi jeudi	génial amusant super	la peinture la cuisine la photographie	la chemise le pantalon la jupe

2 *Quel verbe?* Display the following:
a J'... un petit chat.
b Tu ... un animal à la maison?
c Nous ... un chien et un lapin.
d Vous ... technologie aujourd'hui?
e Ils ... deux cours de géographie par semaine.
1 ont 2 ai 3 avez 4 as 5 avons

Give students one minute to read and work out the answers.

Solution:
a 2, b 4, c 5, d 3, e 1

Introduction

Go through the objectives for this spread.

132

1 Samedi dernier

Look at the images and check that these are recognised and understood. Students then listen to the recording and note the letter by each activity mentioned. The transcript introduces examples of the following phrases in the perfect tense:

j'ai fait, tu as fait; j'ai joué.

Solution:
1 C, 2 G, 3 E, 4 D, 5 I, 6 A, 7 F, 8 H, 9 J, 10 B

CD 5 Track 6

Samedi dernier

1 – Qu'est-ce que tu as fait samedi dernier?
   – J'ai joué au badminton.
2 – Et toi, qu'est-ce que tu as fait?
   – J'ai fait de la natation.
3 – Qu'est-ce que tu as fait samedi dernier?
   – J'ai fait de la voile.
4 – Moi, j'ai joué au rugby.
5 – Et toi, qu'est-ce que tu as fait?
   – J'ai fait du vélo au parc.
6 – Qu'est-ce que tu as fait?
   – J'ai joué aux échecs avec mon ami.
7 – Moi, j'ai joué de la guitare.
8 – Qu'est-ce que tu as fait samedi dernier?
   – J'ai fait du judo au centre sportif.
9 – Moi, j'ai fait de l'équitation.
10 – Et toi, qu'est-ce que tu as fait?
   – J'ai joué du violon avec l'orchestre.

132 Dossier-langue

Nouns and adjectives

This explains the use of *dernier* as a pointer to an action in the past. Students should be able to adapt the pattern to other days. With able students, you could also ask them to work out how to say last summer, last winter, etc.

Tricolore 1 Teacher's Notes   **197**

10D La semaine dernière

132 Dossier-langue

Recognising the perfect tense (1)

Explain that this just introduces two examples (*j'ai joué* and *j'ai fait*) so that students can talk more fully about their free time. If appropriate, explain that the part of *avoir* (*j'ai*) is the auxiliary or helping verb. Explain that the perfect tense will be taught in full in Stage 2.

Presentation

Présent et passé

132

2 Présent ou passé?

Read the sentences aloud. Students decide whether they are past or present. Then in pairs, one student could read the sentences in the present and the other those in the past.

Solution:

présent	passé
1, 2, 6, 8	3, 4, 5, 7

Worksheet

C'est au passé?

133

3 Des journées actives

Students should attempt to use only the verbs in the examples.

a Students write three sentences to describe sport played last Monday.

> **Solution:**
> *J'ai fait du vélo*, etc.

b Students write three sentences to describe musical instruments played last Tuesday.

> **Solution:**
> *J'ai joué de la batterie*, etc.

c For extension, students write a paragraph about last Wednesday, when they played sport in the morning, made music in the afternoon and did a different leisure activity in the evening.

cm 10/5

La semaine dernière

133

4 Le weekend dernier

Students work in pairs to develop a short conversation about past activities, using only *faire* and *jouer à/de*.

133

5 La semaine dernière

Students listen to the recording and note some additional details. Depending on ability, students could aim to note down 1–4 details for each item.

Solution:

	quand	quoi	avec qui	où
1	sam	danse	sœur	club des jeunes
2	ven	badminton	amis	centre sportif
3	dim	promenade	chien	parc
4	lun	clavier	frère	maison
5	jeu	foot	équipe	parc
6	mer	théâtre	club	collège
7	mar	échecs	grand-père	jardin
8	dim	camping	grand-mère	Saint-Malo

CD 5 Track 7

La semaine dernière

1 Samedi dernier, j'ai fait de la danse avec ma sœur au club des jeunes.
2 Vendredi dernier, j'ai joué au badminton avec mes amis au centre sportif.
3 Dimanche dernier, j'ai fait une promenade dans le parc avec le chien.
4 Lundi dernier, j'ai joué du clavier avec mon frère à la maison.
5 Jeudi dernier, j'ai joué au football au parc avec l'équipe.
6 Mercredi dernier, j'ai fait du théâtre au collège avec le club.
7 Mardi dernier, j'ai joué aux échecs avec mon grand-père dans le jardin.
8 Dimanche dernier, j'ai fait du camping avec ma grand-mère à Saint-Malo.

158 Au choix

3 Dans le bon ordre

133

6 Fais des phrases

Students practise forming sentences according to numbered options. This could also be played using just two or three numbers.

133 AfL

7 Dossier personnel

Students could now write a few sentences about last week's activities for their *dossier*. Remind students of the spread objective and indicate that this task will be ideal for them to demonstrate their skills. Discuss what a successful piece of work should include.

10E Au parc d'attractions

gia 1 pp48–49

Recognising the past tense (1) and (2)

This provides more explanation and practice of the perfect tense with *avoir* and regular *-er* verbs (*je* and *tu* forms only). Time phrases are also practised, including *hier*.

Worksheet

Plenary (pages 132–133)

Recognising and using the past tense Ask students how they've found this introduction to using the past tense. What do they find most difficult? Ask them how often they use the past tense when they're speaking in English. Different ways of expressing the past in English could also be discussed, e.g. played, have played, did play.

10E Au parc d'attractions   pages 134–135

- Find out about *Astérix* and the *Parc Astérix*
- Use the 24-hour clock

Grammaire	Stratégies	Phonétique
• None	• Translating from French to English (4)	• The letter 'x'

Resources

Audio: 3 *24 heures*, or CD 5, track 9
Copymasters: 10/6 *24 heures*
Worksheets: Starters and plenaries

Interactive activity: *C'est quand?* (L)
Ph The letter 'x', or CD 5, track 8
PowerPoint: None
Grammar in Action: p46

Worksheet

Starters (pages 134–135)

1 **Times** Write a selection of times on the board for a game of *Effacez!*, e.g. 5h00, 6h05, 9h10, 11h20, 12h00 (*midi*), 1h25, 2h15, 3h30, 4h50, 7h30, 8h25, 9h45.

2 **Chaque mot à sa place** Display the following task. Give students one minute to read and work out the answers, then ask students collectively or randomly to give the number of the box.

Quelle est la bonne boîte pour chaque mot?
samedi (5), seize (3), la piscine (4), janvier (1), la batterie (2)

1	2	3	4	5
février	le violon	quartorze	la patinoire	mardi
juillet	la guitare	vingt	le bowling	mercredi
août	le piano	cinquante	le stade	vendredi

Introduction

Go through the objectives for this spread.

134

1 Astérix

Ask students about comic strip characters in simple French. If possible show the class a comic strip book.
e.g. *Voici une bande dessinée. C'est un livre avec beaucoup d'images. On appelle un livre comme ça, une bande dessinée, ou une BD.*

Les Français aiment beaucoup les bandes dessinées – ou des BD. Il y a même un festival de la bande dessinée.

Qui sont les personnages de BD? Il y a Tintin, Lucky Luke et Astérix.

Astérix, qu'est-ce que c'est? C'est un animal? C'est une ville?

Non – c'est une personne imaginaire – un personnage de bande dessinée.

Qui connait Astérix? Il y a des livres d'Astérix en anglais. On trouve souvent les livres d'Astérix en anglais à la bibliothèque.

Read through the text and check that students understand, and follow this with more oral work on the photos. Students should then do the activity which involves correcting false statements.

Solution:
1 Asterix habite dans **un village**.
2 Obélix est **l'ami** d'Astérix.
3 Obélix a un **chien** qui s'appelle Idéfix.
4 Panoramix fait des **potions** magiques.
5 Astérix et ses amis résistent aux invasions des **Romains**.

Interactive activity

The letter 'x'

134 Phonétique

The letter 'x'

A full explanation of three different ways in which the letter 'x' is pronounced is given on *kerboodle!*, together with interactive practice.

Tricolore 1 Teacher's Notes   **199**

10E Au parc d'attractions

a Explain that before a vowel, the letter 'x' is pronounced rather like the English sound 'gs' in eggs. Say the word *examen*, then *exemple* and *examiner*. Students repeat the words.

Before a consonant, the letter 'x' is pronounced rather like 'ks' as in kicks. Say *extra* with a thumbs up gesture, then, *excusez-moi* and *Astérix*, with students repeating each word.

When 'x' is at the end of the word, the pronunciation varies. In the third group, it is pronounced like an 's'. Say the words: *six*, *dix*, *soixante*, with students repeating each one.

These words are all included on the recording for optional use (part **a**).

If appropriate, explain that in some cases the letter 'x' is not pronounced at all, e.g. *cheveux*, *roux*.

b Students listen to the silly sentence and note down how many times they hear the sound in its various forms (5). They can then repeat the sentence to help them remember this sound.

> CD 5 Track 8
>
> ### The letter 'x'
> Écoutez et répétez:
> a examen, exemple, examiner
> b extra, excusez-moi, Astérix
> c six, dix, soixante
> d Xavier fait six excursions extraordinaires au parc Astérix.

Date and time (revision)

Revise orally the date and the time, using the 12-hour clock. There are several suitable games to help with this, e.g. *Et après?* (write on the board or say a day, month or number and the class have to say the one that follows); *Loto!* (students write down, say, three months and three days); (see also TB pages xvi–xx).

134

2 Le Parc Astérix

Find out if anyone has visited the *Parc Astérix* or knows about it and use this for discussion. Talk through the details and discuss the photos, identifying characters, etc.

As the text includes new language and is quite challenging, discuss reading strategies and refer to the *Stratégies* on page 135.

a Students match the captions to the photos of rides.

> Solution:
> 1 A, 2 E, 3 C, 4 D, 5 B

b Students answer questions about visiting the *parc* (opening times, location, entry tariffs, etc)

Solution:
1 *Le Parc ferme à 18 heures en mai.*
2 *À 19 heures.*
3 *Le Parc est ouvert le weekend en octobre.*
4 *Non, le Parc est fermé à Noël.*
5 *Le Parc, c'est près de Paris.*
6 *L'entrée, c'est 46 euros pour un jour ou 94 euros pour un pass saison.*
7 *C'est 37 euros par jour ou 84 euros pour un pass saison.*

c For extension, students could consult the website to find out current prices and other useful information.

135

The 24-hour clock

Explain that the 24-hour clock is used more widely on the continent, for television and radio programmes, on posters and timetables.

- Draw two columns on the board and, using figures, write a time after noon in the left-hand column, using the 24-hour clock. Then ask a student to write the equivalent time using the 12-hour clock in the right hand column. Begin with hours only and then add in 30, 15, 45, and eventually other times, until you have a list of about twelve times. Say all the times in French as they are written up.
- Next, rub out the original times and do the whole thing again in reverse, this time seeing if the students can supply the times in French.
- Leave the times on the board and play a game of *Effacez!* (TB page xvii).
- For further practice, divide students into teams. Someone from each team in turn says a time in French, using the 24-hour clock, and someone from the other team has to write it on the board in figures.

Interactive activity

C'est quand?

135

3 24 heures

Revise *ouvert* and *fermé* and explain *à partir de*. Students listen and note the time in figures. This task uses times on the hour only.

Solution:
1 15h00   6 16h00
2 13h00   7 14h00
3 20h00   8 18h00
4 21h00   9 20h00
5 17h00   10 22h00

200 Tricolore 1 Teacher's Notes

10F Une journée exceptionnelle

CD 5 Track 9
Vingt-quatre heures
1 Le match de rugby commence à 15 heures.
2 Le déjeuner est à 13 heures.
3 Le film commence à 20 heures.
4 Le concert commence à 21 heures.
5 Le match de football commence à 17 heures.
6 La banque est ouverte jusqu'à 16 heures.
7 L'épicerie est ouverte à partir de 14 heures.
8 Le restaurant est ouvert à partir de 18 heures.
9 L'épicerie ferme à 20 heures.
10 Le match finit à 22 heures.

135 AfL
4 Attention, c'est l'heure!

Students match up the times in words and numbers using the full range of times. This can be used for self-assessment of understanding the 24-hour clock.

Solution:
1 B, 2 F, 3 D, 4 E, 5 C, 6 A

159 Au choix
4 C'est quand?

cm 10/6
24 heures

135 Stratégies
Translating from French to English

This suggests two tips: looking at nouns, adjectives and verbs with the same root as a clue to meaning; and the prefix 're-' which often has the meaning of a repeated action.

Other examples could be given e.g. *la danse – danser, le travail – travailler, une chanson – chanter,* etc.

The stratégies worksheet can be used for further reinforcement.

Solution:
Link verbs and nouns
1 *l'entrée* = entrance
2 *la sortie* = exit
3 *la fermeture* = closing
4 *l'ouverture* = opening
5 *un nageur* = a swimmer

Translate into English
1 Where is the entrance to the park?
2 The shop is near the exit.
3 The dolphins regularly come up to the surface of the lake.

Worksheet
Translating from French to English

gia 1 p46

The 24-hour clock
Further practice of time using the 24-hour clock.

113 Presentation
Chantez! Attention, c'est l'heure!

For revision and for fun, listen again to the rap from *Unité* 8 (see TB page 149). The words also appear on *kerboodle!*. Further notes for using this and other songs appear on TB page xxi.

Worksheet
Plenaries (pages 134–135)

1 **Think, pair and share** Students could discuss the 24-hour clock and its benefits and whether they find it easy to use and would like to see it more widely used in the UK.
2 Students could work in pairs or groups to suggest their top three tips for reading/getting the gist of a text in French. If ideas are slow to emerge, refer them to the reading strategies introduced earlier.

10F Une journée exceptionnelle pages 136–137

- Describe a special day

Grammaire	Stratégies	Phonétique
• Learn how to say 'I went'	• Planning your writing	• None

Resources

Audio: 4 *Tu as passé un bon weekend?*; 6 *Une journée à Paris,* or CD 5, tracks 10 and 11
Copymasters: 10/7 *Qu'est-ce que tu as fait?*
Worksheets: Starters and plenaries; Translating from French to English (Strat); *Une carte postale* (G); *Ma journée idéale* (W)

Interactive activity: *Une journée un peu différente* (R)
PowerPoint: None
Grammar in Action: p47

10F Une journée exceptionnelle

The second page of this spread introduces additional phrases in the perfect tense, including *je suis allé(e)* and *tu es allé(e)*. The perfect tense is taught fully in Stage 2 with detailed explanations. Teachers who do not wish to cover the perfect tense could just use the first page, which provides practice in reading and writing about a special day.

Worksheet

Starters (pages 136–137)

1 *En groupes* Display a list of words in random order or hand this out on slips of paper. Ask students to put these into five groups:

   le hockey, le basket, le rugby

   faire, avoir, aller

   le trombone, le violoncelle, le clavier

   quinze, vingt-cinq, cinquante

   les échecs, les cartes, les jeux vidéo

   Give students a few minutes to work out the groups then ask for volunteers to read out one group each.

2 *Masculin ou féminin* Give out the following list on slips of paper or display the words and ask students to work in pairs to decide whether the words are masculine or feminine. Ask them to show a *masculin* or *féminin* card when checking. Genders have been added for checking purposes.

bibliothèque f	musée m
bowling m	parc m
centre sportif m	patinoire f
château m	piscine f
cinéma m	plage f
club des jeunes m	synagogue f
mosquée f	temple m

Introduction

Go through the objectives for this spread.

136

1 Une journée idéale

Go through the competition details and ask the class what entrants have to do and what they could win.

a Lucie's entry could be read aloud and then students correct the false statements.

   Solution:
   1 Lucie va au **parc Astérix**.
   2 C'est au mois de **mai**.
   3 Lucie et ses amis **mangent à la pizzeria** à midi.
   4 Elle **adore** les pizzas.
   5 Comme boisson, elle prend **une limonade**.
   6 L'après-midi, elle regard **les dauphins au delphinarium**.
   7 À **quatre** heures on prend le goûter.
   8 Lucie **aime bien** faire du shopping.

b Students find the French for some useful phrases. They could also look for suitable phrases they could use in their own work.

   Solution:
   1 *une bande de copains*
   2 *Il n'y a pas de queue*
   3 *On prend beaucoup de photos.*
   4 *d'abord*
   5 *on regarde un spectacle*
   6 *plus tard*

Interactive activity

Ma journée idéale

136

2 Dossier personnel

a Students write a short description of a special day, which could be an ideal day or a disastrous one. Questions and detailed examples are given to help. Students should also read through the *Stratégies*. This could be prepared initially as a class activity.

b For extension, students add more detail and prepare a longer text.

136 Stratégies

Planning your writing

This gives some guidance for preparing a description of a day. Students look for time phrases in Lucie's description, which are used to structure the text.

gia 1 p47

Using regular and irregular verbs

This provides further practice of the present tense of a range of regular and irregular verbs.

Worksheet

Une journée un peu différente

137

3 Bravo Lucie

This presents more examples of the perfect tense with *-er* verbs and introduces *je suis allé(e)* and *tu es allé(e)*. Remind students of the pronunciation of words ending in *-é*.

a Students read the dialogue in pairs.

b For extension, students reply to questions in French. For most students short phrases rather than full sentences will be sufficient.

Tricolore 1 Teacher's Notes

10F Une journée exceptionnelle

Solution:
1 *(Lucie a gagné) une paire de/deux billets*
2 *(Lucie a visité) le Parc Astérix*
3 *(Elle est allée au parc) dimanche dernier*
4 *(Daniel est allé au même parc) pour son anniversaire*
5 *(À son avis) c'est génial*
6 *(Lucie) aime bien*

137 Dossier-langue

Recognising the perfect tense (2)

Ask students about the differences with *je suis allé(e)* and whether the two forms of *allé(e)* sound different.

137

4 Tu as passé un bon weekend?

This gives more examples of *je suis allé(e)* with destinations. Students listen and write down the destinations. Able students could note any additional details.

Solution:
1 *à la plage*, 2 *au château*, 3 *au cinéma*, 4 *à la patinoire*, 5 *au parc*, 6 *aux magasins*, 7 *à l'aquarium*, 8 *à l'église*, 9 *au bowling*, 10 *au centre sportif*

CD 5 Track 10

Tu as passé un bon weekend?

1 – Je suis allé à la plage.
2 – Je suis allée au château.
3 – Lundi dernier, je suis allé au cinéma.
4 – Mardi dernier, je suis allée à la patinoire.
5 – Mercredi dernier, je suis allé au parc avec mon frère.
6 – Samedi dernier, je suis allée aux magasins avec mes copines.
7 – Vendredi dernier, je suis allé à l'aquarium avec le collège.
8 – Dimanche dernier, je suis allée à l'église avec ma famille.
9 – Jeudi dernier, je suis allé au bowling avec ma sœur.
10 – Et moi, je suis allée au centre sportif pour jouer au badminton.

137

5 Je suis allé(e) en ville

Students practise forming sentences on this model.

Solution:
1 *Je suis allé(e) à la bibliothèque.*
2 *Je suis allé(e) à la patinoire.*
3 *Je suis allé(e) à la piscine.*
4 *Je suis allé(e) à la plage.*
5 *Je suis allé(e) au bowling.*
6 *Je suis allé(e) au château.*
7 *Je suis allé(e) au cinéma.*
8 *Je suis allé(e) à l'auberge de jeunesse.*
9 *Je suis allé(e) à l'aquarium.*
10 *Je suis allé(e) au centre commercial/aux magasins.*

137

6 Une journée à Paris

Students could read through the gapped text first and think about what the missing words might be, then they listen to the recording and note down the missing words.

Solution:
1 *b*, 2 *f*, 3 *c*, 4 *h*, 5 *e*, 6 *g*, 7 *a*, 8 *d*

CD 5 Track 11

Une journée à Paris

– Tu as passé un bon weekend?
– Ah oui, j'ai passé un excellent weekend. Je suis allé à Paris.
– Paris, c'est bien?
– Ah oui, il y a beaucoup de choses à faire. D'abord, le matin, je suis allé à la tour Eiffel. C'est vraiment impressionnant. Puis à midi, on a fait un pique-nique près de la Seine.
– Et l'après-midi?
– Ensuite, l'après-midi, je suis allé à la Cité des Sciences. C'est un grand musée avec beaucoup d'activités scientifiques et il y a aussi un planétarium et un grand cinéma IMAX. C'est très intéressant.

Worksheet

Une carte postale

159 Au choix

5 Qu'est-ce que tu as fait?

cm 10/7

Qu'est-ce que tu as fait?

Tricolore 1 Teacher's Notes 203

10G Les loisirs

📖 **159 Au choix**

6 Un bon weekend

🖱 **Worksheet**

Plenary (pages 136–137)
Working in pairs or groups, students see how many sequencing words they can remember and discuss ways of memorising these. Students could also practise in turn making up sentences using a different sequencing word each time.

10G Les loisirs   pages 138–139

- Talk about leisure in general

Grammaire	Stratégies	Phonétique
• None	• Learning and revising vocabulary	• The letters '-sion', '-tion'

Resources

Audio: *Samedi, on part en vacances*, or CD 5, track 17
Copymasters: 10/8 *Tu comprends?*, 10/9 *Sommaire*
Worksheets: Starters and plenaries
e-book: *Les vacances de Margot*

Interactive activity: Classroom commands (V)
Ph The letters '-sion', '-tion', or CD 5, track 12
Video: *En musique*
PowerPoint: *Samedi, on part en vacances* (song)
Grammar in Action: None

🖱 **Worksheet**

Starters (pages 138–139)

1 **5-4-3-2-1** Display the following words in random order; students find groups of 5,4,3,2,1 similar words.

le ski, le judo, la natation, la danse, la voile; suis, est, sont, êtes; le piano, la batterie, la flûte; février, août; les vacances

Students could record their answers on a pre-printed grid and these can then be checked in the usual way.

2 *Quel mot?* Display the following or print them out. Give students a few minutes to read and work out the answers, then ask for them collectively or randomly.

a ... ça va?
b *Tu n'aimes pas la gymnastique – mais ...?*
c *C'est ..., la visite au Parc Astérix?*
d ... va au club de natation, mercredi?
e ... est le concert de musique du collège?
1 qui **2** quand **3** où **4** comment **5** pourquoi

Solution:
a 4, b 5, c 2, d 1, e 3

Introduction
Go through the objectives for this spread.

📖 **138**

1 Un jeu-test

a Students first work out which word is needed for each gap in the text.

Solution:
1 c, **2** i, **3** f, **4** e, **5** b, **6** j, **7** g, **8** d, **9** a, **10** h

b They can then do the light-hearted personality quiz based on leisure activities and read the results.

c For extension, students could work individually or in pairs to prepare some similar questions (requiring *oui/non* answers) for a questionnaire on leisure.

📖 **138 Stratégies**

Learning and revising vocabulary

This encourages students to revise regularly vocabulary for different topics. They could share ideas of useful ways of doing this. Remind them about the *Sommaire* pages at the end of each unit, which summarise the key language covered.

🖱 **Interactive activity**

The letters '-sion', '-tion'

📖 🔊 **138 Phonétique**

The letters '-sion', '-tion'

A full explanation of this sound is given on *kerboodle!*, together with interactive practice.

a Say the word *natation* with the appropriate gesture. Students repeat the word with the same gesture. Then read out the other words with students repeating each one: *excursion*, *attraction*, *solution*. The words are also included on the recording for optional use (part **a**).

204 Tricolore 1 Teacher's Notes

10G Les loisirs

Parts **b** and **c** can be used to practise pronunciation.

b Ask students to listen and repeat the words they hear. Then display the words **a** *confusion*, **b** *ambition*, **c** *version*, **d** *révision*, **e** *situation* for students to match (**b, a, e, c, d**).

c Students listen to the silly sentence and note down how many times they hear the sound (5). They can then repeat the sentence to help them remember this sound.

For further practice write some additional words on the board to check that students recognise the link between spelling and pronunciation, e.g. *sensation, réaction, illusion*.

CD 5 Track 12

The letters '-sion', '-tion'

Écoutez et répétez:
a natation, excursion, attraction, solution
b ambition, confusion, situation, version, révision
c Pour notre excursion, la destination est un grand parc d'attractions où on peut faire de la natation et de l'équitation.

Interactive activity

Rue Danton: En musique

Presentation

Chantez! Samedi, on part en vacances

Interactive activity

Vocabulaire de classe (10)

Worksheet

Les vacances de Margot

Presentation

Les vacances de Margot

cm 10/8

Tu comprends?

139 cm 10/9

Sommaire

A summary of the main structures and vocabulary of this unit.

Interactive activity

Vocabulaire (10)

Worksheet

Plenaries (pages 138–139)

1 Use the *Sommaire* to review the objectives of the unit and what has been learnt. Discuss how the language could be used in different contexts.

2 **Writing challenge** If appropriate, set this challenge: how many lines could students write entirely in French without any prompts?

Hand out blank sheets of paper and give students five minutes' writing time. They can write anything they want in French. Then ask who has written: 1 line/2 lines/3 lines, etc.

(Hopefully many hands will be raised.) When eventually only 3–4 hands are left up (perhaps at 7–10 lines) ask a volunteer from those remaining to read out what they have written.

Review of Stage 1

Students review what they have learnt in Stage 1: which topics they have found most useful/interesting; which grammar points they have found easy/difficult. They discuss their views in pairs and groups and compare their choice with others.

Unité 10 Consolidation and assessment

Épreuves Unité 10

🔊 cm 10/10

Écouter L

A Tu aimes ça?

> **Solution:**
> **1** a, **2** d, **3** e, **4** f, **5** c, **6** b
> **(mark /5)**

> 🔎 🔊 CD 5 Track 13
>
> ### A Tu aimes ça?
> 1 – Est-ce que tu joues du piano?
>   – Oui, je joue du piano.
> 2 – Tu aimes le patin à roulettes?
>   – Le patin à roulettes? Oui, j'aime ça.
> 3 – Tu fais de la voile de temps en temps?
>   – Oui je fais de la voile quand je vais à La Rochelle, chez mes cousins. Ils habitent au bord de la mer.
> 4 – Qu'est-ce que tu fais? Tu dessines?
>   – Oui, je dessine et je fais de la peinture. J'aime la peinture.
> 5 – Tu aimes faire de la natation?
>   – Oui, j'adore la natation. Je vais à la piscine tous les mercredis.
> 6 – Tu aimes jouer aux échecs?
>   – Oui, j'aime bien jouer aux échecs, mais je ne joue pas très bien.

B Quelle heure est-il?

> **Solution:**
> **1** b, **2** a, **3** d, **4** f, **5** e, **6** c
> **(mark /5)**

> 🔎 🔊 CD 5 Track 14
>
> ### Quelle heure est-il
> 1 – Le film commence à 13 heures 10.
>   – C'est vrai? À 13 heures 10!
> 2 – Le musée ferme à 16 heures.
>   – À 16 heures! C'est extraordinaire!
> 3 – Le film finit à quelle heure?
>   – À 22 heures 45.
>   – À 22 heures 45?
>   – C'est ça.
> 4 – Venez ici, tout le monde! Il est 24 heures! Il est minuit!
>   – Hourra, il est minuit!
> 5 – Le train arrive à 17 heures 15.
>   – À 17 heures 15, merci beaucoup.
> 6 – Il est 18 heures 30. Est-ce que le magasin est ouvert?
>   – À 18 heures 30? Mais oui, bien sûr!

C Une présentation

> **Solution:**
> **1** c, **2** a, **3** b, **4** a, **5** b, **6** d
> **(mark /5)**

> 🔎 🔊 CD 5 Track 15
>
> ### Une présentation
> Je vais parler de mon passe-temps: la musique. La musique est très importante pour moi. Ma mère est professeur de musique et elle joue du piano et de la flûte. Moi, je joue du violon. C'est un très bel instrument et j'aime beaucoup écouter des airs de violon. Je joue du violon tous les jours et j'ai un cours de musique chaque semaine, le jeudi soir. Ça dure trente minutes. Pendant la fête de la musique j'ai joué avec des amis à l'église près de ma maison. Je joue dans l'orchestre du collège et dimanche dernier j'ai joué dans un concert à l'hôtel de ville. Plus tard, je voudrais apprendre un autre instrument, peut-être la trompette.

D Au club des jeunes

> **Solution:**
> **1** vrai, **2** vrai, **3** faux, **4** vrai, **5** faux, **6** vrai
> **(mark /5)**

> 🔎 🔊 CD 5 Track 16
>
> ### Au club des jeunes
> 1 Ce soir, au club des jeunes, on fait du sport, on fait de la musique et on fait de l'informatique.
> 2 Deux filles jouent au ping-pong et d'autres jeunes font de la musique.
> 3 Trois filles et un garçon jouent aux cartes et les autres jouent au Monopoly.
> 4 Une jeune fille joue de la batterie – je crois qu'elle adore ça!
> 5 Un garçon joue de la trompette. Il porte un pantalon noir très chic et une chemise blanche.
> 6 Il y a aussi un ordinateur et deux garçons surfent sur le Net.

cm 10/11

Lire

A Un message de Sarah

> **Solution:**
> **1** d, **2** a, **3** b, **4** e, **5** c, **6** f
> **(mark /5)**

B Questions et réponses

> **Solution:**
> **1** b, **2** d, **3** h, **4** c, **5** f, **6** a, **7** e, **8** g
> **(mark /7)**

Tricolore 1 Teacher's Notes

Unité 10 Consolidation and assessment

B Sébastien est en vacances

Solution:
1 V, 2 F, 3 F, 4 V, 5 F, 6 F, 7 V, 8 V, 9 F
(mark /8)

cm 10/12

Écrire et grammaire W

A Un serpent

Solution:
la voile, le volley, la natation
le violon, la flûte
le dessin, la peinture
faire
(mark /4) ½ mark for each item, including the example)

B Un questionnaire sur les loisirs

Solution:
1 au, 2 au, 3 fais, 4 joue, 5 de la, 6 aux
(mark /5)

C Un message

There are additional distracters listed.

Solution:
1 fais, 2 village, 3 joue, 4 promenades,
5 musique, 6 ai
(mark /5)

D À toi!

This is an open-ended task.
(mark /6)

Presse-Jeunesse

140–141

Presse-Jeunesse 4

These magazine-style pages provide material for reading for pleasure and to enhance cultural awareness. The texts and comprehension activities can be used flexibly; by students working alone for extension, for cover lessons etc. Although they mainly use language previously taught, they may also contain a small amount of additional language.

140

Un bon repas pour Mangetout

a Students work out the English for some key words in the story.

Solution:

	français	anglais
1	dormir	to sleep
2	quelque chose	something
3	couverte de	covered in
4	provisions	provisions
5	un peu	a little
6	un gros morceau	a large piece
7	soudain	suddenly
8	s'échapper	to escape

b Students find a word beginning with 'c' for each category.

Solution:
1 un chat, 2 la cuisine, 3 une carotte

c A similar task where students have to find three words beginning with 'd'.

Solution:
1 deux, 2 le déjeuner, 3 le dessert

141

Charter! Samedi, on part en vacances

This just gives a shorter version (verse six) of the song. Play the song first and help students to work out the gist of it. Then go through the text for verse six and explain any vocabulary.

CD 5 Tracks 17–18

Samedi, on part en vacances

Samedi, on part en vacances.
Que nous avons de la chance,
C'est bientôt les vacances!
Sète, Toulouse et Nice et Cannes,
Nous allons en caravane.
Faire du vélo, faire du ski,
Faire du camping, allons-y!
Pour le soleil, mes lunettes,
Pour le volley, mes baskets.
Oui, c'est vrai, on part demain.
Où est mon maillot de bain?
Nice et Cannes, Toulouse et Sète,
Ma valise est presque faite.
Samedi, on part en vacances.
Samedi, on part en vacances.

141

Le volley-ball

This gives some information about the history and rules of volleyball and is followed by questions in French.

Solution:
1 6, 2 simple, 3 de toutes les saisons

Tricolore 1 Teacher's Notes

Unité 10 Consolidation and assessment

141

La planche à voile

This gives some information about windsurfing. Students complete the statements about the sport.

Solution:
1 *individuel*, 2 *un lac*, 3 *une voile*

141

Le judo

This gives some information about judo and is followed by questions in French.

Solution:
1 *le blanc, le jaune, l'orange, le vert, le bleu, le marron, le noir*
2 *5 ans*
3 *le Japon*

Au choix

158 Au choix

1 Qu'est-ce qu'on fait?

Students match questions and answers. If needed, give guidance in looking for the right pronoun in the answer to match with the noun in the question. Students can jot down the matching numbers and letters, but, for more practice, they should read out the questions and answers in pairs like short conversations.

Solution:
1 b, **2** g, **3** c, **4** f, **5** a, **6** e, **7** h, **8** d

158 Au choix

2 Mes loisirs

a In this reading task, students find the correct words to complete the text.

Solution:
1 *ville*, 2 *piscine*, 3 *natation*, 4 *football*, 5 *super*, 6 *surfe*, 7 *surtout*, 8 *livres*, 9 *flûte*, 10 *fais*

b Students can then adapt the text by changing at least six details, and copy out their new version. Students could read out their new version in pairs and comment on one another's work.

For additional oral practice, play one of these games.

1 Chain game

There are several possible versions of this, e.g.
- the first person says *Je joue de la flûte*. The next repeats this and adds another instrument, etc.
- as above, but alternating sports and musical activities
- as above, but adding days of the week, e.g. *Le lundi, je joue de la flûte; le mardi, je fais du dessin*, etc.

2 Qu'est-ce que tu fais?

Students write symbols for an activity or activities that they do (possibly in the form of a diary) and then take it in turns to guess what their partner does. The winner is the first to guess the activity or activities of their partner.

158 Au choix

3 Dans le bon ordre

Students copy the sentences in the correct word order.

Solution:
1 *Mercredi dernier, j'ai joué aux cartes avec mes amis.*
2 *Samedi dernier, j'ai fait de la danse au club des jeunes.*
3 *Dimanche dernier, j'ai fait une promenade avec mon chien.*
4 *Mercredi après-midi, j'ai joué aux échecs avec ma grand-mère.*
5 *Jeudi soir, j'ai fait du judo au centre sportif.*
6 *Mardi matin, j'ai fait du vélo au parc.*
7 *Vendredi dernier j'ai joué du violon dans un concert.*
8 *Lundi dernier, j'ai joué au tennis dans un match.*

159 Au choix

4 C'est quand?

Students listen and choose the correct time from the three options. For extra practice, the answers could be checked orally with students reading out all three possible times listed, then stating the correct one.

Solution:
1 b, **2** c, **3** c, **4** a, **5** b, **6** a

CD 5 Track 19

C'est quand?

1 – Allô! Ici le cinéma Dragon.
– Bonjour, madame. Le film commence à quelle heure, s'il vous plaît?
– À 20 heures 15, monsieur.

2 – Salut, Jacques. C'est à quelle heure, le match de football?
– À 14 heures 30.
– Ah bon.

3 – Le spectacle 'son et lumière' finit à quelle heure, s'il vous plaît, madame?
– Il finit à 22 heures 30.
– À 22 heures 30. Bon, merci, madame.

4 – Pardon, madame. Le concert commence à quelle heure?
– À 20 heures 45, monsieur.

5 – La patinoire ferme à quelle heure le lundi soir?
– Le lundi on ferme à 21 heures.
– À 21 heures. Merci.

6 – La piscine ouvre à quelle heure aujourd'hui, s'il vous plaît?
– À 14 heures, madame.

Tricolore 1 Teacher's Notes

Unité 10 Consolidation and assessment

159 Au choix

5 Qu'est-ce que tu as fait?

a Working in pairs, students make up short conversations using the perfect tense about the previous week or weekend. Two able students could demonstrate this first.

b For extension, students complete sentences to describe where they went or what they did during the previous weekend.

159 Au choix

6 Un bon weekend

Students read through the messages about how people spent the previous weekend and complete the tasks.

a Students reply in English.

> Solution:
> 1 La Rochelle
> 2 went sailing, went to aquarium
> 3 It was very good.
> 4 She went to *Parc Astérix* with her brother and mother.
> 5 Really cool.
> 6 Went horseriding, went to the village, watched a film, played football with his cousins
> 7 Had a picnic
> 8 a huge chocolate ice cream

b Students find the French in the messages for the English phrases.

> Solution:
> 1 *Le weekend dernier*
> 2 *Samedi matin*
> 3 *l'après-midi*
> 4 *Dimanche*
> 5 *je suis allé au village*
> 6 *j'ai joué au football*

Copymasters

cm 10/1

faire

This gives practice of *faire*, with some incline of difficulty.

1 *Faire* – to do, make

Students complete the paradigm:

> Solution:
> *je fais, tu fais, il/elle/on fait, nous faisons, vous faites, ils/elles font.*

2 Des questions

> Solution:
> 1 *fait*, 2 *faites*, 3 *font*, 4 *fais*, 5 *fait*, 6 *fait*, 7 *fait*, 8 *font*

3 Des réponses

> Solution:
> a *fait*, b *fait*, c *fait, fait*, d *faisons*, e *fait*, f *font*, g *fais*, h *fait, fait*

4 Trouve les paires

> Solution:
> 1 *c*, 2 *d*, 3 *f*, 4 *g*, 5 *a*, 6 *b*, 7 *e*, 8 *h*

5 Mots croisés

> Solution:
> *Horizontalement:*
> 1 *faisons*, 4 *il*, 6 *un*, 8 *fais*, 10 *font*, 11 *elles*
> *Verticalement:*
> 1 *faites*, 2 *il*, 3 *nous*, 5 *la*, 7 *fait*, 8 *faire*, 9 *vous*

cm 10/2

Grands mots croisés: la musique

Students interested in music could do this optional crossword at a convenient point.

> Solution:
> *Horizontalement:*
> 1 *violon*, 6 *ne*, 7 *concert*, 10 *sa*, 11 *ou*, 12 *le*, 13 *la*, 15 *du*, 16 *un*, 18 *et*, 20 *clarinette*, 23 *ta*, 24 *flûte*, 25 *piano*, 28 *jouent*, 29 *en*, 30 *trombone*
> *Verticalement:*
> 1 *violoncelle*, 2 *on*, 3 *les*, 4 *en*, 5 *groupe*, 7 *clavier*, 8 *ce*, 9 *tu*, 14 *guitare*, 17 *batterie*, 19 *trompette*, 21 *il*, 22 *salle*, 26 *ne*, 27 *ont*

cm 10/3

Les loisirs

This provides a selection of word games to practise leisure vocabulary.

1 Mots mêlés

Tricolore 1 Teacher's Notes **209**

Unité 10 Consolidation and assessment

Solution:

a

o	r	d	i	n	a	t	e	u	r
d	à	h	s	u	i	l	l	b	é
p	e	i	n	t	u	r	e	o	m
h	t	s	é	c	h	e	c	s	c
o	q	u	s	k	i	a	t	v	a
t	ç	a	n	i	k	j	u	é	r
o	m	l	c	è	n	y	r	l	t
s	a	i	d	u	g	f	e	s	e
t	h	é	â	t	r	e	é	o	s
p	r	o	m	e	n	a	d	e	s

b

1 J'aime faire des **promenades** avec nos chiens.
2 Je n'aime pas jouer aux cartes, mais j'aime jouer aux **échecs**.
3 Je vais faire des **photos** avec mon nouvel appareil.
4 En hiver, j'adore faire du **ski** à la montagne.
5 Quand il fait mauvais, je joue souvent sur l'**ordinateur**.

2 Dans l'ordre alphabétique

Solution:
1 l'athlétisme = athletics
2 la batterie = drums
3 la chorale = choir
4 la danse = dancing
5 l'équitation = horseriding
6 la flûte = flute
7 la guitare = guitar
8 le hockey = hockey
9 le judo = judo
10 la natation = swimming

3 Trouve les paires

Solution:
1 e, **2** f, **3** d, **4** c, **5** a, **6** b

4 Ça ne m'intéresse pas du tout!

Students complete these sentences as they wish.

---

cm 10/4

Manon et Clément

Students work in pairs on this information gap activity. The teacher and an able student could demonstrate the activity first.

---

cm 10/5

La semaine dernière

This provides a range of activities to practise recognition of the perfect tense and controlled practice.

1 Qu'est-ce que c'est en anglais?

Solution:
a 1 c, **2** e, **3** g, **4** i, **5** b, **6** f, **7** d, **8** j, **9** a, **10** h
b Sentences in the perfect tense: **1, 3, 5, 8, 10**

2 Trois jours actifs

This involves productive practice.

Solution:
1 Lundi matin, j'ai fait de la natation.
2 Lundi après-midi, j'ai fait du vélo.
3 Lundi soir, j'ai fait du roller.
4 Mardi matin, j'ai fait de la voile.
5 Mardi après-midi, j'ai fait une promenade avec le chien.
6 Mardi soir, j'ai joué au badminton.
7 Mercredi matin, j'ai joué au football.
8 Mercredi après-midi, j'ai joué de la guitare.
9 Mercredi soir, j'ai joué aux échecs.

3 Un détail en plus

Students copy and complete the sentences and add a further detail of their choice.

---

cm 10/6

24 heures

This provides further practice if required. The first two tasks involve matching times in figures and words (24-hour clock and ordinary time). The third task is harder, involving finding out opening and closing times from posters.

1 Quelle heure est-il?

Solution:
1 b, **2** e, **3** f, **4** h, **5** g, **6** a, **7** d, **8** c

2 Autrement dit

Solution:
1 e, **2** c, **3** b, **4** a, **5** d, **6** f

3 Ça ouvre … ça ferme

Solution:
1 dix heures, dix-huit heures
2 quatorze heures trente, vingt heures
3 dix heures, vingt-deux heures
4 midi, dix-neuf heures trente
5 dix-sept heures, vingt-et-une heures
6 huit heures, treize heures

Unité 10 Consolidation and assessment

cm 10/7

Qu'est-ce que tu as fait?
A sequence of activities to practise *je suis allé(e)* + other details.

1 Dans le bon ordre
Students copy sentences in the correct order.

Solution:
1 *Vendredi dernier je suis allé au Parc Astérix avec mon collège.*
2 *D'abord je suis allé au village d'Astérix.*
3 *À midi, j'ai fait un pique-nique avec mes amis.*
4 *Puis, l'après-midi, j'ai fait une promenade en bateau au grand SPLATCH.*
5 *Finalement je suis allé au magasin de souvenirs.*

2 Où es-tu allé(e)?
Students follow the lines to find the correct destination.

Solution:
a 1 *D'abord, je suis allé au marché.*
  2 *Puis, je suis allé au terrain de football.*
  3 *Ensuite, je suis allé au port.*
  4 *Finalement je suis allé au restaurant.*
b 1 *Samedi dernier, je suis allée à l'office de tourisme à 10 heures.*
  2 *Puis, je suis allée à l'auberge de jeunesse avec mes amis.*
  3 *Dimanche matin je suis allée à la cathédrale en ville.*
  4 *Lundi soir je suis allée au théâtre avec mes parents.*

3 Où es-tu allé(e) en ville?
This is an open-ended task.

cm 10/8

Tu comprends?

1 On fait du sport

Solution:
1 c, 2 h, 3 b, 4 f, 5 g, 6 a, 7 e, 8 d

CD 5 Track 20

On fait du sport

1 – Tu fais du sport, Sophie?
  – Oui, bien sûr. Je fais de l'équitation tous les dimanches.
2 – Et vous, Marc et Luc, est-ce que vous faites du sport?
  – Oui, nous faisons du VTT. Ça, c'est super.
3 – Et Sika, est-ce qu'elle fait du sport?
  – Oui, elle fait de la gymnastique, le mercredi.
4 – Et Claire et Nicole, qu'est-ce qu'elles font comme sport?
  – En été, elles font de la planche à voile. C'est bien, ça.
5 – Est-ce que tu fais du ski en hiver, Charles?
  – Oui, j'adore faire du ski.
6 – Et toi, Karim, qu'est-ce que tu fais comme sport?
  – Pas grand-chose, mais je fais de la natation de temps en temps. J'aime bien la natation.
7 – Et toi, Lucie, qu'est-ce que tu aimes faire comme sport?
  – Moi, j'adore faire du roller avec mes amis. C'est très amusant.
8 – Et Paul et Sanjay, est-ce qu'ils font du sport?
  – Oui, ils font de la voile avec le club de voile, ici à La Rochelle.

2 Enquête loisirs

Solution:

	painting	drama	chess	drums	flute	violin	computer
1			●				
2				●			
3					●		
4		●					
5	●						
6						●	
7							●

CD 5 Track 21

Enquête loisirs

1 – Qu'est-ce que tu aimes faire, à part le sport?
  – Moi, j'aime jouer aux échecs. C'est très intéressant.
2 – Et toi, Charles, tu as d'autres loisirs?
  – Oui, j'aime bien la musique et je joue de la batterie.
3 – Nicole, toi aussi tu joues d'un instrument de musique?
  – Oui, moi, je joue de la flûte. J'aime bien cet instrument.
4 – Et vous, Paul et Sanjay, est-ce que vous avez d'autres loisirs?
  – Oui, nous aimons faire du théâtre. Ça, c'est toujours amusant.
5 – Magali, qu'est-ce que tu as comme loisirs?
  – Moi, je fais de la peinture. J'adore ça.
6 – Marc, est-ce que tu aimes la musique?
  – Oui, j'aime la musique et je joue du violon.
7 – Et vous, Lucie et Paul, est-ce que vous faites autre chose à part le sport?
  – Oui, nous jouons à des jeux vidéo sur l'ordinateur. Ça, c'est vraiment bien.

Tricolore 1 Teacher's Notes

Unité 10 Consolidation and assessment

3 Le weekend dernier

Solution:

	Activité	Détails
1	Ex. e	au concert
2	c	avec des amis
3	a	samedi matin
4	f	avec ma grand-mère
5	b	sur la plage
6	d	avec son frère

CD 5 Track 22

Le weekend dernier

1 – Qu'est-ce que tu as fait le weekend dernier?
 – Moi, j'ai joué du violon avec l'orchestre au concert.
2 – Et toi, tu as passé un bon weekend?
 – Oui, moi j'ai fait de la natation avec des amis.
3 – Est-ce que tu as passé un bon weekend?
 – Oui, j'ai fait du dessin samedi matin. J'adore le dessin.
4 – Et toi, qu'est-ce que tu as fait le weekend dernier?
 – Moi, je suis allée chez mes grands-parents et j'ai joué aux cartes avec ma grand-mère.
5 – Et toi, tu as passé un bon weekend?
 – Oui, très bon. J'ai joué au volley sur la plage – très amusant.
6 – Tu as fait quelque chose de beau dimanche?
 – Oui, dimanche, j'ai fait du VTT avec mon frère.

4 C'est quand?

Solution:
1 21h30, **2** 15h00, **3** 14h30, **4** 18h00, **5** 19h00, **6** 16h20, **7** 20h45, **8** 13h40

CD 5 Track 23

C'est quand?

1 – Le film commence à quelle heure?
 – Il commence à 21 heures 30.
 – À 21 heures 30.
2 – Salut Suzanne, le match commence à quelle heure cet après-midi?
 – À 15 heures.
 – Bon, à 15 heures.
3 – Le musée ouvre à quelle heure aujourd'hui?
 – À 14 heures 30.
 – À 14 heures 30, oui.
4 – Et il ferme à quelle heure?
 – À 18 heures.
 – À 18 heures, bon, merci.
5 – On mange à quelle heure le soir?
 – Normalement, nous mangeons à 19 heures.
 – À 19 heures, d'accord.
6 – Le train pour Paris part à quelle heure?
 – Il part à 16 heures 20.
 – À 16 heures 20, merci.
7 – Le concert commence à quelle heure?
 – Il commence à 20 heures 45.
 – À 20 heures 45, bon merci.
8 – Tes cours commencent à quelle heure l'après-midi?
 – À 13 heures 40.
 – À 13 heures 40, c'est ça.

cm 10/9

Sommaire

A summary of the main structures and vocabulary of this unit.

Contrôles

Contrôles

The three *Contrôles* are available via the Assessment tab in Kerboodle. These provide blocks of formal assessment of the vocabulary and structures introduced during the course. Papers are provided for Listening, Speaking, Reading and Writing at each of the three stages.

Although the former National Curriculum Attainment Target level descriptors no longer apply, Curriculum levels are still provided for teachers who wish to use them for reference. See TB page vi for the Assessment Introduction.

The Listening and Reading sheets are designed to be written on, but the Speaking and Writing sheets are reusable.

Mark scheme:
Do not include a mark for the example. Each *Contrôle* has a total of 100 marks (25 for each Attainment Target).

Record sheets:
A record sheet for students is provided on Kerboodle. They will need one for each block of *Contrôles*.

Listening:
All items are repeated. For Level 1 assessment only, the recording can be played twice (so that students hear it four times altogether). At all levels, the pause button can be used at any time to give students time for reflection and for writing.

Speaking:
Decide how you wish to conduct this assessment:
- invite students out individually and ask the questions yourself;
- invite them in pairs, listen to the conversation and mark the answers;
- offer your students the option of recording the assessment with a partner, for you to listen to and mark afterwards. It is important, if students record their conversations at home, to obtain some assurance that they are not reading the questions and answers. Depending on the facilities available, the assessment could be carried out in a computer suite.

Unités 1–4

> Premier contrôle: Écouter (1)

Premier contrôle: Écouter

A Loto mathématique (NC 1)

Make sure that students understand that they should only put three crosses (not including the example) on each card.

Solution:
Carte numéro un – 24, 30, 45, 3;
Carte numéro deux – 12, 11, 17
(mark /6) 4+ shows understanding of short statements, with no interference and with plenty of repetition

CD 5 Track 24

Loto mathématique
Carte numéro un: vingt-quatre, trente, quarante-cinq, trois
Carte numéro deux: douze, onze, dix-sept

> Premier contrôle: Écouter (1)

B Dans ma chambre (NC 1)

Solution:
1 *a*, **2** *b*, **3** *b*, **4** *a*, **5** *a*, **6** *b*, **7** *a*
(mark /6) 4+ shows understanding of short statements, with no interference and with plenty of repetition

CD 5 Track 25

Dans ma chambre
1. Voici mon baladeur.
2. J'ai une table et deux chaises.
3. Il y a des stylos et une règle.
4. Ça, c'est mon ordinateur.
5. Mon chat s'appelle Tom.
6. Voilà trois cahiers.
7. Et voilà mon poisson.

> Premier contrôle: Écouter (2)

C À la maison (NC 2)

Each item is repeated once, slowly and clearly. It is not necessary to replay the recording for the purposes of assessing at Level 2. It is acceptable, however, to pause the recording at any time to give your students more time for reflection.

Solution:
1 *vrai*, **2** *faux*, **3** *faux*, **4** *faux*, **5** *faux*, **6** *vrai*, **7** *faux*, **8** *vrai*
(mark /7) 5+ shows understanding of a range of familiar statements

CD 5 Track 26

À la maison
1. Maman est dans la cuisine.
2. Le chien est dans le jardin.
3. Le chat est sous la télé.
4. Ma sœur est dans sa chambre.
5. Mon père est dans la salle de bains.
6. Je suis dans le jardin.
7. Le téléphone est sur la chaise.
8. Mon grand-père est dans le salon.

Tricolore 1 Teacher's Notes

Contrôles

▶ Premier contrôle: Écouter (2)

D Deux familles (NC 2)

Solution:

	brother	sister	cat	dog	rabbit
Sylvie	1	0	2	—	—
Richard	1	2	—	1	1

(mark /6) 5+ shows understanding of a range of familiar statements

▶ 🔊 CD 5 Track 27

Deux familles

– Bonjour. Je m'appelle Sylvie. Voilà des photos de ma famille. Voici Paul, mon frère. Je n'ai pas de sœur. Voilà mes deux chats.
– Salut. Je suis Richard. J'ai des photos aussi. Voici Marie et Isabelle, mes sœurs. Voici mon petit frère, Patrick. Marie a un lapin. Moi, j'ai un chien. Le voilà, il s'appelle Bruno.

▶ Premier contrôle: Parler

Premier contrôle: Parler

Students should be given the sheet up to a week before the assessment, to give them time to choose whether they prefer to do 1 and 2 or 2 and 3 or 1 and 3, and to prepare and practise all three conversations (two structured ones and the open-ended one) with their partners.

Mark scheme:

Section A: mark /16: 2 marks per response

1 mark for conveying the requested information, but with a minimal response, e.g. one or two words. Repetition of the question and prompting by pointing to the visuals may be necessary.

2 marks for a response that is clear and conveys all of the information requested, in the form of a complete phrase or sentence, though not necessarily an accurate one. The question and answers may seem disjointed, like separate items rather than part of a coherent conversation.

Section B: mark /9: 2 marks per response, as above, + 1 bonus mark for one or more extra details, e.g. names of animals, their size or their colour. The extra information must be in the form of a complete phrase or sentence, though not necessarily an accurate one.

Summary: Marks 7–15   16–25
           Level   1   2

▶ Premier contrôle: Lire (1)

Premier contrôle: Lire

A Dans la salle de classe (NC 1)

Solution:

1 g, **2** e, **3** b, **4** a, **5** f, **6** d, **7** c

(mark /6) 4+ shows understanding of single words presented in a clear script – illustrations provide context and visual support

▶ Premier contrôle: Lire (1)

B Les animaux (NC 1)

Solution:

1 f, **2** e, **3** d, **4** b, **5** a, **6** h, **7** g, **8** c

(mark /7) 5+ shows understanding of single words presented in a clear script – illustrations provide context and visual support

▶ Premier contrôle: Lire (2)

D Des questions et des réponses (NC 2)

Solution:

1 c, **2** b, **3** g, **4** f, **5** d, **6** a, **7** e

(mark /7) 4+ shows understanding of short phrases presented in a familiar context)

▶ Premier contrôle: Écrire

Premier contrôle: Écrire

A La maison (NC 1)

Solution:

1 la grande salle de bains, **2** la chambre de Lucie, **3** la chambre de Thomas et de Marc, **4** la chambre de Monsieur et Madame Duval, **5** la petite salle de bains, **6** le salon, **7** la salle à manger, **8** la cuisine, **9** le jardin

(mark /8) do not allow spelling mistakes as the vocabulary is given; 6+ shows ability to copy single familiar words or short phrases correctly

▶ Premier contrôle: Écrire

B Quelle image? (NC 2)

Solution:

1 J'ai quatre ans.
2 J'habite en Écosse.
3 J'habite dans une ferme.
4 Voilà un cinéma.
5 J'ai huit ans.
6 Voilà une rue.
7 J'habite dans un appartement.
8 Voilà un café.
9 J'ai six ans.
10 J'habite en France.

(mark /10) do not allow spelling mistakes as the vocabulary is given; 7+ shows ability to copy short familiar sentences correctly

Contrôles

> Premier contrôle: Écrire

C Des questions (NC 2)

> Solution:
>
> **1** *âge*, **2** *habites (accept es)*, **3** *frères*, **4** *animal*, **5** *appelles*, **6** *ordinateur*, **7** *stylo*, **8** *couleur*, **9** *chat*
>
> **(mark /8)** 6+ shows ability to write familiar words from memory – note that, at this level, it does not matter if spelling is approximate, as long as the meaning is clear and unambiguous without reference to the contextual picture

Unités 5–7

> Deuxième contrôle: Écouter (1)

Deuxième contrôle: Écouter

A À Granville (NC 1)

If helpful for students, play the recording again so they hear the information four times altogether. Note, there is an additional distractor, h, so not all symbols are used.

> Solution:
>
> **1** *d*, **2** *e*, **3** *b*, **4** *a*, **5** *g*, **6** *f*, **7** *c*
>
> **(mark /6)** 4+ shows understanding of short statements, with no interference and with plenty of repetition

> 🔊 CD 5 Track 28

À Granville

Qu'est-ce qu'il y a pour les touristes à Granville?
1. Il y a le marché le samedi.
2. Il y a une grande piscine.
3. La tour Saint-Jacques.
4. Le camping n'est pas loin.
5. Il y a un cinéma avec trois salles.
6. La cathédrale est magnifique.
7. L'Escargot, c'est un bon restaurant.

> Deuxième contrôle: Écouter (1)

B Les activités de la famille Giroux (NC 2)

Before the assessment, check that students understand that 20.30 means 8.30pm (item 4).

> Solution:
>
> **1** *faux*, **2** *faux*, **3** *vrai*, **4** *vrai*, **5** *vrai*, **6** *faux*, **7** *vrai*, **8** *vrai*
>
> **(mark /7)** 5+ shows understanding of a range of familiar statements

> 🔊 CD 5 Track 29

Les activités de la famille Giroux

1. – Je cherche un bon cadeau, c'est l'anniversaire de Pierre le 23 mai.
2. – Pierre? Il regarde un match de football avec son copain Alexandre.
3. – C'est la fête des Mères aujourd'hui. Alette a offert des chocolats à Maman.
4. – Il y a un concert à l'église ce soir, à huit heures et demie. Je joue dans l'orchestre.
5. – Alette travaille dans sa chambre avec sa copine Jeanne.
6. – Il y a un match de tennis de table au Collège Émile Zola. Il a lieu le 9 octobre.
7. – Le 15 juin, je vais au musée Maritime avec le collège.
8. – Papa ... papa ... PAPA!
   – Je suis là. J'écoute de la musique.

> Deuxième contrôle: Écouter (2)

C C'est où exactement? (NC 2)

> Solution: 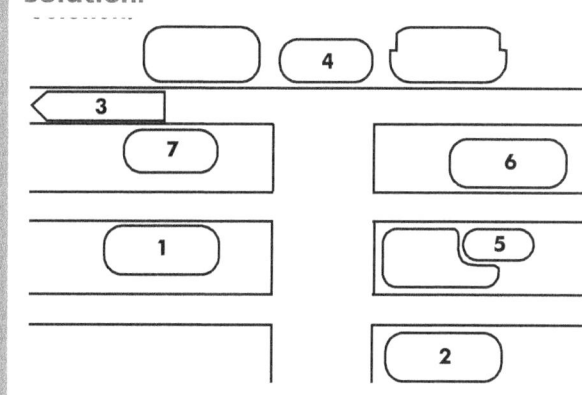
>
> [diagram showing numbered buildings along streets: 4 and 3 at top, 7 and 6 in middle row, 1 and 5 in lower row, 2 at bottom]
>
> **(mark /6)** 4+ shows understanding of a range of familiar questions and answers

> 🔊 CD 5 Track 30

C'est où exactement?

1. – Pour aller à la poste, s'il vous plaît?
   – Prenez la deuxième rue à gauche, et c'est à gauche.
   – Merci, monsieur.
2. – Pardon, il y a un supermarché ici?
   – Oui, voilà, à droite!
   – Oh, pardon.
3. – L'auberge de jeunesse, c'est loin?
   – C'est assez loin, c'est à quinze kilomètres.
   – Quinze kilomètres, ça va.
4. – Le restaurant Renaud, c'est loin?
   – Non, continuez tout droit. C'est entre l'hôtel Pasteur et l'église.
   – Ah, oui, merci.
5. – Maman, il y a des toilettes ici?
   – Oui, derrière l'office du tourisme.
6. – Où est l'hôpital?
   – Ce n'est pas loin. Prenez la deuxième rue à droite, et c'est à gauche.
   – Oh, merci.
7. – Pour aller au marché, s'il vous plaît?
   – Vous prenez la troisième rue à gauche, et le marché est à gauche.
   – Merci beaucoup.

Tricolore 1 Teacher's Notes **215**

Contrôles

> Deuxième contrôle: Écouter (2)

D Quel temps fait-il? (NC 3)

Solution:

	temps	opinion	activité
Charles	e	c	a
Magalie	a	d	d
Robert	d	b	c

(mark /6) 4+ shows understanding of short dialogues, spoken at near normal speed without any interference, identifying personal responses, including opinions)

> CD 5 Track 31

Quel temps fait-il?

– Et voici notre premier joueur. C'est Charles, qui habite à La Rochelle.
– Allô.
– Charles, c'est Annie ici!
– Ah oui, bonjour Annie.
– Il fait beau à La Rochelle?
– Euh, non, il y a du vent. Mais ça va, j'aime le vent.
– C'est vrai?
– Ah oui, je fais de la planche à voile!
– Ah.
– Et maintenant Magalie, à Lyon.
– Allô.
– Salut, Magalie.
– Salut, Annie.
– Quel temps fait-il à Lyon, Magalie?
– Il y a du soleil – j'adore le soleil.
– Moi aussi.
– Je vais à la piscine avec mes amis.
– Super!
– Et le numéro trois habite à Lille. Il s'appelle Robert.
– Allô.
– Salut, Robert.
– Ah, bonjour, Annie.
– Qu'est-ce que tu fais aujourd'hui?
– Oh, il pleut. Je n'aime pas ça. Je reste dans ma chambre et je surfe sur le Net.
– Ah, bon.
– Alors, trois personnes, Robert, Magalie et Charles. On joue!!

> Deuxième contrôle: Parler

Deuxième contrôle: Parler

Students should be given the sheet up to a week before the assessment, to give them time to choose whether they prefer to do 1, 2 or 3, and to prepare and practise both conversations – the structured one (A) and the open-ended one (B) – with their partners.

Mark scheme:

Section A: mark /12: 3 marks per response

1 mark for conveying the requested information, but with a minimal response e.g. one or two words. Repetition of the question and prompting by pointing to the visuals may be necessary.

2 marks for a response that is clear and conveys all of the information requested, in the form of a complete phrase or sentence, though not necessarily an accurate one. The question and answers may seem disjointed, like separate items rather than part of a coherent conversation.

3 marks for a clear and complete response that conveys all of the information requested, in the form of a complete phrase or sentence, though not necessarily an accurate one. The language flows reasonably smoothly, and is recognisable as part of a coherent conversation.

Section B: mark /13: 3 marks per response, as above, + 1 bonus mark for adding one or two items of extra information about personal preferences (i.e. using knowledge of language to adapt and substitute single words and phrases).

Summary: Marks 7–13 14–18 19–25
Level   1   2   3

> Deuxième contrôle: Lire (1)

Deuxième contrôle: Lire

A Cico le clown (NC 1)

Solution:
1 c, **2** g, **3** e, **4** b, **5** a, **6** f, **7** d
(mark /6) 4+ shows understanding of single words presented in a clear script

> Deuxième contrôle: Lire (1)

B Sophie à Cherbourg (NC 2)

Solution:
1 d, **2** b, **3** e, **4** g, **5** f, **6** a, **7** h, **8** i, **9** c
(mark /7) 5+ shows understanding of short phrases presented in a familiar context

> Deuxième contrôle: Lire (2)

C Calais (NC 3)

Solution:
1 f, **2** d, **3** a, **4** g, **5** b, **6** c, **7** e
(mark /6) 4+ shows understanding of a short text in a topic studied

> Deuxième contrôle: Lire (2)

D Les cadeaux de Coralie (NC 3)

Solution:
1 *faux*, **2** *faux*, **3** *vrai*, **4** *faux*, **5** *vrai*, **6** *faux*, **7** *faux*

(mark /6) 4+ shows understanding of a short text, identifying and noting main points, including likes, dislikes and feelings

Contrôles

> Deuxième contrôle: Écrire

Deuxième contrôle: Écrire

A Les activités (NC 1)

Solution:

1 *téléphone,* **2** *dansent,* **3** *surfes,* **4** *jouons,*
5 *dessine,* **6** *écoute,* **7** *allez,* **8** *chantent,*
9 *regarde*

(mark /8) 1/2 mark for correct word; 1/2 mark for correct spelling – round up the odd 1/2 mark; 5+ shows ability to select appropriate words to complete sentences and copy them correctly

B Quel temps fait-il? (NC 2)

Solution:

À Marseille, il fait beau. À Paris, il y a du vent. À Cherbourg, il y a du brouillard. À Bordeaux, il fait chaud. À Grenoble, il fait froid. À Toulouse, il y a du soleil.

(mark /9) 1 mark for key weather word, even if the spelling is inaccurate (this includes completing the Paris sentence); 1 mark for each correctly-constructed sentence, apart from Marseille and Paris, accepting only the smallest spelling errors; 5+ shows ability to adapt given patterns correctly and add further vocabulary from memory

C Le week-end (NC 3)

Solution:

This is an open-ended task.

(mark /8) 1/2 mark for comprehensible phrase, even if the spelling is inaccurate; further 1/2 mark for each of the four phrases that is accurate or virtually accurate; 5+ shows ability to write two or three short sentences on familiar topics, adapting a model and adding own vocabulary

Unités 8–10

> Troisième contrôle: Écouter (1)

Troisième contrôle: Écouter

A La soirée d'Anne-Marie (NC 2)

Solution:

1 *a,* **2** *b,* **3** *a,* **4** *b,* **5** *a,* **6** *a,* **7** *b*

(mark /6) 4+ shows understanding of a range of familiar statements

> 🔊 CD 5 Track 32

La soirée d'Anne-Marie

1 Je quitte le collège à cinq heures.
2 À cinq heures et quart, j'arrive à la maison.
3 Je prends le goûter dans la cuisine.
4 Après le goûter, je regarde la télé.
5 Nous mangeons à sept heures et demie.
6 Je commence mes devoirs après le dîner.
7 Je me couche à dix heures.

> Troisième contrôle: Écouter (1)

B Rendez-vous à quelle heure? (NC 3)

Solution:

1 *1h30, b,* **2** *6h30/18h30, d,* **3** *8h00/20h00, e,*
4 *10h15, c*

(mark /6) 4+ shows understanding of short dialogues, spoken at near normal speed without any interference

> 🔊 CD 5 Track 33

Rendez-vous à quelle heure?

1 – Tu veux aller en ville cet après-midi?
  – Oui, je veux bien.
  – Alors, rendez-vous à la gare à une heure et demie, ça va?
  – Très bien, une heure et demie à la gare.
2 – Tu veux aller voir un film ce soir?
  – Ce soir, ce n'est pas possible, mais vendredi soir oui.
  – Alors, rendez-vous à six heures et demie devant le cinéma?
  – Six heures et demie. À vendredi.
3 – Tu veux fêter l'anniversaire de Pierre avec nous samedi soir?
  – Oui, super!
  – Alors rendez-vous à la maison de Pierre à huit heures?
  – Huit heures. OK. À samedi.
4 – Tu veux jouer au tennis dimanche matin?
  – Oui, nous deux?
  – Et Lucie et Claire. Rendez-vous au parc à dix heures et quart, ça va?
  – Ça va. Dix heures et quart. À dimanche.

> Troisième contrôle: Écouter (2)

C Deux interviews (NC 3)

Solution:

Sabine		Paul	
lettres	opinions	lettres	opinions
d	♥ ♥	c	✗ ✗
h	♥	e	✗

(mark /7) 5+ shows understanding of short dialogues, spoken at near normal speed without any interference, identifying and noting personal responses, including likes and dislikes

> 🔊 CD 5 Track 34

Deux interviews

Sabine
– Sabine, qu'est-ce que tu aimes manger ou boire?
– Moi, j'adore le chocolat chaud, surtout quand il fait froid.
– Et … est-ce qu'il y a quelque chose que tu n'aimes pas?
– Je ne sais pas … Ah oui, le chou-fleur. Je n'aime pas le chou-fleur.

Paul
– Et Paul, il y a quelque chose que tu n'aimes pas manger ou boire?
– Il y a beaucoup de choses que je n'aime pas, mais je déteste surtout le lait.
– Et qu'est-ce que tu aimes? Beaucoup de choses aussi, je suppose.
– Bien sûr, mais j'aime surtout les fraises. Mmm.

Tricolore 1 Teacher's Notes

Contrôles

Troisième contrôle: Écouter (2)

D Théo parle à Hugo (NC 5/6)

Solution:

1 a, **2** c, **3** b, **4** a, **5** c, **6** a, **7** b

(mark /6) 4+ shows understanding of the main points of longer passages, and recognition of people talking about present and past OR future events. Correct answers to questions 4, 5 and 6 shows ability to recognise people talking about present and past and future events.

CD 5 Track 35

Théo parle à Hugo

– Ça va, Théo?
– Oui, ça va. J'adore le ski. Il y a beaucoup de neige pour le ski, mais il fait du soleil!
– Tu fais du ski le matin et l'après-midi?
– Oui, il y a une classe de dix heures à douze heures, et une classe de quatorze heures à seize heures.
– Et qu'est-ce que tu fais à midi?
– Nous allons au restaurant à la montagne et nous mangeons un grand repas chaud.
– Il y a des activités le soir aussi?
– Oui, ce soir, par exemple, je vais faire de la natation. Mercredi prochain, je vais jouer au volley. On va organiser un match à l'auberge de jeunesse.
– Et les autres soirs, qu'est-ce que tu as fait?
– Lundi dernier, j'ai joué au tennis de table. Un autre soir, j'ai fait du shopping. C'est très bien. On organise des activités intéressantes.
– Tu as ton appareil-photo avec toi?
– Oui, j'ai un appareil-photo numérique. Il y a un café avec Internet au village. Je vais t'envoyer un e-mail avec des photos.
– Ah oui. Ça, c'est une bonne idée!

Troisième contrôle: Parler

Troisième contrôle: Parler

Students should be given the sheet up to a week before the assessment, to give them time to choose whether they prefer to do 1, 2 or 3. Conversation 1 is entirely about the present. Conversation 2 includes an exchange about the future (using *aller* + infinitive). Conversation 3 enables students to demonstrate that they can talk about present, past and future. The open-ended conversation B includes a question about future activities using *aller* + infinitive.

Students should prepare and practise both conversations – the structured one (A) and the open-ended one (B) – with their partners.

Mark scheme:

Section A: mark /12: 3 marks per response

1 mark for a response that is clear and conveys all of the information requested, in the form of a complete phrase or sentence, though not necessarily an accurate one. The questions and answers may seem a little disjointed, like separate items rather than parts of a coherent conversation.

2 marks for a response that is clear and conveys all of the information requested, in the form of a complete phrase or sentence, though not necessarily an accurate one. The language must flow reasonably smoothly and be recognisable as part of a coherent conversation.

3 for a clear and complete response that flows smoothly as part of a coherent conversation. The language must be in complete sentences or phrases that are reasonably accurate and consistent as far as grammar, pronunciation and intonation are concerned.

Section B: mark /13: 3 marks per response, as above, + 1 bonus mark for adding one or two items of extra information about personal preferences (i.e. using knowledge of language to adapt and substitute single words and phrases).

Summary: Marks 7–13   14–18   19–25
          Level   2   3   4

Students who talk about present and future or past are operating at Level 5.

Students who talk about present, future and past are operating at Level 6.

Troisième contrôle: Lire (1)

Troisième contrôle: Lire

A L'emploi du temps (NC 2)

Solution:

1 mardi, **2** jeudi, **3** jeudi, **4** lundi, **5** samedi, **6** vendredi, **7** mardi

(mark /6) 4+ shows understanding of short phrases presented in a familiar context

Troisième contrôle: Lire (1)

B Le déjeuner au restaurant (NC 3)

Solution:

	Hors d'œuvre	plat principal	dessert
Mme Dubois	Ex. —	e	h
M. Colin	a	g	j
M. Martin	d	f	—

(mark /7) 5+ shows understanding of short texts, identifying and noting main points, including likes, dislikes and feelings

Troisième contrôle: Lire (2)

C Le message de Richard (NC 4)

Solution:

1 faux, **2** vrai, **3** vrai, **4** faux, **5** faux, **6** faux, **7** vrai

(mark /6) 4+ shows understanding of a longer text, identifying and noting main points and details, including likes, dislikes and feelings

Tricolore 1 Teacher's Notes

Contrôles

> Troisième contrôle: Lire (2)

D Un week-end à Boulogne (NC 6)

Solution:

1f *merci*, **2c** *dernier*, **3a** *ai*, **4b** *allée*, **5d** *intéressant*, **6e** *joué*, **7g** *vas*

(mark /6) 4+, if it includes 7g, shows understanding of a longer text, recognising text relating to present, past and future.

> Troisième contrôle: Écrire

Troisième contrôle: Écrire

A Une boisson ou un fruit? (NC 2)

Solution:

1 *Monsieur Mally prend un café.*
2 *Adèle prend une banane.*
3 *Madame Bijou prend une pomme.*
4 *Robert prend une limonade.*
5 *Julien prend une poire.*

(mark /8) 1 mark for each key word, even if the spelling is inaccurate; 1 mark for each correctly constructed sentence, accepting only the smallest spelling errors; 5+ shows ability to adapt given patterns correctly

> Troisième contrôle: Écrire

B La famille Boulot va au cinéma (NC 3)

Decide whether you want your students to write the times out in full and make sure they are aware of this.

Solution:

1 *Maman travaille, elle rentre à la maison à cinq heures et quart.*
2 *Julien, tu manges/prends le dîner à cinq heures et demie/5h30.*
   (manges/prends = 1 mark, *mange/prend* = 1/2 mark, *manger/prendre* = 0 marks)
3 *Nous prenons le bus à six heures moins dix/ 5h50.*
   (prenons = 1 mark, *prendrons/prennons* = 1/2 mark, *prendre* = 0 marks)
4 *Le film commence à six heures vingt/6h20.*
   (commence = 1 mark, *commences* = 1/2 mark, *commencer* = 0 marks)
5 *Après, maman et moi, nous allons/mangeons/ prenons le dîner au restaurant à neuf heures/9h.* *(allons/mangeons/prenons* = 1 mark, *alons/mangons/prenons* = 1/2 mark, *aller/manger/prendre* = 0 marks)

(mark /8) 1 mark for each correctly conjugated verb, or 1/2 mark for an attempt that shows understanding of the conjugation, rounding up an odd 1/2; 1 mark for each reasonably accurate sentence; 5+ shows ability to write short sentences on familiar topics, adapting a model and vocabulary from a word bank

> Troisième contrôle: Écrire

C Samedi (NC 4/5)

There is potential to use the perfect tense introduced in *Unité* 10, but the task can also be done using just the present tense and *aller* + infinitive.

Solution:

This is an open-ended task.

(mark /9) 6+ shows ability to write simple sentences, relying largely on memorised language

Mark scheme:

for each weekend activity comprehensibly mentioned: 1 mark (up to max. of 2)

for each comprehensible reference to time of activities: 1 mark (up to max. of 2)

for each comprehensible expression of an opinion of an activity: 1 mark (max. of 2)

for fairly accurate spelling throughout (comprehensible with a little effort): 1 mark or for generally accurate spelling throughout (easily comprehensible): 2 marks